RESEARCH ON MOTIVATION IN EDUCATION

Volume 3

Goals and Cognitions

RESEARCH ON MOTIVATION IN EDUCATION

Volume 3

Goals and Cognitions

Edited by

CAROLE AMES
Institute for Research on Human Development
University of Illinois at Urbana-Champaign
Champaign, Illinois

RUSSELL AMES
University of Illinois at Urbana-Champaign
Champaign, Illinois

ACADEMIC PRESS, INC.
Harcourt Brace Jovanovich, Publishers
San Diego   New York   Berkeley   Boston
London   Sydney   Tokyo   Toronto

ACADEMIC PRESS, INC.
San Diego, California 92101

United Kingdom Edition published by
ACADEMIC PRESS LIMITED
24-28 Oval Road, London NW1 7DX

Library of Congress Cataloging-in-Publication Data

(Revised for vol. 3)

Research on motivation in education.

  Carole Ames' name appears first on t.p. of v. 3.
  Vol. 3 published in San Diego.
  Includes bibliographies and indexes.
  Contents: v. 1. Student motivation — v. 2. The
classroom milieu — v. 3. Goals and cognitions.
  1. Motivation in education.   I. Ames, Russell,
Date. II. Ames, Carole. III. Motivation in
education.
LB1065.R47 1984   370.15'4   83-12315
ISBN 0-12-056701-6 (v. 1. : alk. paper)
ISBN 0-12-056703-2 (v. 3. : alk. paper)

PRINTED IN THE UNITED STATES OF AMERICA
89 90 91 92   9 8 7 6 5 4 3 2 1

Contents

PART I. THEORETICAL PERSPECTIVES ON GOALS AND COGNITIONS

2. The Dynamics of Intrinsic Motivation: A Study of Adolescents
Mihaly Csikszentmihalyi and Jeanne Nakamura

3. Intrinsic Motivation in the Classroom
Mark R. Lepper and Melinda Hodell

4. Social Life as a Goal-Coordination Task
Kenneth A. Dodge, Steven R. Asher, and Jennifer T. Parkhurst

PART II. THE CLASSROOM AND SCHOOL CONTEXTS

Contributors

Numbers in parentheses indicate the pages on which the authors' contributions begin.

Carole Ames (1), Institute for Research on Human Development, University of Illinois at Urbana-Champaign, Champaign, Illinois 61820

Russell Ames (1), University of Illinois at Urbana-Champaign, Urbana, Illinois 61801

Steven R. Asher (107), Bureau of Educational Research, University of Illinois at Urbana-Champaign, Champaign, Illinois 61820

David C. Berliner (317), College of Education, Arizona State University, Tempe, Arizona 85287

Mihaly Csikszentmihalyi (45), Department of Behavioral Sciences, University of Chicago, Chicago, Illinois 60637

Kenneth A. Dodge (107), Department of Psychology, Vanderbilt University, Nashville, Tennessee 37240

Jacquelynne S. Eccles (139), Department of Psychology, University of Colorado, Boulder, Colorado 80309

Joyce L. Epstein (259), Center for Social Organization of Schools, Johns Hopkins University, Baltimore, Maryland 21218

Melinda Hodell (73), Department of Psychology, Stanford University, Stanford, California 94305

Mark R. Lepper (73), Department of Psychology, Stanford University, Stanford, California 94305

Martin L. Maehr (299), Institute for Research on Human Development, University of Illinois, Champaign, Illinois 61820

Ronald W. Marx (223), Instructional Psychology Research Group, Simon Fraser University, Burnaby, British Columbia V5A 1S6, Canada

Carol Midgley (139), Institute for Social Research, University of Michigan, Ann Arbor, Michigan 48106

Jeanne Nakamura (45), Committee on Human Development, University of Chicago, Chicago, Illinois 60637

Jennifer T. Parkhurst (107), Department of Psychology, University of Illinois, Champaign, Illinois 61820

Dale H. Schunk (13), School of Education, University of North Carolina, Chapel Hill, North Carolina 27599

Rhona S. Weinstein (187), Department of Psychology, University of California, Berkeley, California 94702

Philip H. Winne (223), Instructional Psychology Research Group, Faculty of Education, Simon Fraser University, Burnaby, British Columbia V5A 1S6, Canada

Preface

This volume is the third of our series, *Research on Motivation in Education*. Each of the volumes in this series has focused on motivation processes, providing varied theoretical perspectives and applications to educational contexts. Each volume also has a special theme, and this one is subtitled *Goals and Cognitions*.

The chapters are grouped in two parts, the first presenting theory and research on student goals and cognitions and the second emphasizing applications to the school and classroom. In this volume, goals are viewed as setting the stage for motivated cognitions and particular cognitive operations. Chapters in the first part of the book consider goals, both general and specific, as filtering mechanisms for beliefs about the self and subsequent action. The second part places special emphasis on specific aspects of the educational environment, including home, school, classroom, and classroom tasks. In the final part, one discussant provides his perspective on the individual chapters and overall contents of Part I, and a second discussant performs the same function for Part II. Throughout the book, the reader will find perspectives about how student goals and cognitions are related to each other and how they are influenced and shaped by the environment. In brief, the theme of the book highlights the place of goals, intentions, cognitions, and moment-to-moment thoughts in specific educational contexts.

The purpose of Volume 3 is to continue to provide a state-of-the-art review and integration of the research on motivation in education. This volume, like the previous ones, should serve a variety of individuals, including educational and psychological scholars interested in advancing research and theory in the field, graduate students interested in this topic, and practitioners trying to improve the quality of the nation's schools. The expanding body of knowledge on motivation and education that this volume represents offers much to our understanding of what influences the quality of motivation in schools.

We thank all the contributors to this volume for enriching the field with their ongoing programs of research. We are also grateful to Academic Press for continued support and commitment to this project. And, finally, we thank our colleagues who continue to advance the field with a richness of perspectives and research approaches.

Introduction

Russell Ames
Carole Ames

PERSPECTIVES ON MOTIVATION

Our purpose in Volume 3 of *Research on Motivation in Education* is to review and integrate some of the most current perspectives on the subject of motivation. Careful attention has been given to how recent advances in motivation theory and research have been applied to a variety of educational issues and problems. As with previous volumes, this one has a theme linking the various chapters, which we have titled "Goals and Cognitions."

Weiner (1986) provides a historical account of various themes that have guided motivational research in this century that is useful to us here. Predating the current cognitive zeitgeist in motivation theory was a conception of motivation as a push, drive, or force behind behavior that was well articulated in the classical theories of Freud and Hull. Other earlier perspectives focused more on external events (e.g., rewards, punishments) and observable indices of achievement-motivated behavior (e.g., time on task, persistence, and achievement level).

As Weiner points out, however, even the influential quasi-cognitive theories of Lewin (field theory), Atkinson (achievement theory), and Rotter (social learning) included extensive implicit and explicit references to internal drives and external rewards and punishments. These

1

classical approaches assumed that these internal drives and forces were not generally available to an individual's conscious experience and, thus, were not subject to conscious control. In contrast to these earlier approaches, the chapters in this volume focus entirely on the conscious experience of the learner and the environmental factors that may affect this conscious experience.

Each chapter in this volume addresses the development of theory that describes and explains conscious, moment-to-moment motivational thoughts of the individual learner. The chapters assume that we have direct access to the thoughts that control how we perceive, learn, and remember. The full range of cognitive processes (see Weiner, 1986), information search and retrieval, short- and long-term memory, categorization, judgment, and decision making are the topics receiving attention in this volume.

Throughout the volume, motivation is viewed as goal-directed behavior that involves different ways of thinking. Motivation is described according to the thought processes that are elicited under various internal and external conditions. Within this framework, the authors ask such questions as when and why certain goals are valued over others, why students attend to different sources of information, how students use various metacognitive processes, and how they evaluate their ability and performance in different contexts.

In preparing this volume, we asked ourselves more than once whether we had confused the theoretical boundaries of learning and motivation. Cognitive learning theorists also focus on goals, information search, memory, problem solving, and decisionmaking. Rather than confusing the boundaries, we believe the chapter authors have begun to show precisely how motivation and learning processes are related. Marx and Winne, for example, suggest that cognitive learning and motivational processing are distinguished by the information and content upon which cognitive operations operate. That is, cognitive learning theorists focus on subject matter content, and motivational theorists focus on processing information about the self and the self in relation to a task or problem.

Although each chapter taken by itself is not a general theory of motivation (cf. Weiner, 1986), the chapters, taken together, broaden our understanding of a cognitive framework of motivation processes. The chapters focus on a wide range of cognitive processes and are concerned with conscious experience, including phenomenal reality of the self. The concepts and theory in each chapter are derived from sets of empirical relations drawn primarily from each author's own extensive program of research. The authors address a wide range of cognitions, but the role of emotions is less well articulated. The chapters focus on describing and explaining sequential, causal sequences of moment-to-moment motivational thought processing in relation to achievement and social goals. In so doing, the chapters represent significant extensions of a cognitive view of motivation that has been evolving since the mid-1960s. Most significantly, the chapters go well beyond the view that attributions are the only or most significant or even primary cognitive events to be described and explained in a theory of motivation.

PLAN OF THE BOOK

The book has been organized into two major parts, "Theoretical Perspectives on Goals and Cognitions" and "The Classroom and School Context." The two discussant chapters are intended to provide an integrative critical look at the four chapters in each part.

The first four chapters attempt to extend relatively extant, previously articulated theories of student motivation. Schunk extends his work on self-efficacy of learning to a self-efficacy for acquiring learning strategies and learning-how-to-learn skills. Lepper and Hodell build on Lepper's classic work on the undermining effects of extrinsic rewards by offering an elaborated cognitive explanation for this effect. Their cognitive-informational analysis leads them to analyze the consequences of a variety of "motivational embellishments" to instruction. Csikszentmihalyi and Nakamura, in their chapter, elaborate on the cognitive components of intrinsic motivation, showing that perceived challenge in the environment and one's perceived skill to meet these challenges are key factors determining the internal state of intrinsic motivation. Finally, Dodge, Asher, and Parkhurst focus on social motivation and look at social skill development in terms of the social goals children are pursuing. They draw theoretical linkages between social skill development and social motivation, using a social goal concept.

In the second part of the book, the chapters again focus on goals, cognitions, and moment-to-moment thoughts of students as they relate to motivation. However, these chapters focus more expressly on specific context factors (such as school, classroom, and home) that influence these individual student motivation variables. Eccles and Midgley examine how changes in the school environment from elementary through junior high to high school affect student motivation. Weinstein focuses on classroom variables, specifically pointing to student perceptions of teacher expectations as a salient feature of the classroom environment.

In their chapter, Marx and Winne attend to specific aspects of classroom tasks and activity structures. And finally, Epstein discusses the overlap between school and home environments, identifying specific, manipulable structures such as the reward structure and authority of the classroom and home environments.

We now turn to an analysis of the major themes of this volume—goals, cognitions, and moment-to-moment thoughts. It is our hope that in presenting an integrative picture of how these themes are addressed in the respective chapters, we can show how this volume contributes to a cognitive theory of motivation.

THEMES

GOALS

It is our view that motivational goals provide the mechanism for filtering perceptions and other cognitive processes. For example, this view suggests that students' goals influence their attributions for a poor grade on an exam and subsequent action plans. If, for example, the student's goal is to learn and master the content, a low grade is likely to be attributed to something that can be controlled and changed in the future. Subsequent action plans might involve more frequent study periods, getting help from teachers or peers, reviewing errors, and so forth. By contrast, if the student's goal had been only to "get by," the student might focus more on estimating, evaluating, and maintaining a minimal level of effort.

In their view of social goals, Dodge and his colleagues discuss how positive and negative social behaviors are a function of the child's social goals. For example, when confronted with a hypothetical social dilemma, children recommend markedly different courses of action depending on whether their goal is to be liked or to achieve retaliation. If the goal is to retaliate, vastly different attributions, thoughts about the other, and social behaviors evolve than if the goal is to be liked. These authors also discuss how individuals typically pursue multiple goals that require goal coordination and goal balancing. Coordinating the goals of being liked with being influential sets up a different perceptual filter than pursuing either of these goals alone.

In the chapters on intrinsic motivation, goals serve as consciously conceived reasons for behavior. Lepper and Hodell contrast intrinsic and extrinsic goals. Extrinsic rewards can provide different information to the student and therefore are viewed as serving different informative functions or goals. Depending on the informational goal, different cognitions follow. According to Csikszentmihalyi and Nakamura, goals define the relative challenge of the situation. When perceived task demands and skills are high, the student's focus of attention on a moment-to-moment basis is on specific task demands and various action possibilities.

In contrast to the chapters on social and intrinsic motivation, where goals are considered as both general and specific, Schunk's theory of self-efficacy focuses on very specific goals. For example, in his research paradigm, students may be presented with a goal of solving 10 math problems and then asked to rate their degree of certainty of solving the problems correctly. Nevertheless, although the goal is presented in specific, unambiguous terms, the goal serves as a filter for subsequent reflections and beliefs about the self and action.

The chapters in the second part address goals from the perspective of how the environmental context influences or establishes particular goal orientations described in Part I. The critical feature of the Part II chapters is that they focus on how the environment influences the motivational cognitions of the individual. In the next section, we elaborate on the nature of these cognitions.

COGNITIONS AND COGNITIVE OPERATIONS

Goals set the framework for eliciting motivational cognitions and particular cognitive operations. Cognitions that are motivational in content include, for example, choices, values, expectations, attributions, and self-evaluations. In addition, Marx and Winne show that there are cognitive operations that are common to both learning and motivational processes, including, for example, mental representations, monitoring, evaluation of responses, and strategic thinking.

Throughout the chapters, propositions about how cognitions are related to each other and to environmental cues are offered. Lepper and Hodell show that cognitions can establish the meaning of incentives for the learner. Specifically, they show that extrinsic rewards can be perceived as being about the social and tangible consequences of task engagement, degree of success or failure at an activity, or degree of external constraint for engaging in an activity. Perceptions about the meaning of the extrinsic reward are related to other cognitions, including expectations about the probability of future rewards, judgments of personal competence, and perceptions of an activity as work or play.

Subjective beliefs about one's competence or level of skill are central to several perspectives in the book. According to Csikszentmihalyi and Nakamura, beliefs about the match of one's level of skill with perceived challenge are a determining factor of intrinsic motivation. Schunk explains that confidence in one's ability to perform a task relates to attributions and subsequent performance behaviors. Eccles and Midgley place primary emphasis on cognitive perceptions of self-esteem and self-concept. Students' understanding and interpretation of teacher expectations and feedback impact students' own self-perceptions of ability, according to Weinstein. In defining the activity structures of home and school, Epstein identifies an array of motivational content associated with these structures, within which cognitions about the self, particularly one's ability and worth, are pivotal.

Most contemporary conceptions of motivation in education focus heavily on describing the cognitive motivational content upon which students operate. These theories also tend to focus on the internal and external conditions that make salient various categories of motivational content. Only a few, however, have attempted to describe and explain the mental operations involved in cognitively manipulating this content. In this volume, Marx and Winne's and Dodge, Asher, and Parkhurst's chapters address this issue in a significant way.

Marx and Winne suggest that motivational content is represented as concepts (e.g., ability), or propositions (e.g., "high ability is required for normatively difficult tasks"), and as schemata (i.e., mental scripts linking concepts and propositions). In addition, they also identify procedural skills that account for how individuals store patterns of content and thought–action sequences. Within this framework, three basic mental prerequisites are necessary for successful task performance: (1) attention, (2) classification of goals and task requirements, and (3) capability. The intermingling of cognitive learning and cognitive motivational content takes place in working memory. A common core of mental operations then manipulates this content. These mental operations are captured in the acronym SMART, representing the operations of stimulating, monitoring, assembling, rehearsing, and translating.

Dodge, Asher, and Parkhurst offer an information processing perspective for explaining goal-coordination tasks. The key cognitions include attention to salient social cues, interpretation of these social cues, cognitive representations of possible behavioral responses to the cues, mental representations of the consequences of the responses, and the evaluation and monitoring of given responses. These cognition that operate on social cues are also dependent on social knowledge.

We now turn to explore how cognitions work together to affect moment-to-moment thought patterns related to mental and physical effort.

MOMENT-TO-MOMENT THOUGHTS

The concept of moment-to-moment motivational thoughts is well captured in William James' (1899) introspective account of conscious awareness:

> When we are studying an uninteresting subject, if our mind tends to wander, we have to bring back our attention every now and then by using distinct pulses of effort, which revivify the topic for a moment, the mind then running on for a certain number of seconds or minutes with spontaneous interest, until again some intercurrent idea captures it and takes it off. Then the process of voluntary recall must be repeated once more. Voluntary attention, in short, is only a momentary affair. (Kirby & Grimley, 1986, p. 11)

According to Schunk, when the task involves learning a skill, cognitive effort is an appropriate index of motivation. In essence, cognitive effort refers to the internal mental dialogue of the learner that is focused on mastering the learning task. In self-efficacy terms, the internal moment-to-moment dialogue focuses on appraising cues during task engagement, coding information about skill acquisition, and making comparison with preexisting efficacy expectations.

Efficacy cues signal to students how well they are learning. If students continue to believe they have "know-how" or strategies for learning, they will maintain a high sense of efficacy for learning. Thus, the learner is likely to keep cognitive efforts focused on applying learning skills to the task. The student's cognitive efforts are directed at understanding and mastering content. Self-efficacy, then, is related to the mental effort expended during instruction, the mental effort involved in trying to comprehend the instructions or task requirements, monitoring one's level of understanding, and rehearsing information to be remembered.

Csikszentmihalyi and Nakamura describe a number of moment-to-moment thought patterns that range from states of apathy, through arousal, to "flow." These thoughts are defined in terms of the individual cognitions regarding perceived skill and challenge of the task at hand. Most interestingly, they address the metacognitive aspects of high intrinsic motivation. How can individuals consciously control whether or not they are in a "flow" state and make the process evolve? They suggest that a series of metacognitions are involved here, including (1) focusing attention on the activity of the moment, (2) defining one's goals and reasons for reaching them, (3) seeking feedback and focusing on the informational aspects of the feedback, (4) recognizing alternative internal states of anxiety and boredom, (5) knowing how to identify new challenges as skills develop, and (6) knowing how to deal with anxiety-provoking interactions and to delay gratification.

Dodge and his colleagues describe five information-processing steps that involve moment-to-moment thoughts associated with encoding information, interpreting information, accessing strategies, evaluating strategies, enacting strategies, and monitoring behavior and outcomes. The attentive child, working toward social-goal coordination, monitors and controls attention to the social task through an internal dialogue that includes generating strategies and continuously monitoring progress toward social-goal attainment. This dialogue demonstrates *social competence*—the sustained strategic effort needed for multiple goal coordination.

The research methodology of some authors also attempts to capture these moment-to-moment thoughts. Csikszentmihalyi's innovative experience-sampling method provides students with a beeper and when they are beeped at random intervals, they record their thoughts on a questionnaire form. Weinstein's inventory of student perceptions of teacher behavior reflects students' conscious attention to moment-to-moment experiences. A quote from one of these students is exemplary of the subtle and complex reasoning process, "Sometimes she say, oh that is very poor reading to someone else and she says pretty good to me, and sometimes I kind of marked myself in the middle in reading because to others and she says excellent reading."

In summary, a major focus throughout this volume is internal, conscious motivational dialogue of the learner, the motivational thoughts that guide the learner. As Marx and Winne put it, we confront the problem of how conscious cognitive activities that concern motivation intermingle with what students know about themselves and the external knowledge they are acquiring. If we assume that this moment-to-moment stream of thought precedes and precipitates motivated behavior, then the more we know about these thoughts the more we can describe the cognitive motivational status of the learner. In the final part, we look at those chapters that have a heavy focus on the classroom and school factors that are related to these thoughts.

CLASSROOM, SCHOOL, AND HOME FACTORS

Thus far, we have tried to elaborate on the nature of goals, cognitions, and moment-to-moment thoughts as they are discussed in the chapters, but the motivational content of one's thinking is also very much related to the environmental context. Substantial research suggests that specific characteristics of schools and classrooms are salient to the learner and central to the form and direction of motivational thought processes.

In their chapter, Eccles and Midgley examine the effects of the transition from elementary to junior high school. They argue that changes in a cluster of classroom organizational- and structural-climate variables accompany the transition to junior high school and that these changes contribute to changes in students' motivation and achievement beliefs. For example, changes in a wide range of environmental variables related to quality of interpersonal relationships, evaluation techniques, opportunities for student autonomy, and grouping practices are shown to have a negative influence on student motivation.

Weinstein focuses on how the organization of the classroom itself influences student perceptions and beliefs. She contrasts different types of classroom environments (e.g., "traditional" versus "open") in terms of students' perceptions of their "treatment." Students' perceptions of differential teacher treatment are shown to be a function of these environments and to be potent mediators of students' expectations and performance.

Winne and Marx also focus on the classroom but attend specifically to the nature of classroom tasks and activity structures as key environmental variables. Classroom tasks are defined in terms of such factors as time allocation, resources, social functions, and teacher factors. Activity structures refer to the temporal and physical boundaries interrelated and overlapping with tasks. Activity structures include functions such as tutoring, remediation, social roles, and sequencing. How task and activity structures are defined in a given classroom elicit different motivational content in cognitive thought.

Finally, Epstein discusses how specific motivational goals, cognitions, and moment-to-moment thoughts are related to TARGET (Task, Authority, Reward, Grouping, Evaluation, and Time) structures that relate to both school and home environments. TARGET structures set the stage for different ways of thinking about the self, about academic tasks, and about significant others in the setting.

Each of these chapters tackles important questions about how the entire setting and features of the setting affect the thinking of the learner. The job of teasing out salient and important characteristics of specific environmental factors is quite onerous, but it is critical to unfolding a general theory of motivation.

CONCLUSION

We hope that we have provided the reader with an appropriate cognitive map of the concepts, theory, and research foci of the chapters in this third volume. We also hope that the thematic structure of goals, cognitions, and moment-to-moment thoughts introduced here highlights the theoretical relationships across the chapters. The chapters in this volume discuss many of the major elements of a cognitive theory of motivation, specifically how student goals and cognitive operations operate on motivational content and resulting moment-to-moment thoughts. An adequate theory, however, must also show how these cognitive-motivational variables are related to a variety of external environmental variables. These variables include, for example, teacher behavior, classroom tasks, activity structures, school organization, peer relationships, and the broader school environment of the home and family. Collectively, the chapters in this volume expand our thinking about the role of goals and cognitions in motivated behavior, and in doing so, elaborate a cognitive theory of motivation.

REFERENCES

James, W. (1899). *Talks to teachers on psychology: And to students on some of life's ideals.* New York: Holt.

Kirby, E. A., & Grimley, L. K. (1986). *Understanding and creating attention deficit disorder.* New York: Pergamon Press.

Weiner, B. (1986). *An attributional theory of motivation and emotion.* New York: Springer Verlag.

PART I

Theoretical Perspectives on Goals
and Cognitions

1

Self-efficacy and Cognitive Skill Learning

Dale H. Schunk

OVERVIEW OF SELF-EFFICACY
AND PERFORMANCE

There is growing evidence that personal expectations influence achievement behaviors. Although research has been conducted within various theoretical traditions, it is united in its emphasis on individuals' beliefs concerning their capabilities to exercise control over important aspects of their lives (Bandura, 1986; Brophy, 1983; Corno & Mandinach, 1983; Dweck, 1986; McCombs, 1984; Schunk, 1984a; Thomas, 1980; Weiner, 1985).

In this chapter, I examine the role of *perceived self-efficacy,* or personal beliefs about one's capabilities to organize and implement actions necessary to attain designated levels of performance (Bandura, 1977, 1982b). My focus is on students' self-efficacy during cognitive skill learning. The central hypothesis is that self-efficacy for learning cognitive skills is an important variable in understanding students' motivation and learning.

Self-efficacy research has explored such facets of behavior change as coping with fearful situations, solving mathematical problems, and eating properly. In much of this work, participants utilize skills that they have previously learned but typically do not perform for various personal and situational reasons (e.g., debilitating anxiety). Snake phobics, for example, possess the skill to touch a snake but do not do so because they fearfully anticipate dire consequences.

In this chapter, I extend the self-efficacy construct to instructional contexts where students are learning cognitive skills. The term *self-efficacy for learning* refers to students' beliefs about their capabilities to apply effectively the knowledge and skills they already possess and thereby learn new cognitive skills. This extension to instructional contexts captures the distinction drawn in many learning theories between learning and performance (Bower & Hilgard, 1981). Performance is not synonymous with learning. We can only infer that learning takes place; we do not observe it directly but rather the behavior presumably brought about by learning. If students successfully perform a new behavior, we safely conclude that they have learned. Conversely, we cannot necessarily infer that students who do not perform a behavior have not learned it. They may be unmotivated, anxious, feeling ill, or believe that performance is unimportant.

This chapter initially provides a historical perspective on self-efficacy theory and research, and then presents a model of school learning that incorporates the self-efficacy construct. Next, research is summarized that bears directly on the operation of self-efficacy for learning, along with some previous work interpreted in light of this model. I conclude the chapter by offering ideas for future research.

SELF-EFFICACY: THEORY AND RESEARCH

ANTECEDENTS AND CONSEQUENCES

Bandura (1977, 1982b) hypothesized that perceived self-efficacy can have diverse effects on behavior. For one, self-efficacy can affect choice of activities. People who hold a low sense of efficacy for accomplishing a task may avoid it, whereas those who believe they are more capable should participate more eagerly. Self-efficacy also is hypothesized to affect effort expenditure and persistence. Especially when facing obstacles, individuals who hold a high sense of efficacy ought to work harder and persist longer than those who doubt their capabilities.

Individuals acquire information about their self-efficacy for performing tasks from performance accomplishments, vicarious experiences, forms of persuasion, and physiological indexes. One's own performances offer quite reliable guides for assessing self-efficacy. In general, successes raise self-efficacy and failures lower it, although once a strong sense of efficacy is developed, an occasional failure is not apt to have much effect.

People also acquire information about their capabilities through knowledge of others. Much research shows that similar others offer the best basis for comparison (Rosenthal & Bandura, 1978). Observing similar peers perform a task can convey to observers that they, too, are capable of accomplishing the task. Information acquired vicariously would probably have a weaker influence on self-efficacy than performance-based information because a vicarious increase in self-efficacy can be negated by subsequent unsuccessful performances.

People often receive information via suggestion or exhortation that they possess the capabilities to perform a task. Although positive persuasory feedback can enhance self-efficacy, this increase is apt to be short-lived if individuals' subsequent efforts turn out poorly. Individuals also derive efficacy information from physiological indexes (e.g., heart rate, sweating). Body symptoms that signal anxiety may convey that one is not especially skillful at the task.

Information acquired from these sources does not automatically influence self-efficacy; rather, it is cognitively appraised (Bandura, 1977, 1982b). Efficacy appraisal is an inferential process in which persons weigh and combine the contributions of such personal and situational factors as their perceived ability, the difficulty of the task, amount of effort expended, amount of external assistance received, task outcomes, patterns of successes and failures, perceived similarity to models, and persuader credibility.

The preceding discussion is not meant to imply that self-efficacy is an important influence on all behaviors. Efficacy appraisal typically does not occur for habitual routines or for tasks requiring skills that are well established (Bandura, 1982b). People are more apt to assess their capabilities for accomplishing a task when they believe that altered personal or situational conditions may thwart performance. In school, for example, students are more likely to assess their self-efficacy for learning new material than for accomplishing drill-and-practice activities.

Self-efficacy is definitely not the only influence on behavior. High self-efficacy will not produce competent performances when requisite skills are lacking. *Outcome expectations,* or one's beliefs concerning the outcomes of one's actions, also are important. Individuals are not motivated to behave in ways that they believe will result in negative outcomes. Another influence on behavior is the relative value people place on perceived outcomes, or how much they desire those outcomes relative to those of other behaviors. In summary, assuming that people possess adequate skills, believe that positive outcomes will result, and value those outcomes, self-efficacy is hypothesized to influence the choice and direction of much human behavior.

RELATED CONCEPTIONS

The notion that personal expectations can influence behavior is not new. Tolman (1959), for example, viewed much learning as the forming of expectancies that certain behaviors will produce given outcomes. Rotter's (1966) *locus of control* emphasizes perceived control over outcomes. In this conception, people differ in whether they believe that outcomes occur independently of how one behaves (external control) or are highly contingent on one's behavior (internal control). Although positive outcome expectations are important in education, they do not guarantee learning. Students who believe that the teacher will praise them for scoring 100% on a spelling test (positive outcome expectation) may nonetheless not study the words very much if they doubt their capabilities to learn how to spell them (low self-efficacy).

Also relevant to the present formulation are *expectancy-value* theories, which stress the idea that motivation is a joint function of one's beliefs concerning the outcomes of one's actions and the value one places on those outcomes (Atkinson, 1964; Vroom, 1964). People are more motivated to act when they believe that an action will lead to positive outcomes and when they value those outcomes. Outcome expectations and values influence motivation and learning, but the former do not guarantee the latter. Students who value high grades and who believe that diligent studying will produce good grades may not be motivated to study if they doubt their capabilities to study effectively.

Attribution theories also are relevant. The basic assumption is that people seek to explain the causes of events in their lives (Heider, 1958; Kelley & Michela, 1980; Weiner, 1985). Research shows that students often attribute their successes and failures to such factors as ability, effort, task difficulty, and luck. In turn, attributions influence expectancies of future successes. Assuming that the conditions under which learning occurs are expected to remain much the same, students who attribute prior successes largely to stable factors (high ability, easy task) are apt to hold higher achievement expectations than students who stress factors that are less stable (high effort, good luck). In the present view, attributions constitute one type of cue that students use to appraise their self-efficacy for learning cognitive skills.

In summary, other conceptions of how cognitions influence achievement behaviors stress the role of outcome expectations, value of outcomes, and attributions concerning prior outcomes. Self-efficacy theory differs from these views in emphasizing students' beliefs concerning their capabilities to employ effectively the skills and knowledge necessary to attain outcomes. This is not to imply that self-efficacy and outcome beliefs are unrelated. Students who attribute prior successes to their abilities feel capable of performing well in the future, and they expect (and usually receive) outcomes that they value (good grades, teacher praise) following successful performances.

EARLY SELF-EFFICACY RESEARCH

Self-efficacy and Coping Behaviors

The focus of the initial self-efficacy research was twofold: (1) to investigate self-efficacy as a predictor of behavioral change, and (2) to determine how different treatments affected self-efficacy. In one study (Bandura, Adams, & Beyer, 1977), adult snake phobics were initially administered a behavioral pretest comprising progressively more threatening encounters with a snake. Given their phobic nature, subjects could perform few, if any, tasks. For the self-efficacy assessment, subjects designated which tasks they felt they could perform and rated their certainty of performance. As a measure of generality, subjects made self-efficacy judgments for the same tasks with a different type of snake.

Following the pretest, subjects were assigned to one of three conditions: participant modeling, modeling, control. Participant modeling subjects initially observed therapists model encounters with a snake. Performance aids (e.g., performing activities jointly with subjects, gradually lengthening performance time) were introduced so that subjects could perform the activities and were withdrawn as treatment progressed. After subjects completed all tasks on the hierarchy, they performed various tasks alone during a short period of self-directed mastery.

Modeling subjects received the same amount of treatment time but they only observed the therapists model the feared activities and did not perform the tasks themselves. Controls received the assessments without intervening training. Following training, subjects were administered the same assessments used during the pretest except that subjects were given a behavioral test with both the training snake and the generalization snake.

Participant modeling subjects demonstrated a substantial increase in self-efficacy from pretest to posttest; modeling subjects evidenced moderate improvement; controls showed no change. Participant modeling subjects judged posttest self-efficacy significantly higher than did subjects in the other two conditions; modeling subjects rated self-efficacy higher than the controls. The two modeling conditions showed significant increases in approach behaviors toward both snakes, with participant modeling producing the greater increases. Participant modeling promoted self-efficacy more than modeling alone.

The relationship between posttest self-efficacy and performance was explored by comparing each subject's self-efficacy judgment for each task with his or her performance on that task. Congruence was defined as subjects judging that they could perform a task and then performing it, or as judging that they could not perform a task and then not performing it. Congruence percentages were high: 89% for participant modeling, 86% for modeling, and 90% for control.

Bandura and Adams (1977) administered phobics a systematic desensitization treatment in which they imagined themselves performing the feared activities while deeply relaxed until they no longer experienced anxiety. Desensitization increased subjects' self-efficacy, and the congruence percentage was 84%.

In a second experiment, Bandura and Adams gave subjects participant modeling until they successfully performed all tasks up to a prespecified level. Following treatment, subjects judged self-efficacy for performing tasks and received the behavioral posttest. Although all subjects demonstrated comparable treatment performance, there was considerable variability in their efficacy judgments and in their posttest performances: Some subjects failed to perform tasks that they had successfully performed, some moved slightly beyond treatment level, and others achieved terminal performance. Subjects' self-efficacy judgments prior to the posttest predicted their actual posttest performances better than did their performances during the treatment phase. Self-efficacy was influenced by treatment performance but was not merely a reflection of it.

Self-efficacy and Achievement Behaviors

In the initial self-efficacy research in an achievement context, low-achieving children participated in a long-division training program and received either cognitive modeling or didactic instruction (Schunk, 1981). Children in the modeling condition observed an adult verbalize aloud division operations while simultaneously applying them to problems. Didactic subjects reviewed instructional pages that portrayed the solution of division problems step by step. Modeling was expected to be more effective because of evidence that coupling explanatory principles with exemplary modeling promotes skills better than principles alone (Rosenthal & Zimmerman, 1978).

This study also explored the effects of effort attributional feedback. Within each instructional condition, half of the children periodically received effort feedback as they solved problems; children were told that they had worked hard after their efforts led to success and that they needed to work harder when difficulties followed lackadaisical efforts. The other half received no attributional feedback.

The role of effort in attributional theories has received considerable attention because—unlike ability, task ease or difficulty, and luck— effort presumably is under volitional control and amenable to change. Ascribing past failures to insufficient effort is hypothesized to exert motivational effects. When students believe that increased effort will produce success they should persist longer at the task and thereby increase their level of performance (Weiner, 1985). Attribution retraining programs often concentrate on changing children's causal ascriptions for failure from low ability to insufficient effort (Andrews & Debus, 1978; Dweck, 1975).

Effort attributional feedback is a persuasive source of self-efficacy information. To be told that one can achieve results through hard work can motivate one to do so because such information conveys that one possesses the necessary capability to perform well. Providing effort feedback for task success can support students' perceptions of their successes and lead to further increases in self-efficacy and skills. In these situations, children view outcomes as highly dependent on effort and often equate effort with ability (Harari & Covington, 1981; Nicholls, 1978).

In the long-division training program, both cognitive modeling and didactic instruction significantly increased self-efficacy, division skill, and task persistence, but modeling led to higher skill than did didactic instruction. Surprisingly, attributional feedback exerted no benefits on achievement outcomes. To explore the hypothesized relationship between self-efficacy and subsequent skillful performance, the probability of an accurate solution as a function of the level of self-efficacy was computed. Regardless of treatment condition, higher self-efficacy was associated with progressively higher division skill.

The hypothesized influences on achievement outcomes were explored further using path analysis to reproduce the correlation matrix compris-

ing instructional treatment (modeling–didactic), self-efficacy, persistence, and skill. The most parsimonious model that reproduced the data
showed that: (1) treatment exerted both a direct effect on skill as well as
an indirect effect through persistence and self-efficacy, (2) the effect of
treatment on persistence operated indirectly through self-efficacy, and
(3) self-efficacy influenced skill and persistence.

The failure of the attributional feedback may have resulted because
providing effort feedback for success and difficulty conveyed markedly
different efficacy information. As children work at a task and observe
their successes, they should begin to develop a sense of efficacy. Telling
children that effort is the reason for their successes should support their
perceptions of skill improvement and convey that they can continue to
perform well with hard work; telling them that they need to work hard
following difficulty might convey that they are not doing well. They may
conclude that they are not very capable and may wonder whether more
effort will produce better results. A subsequent study (Schunk, 1982;
summarized later in this chapter) disentangled these effects.

Substantive Issues

Learning versus Performance. Early self-efficacy research did not
clearly distinguish between learning new skills and performing previously learned behaviors. Activities such as approaching and touching a
snake involve behaviors that people know how to perform but typically
do not because of such factors as anxiety and negative outcome
expectancies (e.g., "If I get near the snake, it will bite me"). Treatments
that promote people's interactions in feared situations do so by raising
their self-efficacy for successfully managing threatening activities.

Some school activities involve performance of previously learned
skills, but much time is spent on cognitive learning. Students acquire
declarative knowledge in the form of facts, scripts (e.g., events of a story),
and organized passages (the Declaration of Independence). Students
also acquire *procedural knowledge*—concepts, rules, algorithms. A third
type of cognitive learning involves *cognitive strategies,* or knowledge of
when and how to employ forms of declarative and procedural knowledge (Gagne, 1984). Cognitive strategies apply to learning, memory, and
problem-solving, and include such processes as rehearsal, elaboration,
and means–ends analysis.

Self-efficacy should influence new learning as well as the performance
of previously learned skills. In assessing self-efficacy for learning,
students make judgments about what they will need to learn, what

knowledge and skills are prerequisites for the new learning, how well they can recall the prerequisite information from memory, how easily they have learned similar skills in the past, how well they can attend to the teacher's instruction and rehearse material to be learned, and how skillfully they can monitor their level of understanding. Self-efficacy for learning, then, involves assessing what will be required in the learning context and how well one can use one's knowledge and skills to produce new learning.

Self-efficacy and Motivation.   Self-efficacy theory postulates that self-efficacy influences choice of activities, persistence, effort expenditure, and task accomplishments (Bandura, 1982b). Individuals who feel more efficacious about effectively managing situations are apt to choose to engage in the activities more often, persist in the face of difficulties, expend greater effort to attain their goals, and attain a higher level of performance. Each of these hypotheses seems reasonable in contexts where behaviors reflect performance of previously learned skills. When self-efficacy is applied to classroom situations involving learning, however, these propositions require some modification. For example, choice of activities is not a good index of motivation in schools because students typically do not choose whether to participate in learning activities (Brophy, 1983). Choice of activities is meaningful under a limited set of conditions (e.g., activities during free time).

Similarly, higher self-efficacy may not always lead to greater persistence. At the outset of a learning activity, students persist at tasks not so much due to high self-efficacy but rather because of contextual factors, such as the teacher's efforts to keep students on task. As skills develop we might expect that self-efficacy would bear a negative, rather than a positive, relationship to persistence; students should not have to persist as long to correctly answer questions, solve problems, and so on.

Where skill learning is involved, cognitive effort seems to be an appropriate index of motivation (Corno & Mandinach, 1983). A large part of students' time during instruction is spent attempting to understand the content (Peterson, Swing, Braverman, & Buss, 1982). Students with higher self-efficacy for learning ought to expend greater mental effort during instruction on activities that they believe will promote learning (rehearsing information, monitoring their level of understanding).

Self-efficacy and Outcomes.   In general, successes should raise self-efficacy and failures should lower it, although an occasional failure (or success) occurring after many successes (failures) may not have much impact on self-efficacy (Bandura, 1982b). To accurately judge self-efficacy, people must be able to distinguish successes from failures. In situations that require performance of previously learned skills, individuals usually can determine whether they have succeeded or failed.

Judging self-efficacy in cognitive skill learning contexts is more complex. Students may learn some component subskills of a task but not others. To the extent that students are unaware of the full range of task demands, they could misjudge self-efficacy due to incomplete information. In mathematics, students often employ *buggy algorithms* (erroneous strategies) that result in a problem solution (whether the solution is correct or incorrect) (Brown & Burton, 1978). Because buggy algorithms produce solutions, employing them may lead to a false sense of competence, especially in the absence of teacher feedback. Similarly, students who solve problems correctly but are unsure of whether their answers are correct may not feel more efficacious. In short, feedback to students concerning their progress in learning is important when students cannot determine progress on their own.

SELF-EFFICACY AND COGNITIVE SKILL LEARNING

Figure 1 portrays the operation of self-efficacy in a model of cognitive skill learning. I have discussed various aspects of this model in prior reviews (Schunk, 1984a, 1985b). It is derived from different theoretical traditions, including social learning, attribution, and instructional psychology (Bandura, 1977, 1982b; Corno & Mandinach, 1983; Marx, 1983; McCombs, 1984; Nicholls, 1983; Weiner, 1985; Winne, 1985).

ENTRY CHARACTERISTICS

Students who enter learning situations differ in aptitudes and prior experiences. Aptitudes include general abilities, skills, strategies, interests, attitudes, and personality characteristics (Cronbach & Snow, 1977; Peterson et al., 1982). Educational experiences derive from prior schools attended, interactions with teachers, time spent on different subjects, and so on. These two factors are not independent. For example, students high in reading ability ought to perform better on tasks requiring reading, which should earn them teacher praise and good grades. In turn, these outcomes may lead students to develop greater interest in reading, which may further improve their ability.

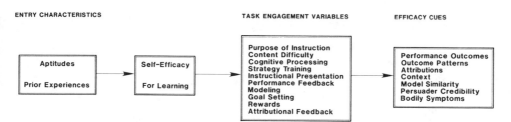

Figure 1.   Self-efficacy model of cognitive skill learning.

SELF-EFFICACY FOR LEARNING

At the outset of a learning endeavor, we may speak of *self-efficacy for acquiring knowledge, developing skills,* or *mastering material* (Schunk, 1985b). Aptitudes and prior experiences will affect students' initial beliefs about their capabilities for learning. Students who previously have performed well in a subject area ought to believe that they are capable of learning a new task in that area, whereas students who have experienced difficulties may doubt their capabilities.

Although self-efficacy is influenced by aptitudes and prior experiences, it is not merely a reflection of them. Collins (1982) administered standardized tests to students and identified those with high, average, and low mathematical ability. Within each ability level, she also identified students of high and low mathematical self-efficacy, and gave all students problems to solve and opportunities to rework those they missed. Ability was positively related to skillful performance, but regardless of ability level, students with higher self-efficacy solved more problems correctly and chose to rework more problems they missed.

EFFICACY CUES

Before discussing task-engagement variables, I wish to emphasize that they make various efficacy cues salient. Efficacy cues signal to students how well they are learning, and students use the cues to appraise their own self-efficacy for continued learning. In turn, self-efficacy for learning affects students' motivation and actual skill acquisition.

The actual cognitive processing involved in appraising self-efficacy may be very similar to how students cognitively process instructional information. Winne (1985) suggests that efficacy expectations are represented in memory as propositions, much the same as declarative and procedural knowledge. In appraising self-efficacy for learning, students may attend to cues during task engagement, code information about skill acquisition in a form compatible with preexisting efficacy representations, and periodically alter the latter.

Performance outcomes are important cues used by students to appraise self-efficacy for learning. As noted previously, successes generally raise and failures generally lower self-efficacy; however, after many successes, an occasional failure would have little impact, as would one success after many failures (Schunk, 1984a, 1985b).

Outcome patterns constitute a second type of cue. Early learning is often fraught with failures, but the perception of progress can promote self-efficacy for learning (Schunk, 1985b). Self-efficacy may not be aided much if students believe that their progress is slow or that their skills have stabilized at low levels.

Attributions for prior successes and failures are used to appraise self-efficacy for learning. Achievement outcomes often are attributed to such causes as ability, effort, task difficulty, and luck (Freize, 1980; Weiner, 1985). Children view effort as the prime cause of outcomes and ability-related terms as closely associated, but as they gain experience and develop, a distinct conception of ability emerges (Nicholls, 1978). Ability attributions become increasingly important influences on expectancies, whereas the role of effort declines in importance (Harari & Covington, 1981). Success achieved with great effort should raise self-efficacy less than if minimal effort is required, because the former situation implies that skills are not well developed (Bandura, 1982b).

Students also derive cues from the learning *context*. Consider the role of help from others. Teachers who provide much assistance to students may improve their skills but do little to raise students' self-efficacy for learning, because students may believe that they could not succeed on their own. Another cue that affects self-efficacy for learning is teacher praise, because it can convey how the teacher views student abilities (Weiner, Graham, Taylor, & Meyer, 1983). Especially when students believe that a task is easy, praise combined with effort information (e.g., "That's good. You've been working hard") signals low ability. Students who believe that the teacher does not expect much of them are apt to doubt their capabilities. Other contextual factors include students' perceptions of the working conditions and distractions from others.

Model similarity ought to be an important cue used to appraise self-efficacy. Observing similar peers improving their skills can convey a vicarious sense of self-efficacy that students can learn as well, whereas observed failures cast doubt on students' own capability to succeed (Schunk, 1985b). Model similarity can be based on perceived competence or on personal attributes (e.g., age, gender, ethnic background), even when the attributes have little bearing on the modeled behaviors (Rosenthal & Bandura, 1978).

Students' judgments of *persuader credibility* should affect self-efficacy for learning. Students may experience higher self-efficacy when they are persuaded that they are capable of learning by a trustworthy source (e.g., the teacher), whereas they may readily discount the advice of less credible sources. Students also may discount the advice of an otherwise credible source if they believe that the source does not fully understand the nature of the task demands (e.g., difficult for students to comprehend) or the effect of contextual influences (e.g., too many distractions).

Various *physiological symptoms* serve as cues for appraising self-efficacy. Sweating and trembling may signal that students are not very capable of learning. Conversely, students who notice that they are reacting in a less-agitated fashion to academic tasks may feel more efficacious about continuing to learn. Included in this category are cues emanating from fatigue and physical illness.

TASK-ENGAGEMENT VARIABLES

Task engagement refers to students' cognitive activities (i.e., attending, processing and integrating information, thinking, mentally solving problems) as well as their overt verbalizations and behaviors (Brophy, 1983; Corno & Mandinach, 1983). Cognitive activities and overt behaviors are related. Students act on the basis of what they think (e.g., they volunteer answers and write answers to problems), and cognitive processes are themselves altered by the consequences of their actions (corrective feedback, teacher praise). Although students' activities typically are initiated by aspects of instruction (Marx, 1983), students' activities also can influence instructional processes. For example, students with high self-efficacy for learning are likely to engage in cognitive processes conducive to learning (attend to the teacher, rehearse material to be remembered, monitor own level of comprehension). In turn, these students master the material more rapidly and thereby require less instruction.

In this section, I discuss some types of task engagement variables that may have important effects on students' self-efficacy for learning. This discussion is not meant to be exhaustive but rather to be suggestive of the kinds of variables that seem especially germane to school learning settings.

The *purpose of instruction,* or what uses students will be expected to make of the material to be learned (Marx, 1983), can affect self-efficacy for learning. When teachers announce that material will be covered on a test, students who have performed poorly on tests in the past may experience anxiety, which could lead to low self-efficacy. Conversely, students who previously have earned good grades on term papers may react with high self-efficacy to the announcement that they will have to write a term paper.

Content difficulty would seem to be an especially important variable. Subject matter that is perceived as difficult to learn may lead to attributions of high task difficulty, which can negatively affect self-efficacy for learning. Conversely, material that students believe is easy to learn ought to result in high self-efficacy. For example, many students have qualms about learning how to reduce fractions to lowest common denominators. Those who believe that they are competent in the component skills (multiplication, division) may feel more efficacious about learning than students who doubt their capabilities.

Self-efficacy for learning ought to be affected by the type of *cognitive processing* required by the content. Students who have difficulty processing information required by a task may conclude that they have low ability and thereby feel less efficacious about learning than students who believe that they can effectively process the information. In memorizing spelling words, students who believe that they are poor memorizers are apt to feel less efficacious about learning a list of spelling words than those who believe they can apply a memorization strategy. Salomon (1984) has shown that students perceive learning from television to be easier than learning from print, hold higher self-efficacy about learning from television, and consequently invest less mental effort in learning. For written materials, on the other hand, self-efficacy relates positively to mental effort.

Much classroom learning depends on being able to effectively apply cognitive strategies. *Strategy training* can foster self-efficacy for learning (Schunk, 1985b). The belief that one understands and can effectively apply a strategy leads to a greater sense of control over learning outcomes, which can promote self-efficacy (Bandura, 1982a). We might expect that strategy training would foster ability attributions in students and enhance their self-efficacy for learning.

Modeling (discussed more fully later) is an important component of strategy training. Observing a strategy modeled can convey to students that they possess the capabilities to learn to apply the strategy (Schunk, 1985b). Cognitive modeling, in which models verbalize aloud task rules and operations while simultaneously demonstrating their application, is useful for training students to use strategies (Meichenbaum, 1977).

At the same time, consistent and effective strategy use is enhanced by conveying information about task demands, such as how using the strategy will help overcome difficulties and promote success at various tasks (Baker & Brown, 1984; Borkowski & Cavanaugh, 1979). For example, models can verbalize while working at the task (e.g., "This isn't so hard"). Understanding the demands of a task and how to utilize strategies to surmount difficulties can engender a sense of control over learning outcomes among students and raise self-efficacy (Bandura, 1982a). Students also can be given information directly by the model (e.g., "Remember to . . ."), or receive information on what other similar students did to succeed at the task (e.g., "Other students did best when they . . .").

Brown and her colleagues emphasize that effective strategy training needs to include three components: instruction and practice in applying a strategy, training in self-regulated implementation and monitoring of strategy use, and information on strategy value and on the range of tasks to which the strategy can be applied (Baker & Brown, 1984; Brown, Palincsar, & Armbruster, 1984). Each of these aspects should have a positive influence on students' self-efficacy for continued skill improvement.

Research on instruction has addressed how variations in teachers' presentations affect students' cognitive processes and learning. Although empirical data are lacking, *instructional presentation* may influence self-efficacy for learning. Teachers who present material in a fashion that students can comprehend are apt to engender high self-efficacy for learning. Teachers' use of instructional time also may be important. Teachers who provide students with multiple opportunities for task engagement (instruction, practice, review) enhance students' opportunities to experience success.

In judging self-efficacy, students also may take into account how well they learn from the instructional methods employed by the teacher. Students who believe that they can capture the main points from a lecture and take good notes may hold higher self-efficacy for learning from a lecture than students who doubt their capabilities. Shy students may experience anxiety about participating in group discussions, which may lead them to believe that they will not learn much from the experience.

Brophy (1983) has shown that an important aspect of instructional presentation is how the teacher opens the lesson. Teachers often give no introduction but rather move directly into task. Other ways of opening lessons are to cue positive (negative) expectations by asserting that students will enjoy (not enjoy) the task and do well (poorly) on it. To the extent that students view the teacher as a credible judge of their abilities, these statements ought to have quite different effects on self-efficacy for learning.

When and how the teacher provides students with *performance feedback* can influence self-efficacy. The role of teacher feedback is minimal where students can derive their own feedback to determine how well they are learning. Some mathematical exercises allow for students to check their answers. But many times, students require teacher feedback because otherwise they do not know whether they are making progress in learning. In these instances, teacher feedback that highlights progress (e.g., "That's right. You're getting good at this") ought to be especially beneficial.

Students are exposed to many teacher and peer models daily. *Modeling* occurs not only when a teacher explains a skill and demonstrates its application but also when students compare their performances with those of their peers. An important cue used to assess self-efficacy may be the perceived similarity between observers and models. Perceived similarity can be based on personal attributes (e.g., age, gender, background) or competence. Models who are perceived as similar or slightly higher in competence provide the best information for assessing one's own capabilities (Suls & Miller, 1977). Students who observe a similar peer learn a task are apt to believe that they can learn as well (Schunk, 1985b).

At the same time, models who are high in prestige and power lead to greater observational learning than models of lower status (Rosenthal & Bandura, 1978). Although students attend to and emulate their teachers despite dissimilarity in personal attributes and perceived competence, observation of a peer (student) model may exert more beneficial effects on self-efficacy, especially among low achievers who may doubt that they are capable of attaining the teacher's level of competence (Schunk, 1985b). Remedial students, for example, may not feel highly efficacious about learning to divide fractions by observing a flawless teacher model, whereas they should feel more capable of learning when they observe a peer successfully solving problems.

Another influential modeling variable is the number of models. Compared with a single model, multiple models increase the probability that observers will perceive themselves as similar to at least one of the models (Thelen, Fry, Fehrenbach, & Frautschi, 1979). Students who might easily discount the successes of a single model may be especially swayed by observing several peers performing a task; they might believe that if several peers can learn, they can as well. Multiple models could be highly influential with students who have encountered difficulties in school.

The use of coping rather than mastery models also could increase model–observer similarity. Coping models initially demonstrate the typical fears and deficiencies of observers but gradually improve their performance and gain confidence in their capabilities, whereas mastery models demonstrate faultless performance and high confidence from the outset (Kazdin, 1978; Thelen et al., 1979). Coping models illustrate how determined effort and positive self-thoughts can overcome difficulties.

In academic settings, the effects of mastery and coping models may depend on such factors as the type of learner and the difficulty of the task. For example, coping models might promote self-efficacy for learning better among students likely to view the coping models' initial difficulties and gradual progress as more similar to their typical performances than the rapid learning of mastery models. Normal learners might benefit more from observing mastery models; observation of a peer having difficulty learning could convey high task difficulty, which will not raise self-efficacy for learning (Schunk, 1985b).

In addition to perceived similarity, students also use modeled outcomes and outcome patterns as cues for assessing self-efficacy (Bandura, 1986). Observing a superior model, such as the teacher, succeed using a strategy that students believe they can apply should raise self-efficacy; when students observe similar peers fail using inferior tactics, students might nonetheless feel they can learn if they believe that they could work more effectively. Conversely, observing a similar model succeed only after expending much effort and utilizing an effective strategy may not raise observers' self-efficacy.

Another important task engagement variable that can affect self-efficacy for learning is *goal setting*, which involves comparing one's present performance against a standard (Bandura, 1986). When students are given or select a goal, they may experience a sense of self-efficacy for attaining it, which is substantiated as they work at the task and observe their goal progress. A heightened sense of learning efficacy helps sustain task motivation (Schunk, 1985b).

Goals exert their effects through their properties: specificity, difficulty level, proximity (Bandura, 1986; Locke, Shaw, Saari, & Latham, 1981). Goals that incorporate specific performance standards are more likely to raise learning efficacy because progress toward an explicit goal is easier to gauge. General goals (e.g., "Do your best") do not enhance motivation. Goal difficulty refers to the level of task proficiency required as assessed against a standard. Although students initially may doubt their capabilities to attain goals they believe are difficult, working toward difficult goals can build a strong sense of efficacy, because they offer more information about learning capabilities than easier goals. Goals also are distinguished by how far they project into the future. Proximal goals, which are close at hand, result in greater motivation than more distant goals. As students observe their progress toward a proximal goal, they are apt to believe that they are capable of further learning.

Goal setting may be especially influential with long-term tasks and assignments. For example, many students have initial doubts about writing a good term paper. Teachers can assist students by breaking the task into a series of short-term goals (e.g., select a topic, conduct background research, write an outline). Students are apt to feel more efficacious about accomplishing the subtasks, and the attainment of each subgoal should help develop their overall sense of efficacy for producing a good term paper.

Much research shows that offering rewards can promote task performance (Lepper & Greene, 1978). *Rewards* also constitute an important influence on students' learning efficacy. Rewards are likely to enhance self-efficacy when they are tied to students' actual accomplishments. Telling students that they can earn rewards based on what they accomplish can instill a sense of self-efficacy for learning (Schunk, 1985b). As students then work at a task and note their progress, this sense of efficacy is validated. Receipt of the reward further validates self-efficacy, because it symbolizes progress. When rewards are not tied to actual performance, they may actually convey negative efficacy information; students might infer that they are not expected to learn much because they do not possess the requisite capability.

Research has examined how classroom reward structures influence students' motivation and social comparisons of abilities. Competitive reward structures reduce the possibilities for students receiving rewards when others are successful (Ames, 1984). Under competitive conditions, students who do not receive rewards may form low ability attributions, which ought to negatively affect self-efficacy. In contrast, cooperative reward structures are characterized by group members sharing rewards based on their collective group performance. When groups are successful, the group's success may be a salient cue for assessing learning efficacy (Schunk, 1985b). Cooperative groups that fail, however, may stifle motivation and negatively affect self-efficacy. In individualistic reward structures, students' achievements are independent of one another, and the opportunity for reward is equal across students. This structure ought to highlight progress in skill development as a cue for gauging self-efficacy; however, the perception of little or no progress will not promote efficacy.

Finally, *attributional feedback,* or feedback linking students' successes and failures with one or more causes, should influence self-efficacy for learning. Attributional feedback is a persuasive source of efficacy information. Being told that one can achieve better results through harder work can motivate one to do so and convey that one possesses the necessary capability to succeed (Andrews & Debus, 1978; Dweck, 1975). Providing effort feedback for prior successes can support students' perceptions of their progress in learning, sustain motivation, and increase self-efficacy for continued learning (Schunk, 1985b). Ability information becomes more important with increasing experience and development. To the extent that ability attributions are accompanied by less emphasis on effort as a cause of success, students should feel exceptionally self-confident for being able to learn.

The timing of attributional feedback also seems important. Early task successes constitute a prominent cue used to formulate ability attributions (Weiner, 1974). Teacher feedback that links students' early successes with ability (e.g., "That's correct. You're really good at this") could result in an enhanced sense of learning efficacy. Many times, however, effort feedback for early successes may be more credible, because when students lack skills they realistically have to expend some effort to succeed. As students develop skills, switching to ability feedback may better enhance self-efficacy. Continuing to attribute students' performances to effort may lead students to wonder why they must continue to work hard to succeed.

RESEARCH EVIDENCE

This section summarizes some previous work that investigated the effects of attributional feedback, goal setting, and strategy training on achievement behaviors. These studies, which are discussed in depth elsewhere (Schunk, 1984a, 1985b), did not specifically address self-efficacy for learning. They are relevant to this chapter, however, because they explored the effects of task engagement variables during cognitive skill learning. I conclude this section by summarizing more-recent research on peer models that specifically explored the operation of self-efficacy for learning cognitive skills.

ATTRIBUTIONAL FEEDBACK

As noted earlier, the failure of the attributional feedback treatment in the Schunk (1981) study may have occurred because students received conflicting efficacy information. In a follow-up experiment (Schunk, 1982), children periodically received effort feedback as they solved problems during a subtraction training program. Some children's prior achievement was linked with effort ("You've been working hard"), other children's future achievement was linked with effort ("You need to work hard"), and those in a third condition did not receive effort feedback. Linking prior achievement with effort led to the highest posttest subtraction skill and self-efficacy, as well as task motivation (measured by rate of problem solving during training). These results support the idea that linking prior achievement with effort validates children's beliefs concerning their progress and conveys that they are capable of further learning with hard work.

Using similar methodology (Schunk, 1983a), we investigated whether ability feedback might exert stronger effects on achievement outcomes than effort feedback. Children participated in a subtraction training program and periodically received ability feedback for prior successes ("You're good at this"), effort feedback ("You've been working hard"), ability and effort (combined) feedback, or no feedback. Children who received only ability feedback demonstrated higher self-efficacy and skill on the posttest compared with the effort-only and the ability-plus-effort conditions. The latter subjects judged their effort expenditure during training to be greater than did ability-only students. Children in the combined condition may have discounted some ability information in favor of effort. They might have wondered how well they were learning if they had to continue to work hard to succeed. Information that children were good in subtraction and that they had been working hard may have implied lower ability than ability feedback alone.

Schunk (1984b) tested the idea that the sequence of attributional feedback influences achievement outcomes. Children lacking subtraction skills received training and solved subtraction problems during the treatment sessions. One group of children periodically received ability feedback, a second group received effort feedback, a third condition was given ability feedback during the first half of training and effort feedback during the second half, and for a fourth condition this sequence was reversed. Providing ability feedback for early successes, regardless of whether it was continued or children later received effort feedback, led to higher ability attributions, posttest self-efficacy and subtraction skill, compared with providing effort feedback for early successes. These results suggest that early ability feedback instilled higher expectations for continued learning.

A 1986 study explored how the sequence of effort feedback affected learning disabled students' motivation, self-efficacy, and subtraction skill (Schunk & Cox). Students received subtraction training and (a) effort feedback during the first half of training, (b) effort feedback during the second half, or (c) no effort feedback. Each type of effort feedback promoted posttest self-efficacy and skill better than no feedback, but effort feedback during the first half of training enhanced students' effort attributions for success. Given students' learning disabilities, the effort feedback for early or later successes may have seemed highly credible, because they realistically had to expend effort to succeed. They may have interpreted the effort feedback as indicating that they were becoming more skillful and were capable of further learning. Over a longer time, however, effort feedback might lower self-efficacy, because as students become more skillful they might wonder why they still have to work hard to succeed.

In summary, the effects of attributional feedback on students' achievement behaviors depends on such factors as the sequence of feedback, the type of student, and the difficulty of the task. Effort feedback is most influential when students realistically have to expend effort to succeed. When students learn skills readily, ability feedback exerts stronger effects on self-efficacy and motivation. Future research should examine students' perceptions of the meaning of attributional feedback to determine how various forms of feedback influence their self-efficacy for continued learning.

GOAL SETTING

Self-set Goals versus Assigned Goals

Schunk (1985a) tested the idea that self-set goals promote achievement behaviors better than either externally imposed goals or no goals. The rationale for this study derived from the idea that participation in goal setting can lead to high goal commitment, which is necessary for goals to enhance performance (Locke et al., 1981).

Subjects were sixth graders classified as learning disabled in mathematics. Children received subtraction training that included instruction and practice opportunities over several sessions. Some children set performance goals each session, others had comparable goals assigned to them, and children in a third condition received training but no goals. Children in each of the goal conditions judged their expectancy of goal attainment at the start of each session.

Self-set goals led to the highest posttest self-efficacy and subtraction performance. Although children in each of the goal conditions demonstrated higher task motivation during training (measured by number of problems completed), children in the self-set condition expected their goal attainment to be higher. The latter finding suggests that allowing students to set their own learning goals enhanced their self-efficacy for attaining them.

Proximal versus Distant Goals

Subtraction Training. To test the idea that proximal goals enhance achievement behaviors better than distant goals, Bandura and Schunk (1981) presented children with a subtraction training program over several sessions. The program consisted of individual sets of written material that included both the didactic instruction and the problems to be solved. Some children pursued a proximal goal of completing one set each session; a second group was given a distant goal of completing all sets by the end of the last session; a third group was advised to work productively.

Proximal goals heightened task motivation and led to the highest posttest subtraction skill and self-efficacy, whereas the distant goal resulted in no benefits compared with the general goal. These findings support the idea that when children can easily gauge their progress against a goal, the perception of improvement enhances self-efficacy. Gauging progress against a distant goal is more difficult, and uncertainty about one's learning should not instill high self-efficacy for improving one's skills.

Division Training. That short-term performance goals can enhance self-efficacy was also demonstrated during a division training program in which children received instruction and individually solved problems throughout treatment sessions (Schunk, 1983b). Half of the children were given goals each session, whereas the other half were advised to work productively. This study also explored how providing social comparative information about other students' performances affected subjects' achievement outcomes. Within each goal condition, half of the subjects were informed of the number of problems that other similar children had been able to complete (which matched the session goal); the other half were not given comparative information. The comparative information was designed to convey that the goals were attainable.

Goals enhanced division self-efficacy on the posttest; comparative information promoted motivation during training. Subjects who received both goals and comparative information demonstrated the highest posttest division skill. These results suggest that providing children with a goal and information that it is attainable may lead to a sense of self-efficacy for learning, which contributes to more productive performance during training and to greater skill development.

Summary

Goal properties exert important effects on students' achievement behaviors. These effects are hypothesized to occur in part by enhancing students' self-efficacy for learning. Future research should assess students' self-efficacy at the outset of learning tasks and determine how sources of information concerning progress toward a goal affect students' self-efficacy for continued learning.

STRATEGY TRAINING

One means of teaching strategies involves *overt verbalization* (having students verbalize aloud the component steps while applying them to academic tasks). Overt verbalization is a form of *private speech* (the set of speech phenomena that has a behavioral self-regulatory function but is not socially communicative; Harris, 1982; Vygotsky, 1962). Overt verbalization can facilitate learning because it (1) directs students' attention to important task features, (2) assists strategy encoding and retention, and (3) helps students work in a systematic fashion (Schunk, 1985b). Verbalization seems most beneficial for students who typically perform in a deficient manner, such as impulsive, remedial, learning disabled, or emotionally disturbed children (Borkowski & Cavanaugh, 1979; Hallahan, Kneedler, & Lloyd, 1983). By highlighting a strategy that can improve performance, verbalization conveys to students a sense of personal control over learning outcomes, which can enhance performance expectancies (Licht & Kistner, 1986).

To determine the effects of strategy verbalization on achievement outcomes, Schunk and Rice (1984) presented language-deficient children in grades two through four with instruction in listening comprehension. Half of the children in each grade verbalized strategic steps prior to applying them to questions; the other half received strategy instruction but did not verbalize the steps. Strategy verbalization led to higher self-efficacy across grades and promoted performance among third and fourth graders but not among second graders. Perhaps the demands of verbalization, along with those of the comprehension task itself, were too complex for the youngest subjects. These children may have focused their efforts on the comprehension task, which would have interfered with strategy encoding and retention.

In a follow-up study (Schunk & Rice, 1985), children in grades four and five with reading comprehension deficiencies received instruction and practice opportunities. Within each grade, half of the subjects verbalized a strategy prior to applying it. Strategy verbalization led to higher reading comprehension, self-efficacy, and ability attributions across grades. The latter finding suggests that strategy verbalization may enhance self-efficacy through its effect on ability attributions.

Subjects in the Schunk and Cox (1986) study received one of three verbalization treatments. One group verbalized aloud the steps to subtraction solution and their application to problems (continuous verbalization), a second group verbalized aloud during the first half of training but not during the second half (discontinued verbalization), and a third group did not verbalize at all (no verbalization). Continuous verbalization led to higher posttest self-efficacy and skill than discontinued and no verbalization, which did not differ. It is possible that when instructed to stop verbalizing aloud, the discontinued-verbalization students had difficulty internalizing the strategy; they may not have utilized covert instructions to regulate their performances. They also may have believed that although the strategy was useful, other factors (e.g., effort) were more important for solving problems (Fabricius & Hagen, 1984). Conversely, continuous verbalization may have made highly salient to students the effectiveness of the strategy for solving problems. Students' self-efficacy for learning likely was validated during training as they successfully applied the strategy.

Future research should examine students' beliefs concerning the effectiveness of strategies to determine how such beliefs relate to perceived capabilities for learning. As a form of self-regulation, verbalization of specific strategies may highlight students' success at the task and better link success with strategy use. The belief that one can effectively apply a strategy that will improve performance should enhance one's belief concerning further learning. Among students who often experience difficulties in learning, strategy verbalization may help to build skills and a sense of self-efficacy for applying them.

PEER MODELS

In the initial study assessing self-efficacy for learning (Schunk & Hanson, 1985), elementary school children who were low achievers in mathematics observed videotapes portraying an adult teacher and a same-sex peer (student) model. The teacher repeatedly provided instruction on subtraction with regrouping, after which the model solved problems using that technique. Other students viewed videotapes that portrayed only the teacher presenting instruction, and a third group of students were not exposed to models. After viewing the tapes, subjects who had observed a peer model were asked to judge perceived similarity in competence to the model. Next, all students assessed self-efficacy for learning to subtract and they all received subtraction instruction.

This study also investigated the effects of mastery and coping models: Children exposed to a peer observed either a mastery or a coping model. The peer-mastery model easily grasped subtraction operations, solved all problems correctly, and verbalized positive achievement beliefs reflecting high self-efficacy (e.g., "I can do that one"), high ability ("I'm good at this"), low task difficulty ("That looks easy"), and positive attitudes ("I like doing these"). The peer-coping model initially made errors and verbalized negative achievement beliefs reflecting low self-efficacy and ability, high task difficulty, and negative attitudes. Over time, the model made fewer errors and began to verbalize coping statements (e.g., "I'll have to work hard on this one"). The coping model's problem-solving behaviors and verbalizations eventually matched those of the mastery model.

Observing a peer model enhanced self-efficacy for learning more than either observing the teacher model or not observing a model; and subjects who viewed the teacher model judged self-efficacy higher than no-model subjects. On posttest measures of self-efficacy and subtraction skill, peer-model subjects outperformed teacher-model and no-model subjects; and the teacher-model condition scored higher than the no-model condition. There were no differences on any measure between the peer-mastery and peer-coping conditions. These negative effects may have been due to students' prior classroom experiences with subtraction. Even though their prior successes had been limited to problems without regrouping, they nonetheless had these experiences to draw on and may have concluded that if the peer could learn to regroup, they could as well. Students may have focused more on what the models had in common (task success) than on their differences (rate of learning, number of errors, type of achievement beliefs). This is not to suggest that observing a teacher model necessarily exerts weak effects on students' self-efficacy. Students who typically learn more rapidly than these subjects might feel quite self-confident after observing a teacher model.

Follow-up research comprising two experiments further explored the effects of mastery and coping models (Schunk, Hanson, & Cox, 1987). Low-achieving children observed videotapes portraying a peer model who demonstrated either rapid (mastery model) or gradual (coping model) acquisition of skill in adding and subtracting fractions. These children had experienced little, if any, prior success with fractions. We expected that children would perceive the coping model's gradual learning more similar to their typical performances than the rapid learning of the mastery model, and thereby experience higher self-efficacy for learning after observing coping models.

Experiment 1 also explored the effects of the gender of the model: Children observed either a same- or opposite-sex peer-mastery or peer-coping model. Although some theories suggest that children are more likely to imitate same-sex models, research shows that gender of the model affects performance of behaviors more than it affects learning (Perry & Bussey, 1979). That is, children learn from models of both sexes, but they are more likely to perform behaviors demonstrated by models whom they believe are good examples of their own gender role. Given that this study investigated cognitive skill learning of a school subject appropriate for children of both genders, effects due to gender of the model were not anticipated.

Experiment 2 investigated the effects of number of models: Children observed either one or three same-sex peer models display mastery or coping behaviors. Observing multiple models presumably increases the probability that observers will perceive themselves as similar to at least one of the models, which should enhance self-efficacy. Given that subjects had encountered difficulties in learning mathematical skills, we felt that they might be more likely to discount the successes of a single model than the diverse instances of successful learning displayed by multiple models.

In both experiments, children who observed coping models judged themselves more similar in competence to the models than did subjects who observed mastery models. In Experiment 1, observation of a coping model led to higher self-efficacy, skill, and training performance, compared with observation of a mastery model. There were no differences on any measure due to sex of model. In Experiment 2, children in the single coping model, multiple coping model, and multiple mastery model conditions demonstrated higher self-efficacy, skill, and training performance, compared with subjects who observed a single mastery model. These latter results show that the benefits of multiple models did not depend on perceptions of similarity in competence. Perceived similarity in competence is not the only means of conveying information about one's self-efficacy for learning. Similarity in competence may be a more important source of efficacy information when children are exposed to a single model and have a less-diverse set of modeled cues to use in judging self-efficacy.

To summarize, the observation of peers learning cognitive skills has positive effects on self-efficacy for learning among children who have encountered prior difficulties with the subject matter. The research to date suggests that coping models and multiple models are particularly beneficial; however, much more research is needed to explore the mechanisms whereby various attributes of models influence children's beliefs about their own learning capabilities. For example, research ought to examine whether teacher modeling of coping behaviors also promotes students' self-efficacy for learning. Such research would have valuable implications for teaching practices.

CONCLUSIONS AND NEW DIRECTIONS

The model outlined in this chapter proposes that students enter learning tasks with varying levels of self-efficacy for learning that are a function of aptitudes and prior experiences. As students engage in learning activities, cues emanating from task engagement variables signal to students how well they are learning. This information affects their beliefs about their capabilities for further skill improvement. In turn, self-efficacy bears a positive relationship to task motivation and learning.

Many of the points made in this chapter require empirical investigation. In particular, research emphasis should be given to exploring (1) how students integrate efficacy information from diverse sources, (2) how developmental factors influence self-efficacy, and (3) how treatments designed to promote students' self-efficacy can be integrated into the context of regular classroom instruction.

INTEGRATION OF EFFICACY INFORMATION

Research is needed on how students cognitively process different pieces of information in forming and modifying their perceptions of self-efficacy for acquiring cognitive skills. In school, students routinely acquire self-efficacy information in diverse ways. As they work on tasks, they gain efficacy information directly from their own accomplishments. They also observe their peers' performances. Teachers periodically provide persuasory information as they monitor students' efforts (e.g., "You can do better").

Information from direct, vicarious, and persuasory sources may not be consistent. A student may perform poorly but observe peers succeed and be told by the teacher, "You can do better." An important research issue concerns how students resolve such discrepancies. We might expect that actual performance information would "count" more heavily than other sources, but perhaps, as suggested by the Schunk et al. (1987) study, observing several peers succeeding would enhance self-efficacy for learning despite prior failures.

DEVELOPMENTAL INFLUENCES ON SELF-EFFICACY

Developmental factors should influence the cues that students derive from task engagement variables and how students cognitively process these cues to form and alter perceptions of self-efficacy. Research is needed on each of these aspects. For example, short-term and specific goals should be maximally motivating and provide clear information to young children concerning their progress. With development, students become able to represent long-term objectives in thought, break such objectives into a series of subgoals, and self-regulate their performances over time. Children's social comparisons also undergo developmental changes. Young children's comparisons focus on the overt performances of their peers. As children gradually acquire a conception of underlying abilities, the basis for perceived similarity may shift from tangible outcomes to underlying abilities.

I already have mentioned some developmental considerations involved in the effects of various forms of attributional feedback. Young children stress effort as a cause of outcomes, but with increasing development and experience, ability attributions become increasingly important influences on self-efficacy. An important question concerns how children weigh and combine effort and ability information to form self-efficacy judgments at various stages of development.

CLASSROOM RESEARCH

Although the research summarized earlier employed school tasks, most of these studies were not conducted in the context of actual classroom instruction. As a consequence, the ways that task engagement variables might actually operate in classroom contexts have not been adequately explored. Classroom-based research using teachers, text-books, and computers is needed. To this end, researchers need to work directly with classroom teachers. This type of research strategy would involve training teachers to administer treatments that systematically explored the effects of various task engagement variables on students' self-efficacy. Once trained, these teachers can become active collaborators in the research process. Such research also could explore how perceptions of self-efficacy change over the course of a semester or school year. In short, research is needed on how classroom task engagement variables can be systematically employed to enhance students' self-efficacy, motivation, and learning.

ACKNOWLEDGMENTS

The research reported in this chapter was supported by grants from the National Institute of Mental Health (MH35459 and MH38147), the National Science Foundation (BNS-8011753), The Spencer Foundation, and the University of Houston.

REFERENCES

Ames, C. (1984). Competitive, cooperative, and individualistic goal structures: A cognitive-motivational analysis. In R. Ames & C. Ames (Eds.), *Research on motivation in education: Vol. 1. Student motivation* (pp. 177–207). Orlando, FL: Academic Press.

Andrews, G. R., & Debus, R. L. (1978). Persistence and the causal perception of failure: Modifying cognitive attributions. *Journal of Educational Psychology, 70,* 154–166.

Atkinson, J. W. (1964). *An introduction to motivation.* Princeton, NJ: Van Nostrand.

Baker, L., & Brown, A. L. (1984). Metacognitive skills and reading. In P. D. Pearson (Ed.), *Handbook of reading research* (pp. 353–394). New York: Longman.

Bandura, A. (1977). Self-efficacy: Toward a unifying theory of behavioral change. *Psychological Review, 84,* 191–215.

Bandura, A. (1982a). The self and mechanisms of agency. In J. Suls (Ed.), *Psychological perspectives on the self* (Vol. 1, pp. 3–39). Hillsdale, NJ: Erlbaum.

Bandura, A. (1982b). Self-efficacy mechanism in human agency. *American Psychologist, 37,* 122–147.

Bandura, A. (1986). *Social foundations of thought and action: A social cognitive theory.* Englewood Cliffs, NJ: Prentice-Hall.

Bandura, A., & Adams, N. E. (1977). Analysis of self-efficacy theory of behavioral change. *Cognitive Therapy and Research, 1,* 287–310.

Bandura, A., Adams, N. E., & Beyer, J. (1977). Cognitive processes mediating behavioral change. *Journal of Personality and Social Psychology, 35,* 125–139.

Bandura, A., & Schunk, D. H. (1981). Cultivating competence, self-efficacy, and intrinsic interest through proximal self-motivation. *Journal of Personality and Social Psychology, 41,* 586–598.

Borkowski, J. G., & Cavanaugh, J. C. (1979). Maintenance and generalization of skills and strategies by the retarded. In N. R. Ellis (Ed.), *Handbook of mental deficiency, psychological theory and research* (2nd ed., pp. 569–617). Hillsdale, NJ: Erlbaum.

Bower, G. H., & Hilgard, E. R. (1981). *Theories of learning* (5th ed.). Englewood Cliffs, NJ: Prentice-Hall.

Brophy, J. (1983). Conceptualizing student motivation. *Educational Psychologist, 18,* 200–215.

Brown, A. L., Palincsar, A. S., & Armbruster, B. B. (1984). Instructing comprehension-fostering activities in interactive learning situations. In H. Mandl, N. L. Stein, & T. Trabasso (Eds.), *Learning and comprehension of text* (pp. 255–286). Hillsdale, NJ: Erlbaum.

Brown, J. S., & Burton, R. R. (1978). Diagnostic models for procedural bugs in basic mathematical skills. *Cognitive Science, 2,* 155–192.

Collins, J. (1982, March). *Self-efficacy and ability in achievement behavior.* Paper presented at the meeting of the American Educational Research Association, New York.

Corno, L., & Mandinach, E. B. (1983). The role of cognitive engagement in classroom learning and motivation. *Educational Psychologist, 18,* 88–108.

Cronbach, L. J., & Snow, R. E. (1977). *Aptitudes and instructional methods.* New York: Irvington.

Dweck, C. S. (1975). The role of expectations and attributions in the alleviation of learned helplessness. *Journal of Personality and Social Psychology, 31,* 674–685.

Dweck, C. S. (1986). Motivational processes affecting learning. *American Psychologist, 41,* 1040–1048.

Fabricius, W. V., & Hagen, J. W. (1984). Use of causal attributions about recall performance to assess metamemory and predict strategic memory behavior in young children. *Developmental Psychology, 20,* 975–987.

Frieze, I. H. (1980). Beliefs about success and failure in the classroom. In J. H. McMillan (Ed.), *The social psychology of school learning* (pp. 39–78). New York: Academic Press.

Gagne, R. M. (1984). Learning outcomes and their effects: Useful categories of human performance. *American Psychologist, 39,* 377–385.

Hallahan, D. P., Kneedler, R. D., & Lloyd, J. W. (1983). Cognitive behavior modification techniques for learning disabled children: Self-instruction and self-monitoring. In J. D. McKinney & L. Feagans (Eds.), *Current topics in learning disabilities* (pp. 207–244). Norwood, NJ: Ablex.

Harari, O., & Covington, M. V. (1981). Reactions to achievement behavior from a teacher and student perspective: A developmental analysis. *American Educational Research Journal, 18,* 15–28.

Harris, K. R. (1982). Cognitive-behavior modification: Application with exceptional children. *Focus on Exceptional Children, 15,* 1–16.

Heider, F. (1958). *The psychology of interpersonal relations.* New York: Wiley.

Kazdin, A. E. (1978). Covert modeling: The therapeutic application of imagined rehearsal. In J. L. Singer & K. S. Pope (Eds.), *The power of human imagination: New methods in psychotherapy* (pp. 255–278). New York: Plenum.

Kelley, H. H., & Michela, J. L. (1980). Attribution theory and research. *Annual Review of Psychology, 31,* 457–501.

Lepper, M. R., & Greene, D. (1978). *The hidden costs of reward: New perspectives on the psychology of human motivation.* Hillsdale, NJ: Erlbaum.

Licht, B. G., & Kistner, J. A. (1986). Motivational problems of learning-disabled children: Individual differences and their implications for treatment. In J. K. Torgesen & B. W. L. Wong (Eds.), *Psychological and educational perspectives on learning disabilities* (pp. 225–255). Orlando, FL: Academic Press.

Locke, E. A., Shaw, K. N., Saari, L. M., & Latham, G. P. (1981). Goal setting and task performance: 1969–1980. *Psychological Bulletin, 90,* 125–152.

Marx, R. W. (1983). Student perception in classrooms. *Educational Psychologist, 18,* 145–164.

McCombs, B. L. (1984). Processes and skills underlying continuing intrinsic motivation to learn: Toward a definition of motivational skills training interventions. *Educational Psychologist, 19,* 199–218.

Meichenbaum, D. (1977). *Cognitive behavior modification: An integrative approach.* New York: Plenum.

Nicholls, J. G. (1978). The development of the concepts of effort and ability, perception of academic attainment, and the understanding that difficult tasks require more ability. *Child Development, 49,* 800–814.

Nicholls, J. G. (1983). Conceptions of ability and achievement motivation: A theory and its implications for education. In S. G. Paris, G. M. Olson, & H. W. Stevenson (Eds.), *Learning and motivation in the classroom* (pp. 211–237). Hillsdale, NJ: Erlbaum.

Perry, D. G., & Bussey, K. (1979). The social learning theory of sex differences: Imitation is alive and well. *Journal of Personality and Social Psychology, 37,* 1699–1712.

Peterson, P. L., Swing, S. R., Braverman, M. T., & Buss, R. (1982). Students' aptitudes and their reports of cognitive processes during direct instruction. *Journal of Educational Psychology, 74,* 535–547.

Rosenthal, T. L., & Bandura, A. (1978). Psychological modeling: Theory and practice. In S. L. Garfield & A. E. Bergin (Eds.), *Handbook of psychotherapy and behavior change: An empirical analysis* (2nd ed., pp. 621–658). New York: Wiley.

Rosenthal, T. L., & Zimmerman, B. J. (1978). *Social learning and cognition.* New York: Academic Press.

Rotter, J. B. (1966). Generalized expectancies for internal versus external control of reinforcement. *Psychological Monographs, 80* (Whole No. 609).

Salomon, G. (1984). Television is "easy" and print is "tough": The differential investment of mental effort in learning as a function of perceptions and attributions. *Journal of Educational Psychology, 76,* 647–658.

Schunk, D. H. (1981). Modeling and attributional effects on children's achievement: A self-efficacy analysis. *Journal of Educational Psychology, 73,* 93–105.

Schunk, D. H. (1982). Effects of effort attributional feedback on children's perceived self-efficacy and achievement. *Journal of Educational Psychology, 74,* 548–556.

Schunk, D. H. (1983a). Ability versus effort attributional feedback: Differential effects on self-efficacy and achievement. *Journal of Educational Psychology, 75,* 848–856.

Schunk, D. H. (1983b). Developing children's self-efficacy and skills: The roles of social comparative information and goal setting. *Contemporary Educational Psychology, 8,* 76–86.

Schunk, D. H. (1984a). Self-efficacy perspective on achievement behavior. *Educational Psychologist, 19,* 48–58.

Schunk, D. H. (1984b). Sequential attributional feedback and children's achievement behaviors. *Journal of Educational Psychology, 76,* 1159–1169.

Schunk, D. H. (1985a). Participation in goal setting: Effects on self-efficacy and skills of learning disabled children. *Journal of Special Education, 19,* 307–317.

Schunk, D. H. (1985b). Self-efficacy and classroom learning. *Psychology in the Schools, 22,* 208–223.

Schunk, D. H., & Cox, P. D. (1986). Strategy training and attributional feedback with learning disabled students. *Journal of Educational Psychology, 78,* 201–209.

Schunk, D. H., & Hanson, A. R. (1985). Peer models: Influence on children's self-efficacy and achievement. *Journal of Educational Psychology, 77,* 313–322.

Schunk, D. H., Hanson, A. R., & Cox, P. D. (1987). Peer model attributes and children's achievement behaviors. *Journal of Educational Psychology, 79,* 54–61.

Schunk, D. H., & Rice, J. M. (1984). Strategy self-verbalization during remedial listening comprehension instruction. *Journal of Experimental Education, 53,* 49–54.

Schunk, D. H., & Rice, J. M. (1985). Verbalization of comprehension strategies: Effects on children's achievement outcomes. *Human Learning, 4,* 1–10.

Suls, J. M., & Miller, R. C. (1977). *Social comparison processes: Theoretical and empirical perspectives.* Washington, DC: Hemisphere.

Thelen, M. H., Fry, R. A., Fehrenbach, P. A., & Frautschi, N. M. (1979). Therapeutic videotape and film modeling: A review. *Psychological Bulletin, 86,* 701–720.

Thomas, J. W. (1980). Agency and achievement: Self-management and self-regard. *Review of Educational Research, 50,* 213–240.

Tolman, E. C. (1959). Principles of purposive behavior. In S. Koch (Ed.), *Psychology: A study of a science* (Vol. 2, pp. 92–157). New York: McGraw-Hill.

Vroom, V. H. (1964). *Work and motivation.* New York: Wiley.

Vygotsky, L. S. (1962). *Thought and language.* Cambridge, MA: MIT Press.

Weiner, B. (1974). An attributional interpretation of expectancy-value theory. In B. Weiner (Ed.), *Cognitive views of human motivation* (pp. 51–69). New York: Academic Press.

Weiner, B. (1985). An attributional theory of achievement motivation and emotion. *Psychological Review, 92,* 548–573.

Weiner, B., Graham, S., Taylor, S. E., & Meyer, W. (1983). Social cognition in the classroom. *Educational Psychologist, 18,* 109–124.

Winne, P. H. (1985). Cognitive processing in the classroom. In T. Husen & T. N. Postlethwaite (Eds.), *The international encyclopedia of education* (Vol. 2, pp. 795–808). Oxford, England: Pergamon.

2

The Dynamics of Intrinsic Motivation: A Study of Adolescents

Mihaly Csikszentmihalyi
Jeanne Nakamura

A BRIEF HISTORY

Almost 700 years ago, William of Ockham proposed his famous rule that "entities should not be increased without necessity," thereafter known as "Ockham's razor." During the heyday of behavioral psychology a generation ago, it was thought that "motivation" was one of those unnecessary entities that could be deleted from scientific vocabulary. If behavior was partly a direct function of some genetic programming and partly of some stimulus–response learning, then motivation was indeed a superfluous concept.

Before the advent of mechanistic psychology, motivation referred to goals, desires, or ideas that moved people to act in certain predictable directions. One person might be motivated to become a saint, another to explore a new continent. It was assumed that motivation was largely under the control of a person's will, which itself was relatively free to determine its own direction. With the spread of modern psychology, however, this autonomy of the will was discredited. People did not "want" to do things; they did them because they had to do them.

The resurgence of interest in cognitive processes in the 1950s granted motivation a slight reprieve. From a cognitivistic perspective, it was possible to view motivation as a mental representation that people made of those instinctive and learned programs that ruled their behavior. But even according to this view, motivation was essentially powerless to affect behavior; it was just a mirror held up to genes and learning that reflected a reality it had no power to change.

The real resurgence of interest in motivation can probably be dated to the late 1950s. It started, ironically, with some unexpected findings with monkeys and rats, in the laboratories of Harry Harlow and others. These results suggested that, given a chance, even rats will "behave" in order to see novel sights, explore new territory, or experiment with challenging tasks. The findings forced psychologists to extend the list of "drives" motivating behavior by adding novelty, curiosity, and competence drives (Butler, 1958; Montgomery, 1954; White, 1959). But how could such results be explained theoretically? J. McV. Hunt, among others, proposed a solution: Organisms were driven not just to restore a homeostatic balance in their nervous systems, as previous drive theories had held, but also to satisfy a need for "optimal arousal." When the nervous system was understimulated, the organism would need to seek out additional stimulation (Berlyne, 1966; Day, Berlyne, & Hunt, 1971; Hunt, 1965). The "optimal arousal hypothesis" was still a mechanistic concept because it postulated a direct effect of the chemistry of the nervous system on behavior. But it opened up some interesting possibilities because it no longer claimed a rigid link between what happened at the molecular level and what the organism did. A certain amount of freedom had crept back into motivation. One of the most influential summaries of this early phase was the volume edited by Fiske and Maddi (1961).

The effect of this new way of thinking about motivation was to split the old concept into two forms. "Extrinsic motivation" remained a label that described the old notion of behavior determined by physiological drives and by stimulus–response learning. "Intrinsic motivation" became a separate topic and referred to things done for reasons that seemed to be better explained as resulting from some decision of the acting organism—a decision that took into account the goal of the organism as well as the situation. Thus, the behavior was interpreted as being less predictable, and hence apparently more "free," than earlier mechanistic theories would have allowed for.

The first generation of researchers to focus directly on intrinsic motivation included Richard deCharms (1968, 1976), who earlier had investigated the achievement motive with David McClelland. His review of the literature on social motivation written more than a decade ago helped put the concept of intrinsic motivation on the intellectual agenda of psychologists (deCharms & Muir, 1978). In his research, deCharms found striking differences among schoolchildren in terms of whether they did or did not feel in control of their lives. He called the first type "Origins," because they believed that what they did was what they wanted to do; and he called the second type "Pawns," because they felt that they were just being pushed around by outside forces. An important characteristic of the Origins was their intrinsic motivation: Because they felt they owned their behavior, they took it more seriously and enjoyed it regardless of outside recognition. Indeed, deCharms hypothesized that in contrast to what drive theories might predict, if people were rewarded for doing things they had initially chosen spontaneously, their intrinsic motivation to do them would decrease.

At the University of Rochester, Edward Deci tested deCharms's prediction (1971, 1975). He found that if people were given money for doing things they enjoyed, they lost interest in those things faster than when they were not rewarded. Deci agreed with deCharms that under such conditions people came to see their involvement in the activity as being instrumental, controlled by external forces rather than freely chosen. Recognition of the reality of intrinsic motivation led Deci and his colleagues by an inevitable logic to investigations of autonomy and self-determination (Deci & Ryan, 1985).

Mark Lepper's team of researchers at Stanford University discovered intrinsic motivation at about the same time. Influenced (1) by the social psychology of Heider (1958) and Kelley (1967, 1973), which ascribed greater importance to causal attributions than earlier cognitive theories of motivation had done, and (2) by the self-perception theory of Bem (1967, 1972), which assigns a similar autonomous power to the self construct, they labelled the proposition the "overjustification hypothesis." Studying children engaged in play activities, Lepper's team replicated and refined the overjustification findings, specifying the conditions under which rewards interfere with behavior, and thus clarifying the dynamics of intrinsic motivation (Greene & Lepper, 1974; Lepper & Greene, 1975; Lepper, Greene, & Nisbett, 1973). The literature on this topic was summarized in a volume appropriately entitled *The Hidden Costs of Reward* (Lepper & Greene, 1978).

The recognition of intrinsic motivation might yet have an important liberating effect on psychology. If psychology is to be a science limited to explaining the behavior of organisms restricted to absurdly simplified laboratory environments, then it makes sense to invoke Ockham's razor and forget about motivation. There is indeed no need to use such a concept to explain why a rat will press a bar in a box that has nothing else in it. But if we wish to say something about why people act in complicated ways in complex natural environments, motivation becomes again a useful concept. And intrinsic motivation alerts us to several facts: (1) People are moved by curiosity and novelty; (2) people need to feel in charge of their own actions; and (3) autonomy and self-determination will lead people to act in ways that often override the instructions built into their nervous systems by genes and by learning. In other words, intrinsic motivation highlights the existence of another system that determines behavior, in addition to genetic programming and stimulus–response pathways. This other system is the self, a configuration in consciousness that has its own needs and its own power to direct behavior (Csikszentmihalyi, 1978, 1982, 1985).

MOTIVATION AS THE ORDERING OF PSYCHIC ENERGY

To illustrate how motivation manifests itself in human behavior in daily life, we draw on data collected from several samples of adolescents over a period of a dozen years. These teenagers were studied with a method devised for recording ongoing inner experience and its setting. The method is called the Experience Sampling Method, or ESM, and it involves giving each respondent an electronic pager, or beeper, and a block of Experience Sampling Forms, or ESFs, to carry for a week. A radio transmitter is programmed to send a signal at random times, about eight times a day, for a week. When the pagers signal, the respondents write down where they are, what they are doing, who else is there, and what they are thinking about; they then fill out 20 or so rating scales that try to assess moods and other states of consciousness at the moment the pagers went off. In the course of a week, each respondent provides 30 to 50 snapshots of daily life, including states of intrinsic motivation. In addition to lengthy interviews after the week of signalling, as well as other standard test information, this method allows the investigator to obtain a rather precise and dynamic account of how motivation changes in response to variations in external and internal conditions (Csikszentmihalyi & Larson, 1984; Csikszentmihalyi & Nakamura, 1986; Csikszentmihalyi, Larson, & Prescott, 1977; Graef, Csikszentmihalyi, & Mc-Manama Giannino, 1983; Mayers, 1978). It is on these studies that the rest of this chapter draws.

On a Monday morning in May, Ted, a senior we studied at the Academy High School in Chicago, started the day out by having an intense argument with some of his friends in the hallway next to his locker. Before noon of the same day, he was sitting in English class, bored. The pre-law class after lunch was slightly better, but Ted began to get himself in high gear only by midafternoon, when he started programming his PC at home. Before supper, Ted spent some time reading an article by Hofstadter about social class and political power in America, and after that he watched a movie on TV. By now it was past 10 o'clock, and because it was Monday, Ted wisely decided to retire for the night.

Ted's day is in some ways typical of the thousands of days we have studied with the ESM. The question we explore is a very simple one: What makes Ted, and the other people who reported on their lives in our studies, do the things they do, day in, day out?

Earlier psychological theories would have explained motivation either in terms of innate drives or in terms of operant learning (Brody, 1980; Gleitman, 1981; Millenson, 1967). For instance, in Ted's case, his argument with friends in the morning might be explained in terms of aggressive drives helpful in establishing dominance hierarchies, drives he has inherited from his primate ancestors. Studying in class and at home could be explained in terms of Ted having learned to associate study with the absence of punishment and the presence of positive rewards from his parents and teachers. The reason Ted watched TV could have been due to an instinctive effort on his part to reduce stimulation to a pleasing homeostatic level.

Some of the things Ted did that Monday, however, are more puzzling. For instance, he spent the best part of the afternoon writing programs for his computer. Strictly speaking, he did not have to do this. Programming was not part of his coursework, nor was it in any direct way related to his future earnings or social status. It was clearly something beyond the call of duty. Nor was writing programs an automatic activity, like watching TV, that he could do almost accidentally. It required a concentration of psychic energy—or attention—that could not have occurred by chance. Why did he try to do this in the absence both of innate drives to do so and of previous conditioning? More recent motivational theories might explain Ted's behavior in terms of "optimal arousal"—as an attempt to set stimulation to the most comfortable level.

Motivational constructs based on drives, operant learning, and even optimal arousal assume that the organism is a system that automatically adjusts and responds to mechanical forces impinging on it. But such models of behavior do not account for one obvious feature of human experience—namely, that people are aware of their own actions. For a person reflecting on his or her own behavior, the major question is not whether that behavior is motivated by drives or by learning; the real question is whether it is something he or she *wants* to do.

Our approach to motivation does not deal with the metaphysical question that drive-oriented psychology tried to resolve and that learning theory tried to avoid: "What causes behavior?" Instead, we more modestly try to address the question, "How do people consciously choose one course of action over another?" In taking such an approach, we need only deal with the objective facts of subjective experience, instead of engaging in speculations about the ultimate causes of action. According to current wisdom, subjective reality is simply a by-product of external forces—of genetic programs, libidinal drives, learning schedules, social controls, cultural ideologies, and so on. In line with these views, there is no autonomous process in consciousness that causes behavior. Our position, however, is different: It is based on the assumption that the self is a system with its own energy, its own structure, and its own capacity to initiate and direct action (Csikszentmihalyi, 1985; Csikszentmihalyi & Massimini, 1985). From this perspective, motivation is to be understood in terms of processes that take place in consciousness.

A concept such as motivation is necessary for explaining behavior only when the behavior involves conscious choice. A good deal of human behavior does not need a concept like motivation to explain its occurrence because it can be accounted for by (1) genetically preprogrammed goal seeking, (2) learned responses, or (3) random shifts of consciousness. None of these processes are motivated in the sense that we use the term because they can be explained just as well by simpler psychological mechanisms.

In its ordinary, normal state, the information-processing system that constitutes consciousness does not focus on any particular range of stimuli. Like a radar dish, attention sweeps back and forth across the stimulus field, noting movements, colors, shapes, objects, sensations, memories, one after the other in no particular order or pattern. This is what happens when we walk down a street, when we lie awake in bed, when we stare out a window—in short, whenever attention is not focused in an orderly sequence. One thought follows another without rhyme or reason, and usually we cannot link one idea to the other in a sensible chain. As soon as a new thought presents itself, it pushes out the one that was there before. Knowing what is in the mind at any given time does not predict what will be there a few seconds later.

This random shift of consciousness, although it produces unpredictable information, is the *probable* state of consciousness. It is probable because that is the state to which consciousness reverts as soon as there are no demands on it; it is the natural state of our information-processing apparatus. In other words, *entropy* (the lack of pattern or order in the information processed by attention) is the baseline state that requires no explanation. The deviations from this random baseline are what need to be explained.

To focus attention on a given set of related stimuli, to the exclusion of irrelevant thoughts and sensations, requires effort, or the expenditure of psychic energy. For instance, when Ted sat for several hours at his PC, his attention was mainly processing information related to the logic of Pascal, the programming language he was learning to use. If we had repeatedly asked him during this period: "What are you thinking about?" most of the time Ted would have answered: "I am looking for the bugs in this program." The fact that his consciousness was relatively predictable for hours at a time is an extremely *improbable* event that could not happen by chance. Therefore, it requires an explanation. Motivation is supposed to provide this explanation. Whenever we encounter human activity that requires concentrated investment of psychic energy, we assume that this event is not random but the product of conscious effort. Motivation is what makes such effort possible.

THE ROLE OF INTRINSIC MOTIVATION

But what motivates a person to pay attention to a given set of information? Again, we do not seek the answer in causal mechanisms such as instincts, drives, or operant learning (i.e., in inferential constructs). They are not the forces one finds operating in consciousness when a person makes a choice. Instead, we consider motives—information that the actor actually considers when making a decision about how to act. Of these motives, it is useful to distinguish two main types: extrinsic and intrinsic motives.

When the only reason for doing a thing is to get something outside the activity itself, the motivation is *extrinsic*. For instance if on Monday morning Ted had been told: "You can leave English class; it will in no way affect your grades," he would have packed up his books and left because what kept his attention on the English class was not anything happening then and there, but the goal of graduation still months away in the future. Most of the time, we do things for extrinsic reasons—not because we want to do them, but in order to reach goals that depend on our expending psychic energy on something else first. We learn to behave like civilized members of society—eating with forks and knives, combing our hair, washing our faces, going to work, respecting the laws, and so on—not because we particularly like to do these things, but because we expect that by acting this way we will get some entirely different things in return—things like money, respect, and free time to use at our discretion. The best way to recognize extrinsic motivation is to ask: "Would a person do this even if no reward or punishment followed from the activity?" If the answer is "No, he or she would not," it makes sense to assume that the motivation was extrinsic.

On the other hand, if the answer to the question was "Yes," it makes sense to talk of intrinsic motivation. When a person does something because he or she gets a reward directly from doing the activity itself, rather than because of a reward that comes after, the motivation is *intrinsic*.

The reward of intrinsic motivation is not a tangible object like the pellets of food that experimenters give rats to reward them for pressing the right bar in the laboratory; neither is it an abstract, symbolic reward like money or status. Instead, intrinsic rewards consist of a direct experience, a state of consciousness that is so enjoyable as to be *autotelic* ("having its goal within itself").

In everyday life, the things we do are often motivated by varying mixtures of extrinsic and intrinsic rewards. For Ted, reading the article on political science at 5:55 P.M. Monday evening was in part a course requirement (and hence extrinsically motivated). But as he went on reading, Ted became engrossed in the argument Professor Hofstadter had woven, and if we had interrupted him with the fateful question "Would you go on reading if you didn't have to?" Ted would probably have answered, "Yes." Similarly, programming the PC was also a mixture of the two sources of motivation. Basically, Ted enjoys playing with the computer; he does not have to do it, so his rewards are primarily intrinsic. Yet Ted also knows that computer literacy is a useful skill that might get him a desirable job later on in life; so it is unavoidable that some extrinsic motives are also present in Ted's consciousness as he works on the computer.

Pleasure and enjoyment are the names we give to those autotelic experiences that are their own reward, and life would be grim without them. Indeed, when people forego for just 48 hours the activities that they enjoy, they report functioning significantly less well afterward (Csikszentmihalyi, 1975). If everything we did was for some extrinsic reason, if nothing we did was worth doing for itself, it is unlikely that we could survive.

On the other hand, social life would be unimaginable if people were not motivated also by extrinsic rewards. As Freud (1961) and many others before and since have pointed out, civilization is possible only because people learn to postpone immediate gratification. Instead of always doing what we want to do, we learn instead to do what others expect us to do, hoping that in the long run we shall enjoy the rewards society dispenses to those who have invested their psychic energy in its goals. Over 2000 years ago, Aesop set down the basic message in his parable of the ant and the grasshopper: The grasshopper made music and had fun all summer long, and laughed at the ant who slaved away the mellow summer days storing surplus food for the winter. But when winter did come, the grasshopper was struck with panic: He was starving while the ant, snug in his underground labyrinth, quietly feasted.

It almost seems that the more complex a culture becomes, the more people have to learn to behave like the ant did in Aesop's fable. As the skills required to be a productive worker become increasingly difficult, it takes proportionately longer for a person to become a competent contributor to society. In the meantime, he or she has to spend more and more years preparing for the future. And when these persons begin to work, they cannot spend much of their earnings on intrinsically rewarding activities; more and more of the money has to go into taxes, insurance premiums, medical plans, social security, investments, pensions, and other savings for the future.

This is not a problem if studying, working, and saving—all this preparation for the future—is to a certain extent also intrinsically rewarding. The long years of schooling, the half of waking life that goes into a job, are tolerable as long as a person enjoys what he or she is doing. Unfortunately, however, teenagers seldom say that they get intrinsic rewards from studying (Csikszentmihalyi & Larson, 1984), and adults rarely see their work as being intrinsically motivated (Graef et al., 1983). Too often, people experience the productive side of everyday life—work, study, housework—as drudgery to be endured only for the sake of future rewards. Enjoyment in the present comes from doing things that are culturally designed for the express purpose of providing it—in other words, from leisure activities. Watching TV, taking drugs, playing Trivial Pursuit, going to a restaurant, getting drunk, or taking a vacation become the rewards that keep people working away at jobs they basically dislike.

The most synergistic use of human potential is when psychic energy gets invested in activities that are simultaneously autotelic and productive. In such cases, persons feel that what they do is worth doing for its own sake, so it is not a waste of time in the present. At the same time, if the activity is also productive, it is not a waste of time for the future either. It is the ideal solution—a combination of the ant's and the grasshopper's way. In Ted's case, programming the PC and reading the article about class and power were good examples of this happy synergy.

Societies in which people cannot get intrinsic rewards from work and family life, and must seek them exclusively in leisure, are usually headed for trouble. Less and less psychic energy goes into productive goals and social ties; an increasingly large amount is wasted in activities that give immediate satisfaction but fail to increase future adaptation. The late Roman empire, the last decades of Byzantium, the French court in the second half of the 18th century are only a few of the most notorious examples of what can happen when large segments of society fail to find pleasure in productive life. To provide enjoyable experiences, the rulers of society had to resort to increasingly elaborate and expensive artificial stimulations—circuses, chariot races, balls, and hunts—which drain psychic energy without leaving any useful residue.

Given these facts, it is not too much to claim that one of the central issues of psychology is learning how to combine intrinsic rewards with activities that are useful in the long run. To achieve this aim, however, we must first understand the dynamics of intrinsic motivation. What makes an activity autotelic? Why do we enjoy doing some things while we get bored or anxious doing others? These are the questions we try to answer in the remainder of this chapter, by presenting first a theoretical model of intrinsic motivation and then a variety of data that illustrate how the theory accounts for events in real, everyday life.

A THEORETICAL MODEL OF
INTRINSIC MOTIVATION

If you ask persons who enjoy what they are doing to describe how they feel, it is likely that they will tell you some or all of the following: (1) that all of their minds and bodies are completely involved in what they are doing, (2) that their concentration is very deep, (3) that they know what they want to do, (4) that they know how well they are doing, (5) that they are not worried about failing, (6) that time is passing very quickly, and (7) that they have lost the ordinary sense of self-consciousness and gnawing worry that characterize so much of daily life (Csikszentmihalyi,

1975). Because of these dimensions of experience, they feel that the activity is worth doing for its own sake even if nothing else were to come of it; in other words, the activity has become autotelic.

These are what hundreds of respondents mentioned when we asked them to describe experiences that were autotelic, or intrinsically motivated—occasions when the doing of an activity was so enjoyable that no external rewards were needed to keep doing it. The same accounts were given by groups of people from very different cultures, ages, and social classes such as chess masters, rock climbers, basketball players, music composers, and surgeons in the United States (Csikszentmihalyi, 1975), American high school students (Mayers, 1978), elderly Korean men and women (Han, 1988), long-distance sailors interviewed in the South Pacific (Macbeth, 1985), teenage members of Japanese motorcycle gangs (Sato, 1988), and old men and women living in mountain villages in Europe (Csikszentmihalyi & Csikszentmihalyi, 1988; Massimini, Csikszentmihalyi, & Della Fave, 1986).

This autotelic state of consciousness is what we have called the "flow experience." Flow is what people feel when they enjoy what they are doing, when they would not want to do anything else. What makes flow so intrinsically motivating? The evidence suggests a simple answer: in flow, the human organism is functioning at its fullest capacity. When this happens, the experience is its own reward.

In theory, the flow experience can occur anytime, anywhere. But in practice, it is easier to find it in activities designed to provide it, such as games, athletic contests, rituals, or art. These leisure activities were developed over time to enable people to get involved in goal-directed action with clear feedback, in settings more or less sharply differentiated from the confusing and contradictory events of everyday life. But flow is not restricted to these protected preserves of optimal experience: it can occur at work, in school, in the spontaneous interaction between people. In short, this intrinsically motivated experience is potentially available to every person, at any time.

In reality, however, most people experience flow rarely. In a sample of average U.S. working men and women we interviewed, 13% claimed never to have experienced anything resembling it, while of the remaining 87% the majority reported it as a rare event; fewer than 10% reported it as occurring daily. The flow experience is relatively rare because it requires an unusual match between the person and the environment. Specifically, a person experiences flow when personal capacities to act fit the opportunities for action in the environment.

At any given moment, persons are aware of a certain range of challenges available in the environment, of things to do, of demands to meet, of possibilities for action. At the same time, they have a sense of how adequate are their skills to meet the available challenges. For instance, a student waiting for a math test to begin may recognize the imminent assignment as her challenges and may view her present knowledge of math as her skills.

If the person sees the challenges as much greater than her skills, then the experience will be characterized by feelings of anxiety. If the challenges are considerably less than the person's skills, the feeling will be that of boredom. When challenges and skills are equal, then the intrinsically rewarding flow experience is present. It is important to note that the challenges and skills in question are based on real elements of the situation—such as the difficulty of the math test and the student's objective skills in math—but that what effectively determines the quality of the experience is the person's subjective estimation of what the level of challenges and skills are at any given time. It appears, for example, that the level of challenge an individual perceives in an activity reflects his or her judgment of how important the activity is. Students taking the same math test will see in it different challenges, different opportunities for action, depending on the degree to which they believe the task matters.

This relationship between challenges and skills has been the central axiom of the flow theory from its inception (Csikszentmihalyi, 1975, 1978, 1982). More recent empirical research has confirmed the validity of the theoretical model, but with an important qualification: Both the challenges and the skills must be relatively high before anything resembling the flow experience comes about (Carli, 1986; Massimini, Csikszentmihalyi, & Carli, 1987).

Flow is important as a source of intrinsic motivation on two counts. In the first place, flow is important because the experience is so positive. At the same time, the logic of the theoretical model which we have proposed suggests that the experience of flow can provide the impetus to growth. An activity is initially absorbing because its challenges match an individual's ability. With practice, skills improve; unless one then takes on new challenges, the activity becomes boring. To recover the state of flow, it seems that the individual must seek greater challenges, developing an ever more complex relationship with the environment.

In practice, we have operationalized the conditions for the flow experience as those situations in which people estimate both the opportunities for action to be above average and their own ability to act as above average. In terms of the ESM data, this means that one would expect persons to be closest to the flow experience whenever they score the levels of both the challenges and the skills as being above the mean

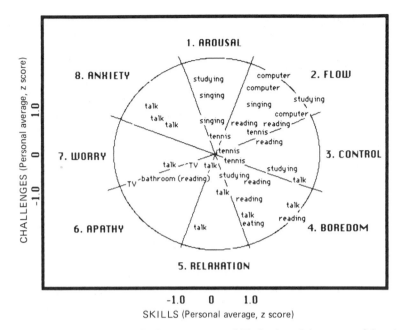

Figure 1. Flow analysis of ESM responses of Ted, plotted in terms of 8 ratios of challenge : skill.

for the week (z Challenge > 0, and z Skills > 0). This procedure, of course, makes flow a much more frequent experience than one would estimate through interviews or other qualitative means. By definition, everybody will be in flow at least some of the time each week, and possibly much more often because half of each person's responses will be above the mean on each of the two variables.

THE MEASUREMENT OF FLOW IN EVERYDAY LIFE

How does this procedure work? It is easiest to demonstrate it with the example of a single person, the senior we have called Ted earlier in this chapter. The responses he gave to the pager throughout the week are reported in terms of the ratio of challenges and skills in Figure 1. His raw scores on these two dimensions have been transformed into z scores with a standard deviation of ±1.0 around an individual mean of 0.

The ratio between challenges and skills can be described in terms of eight slices of an imaginary pie, or eight "channels." Each of these channels has been found to be characterized by a distinct experiential state. The formula by which the channels were determined is described in Carli (1986) and in Massimini et al. (1987). Other options are also possible: for example, a 16-channel model that gives a finer resolution, or a 4-channel model that gives a more global picture.

The first channel includes situations in which skills are average, but challenges are above average. These situations should have the property of *arousal*. In channel 1, Ted was either studying, singing in choir, or playing tennis (see figure 1). The next is channel 2, and this corresponds theoretically to those situations in which a person experiences *flow*, because here challenges and skills are approximately equal and both are above the individual's average levels (that is, greater than zero, in terms of z scores). Ted was either programming his computer, studying, reading a book, singing, or playing tennis in these moments that most closely approximate the flow state. Channel 3 should provide a sense of *control*, because high skills are paired with moderate challenges. In these situations, Ted was either reading, studying, talking, or playing tennis. These three channels all correspond to situations that should be experienced as enjoyable; in fact, if one used a 4-channel model to represent the ratio of challenges and skills, most of the responses in these three channels would be recoded as flow. And indeed what Ted does in these channels—programming computers, singing, reading, playing tennis—are things he enjoys doing and is intrinsically motivated to pursue. Perhaps more important, when studying, Ted is more likely to be in these three channels than in the other five, which suggests that schoolwork might often be intrinsically rewarding for him.

The next two channels describe situations of low challenge, coupled with high skills in channel 4, and with average skills in channel 5. Thus channel 4 is theoretically a condition of *boredom;* for Ted it involved such activities as listening to his teacher in class, reading the comics, talking, and eating. Channel 5 might be best described as involving *relaxation*, and Ted was talking with friends when he was in this condition. In channel 6, both skills and challenges are below average. This is associated with a low point of psychic functioning which has come to be called the condition of *apathy*. In it Ted was either watching TV or reading in the bathroom.

The next two contexts are characterized by low skills. Channel 7 matches these with average challenges, so the expected condition is one of *worry*. Channel 8 matches low skills with high challenges, so it represents occasions of *anxiety*. In both of these channels, Ted was talking; these were the arguments he was having with his classmates in the hallway of the school on the Monday morning he started the ESM procedure.

Ted's week, as represented by the pattern of activities in Figure 1, is similar in several ways to that of average high school students (Csikszent-mihalyi & Larson, 1984). For instance, it is typical of teenagers to be more frequently bored than anxious. It is typical for them to be apathetic when watching TV. It is generally true that active leisure like singing and tennis provide intrinsically rewarding flow experiences. It is also true for most teenagers that talking to other teens is one of the most frequent activities, and that it spans the widest range of conditions, from control and boredom to worry and anxiety. Talking to others can be soothing, boring, numbing, or worrisome, depending on the person and the topic of conversation. Other activities have a much narrower range: TV is rarely anything but a low-involvement activity accompanied by apathy, whereas singing or tennis are generally flow-producing activities.

In some ways, however, Ted stands out from his peers. For one thing, he practices more active leisure pursuits such as tennis and singing. In part, this is possible because he spends less time doing routine maintenance activities such as household chores, and he does not have a part-time job as some of his peers do. At the same time, he watches TV less than the average U.S. teenager, and he reads much more. Reading, especially literature, is sometimes a flow experience for Ted; at other times it is relaxing or boring, but it is generally a positive experience and this distinguishes him from his peers. Compared to other adolescents, Ted also finds study more challenging, and he enjoys it more. These features of his week provide a very encouraging prognosis for Ted's future; it looks as if he is on the way to finding enjoyment in complex and productive activities. By linking up intrinsic motivation with challenging activities, he is likely to become a skilled adult who will lead a productive and personally satisfying life.

The prognosis is not as positive for many of Ted's schoolmates. To take an extreme example, one of the boys in the same sample tried to commit suicide during the week of the study. His problems were reflected in the fact that his responses very seldom fell in the flow channel; instead, he was almost always either bored, apathetic, or anxious. The next section presents a more representative picture of the ups and downs of adolescent motivation, comparing three different groups that total approximately 150 young people.

FLOW AND MOTIVATION IN ADOLESCENCE

How often do teenagers approximate the flow state in ordinary life, and how is their motivation affected by whether they are in flow? To answer this question, we compared the responses of three groups of

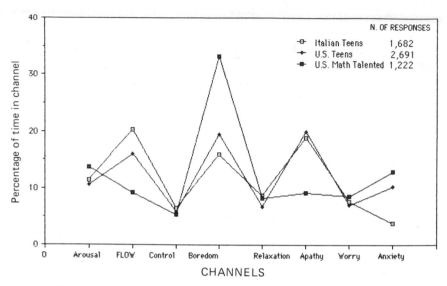

Figure 2.   Percentage of time spent in flow channels for U.S. and Italian teenagers.

adolescents. The first was a group of 47 Italian teenagers from Milan, a representative sample of students from one of the select public "Licei Classici" that have the highest academic reputations in the city (Massimini & Inghilleri, 1986). The second was a representative sample of 75 U.S. teenagers from an above-average suburban high school near Chicago (Csikszentmihalyi & Larson, 1984). The third group included 37 talented math students—all scoring above the 95th percentile on standard math tests—from one of the top three Chicago public city schools (Robinson, 1985). These groups were matched as closely as possible on variables such as gender and socioeconomic class. The Italian group, however, was on the average about 2 years older than the U.S. samples and was probably more academically inclined because their school traditionally stressed a classical curriculum. All students were tested with the ESM for a week, and they filled out a total of 5595 responses.

When these students' responses were coded by the eight channels of the flow model, as they were with the single case of Ted, the pattern reported in Figure 2 results. As the graph indicates, the Italian teenagers spend considerably more time in the flow channel than the normal U.S. teens ($\chi^2 = 18.9$, $p \le .001$) and twice as much time as the U.S. adolescents who were talented in math ($\chi^2 = 75.32$, $p \le .001$). The average American adolescents also spend significantly more time in flow

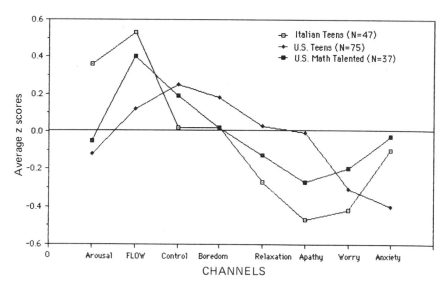

Figure 3.   Levels of intrinsic motivation as related to flow in U.S. and Italian teenagers.

than the talented ones (χ^2 = 32.6, p ≤ .001). While the talented math students are seldom in flow, they are bored a great deal of the time. They respond in the boredom channel a striking 34% of the time, as opposed to 19% for the normal U.S. high schoolers, and 17% for the Italians. In addition, the frequency of anxiety is significantly higher for the talented than for either the normal U.S. students (χ^2 = 5.56, p ≤ .02) or the Italians (χ^2 = 25.5, p ≤ .001). On the other hand, both the Italians and the normal U.S. students are in channel 6 (apathy) about twice as often as the teens talented in math: 20% for the first two groups, 9% for the latter.

In general, the frequencies are very similar for the Italian and the normal U.S. samples. The largest difference between them is only 6% (in the anxiety channel). The talented math students, however, show a different distribution of responses. In the boredom channel, they differ by as much as 16 and 14 percentage points, respectively, from the Italians and from their more average U.S. counterparts. Apparently, the structure of experience is quite comparable for bright normal high school students in the two cultures. But for the U.S. teenagers who have a special talent in mathematics, both flow and apathy are more rare, whereas boredom and anxiety are more frequent experiences.

The frequency of responses in the various channels indicates how often the theoretical conditions for intrinsic motivation were met, but it does not show whether the level of motivation actually reported by the three samples varied as the flow model would have predicted. Figure 3 shows the variation in the level of response, in the three samples, to the ESM item: "When you were beeped, did you wish you had been doing something else?" Respondents answered this item on a 10-point scale, from 0 = "not at all" to 9 = "very much." The scores were then reversed, to indicate positive motivation. This item has repeatedly been found to be the best single index of intrinsic motivation both for adults (Graef et al., 1983), and for adolescents (Csikszentmihalyi & Larson, 1984).

As Figure 3 indicates, the level of intrinsic motivation was the highest in channel 2 (flow), as predicted, for two of the groups: the Italians and the U.S. talented students. For the normal U.S. teenagers, the peak of positive motivation was in the control channel, followed by boredom and flow. In general, the motivational pattern of the Italian teenagers is closest to the predicted pattern. The two U.S. groups show less effect on their motivation due to challenges and skills; and when they do, they seem to decidedly prefer a surfeit of skills to a preponderance of challenges.

It is instructive to compare the two groups that differ most strongly. The Italian adolescents were significantly more motivated than average in channel 2 (flow; t [45], $p \leq .001$) and channel 1 ($p \leq .05$). They were significantly less motivated in channels 6 and 7 ($p \leq .01$). The average U.S. high schoolers were significantly more motivated than their own mean levels in channel 3 (control; t [73], $p \leq .05$); they were significantly less motivated in channel 8 ($p \leq .01$) and in channel 7 ($p \leq .05$). In other words, for the Italians flow is most motivating, while apathy and worry are the least motivating; for the U.S. teens, the most motivating condition is control, the least motivating, anxiety and worry.

DISCUSSION

The patterns reviewed in the preceding section might help to clarify the interaction between the teenagers' motivation and the social system that assigns rewards and punishments in real life. In general, we have seen that the students' motivation tends to correspond to the flow model. The fit is best for the Italian students, it is less good for the U.S. students with math talent, and least good for the normal U.S. high school students, for whom an absence of anxiety, rather than the presence of flow, seems to be the strongest motivating force.

It is possible that these differences are in part the result of different socialization practices. For the Italian adolescents, who are both somewhat older and committed to a rigorous classical education, the balance of high challenges and skills creates an optimal state of experience because their socialization has prepared them to confront high challenges with an expectation of mastering them and finding them intrinsically rewarding. On the other hand, they find situations that provide few challenges extremely aversive, so their motivation drops precipitously in the conditions of relaxation and apathy (as well as in worry, but that response they share with the U.S. students).

The motivational structure of the average American adolescents is no less a product of socialization. The attenuated motivation which they experience in the flow channel seems to be the result of having learned a different set of expectations concerning what is enjoyable and what is not. That is, their socialization has tended to introduce a split between schoolwork and free time, and has created the expectation that the latter is the only arena in which enjoyment can be found.

That possibility is reinforced by the fact that the American teens rated the class they liked best only slightly, although significantly, less enjoyable than their favorite activity (Csikszentmihalyi & Larson, 1984). On the positive side, the ratings of classes suggest that the American teenagers find at least some schoolwork experientially rewarding. However, because none of the teenagers listed their favorite academic subjects among the activities they enjoyed, despite how highly they subsequently rated them, their spontaneous choices seem to reflect an implicit distinction between work and leisure as contexts for enjoyment and therefore as domains in relation to which the idea of being intrinsically motivated even makes sense. Once this dichotomy is internalized, it seems that boredom and even apathy come to be accepted as long as they are experienced within the context of freely chosen pursuits. Viewing TV is the exemplar of such activities. ESM studies have repeatedly shown that people find little challenge and few experiential rewards in watching TV (Kubey, 1984), yet teenagers (and adults) devote as much time to it as they do to the active leisure pursuits in which they experience flow.

The contrast between the Italian and American teenagers' academic experience accords with this interpretation. In all three samples, schoolwork is the most frequently represented activity in flow, channel 2. High-challenge, high-skill situations tend to involve learning more than anything else. Yet when schoolwork falls in channel 2, which should produce flow experiences, the U.S. adolescents tend to be less motivated than predicted (as well as less happy, alert, and so on) simply because they are doing schoolwork. That is, they are more motivated than average, but less so than when they are in channel 2 but engaged in other activities. The Italian adolescents seem less inclined to find the experience of learning negative simply because it takes place in an academic setting.

This pattern might be a real-life manifestation of the overjustification hypothesis demonstrated in so many laboratory experiments (deCharms, 1968; Deci, 1972a, 1972b; Lepper & Greene, 1978). The American adolescents are not motivated as much by flow conditions because these often consist of formal learning; and learning is seen as an extrinsically controlled activity which, ipso facto, cannot be enjoyable and intrinsically rewarding. If this is true, the Italian teenagers must not have come to see the rewards and punishments of schoolwork as being so much under the control of external agents.

The plight of the U.S. students with math talent is particularly instructive. Their motivation is highest in flow, channel 2 (t [35], $p \leq$ .01), and it is not depressed by a surplus of challenges, as is the motivation of the more typical U.S. students. So their motivational structure is more in line with theoretical expectations and shows a positive adaptation to the challenges of the academic environment. But as Figure 2 shows, the environment is not well adapted to the skills of these talented teens, who are rarely in the flow state, and spend a very large part of the time in boredom. The talented students are ready to enjoy high challenges, but they rarely find them in their daily lives. And when they do find them, they are quite likely to be in areas where their skills are low.

The empirical explorations reported here are not attempts at proving a point. We are not trying to clinch an argument about cross-national differences or to drive home a critique of the American school system. Rather, the data in the previous sections were presented in order to show the potential usefulness of both a theoretical model of motivation and a method for exploring it. It is our belief that complex human behavior in real sociocultural environments cannot be explained or predicted unless one takes into account the needs of the self. Foremost among these is the need for the self to determine its own choices and to maximize optimal experience in high-challenge, high-skill situations while avoiding boredom, apathy, and anxiety. Socialization and social structure might either help this normal development or hinder it in various ways—by withholding challenges, by imposing extrinsic controls on intrinsically rewarding situations, or by expecting too much without providing adequate training in skills.

FUTURE DIRECTIONS IN THE STUDY OF
INTRINSIC MOTIVATION

The flow model and the ESM have been offered as suitable tools for studying the dynamics of intrinsic motivation in natural settings. It is hoped that other investigators will find these tools useful as well. Before concluding, we wish to indicate one set of questions that the flow model might help frame, and to which both the model and the method might be fruitfully applied.

Earlier in this chapter we recounted a typical week in the life of the high school student, Ted. We observed that he enjoyed schoolwork and reading more than his peers did; and we noted that, compared to at least some of his classmates, Ted spent much more time overall in flow. People differ both in the activities that give them enjoyment, and in how often they get intrinsic rewards from what they do. Here, we wish to suggest how the flow model might guide attempts to explain, as well as describe, these differences.

Over 100 different activities were identified as enjoyable by the American teenagers studied by Csikszentmihalyi and Larson (1984). American adults also named a diverse set of activities in which they experienced flow (Csikszentmihalyi, 1985). The range of activities that people enjoy is thus extremely wide, and different people derive very different amounts of enjoyment from any particular activity.

The issue of enjoyable activities tends to be framed in terms of explaining individual differences in the intrinsic motivation to engage in specific, societally valued pursuits such as work. For educators, the crucial differences are in students' enjoyment of formal learning experiences. This is particularly so because intrinsic enjoyment of learning appears to be associated with greater creativity (e.g., Amabile, 1985) and higher school achievement (e.g., Gottfried, 1985; Mayers, 1978; Whitehead, 1984). For example, among the math-talented American students, we found that when doing schoolwork, the high achieving members of the group were more often in the flow channel than were the equally talented low achievers (Csikszentmihalyi & Nakamura, 1986). What sorts of reasons might account for differences such as this?

The flow model directs attention to factors that influence the subjective challenges perceived in an activity and the skills brought to it. The skill side of the interaction includes factors such as inherent capacities and sensitivities, and one's perception of them in oneself. The challenge side includes factors determined by individual and cultural values, such as (1) the degree of importance attached to the activity and to the skills it brings into play, (2) the normative status of the activity, and (3) the position of the activity within larger meaning systems. And the subjective experience of challenge includes factors determined by social and historical location, such as prior exposure to the particular activity's challenges and access to those challenges. Finally, as postulated earlier in relation to the cross-cultural findings, the socially determined definition of a given activity as a potential source of enjoyment (as opposed to a burdensome duty, a means to an end, or whatever) might also influence the degree to which the activity is enjoyed.

These factors are proposed as potentially important determinants of individuals' differential enjoyment of a particular activity. Put another way, these factors might help explain why individuals invest their energy in, and derive enjoyment from, diverse pursuits. However, we hypothesize that there is also a set of factors that influence the capacity to find enjoyment in whatever domain one enters. These affect the capacity to find enjoyment in life more generally. They therefore introduce a second goal, that of explaining the overall differences in the experiential rewards that people find in their everyday lives.

Research has repeatedly shown that people spend widely varying amounts of time in interactions with the environment that they find intrinsically rewarding. We have already noted the differences found within the sample of American workers. By the same token, among the math-talented students, there were some who spent one-fifth of their time in the flow channel during the week that they participated in the study, while others spent practically none. Drawing on the flow model, it is possible to propose one kind of answer to the question of why some of these people are in flow so often, and others so seldom.

In the first place, it is obvious that social location acts to constrain some individuals' overall opportunities for action, but may facilitate them for others. We wish, however, to focus on a different set of factors. These factors might be called *metaskills*.

The flow model suggests that to derive enjoyment from life reliably requires the ability to get into flow, stay in it, and make the process evolve. We hypothesize that this depends on a capacity to structure interactions with the environment in ways that facilitate flow (Csikszentmihalyi, 1975; Rathunde, 1988). In large part, this would seem to depend on having assigned to other experiences the functions performed by games and other autotelic activities that are deliberately structured to provide experiential rewards. Specifically, the characteristics of the autotelic activity correspond to capacities (1) to focus attention on the present moment and the activity at hand; (2) to define one's goals in an activity and identify the means for reaching them; and (3) to seek feedback and focus on its informational aspects. In addition to these abilities, the dependence of enjoyment on a balancing of challenges and skills suggests the importance of a capacity to continuously adjust this balance, by using anxiety and boredom as information, and identifying new challenges as skills grow. In relation to this, a capacity to tolerate the anxiety-provoking interactions that test one's skills also appears to be important. Finally, we suspect other metaskills have their effect outside of the particular interaction; these would include the ability to delay gratification, which seems necessary for the eventual enjoyment of activities that require a significant investment of energy before they start providing intrinsic rewards.

Individuals who acquire metaskills might be less at the mercy of the environment for opportunities to experience flow. Indeed, a new range of activities may be opened to them as avenues to enjoyment. We hypothesize that it is largely because of such capacities that some people derive a great deal of enjoyment from their daily lives and spend relatively little time feeling apathetic, anxious, or bored.

Where do individual differences in these skills come from? Ongoing research employing the ESM method provides evidence that the family plays a central role in the acquisition of metaskills (Rathunde, 1988). In a sample of gifted teenagers, Rathunde distinguished between those who perceived their parents as autotelic, creating the conditions for flow at home, and those who perceived their parents as nonautotelic, creating the conditions for either boredom or anxiety rather than flow in their family interactions. He found that the teenagers from autotelic family contexts reported significantly higher intrinsic motivation when inter-acting with their families, as well as higher self-esteem and cognitive efficiency, and a more ordered state of consciousness. Moreover, he found that most of these differences continued to hold when the teenagers were engaged in schoolwork—that is, when doing precisely those high-challenge activities for which the possession of metaskills would seem to matter most.

More work is needed to clarify the nature of the metaskills acquired in the home, and the ways in which they are acquired. For example, important aspects of the family context may include modeling of intrinsically motivated interactions with the environment as well as providing the supports for autotelic experience to which Rathunde has pointed. As more is learned, it should become clearer how educators can also foster these kinds of competences in their students. The educator's challenge tends to be thought of as one of making formal learning experiences a source of enjoyment for students. However, development of the metaskills we have described seems at least as important a goal.

These capacities empower students in a double sense: by fostering their intrinsic enjoyment of learning and by increasing the likelihood that they can derive experiential rewards from pursuits outside of the classroom.

THE NEED FOR A CONCEPT OF
INTRINSIC MOTIVATION

In closing, we revisit the question of whether cutting out the concept of intrinsic motivation from academic psychology is a well-advised use of Ockham's razor. We tried in the opening pages of this chapter to indicate how the progress of motivational research since the 1950s has led psychologists to believe that certain behavioral propensities could not be explained without such a concept. The behavior of an individual who endures significant hardships to pursue an activity that carries no extrinsic rewards or of a child who becomes absorbed in a new activity and forgoes proffered treats cannot be easily explained via drive or operant-learning models. Nor do mechanistic models explain the hidden costs of reward or account for people's greater creativity and higher achievement when crediting intrinsic rather than extrinsic reasons for their actions.

Employing the flow model to conceptualize such phenomena illuminates the manner in which properties of the here-and-now transaction with the environment foster attainment of the inherently pleasurable subjective states that motivate action. Intrinsic motivation has thus also been called "emergent," to stress the fact that the impetus to act seems to come out of the ongoing interaction (Csikszentmihalyi, 1978, 1985).

As we have noted, in embracing the notion that people sometimes choose to act for the sake of emergent rewards, we assume a capacity for intentional action. We assume, that is, that people's conscious intentions and beliefs can, at times, guide what they do. Systematic arguments to this effect have been made (e.g., Gauld & Shotter, 1977), and we find these compelling. Of the two models of human functioning that dominate academic psychology—the "mechanistic" and "organismic"—it is thus the latter that informs our conceptualization of human motivation, as it does that of others mentioned here (e.g., deCharms, 1968; Deci & Ryan, 1985).

Ultimately, it may be impossible to prove the necessity of a concept of intrinsic motivation, in the same way that it is impossible to prove the truth of the organismic model to which it is logically tied. It has been rather convincingly argued (Overton & Reese, 1973; Reese & Overton, 1970) that, as metaphors for the phenomena they represent, neither mechanistic nor organismic models can be shown to be true. However—and particularly if this is the case—it is important to address the real-life implications of these competing conceptualizations. If we conceive of human behavior mechanistically and explain phenomena in mechanistic terms, we stand to treat people accordingly. On the other hand, if we conceive of humans as intentional agents, who sometimes choose to act for the sake of intrinsic enjoyment alone, we might be able to facilitate people's enjoyment of the activities in which they engage.

ACKNOWLEDGMENT

The research in this chapter has been supported by grants from the Spencer Foundation.

REFERENCES

Amabile, T. M. (1985). Motivation and creativity: Effects of motivational orientation on creative writers. *Journal of Personality and Social Psychology, 48,* 393–397.

Bem, D. J. (1967). Self-perception: An alternative interpretation of cognitive dissonance phenomena. *Psychological Review, 74,* 183–200.

Bem, D. J. (1972). Self-perception theory. In L. Berkowitz (Ed.), *Advances in experimental and social psychology* (Vol. 6). New York: Academic Press.

Berlyne, D. E.. (1966). Exploration and curiosity. *Science, 153,* 25–33.

Brody, N. (1980). Social motivation. *Annual Review of Psychology, 31,* 143–168.

Butler, R. A. (1958). Exploratory and related behavior: A new trend in animal research. *Journal of Individual Psychology, 14,* 111–120.

Carli, M. (1986). Selezione psicologica e qualita dell'esperienza. [Psychological selection and the quality of experience.] In F. Massimini & P. Inghilleri (Eds.), *L'esperienza quotidiana.* Milan: Franco Angeli.

Csikszentmihalyi, M. (1975). *Beyond boredom and anxiety.* San Francisco: Jossey-Bass.

Csikszentmihalyi, M. (1978). Intrinsic rewards and emergent motivation. In M. R. Lepper & D. Greene (Eds.), *The hidden costs of reward.* Hillsdale, NJ: Erlbaum.

Csikszentmihalyi, M. (1982). Toward a psychology of optimal experience. In L. Wheeler (Ed.), *Review of personality and social psychology* (Vol. 2). Beverly Hills, CA: Sage.

Csikszentmihalyi, M. (1985). Emergent motivation and the evolution of the self. In D. A. Kleiber & M. L. Maehr (Eds.), *Advances in motivation and achievement* (Vol. 4). Greenwich, CT: JAI Press.

Csikszentmihalyi, M., & Csikszentmihalyi, I. (1988). *Optimal experience: Psychological studies of flow in consciousness.* New York: Cambridge University Press.

Csikszentmihalyi, M., and Larson, R. (1984). *Being adolescent.* New York: Basic.

Csikszentmihalyi, M., Larson, R., & Prescott, S. (1977). The ecology of adolescent activity and experience. *Journal of Youth and Adolescence, 6,* 281–294.
Csikszentmihalyi, M., & Massimini, F. (1985). On the psychological selection of bio-cultural information. *New Ideas in Psychology, 3,* 115–138.
Csikszentmihalyi, M., & Nakamura, J. (1986, August). *Optimal experience and the uses of talent.* Paper presented at the 94th Annual Meeting of the American Psychological Association, Washington DC.
Day, H. I., Berlyne, D. E., & Hunt, D. E. (Eds.). (1971). *Intrinsic motivation: A new direction in education.* New York: Holt, Rinehart and Winston.
deCharms, R. (1968). *Personal causation: The internal affective determinants of behavior.* New York: Academic Press.
deCharms, R. (1976). *Enhancing motivation: Change in the classroom.* New York: Irvington.
deCharms, R., & Muir, M. S. (1978). Motivation: Social approaches. *Annual Review of Psychology, 29,* 91–113.
Deci, E. L. (1971). Effects of externally mediated rewards on intrinsic motivation. *Journal of Personality and Social Psychology, 18,* 105–115.
Deci, E. L. (1972a). Intrinsic motivation, extrinsic reinforcement, and inequity. *Journal of Personality and Social Psychology, 22,* 113–120.
Deci, E. L. (1972b). Effects of contingent and non-contingent rewards and controls on intrinsic motivation. *Organizational Behavior and Human Performance, 8,* 217–229.
Deci, E. L. (1975). *Intrinsic motivation.* New York: Plenum.
Deci, E. L., & Ryan, R. M. (1985). *Intrinsic motivation and self-determination in human behavior.* New York: Plenum.
Fiske, D. W., & Maddi, S. R. (Eds.). (1961). *Functions of varied experience.* Homewood, IL: Dorsey.
Freud, S. (1961). *Civilization and its discontents.* New York: Norton.
Gauld, A., & Shotter, J. (1977). *Human action and its psychological investigation.* London: Routledge and Kegan Paul.
Gleitman, H. (1981). *Psychology.* New York: Norton.
Gottfried, A. E. (1985). Academic intrinsic motivation in elementary and junior high school students. *Journal of Educational Psychology, 77,* 631–645.
Graef, R., Csikszentmihalyi, M., & McManama Giannino, S. (1983). Measuring intrinsic motivation in everyday life. *Leisure Studies, 2,* 155–168.
Greene, D., & Lepper, M. R. (1974). Effects of extrinsic rewards on children's subsequent intrinsic interest. *Child Development, 45,* 1141–1145.
Han, S. (1988). The relationship between life satisfaction and flow in elderly Korean immigrants. In M. Csikszentmihalyi & I. Csikszentmihalyi (Eds.), *Optimal experience: Psychological studies of flow in consciousness.* New York: Cambridge University Press.
Heider, F. (1958). *The psychology of interpersonal relations.* New York: Wiley.
Hunt, J. McV. (1965). Intrinsic motivation and its role in psychological development. In D. Levine (Ed.), *Nebraska symposium on motivation* (Vol. 13). Lincoln: University of Nebraska Press.
Kelley, H. H. (1967). Attribution theory in social psychology. In D. Levine (Ed.), *Nebraska symposium on motivation* (Vol. 15). Lincoln: University of Nebraska Press.
Kelley, H. H. (1973). The processes of causal attribution. *American Psychologist, 28,* 107–128.
Kubey, R. (1984). *Leisure, television, and subjective experience.* Unpublished doctoral dissertation, The University of Chicago.
Lepper, M. R., & Greene, D. (1975). Turning play into work: Effects of adult surveillance

and extrinsic rewards on children's intrinsic motivation. *Journal of Personality and Social Psychology, 31,* 479–486.

Lepper, M. R., & Greene, D. (1978). *The hidden costs of reward: New perspectives on the psychology of human motivation.* Hillsdale, NJ: Erlbaum.

Lepper, M. R., Greene, D., & Nisbett, R. E. (1973). Undermining children's intrinsic interest with extrinsic rewards: A test of the overjustification hypothesis. *Journal of Personality and Social Psychology, 28,* 129–137.

Macbeth, J. (1985). *Ocean crusing: A study of affirmative deviance.* Unpublished doctoral dissertation, Murdoch University, Western Australia.

Massimini, F., Csikszentmihalyi, M., & Carli, M. (1987). The monitoring of optimal experience: A tool for psychiatric rehabilitation. *Journal of Nervous and Mental Diseases, 175,* 545–549.

Massimini, F., Csikszentmihalyi, M., & delle Fave, A. (1986). Selezione psicologica e flusso di conscienza. [Psychological selection and the flow of consciousness.] In F. Massimini & P. Inghilleri (Eds.), *L'esperienza quotidiana.* Milan: Franco Angeli.

Massimini, F., & Inghilleri, P. (Eds.). (1986). *L'esperienza quotidiana.* [Everyday experience.] Milan: Franco Angeli.

Mayers, P. (1978). *Flow in adolescence and its relation to school experience.* Unpublished doctoral dissertation, The University of Chicago.

Millenson, J. R. (1967). *Principles of behavioral analysis.* New York: Macmillan.

Montgomery, K. C. (1954). The role of the exploratory drive in learning. *Journal of Comparative Physiological Psychology, 47,* 60–64.

Overton, W. F., & Reese, H. W. (1973). Models of development: Methodological implications. In J. R. Nesselroade & H. W. Reese (Eds.), *Life-span developmental psychology: Methodological issues.* New York: Academic Press.

Rathunde, K. (1988). Optimal experience and the family context. In M. Csikszentmihalyi & I. Csikszentmihalyi (Eds.), *Optimal experience: Psychological studies of flow in consciousness.* New York: Cambridge University Press.

Reese, H. W., & Overton, W. F. (1970). Models of development and theories of development. In L. R. Goulet & P. B. Baltes (Eds.), *Life-span developmental psychology: Research and theory.* New York: Academic Press.

Robinson, R. E. (1985, April). *The experience of giftedness in adolescence.* Paper presented at the Society for Research in Child Development Biennial Conference, Toronto.

Sato, I. (1988). *Bosozoku:* flow in Japanese motorcycle gangs. In M. Csikszentmihalyi & I. Csikszentmihalyi (Eds.), *Optimal experience: Psychological studies of flow in consciousness.* New York: Cambridge University Press.

White, R. W. (1959). Motivation reconsidered: The concept of competence. *Psychological Review, 66,* 297–333.

Whitehead, J. (1984). Motives for higher education: A study of intrinsic and extrinsic motivation in relation to academic attainment. *Cambridge Journal of Education, 14,* 26–34.

3

Intrinsic Motivation in the Classroom

Mark R. Lepper
Melinda Hodell

> *The most important attitude that can be formed is that of desire to go on learning.*
>
> *Dewey, 1938*

INTRODUCTION

It is one of the persistent paradoxes of educational psychology that so many children seem to have motivational problems in our schools. As potential educational reformers have noted time and again (e.g., Holt, 1964, 1968; Jackson, 1968; Silberman, 1970), the young child, outside of school, seems blessed with a seemingly limitless curiosity, a thirst for knowledge, a will to learn. Young children begin to acquire a first language, and sometimes a second and third, with remarkable facility and minimal confusion; and they do so at the tender age of two and in the relative absence of formal instruction. They learn a great deal about the social and physical environments in which they live and how to navigate through those complex environments, with limited overt tuition. Some even learn significant amounts about the process of reading or the rudiments of arithmetic without being explicitly taught these subjects. Rarely, if ever, does one find a parent complaining about his or her preschooler's lack of motivation for learning.

RESEARCH ON MOTIVATION IN EDUCATION
VOLUME 3: GOALS AND COGNITIONS

73

Observe these same children a few years later, however, as they sit in elementary-school classrooms, and one sees a different picture. For many of these children, motivation is now a problem. Attention strays; minds wander. Extrinsic incentives and sanctions are now required to motivate children to learn their assigned lessons.[1] In this, as in many other ways, schools seem to have changed little in the last half century (Cuban, 1982; Sirotnik, 1983). Walk into most elementary-school classrooms, and take a look around. Most likely, you will see students' stories and art works stapled on the bulletin boards, bearing red-inked evaluations such as "excellent" or "good job." Likely there will be a chart of book reports or science projects, with Marjorie or Roberto obviously out in front with many more stars, or X's, or colored-in squares. On the blackboard might be a chalked list of class monitors, lunch-money collectors, and children who have to stay in at recess to do spelling. You may see attendance records posted conspicuously, along with 100% math papers and exemplary student artwork.

What has happened to these formerly excited, curious, intrinsically motivated children? They have met, and have been enveloped by, a system that necessarily constrains and standardizes their learning opportunities. The content of what they are taught is governed by a general curriculum that defines in advance not only what, but also when, particular subjects will be taught to students at each grade level. The result, as Bruner (1962, 1966) and many others have pointed out, is a *decontextualization* of the knowledge children are asked to acquire in school (Condry, 1978; Ginsberg, 1977). Information is presented in an abstract form, dissociated from the contexts in which it might be of obvious, everyday use to children. Topics are presented when the schedule calls for them, not when particular children are especially interested or "ready" to learn about them.

Likewise, the methods by which children learn in school are limited by a variety of constraints inherent in our system of separate classrooms in which individual teachers have sole and simultaneous responsibility for 30 students or more. Much of school, as Jackson (1968) and others have so eloquently illustrated, revolves around a hidden curriculum of social control and classroom management. Children spend many hours in crowded classrooms, waiting, in transition, and in passive observation of the teacher's interactions with other students (Dreeben, 1968; Winnett & Winkler, 1972).

---

[1] As is explicated later in this chapter, it is likely that the overuse of extrinsic incentives may be one *cause* of decreases in intrinsic motivation among more advanced students. Once intrinsic motivation declines for any reason, however, extrinsic incentives do become increasingly necessary if students are to be kept on task.

As a result, motivation can become a problem for many students in our educational system. Indeed, though it is a difficult claim to evaluate, there is some evidence to suggest that such effects may be cumulative through the years. Harter (1981), for example, has found that as students move from third through ninth grade in our school system, they report activity preferences that show them to be less and less intrinsically motivated, but instead, more and more extrinsically motivated. The older the students, the more likely they are to indicate, for instance, that they would prefer a simple but boring task that would clearly please the teacher to a more challenging and interesting task that is not on the teacher's immediate agenda.[2]

What might the significance of such effects be? Since the mid-1970s, there has been something of a revival of interest in the study of intrinsic motivation and its determinants (e.g., Csikszentmihalyi, 1975; Deci, 1975, 1981; Deci & Ryan, 1985; Harter, 1978, 1981; Lepper, 1981, 1983a; Lepper & Greene, 1978b; Lepper & Malone, 1987; Malone, 1981; Malone & Lepper, 1987; Ryan, Connell, & Deci, 1985). In the present chapter, we examine this literature with respect to two basic questions.

First: What difference does it make? Should we really be concerned if, in school, intrinsic motivations are gradually supplanted by extrinsic motivations? In this case, we focus on a literature that has examined the ways in which the use (or, more accurately, the misuse) of overly powerful extrinsic rewards and sanctions may unwittingly undermine children's intrinsic motivation. In particular, we consider research regarding the *consequences* of decreases in students' intrinsic motivation in classrooms.

Second: What might be done? What methods might schools use to maintain or enhance children's intrinsic motivation—to make classroom learning more interesting or enjoyable? In this case, we examine a more recent line of investigation that has involved the study of techniques of instructional design, of methods for altering the structure of educational activities so as to enhance students' intrinsic motivation. Here, we focus especially on what difference it might make if one were successful in making learning activities more intrinsically motivating for children. Are there actually important differences in the ways children learn from activities, for instance, as a function of their level of intrinsic motivation?

[2] It would be of considerable interest to know whether these changes actually involve an increase in students' extrinsic motivation, a decrease in their intrinsic motivation, or both. Unfortunately, the existing data do not permit one to differentiate among these possibilities.

UNDERMINING CHILDREN'S INTRINSIC MOTIVATION

The recent revival of interest in the experimental study of intrinsic motivation has its immediate origins in a set of studies initially undertaken independently by three different groups of investigators, all concerned with the possibility that the inappropriate use of tangible rewards and sanctions might have detrimental effects on children's intrinsic interest (Deci, 1971; Kruglanski, Friedman, & Zeevi, 1971; Lepper, Greene, & Nisbett, 1973). Though involving very different activities, rewards, and subject populations, each of these initial investigations seemed to provide convergent evidence concerning some potential "hidden costs" of a reliance on extrinsic rewards and punishments to motivate and control children's behavior (Lepper & Greene, 1978b). Consider, first, the literature derived from these early investigations.

DETERMINANTS OF UNDERMINING EFFECTS

The parallel demonstrations of detrimental effects of the use of functionally superfluous extrinsic rewards in three geographically disparate laboratories, then, provided the initial impetus toward a concern with intrinsic motivation. In the first of these, Deci (1971) compared the subsequent responses of college subjects who had been offered money to work with a geometric puzzle of high initial intrinsic interest with those who had played with the same puzzle without pay. In a subsequent session involving no extrinsic rewards, he found that previously rewarded subjects chose to spend less time playing with the puzzle than did previously nonrewarded subjects.

By contrast, Kruglanski, Friedman, and Zeevi (1971) offered half of a sample of Israeli high-school subjects a personal tour of nearby university facilities in exchange for their engagement in a series of experimental tasks. Compared to other subjects who had undertaken these same activities without the promise of any extrinsic reward, rewarded subjects reported more negative attitudes toward the experimental tasks. These authors also report a number of other adverse effects of reward on various indices of task performance that we consider in more detail later in this chapter.

In a third study, Lepper, Greene, and Nisbett (1973) worked with preschool children selected on the basis of their initial high intrinsic interest in a particular art activity in their regular classrooms. These subjects were then asked to engage in this same art activity in a different setting, under one of three conditions. Some were offered the chance to win an attractive tangible award for engaging in this activity; others were offered no such award, although half of these other children did receive the same award unexpectedly. Three weeks later, in their normal classrooms where awards were no longer present, children who had previously agreed to engage in the target activity in order to receive an award showed significantly decreased interest, compared both to their own baseline levels of interest and to the levels of postexperimental interest shown by children who had received no award or an unexpected award.

These comparable results of the three studies, obtained across such a wide array of tasks, incentives, and subjects, suggested the potential generality of detrimental effects of extrinsic rewards on intrinsic motivation. At the same time, these results also seemed to fly in the face of traditional wisdom, and to contradict the results of a variety of behavioral treatment programs that had demonstrated the potential beneficial effects of appropriate uses of tangible extrinsic rewards and punishments (Lepper & Greene, 1978a). As a result, a considerable literature has developed concerning the conditions under which such salient extrinsic constraints or incentives are likely to decrease, or to increase, students' subsequent intrinsic motivation.

As recent reviews of this literature suggest (e.g., Deci, 1981; Deci & Ryan, 1985; Lepper, 1981, 1983a, 1983b; Quattrone, 1985; Ryan, Connell, & Deci, 1985), some controversy continues concerning the specific processes by which extrinsic rewards may have detrimental effects on intrinsic motivation. The basic outlines of the phenomenon, however, seem fairly clear. Such effects are most likely to occur, for example, when initial interest is high, when extrinsic constraints are superfluous and salient, and when they provide a psychologically plausible explanation for one's engagement in the activity—when the reward, in short, can be easily viewed as a "bribe." Unnecessarily powerful extrinsic rewards, functionally superfluous temporal deadlines, and excessive adult surveillance all can be shown to have negative effects on children's later intrinsic interest in the activity for which those constraints were imposed (Lepper, 1981). Indeed, the mere creation of an instrumental, contingent, means–end relationship, even between two activities of high and initially equivalent interest to the child, may be sufficient to create a decrease in the child's later intrinsic interest in the activity undertaken as a means to some ulterior end (Lepper, Sagotsky, Dafoe, & Greene, 1982).

Such adverse effects are less likely to occur, by contrast, when extrinsic rewards are seen as "bonuses," rather than "bribes." When tangible rewards are based on task performance, for example, and convey to children clear positive information about their high competence and ability at an activity, the rewards will generally be less likely to undermine later intrinsic interest than when they are offered simply for task engagement (Lepper, 1983a). Similarly, rewards that have some integral or endogenous relationship to the activity for which they have been provided will be less likely to undermine interest than those that bear a more arbitrary or exogenous relationship to the task undertaken (Kruglanski, 1978).

The conditions under which the use of inappropriately powerful extrinsic rewards may undermine intrinsic interest have been discussed at length in a number of other sources (e.g., Deci & Ryan, 1985; Lepper, 1981, 1983a). One final point concerning this first literature bears emphasis, however. Very few of the experiments in which subjects are initially intrinsically motivated have yet found any reliable method for using extrinsic rewards to increase intrinsic motivation further, whereas a number of investigations have found that such rewards may be important in enhancing interest among subjects who do not find the activity of initial intrinsic interest (Bandura & Schunk, 1981; Calder & Staw, 1975; Loveland & Olley, 1979; McLoyd, 1979).

CONSEQUENCES OF UNDERMINING INTRINSIC INTEREST

What happens, then, when a student's intrinsic interest is undermined through the use of superfluous extrinsic rewards or the application of other unnecessarily powerful techniques of social control? Although the central focus of this research literature has historically been the finding that children subsequently choose the activity less when tangible rewards are no longer available, a number of authors have studied and reported other conceptually related effects as well. Some of these effects concern aspects of performance or learning that occur immediately (i.e., in the setting in which a superfluous tangible reward has been offered for task performance or engagement). Others involve effects that may appear days or weeks later, when the same activity, or one similar to it, is subsequently encountered.

Immediate Effects

Consider the ways in which the presence of an unnecessarily powerful extrinsic incentive or sanction may have immediate effects on the child's response to the activity undertaken in order to obtain that incentive or avoid that sanction. Given that the incentive is indeed superfluous (i.e., not needed to induce the child to engage in the activity), two general sorts of negative consequences have been observed. Some involve detrimental effects on *peripheral* or *incidental performance* measures—aspects of task performance that are irrelevant to the attainment of the extrinsic reward. Others involve deleterious effects on *central performance* measures—aspects of task performance on which the receipt of extrinsic reward is clearly contingent.

Effects on Peripheral Performance Measures. One of the most common, and certainly the most thoroughly studied, potential adverse consequence of offering extrinsic rewards for task performance is a decrease in performance on aspects that are *peripheral* to reward attainment—for example, dimensions of performance on which students do not expect to be graded or evaluated. To the extent that extrinsic constraints may serve as a powerful incentive for the individual, their availability will provide a stimulus to the individual to concentrate his or her energy, effort, and attention on those aspects of the task perceived as instrumentally relevant. As a result, less energy and attention is likely to be devoted to parameters of performance on which extrinsic rewards are known not to be contingent.

Such an idea, of course, considerably predates the recent literature on intrinsic motivation, as McGraw (1978) ably documents. For example, evidence illustrating that the offer of tangible rewards may undermine performance on incidental learning tasks has been around for many years (e.g., Bahrick, 1954; Bahrick, Fitts, & Rankin, 1952). Even so, recent studies have highlighted some of the potentially less obvious implications of such a mechanism.

Garbarino (1975), for example, found the presence of extrinsic incentives to produce a variety of negative, peripheral social effects in a peer-tutoring situation. In particular, Garbarino compared the performance of sixth-grade children either offered or not offered a tangible reward contingent on their success in tutoring a first-grade pupil on a novel activity. Receipt of the reward in this situation was, thus, not contingent on the use of any particular tutoring style or technique. Nonetheless, tutors who expected a reward for their efforts if successful made more demands of the tutee, provided more criticism, and generally created a social context characterized by a more negative emotional tone.

In a similar vein, Harter (1978) examined the effects of the offer of a reward, contingent only on the number of problems children solved correctly, on children's choices of which problems to attempt. In a setting in which children were permitted to choose a set of problems from a number of levels of expected difficulty, Harter found that the presence of such extrinsic rewards led children to select easier problems than they would have in the absence of rewards. Because the solution of more difficult problems did not, in this setting, yield larger extrinsic rewards, the difficulty of the problems was incidental to receipt of reward; yet the offer of rewards led children to opt for simpler problems for which success was more certain—even though, as Harter also showed, those children found these easier problems less intrinsically interesting. Extrinsic incentives, in a sense, drove out intrinsic incentives.

Finally, when the criteria determining the receipt of a salient extrinsic reward are not clearly specified, it can also be shown that students will tend to take the apparent path of least effort. In studies by Greene and Lepper (1974) and Lepper et al. (1973), for instance, young children who were asked simply to draw pictures in order to obtain a proffered reward tended to work more quickly and to produce pictures of lower rated average quality than their peers who had undertaken the same activity without expectation of any tangible reward. Since receipt of a reward was not explicitly tied to the quality of their artwork, children working for a reward put less time and effort into their drawings.

Effects on Central Performance Measures.   The aforementioned effects are, of course, easily understood from a number of theoretical perspectives (Lepper & Greene, 1978c). Somewhat more surprising and more difficult to explain, however, are findings of detrimental effects of superfluous extrinsic rewards on measures of central task performance, because here a focusing of attention and effort on instrumentally relevant parameters might be expected to enhance, rather than to undermine, performance. The literature reveals a surprising number of cases, however, in which this second, more subtle type of detrimental effect also occurs.

One class of activities for which such effects seem particularly common is the category of tasks that require creativity or insight for their solution. If extrinsic rewards or external evaluation standards, for instance, are imposed on students working on tasks where creativity of response is the central criterion of performance, the consequences are typically negative. In the earliest demonstrations of such effects, Glucksberg (1962, 1964) found that subjects offered a reward for solving two classic *functional fixedness* problems (in which creative, nonstandard uses of everyday materials are required for success) took significantly longer to reach acceptable solutions than subjects offered no such reward. Kruglanski et al. (1971) demonstrated similar effects of rewards on the performance of Israeli high-school students asked to suggest novel titles for a set of stories or to compose an original story from a selected list of words. In both cases, students offered an extrinsic reward were rated as showing less creativity than those not offered any tangible reward.

Similarly, McGraw and McCullers (1979) observed differences in the ability of college students to reach an insightful solution to a Luchins water-jar problem. Here again, students not expecting a reward performed more effectively. After the complex solution that had led to success on previous trials had suddenly failed, these students found it easier to "break set" and to uncover the simple solution that would now solve the problem. Most recently, Amabile's investigations of the determinants of artistic creativity have found that the offer of unnecessary extrinsic rewards (Amabile, Hennessey, & Grossman, 1986) and the imposition of salient evaluative pressures (Amabile, 1979) both undermined the rated creativity of students' efforts.

Other tasks in which central performance indices seem to show impairment in the face of superfluous extrinsic pressures are those described by McGraw (1978) as requiring insightful or heuristic, rather than formal and algorithmic, solutions. Several investigators, for example, have studied the effects of proffered extrinsic rewards on performance on complex concept- or discrimination-learning problems, which proved (for their respective subject populations) too complex to permit algorithmic solutions (cf. McGraw, 1978). Moreover, demonstrations of such effects have once again been available for a considerable time (e.g., Miller & Estes, 1961; Terrell, Durkin, & Wiesley, 1959).

In addition to differences in eventual learning outcomes, more recent investigations have been able to show detrimental effects of superfluous extrinsic incentives offered for task performance on a variety of trial-by-trial measures of learning efficiency. Thus, Condry and Chambers (1978) found that rewarded subjects working on a concept-attainment task made a higher proportion of illogical and redundant requests for information, as well as more incorrect guesses, than did nonrewarded students. Similarly, in Garbarino's (1975) study of tutoring, those tutors offered a reward were not only incidentally more critical and demanding of their pupils, but they also proved significantly less effective in the central task of actually teaching the material to their younger charges.

Such effects, of course, are considerably more interesting than those that reflect a simple redirection of attention toward instrumental goals. Here, one needs to postulate some additional mechanism—an involuntary narrowing of the range of cues and dimensions to which a person can simultaneously attend (Easterbrook, 1959) or a strengthening of existing prepotent responses by increases in drive level (Spence, 1956), as a function of the presence of an extrinsic incentive—to explain the results that have been reported. The implications of these results for classroom practices, however, are potentially considerable.

Subsequent Effects

Such immediate performance effects, naturally, carry no necessary implications for students' responses to the activities involved, once the student is outside the specific setting in which rewards have been offered or sanctions threatened. Potentially more significant, and socially pernicious, would be effects that persist or generalize to later encounters with these activities outside the context in which extrinsic constraints had been encountered.

Subsequent Choice of Activities. One such effect is evident and provided a focus of interest for some of the earliest studies in this area—that students will be less likely to choose to engage in previously (and superfluously) rewarded or constrained activities in later settings in which salient rewards or constraints are no longer present. What might deserve emphasis, however, is the apparent strength of these effects. In studies with preschool children, for example, not only were significant differences in children's willingness to choose the experimental activity observed 3 weeks after the conclusion of experimental sessions, but these differences occurred in a different setting from that in which subjects had had previous experience with the same activity (e.g., Greene & Lepper, 1974; Lepper & Greene, 1975; Lepper et al., 1973).

Subsequent Task Performance. Other research suggests that the prior use of superfluous extrinsic rewards or sanctions may also have other sorts of persistent effects. As mentioned earlier, Condry and Chambers (1978) compared the strategies of subjects offered and subjects not offered tangible rewards for success on a complex concept-attainment task and found clear evidence that the offer of rewards led students to pursue less logically efficient strategies for information seeking and hypothesis testing. More importantly, these investigators also observed these subjects several weeks later, when they were again confronted with a complex concept-attainment task. This second time, however, Condry and Chambers made quite explicit an important change in the ground rules for engaging in this task. In this second session, students were to wait before venturing an answer until they were absolutely certain that they had solved the problem and had completely eliminated all possible alternative hypotheses. Strikingly, even in this second setting in which the rules for successful performance at the task had been changed, students continued to show adverse effects of the prior reward manipulation. Once again, rewarded subjects made a higher proportion of illogical guesses, made more redundant moves, and proceeded in a less systematic fashion. In addition, they offered answers to the problem, about which they claimed to be positive, before they could logically have eliminated alternative possibilities.

Such persistent changes in the ways in which activities are later approached or undertaken, although of enormous potential importance, have, unfortunately, been only rarely studied. One other relevant demonstration of this sort derives from work by Pittman, Emery, and Boggiano (1982), who examined the effects of prior receipt of tangible rewards for task engagement on students' later choices among different versions of an activity that varied in complexity or difficulty. In the initial session of this study, the offer of a tangible reward produced a significant shift in children's choices toward the selection of generally easier and less complex problems, as in the aforementioned Harter (1978) study. More importantly, when these same children were later afforded a chance to engage in the activity at different levels of difficulty, they continued to show a preference for less difficult problems and less complex versions of the activity.

THE MULTIPLE FUNCTIONS OF REWARDS AND SANCTIONS

From this research tradition, then, it is clear that the misuse of extrinsic incentives and sanctions can have a variety of detrimental effects on children's intrinsic motivation, task performance, and learning. Even within this same experimental literature, however, it is equally clear that the use of extrinsic rewards and punishments does not always, or necessarily, produce negative consequences. Indeed, under appropriate conditions in this work, extrinsic rewards have been shown to enhance motivation and to promote learning (e.g., Condry, 1977; Lepper & Greene, 1978a; McGraw, 1978). What is needed, obviously, is an analysis that would serve to specify the circumstances under which extrinsic rewards are likely to have detrimental, versus beneficial, effects on students.

One potentially useful perspective for considering such questions involves an analysis of the several conceptually distinct functions that extrinsic rewards may serve (cf. Lepper & Gilovich, 1981). As illustrated

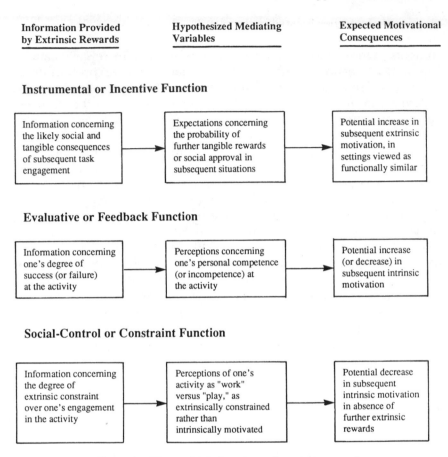

Information Provided by Extrinsic Rewards	Hypothesized Mediating Variables	Expected Motivational Consequences

Instrumental or Incentive Function

| Information concerning the likely social and tangible consequences of subsequent task engagement | Expectations concerning the probability of further tangible rewards or social approval in subsequent situations | Potential increase in subsequent extrinsic motivation, in settings viewed as functionally similar |

Evaluative or Feedback Function

| Information concerning one's degree of success (or failure) at the activity | Perceptions concerning one's personal competence (or incompetence) at the activity | Potential increase (or decrease) in subsequent intrinsic motivation |

Social-Control or Constraint Function

| Information concerning the degree of extrinsic constraint over one's engagement in the activity | Perceptions of one's activity as "work" versus "play," as extrinsically constrained rather than intrinsically motivated | Potential decrease in subsequent intrinsic motivation in absence of further extrinsic rewards |

Figure 1.   The multiple functions of extrinsic rewards.

in Figure 1, the available literature suggests at least three quite different sources of information that extrinsic rewards may provide to children in school. Each of these sources of information, in turn, may exert an independent influence on children's later motivation in subsequent settings. Hence, the net influence of the introduction of any given reward procedure on children's later behavior may depend on each of these three separate, and potentially conflicting, factors.

Instrumentality

First, and most obviously, extrinsic rewards may serve an instrumental or incentive function. That is, whether perceived as "bribes" or "bonuses," rewards may contain information that the rewarded activity is one that may lead to additional extrinsic rewards in the future. Activities that have led to the receipt of tangible rewards in the past may produce similar consequences in the future—at least in situations that the child sees as functionally related to the setting in which rewards were initially received. This is, of course, the fundamental assumption of classical social-learning theory accounts of reinforcement processes (e.g., Bandura, 1969, 1977; Lepper & Greene, 1978a; Mahoney, 1974; Mischel, 1973).

Thus, a first process by which the introduction of extrinsic rewards may affect subsequent motivation involves the effects of those rewards on children's expectations regarding the continued instrumentality of the previously rewarded activity. The power of such processes is amply attested by the extensive literature documenting the effectiveness of token-economy programs as a means of increasing appropriate, and decreasing disruptive, classroom behaviors—as long as children expect that they will continue to receive tangible rewards for their actions (e.g., Kazdin, 1977; O'Leary & Drabman, 1971). In the case of this first variable, note that there is no assumption that children's *intrinsic* motivation has been affected by the provision of rewards, but simply that children may choose to engage in activities even though they find them intrinsically aversive if the extrinsic payoff is sufficiently large.

Furthermore, especially in institutions such as schools, the provision of tangible rewards for certain types of activities will typically convey to children a more general message concerning the sorts of activities that are differentially valued by their parents and teachers. As a result, children may come to believe that engagement in highly valued activities is likely to produce social recognition and approval even if no further tangible rewards are available. That the teacher has awarded students points and privileges for taking turns, raising their hands, or sitting quietly while others speak, for example, may indicate to children that these are behaviors of which he or she particularly approves (Winnett & Winkler, 1972). Under such circumstances, children may choose to continue to engage in the activity in order to obtain further social approval—though, once again, only in those similar situations in which such further social rewards might reasonably be expected and only in those circumstances in which children sufficiently value the approval of the teacher. The typical lack of transfer of effects from classroom token-economy programs, despite the obvious social messages they convey, for instance, may suggest that the children who are the targets of such programs place little value on earning the approval of their teachers (Lepper & Greene, 1978a; O'Leary & Drabman, 1971).

Evaluation

A second function that extrinsic rewards may serve is the provision of evaluation or feedback regarding one's performance. Thus, extrinsic rewards may provide children with important information concerning their success, and more generally their competence, at particular activities. In some cases, extrinsic rewards may simply signal success at the task; in others, they may provide considerably more specific information about the quality of one's performance, relative either to social norms or to measures of one's own past performance on the same, or closely related, tasks. Grades, gold stars, honor rolls, and the like are generally intended to serve such an evaluation or feedback function in schools.

This feedback function, through which extrinsic rewards may influence children's subsequent motivation, focuses on the ways in which extrinsic rewards may influence children's perceptions of their competence at the activity and their expectations concerning the likelihood that they may succeed or fail at that activity in the future. Historically, such concerns have played a central role in analyses of children's achievement motivation and achievement-related behaviors (e.g., Atkinson, 1964; McClelland, 1961; McClelland, Atkinson, Clark, & Lowell, 1953). More recently, they have proved a focus of attribution theorists concerned with the analysis of achievement-related behaviors and children's understandings of the causes of their successes and failures (e.g., Dweck, 1986; Dweck & Elliott, 1983; Weiner, 1974, 1979, 1985).

Through this evaluation process, reward procedures that lead to increases in children's perceptions of their own competence and self-efficacy at the rewarded activity are expected to increase children's subsequent intrinsic motivation toward the previously rewarded activity in the future, whether or not additional extrinsic rewards are expected (e.g., Bandura & Schunk, 1981; Deci, 1975; Deci & Ryan, 1981; Harackiewicz, Manderlink, & Sansone, in press; Harter, 1978; Lepper & Greene, 1978c; Schunk, 1984, 1985; Weiner, 1979). Conversely, extrinsic incentive systems that serve to lower students' perceptions of competence and self-efficacy (as may be the case for some students with grades or other comparative evaluation systems) may decrease the subsequent intrinsic motivational appeal of the activity.

Social Control

Finally, rewards may also serve a social-control or constraint function, as illustrated in the literature concerning the potential deleterious effects of the use of functionally superfluous extrinsic rewards (Condry,

1977; Deci, 1975; Deci & Ryan, 1985; Lepper, 1981, 1983b; Lepper & Greene, 1978c; Quattrone, 1985; Ryan et al., 1985). In this third case, the relevant conceptual variable involves children's perceptions of their reasons for engaging in particular activities (e.g., Lepper et al., 1982). Here, the central issue is whether the introduction of extrinsic rewards leads children to view their engagement in the activity as extrinsically constrained and instrumentally controlled rather than intrinsically motivated. If so, their subsequent intrinsic interest in the activity, in terms of this third process, will be reduced.

Such decreases in later intrinsic motivation, of course, will necessarily run counter to any increases in extrinsic motivation that may be produced by reward systems that lead children to believe that further engagement in a previously rewarded activity will continue to produce further tangible rewards. Such decreases may also stand in opposition to any positive effects the reward system may have had on students' perceptions of their own competence at the activity. Thus, predicting the effects of a given reward procedure on children's later motivation may require attention to each of these three conceptually independent processes. In traditional "overjustification" studies, it should be noted, both the evaluation and the instrumentality functions are typically held constant; rewards are used in ways that do not convey to children salient information about their competence at the activity, and their responses are observed only in subsequent settings in which there is no longer any expectation that further engagement in the activity will lead to additional extrinsic rewards. Under these controlled conditions, children previously rewarded for engaging in activities of high initial interest will show consistent decreases in interest in those activities, as illustrated in the research discussed in the preceding sections of this chapter.

IMPLICATIONS FOR THE CLASSROOM

The direct application of this analysis to classroom practice, of course, is necessarily complex (e.g., Lepper, 1983a). The foregoing literature clearly establishes the potential difficulties that may result when one attempts to overcome a lack of intrinsic interest in learning through the use of extrinsic rewards and sanctions. Any particular reward procedure, any specific extrinsic incentive, may simultaneously produce multiple effects on subsequent motivation through the existence of potentially opposing processes; therefore, predicting its precise effects on children's behavior in some later setting will require attention to each of these individual component processes and to their conjoint effects on children's subsequent motivation.

One straightforward implication of the preceding literature, for example, might be that programs in which extrinsic rewards are contingent simply on the child's conformity to rules (such as those involved in many token economies) ought only to be used when their use is necessary to get children to comply with those rules. If children were initially willing to comply with the same rules without the offer of extrinsic rewards, that is, the use of superfluous extrinsic incentives would be likely to undermine children's motivation to comply in subsequent settings in the later absence of further rewards. The difficult question here, however, would be how to know precisely when, and what type of, rewards are actually necessary to produce particular behaviors.

Moreover, there are other potential consequences of the imposition of an effective reward system, even in cases where the rewards are absolutely necessary. If children who had been offered rewards simply for sitting quietly in their seats, for instance, now spend more time working on their homework, they may be acquiring new skills or knowledge that will lead them to feel more competent in the subject. Such increases in perceived competence may produce increases in intrinsic motivation that more than offset any decreases in motivation created by an increased sense of constraint. In addition, for many academic tasks, it may not be possible to experience the intrinsic satisfactions of activity until one has acquired a minimal level of proficiency. If extrinsic rewards can be used to start children reading or playing an instrument, those children may begin to experience new sources of motivation from the activity itself. Once this is so, however, one might then wish to withdraw extrinsic incentives, gradually, so as not to undermine these newly found sources of intrinsic interest. Indeed, the process of effectively withdrawing extrinsic rewards and sanctions when they are no longer necessary represents perhaps the single topic most in need of systematic further study (Deci & Ryan, 1985; Lepper, 1981; 1983b).[3]

Finally, the effects of any given reward program on later interest should be likely to vary as a function of individual differences among the students to whom rewards have been offered. What may be a necessary incentive or bribe to students who do not find a particular activity of high initial interest may also prove a wholly superfluous and unnecessarily powerful constraint for other students who already find that activity of inherent interest (Lepper & Gilovich, 1981; Lepper & Greene, 1978c). Similarly, receipt of a "B" on the semester exam may prove an

[3] A more detailed discussion of the potential trade-offs between different competing functions of extrinsic reward systems in schools is beyond the scope of the present chapter. More extended discussions of a number of these issues, however, can be found in previous papers (Lepper, 1983a, 1983b; Lepper & Gilovich, 1981).

enormously powerful boost to students who arrive in class with histories of failure and low levels of self-esteem, whereas receipt of the same grade to the budding, highly confident valedictorian may seem a personal tragedy. Detrimental effects of extrinsic rewards seem especially likely, therefore, in cases in which a single set of constraints (designed, typically, to motivate the least attentive student in the class) is applied to an entire classroom of students of varying abilities and initial interests.

ENHANCING CHILDREN'S
INTRINSIC MOTIVATION

In contrast to the preceding literature, which focused, for a variety of historical reasons, on the study of variables that undermine intrinsic interest, a few more recent analyses have tried to examine the opposite side of this coin—to investigate techniques for enhancing children's intrinsic motivation toward particular activities. These more recent approaches, in addition, have turned from the study of social and contextual variables (such as the offer of extrinsic rewards or the imposition of temporal deadlines) to the study of how activities themselves might be structured and designed so as to be more intrinsically motivating to children. These later studies have also begun to focus more clearly on activities of obvious educational value.

FORMS OF MOTIVATIONAL EMBELLISHMENT

The starting point for this more recent work involved an attempt by Malone (1980, 1981) to propose a conceptual framework for thinking about features of activities that might determine their intrinsic interest to children. Malone's goal, in part, was to create a useful taxonomy of sources of intrinsic motivation that could contribute to making an activity more intrinsically interesting. As revised and elaborated by Malone and Lepper (1987), this taxonomy suggested that there are four primary sources of intrinsic motivation that an activity might provide an individual. A brief sketch of their analysis is presented in Figure 2.

Challenge

Perhaps the most obvious and ubiquitous source of intrinsic motivation that activities may offer to students is the provision of an effective challenge to their skills. To provide the student an appropriate level of

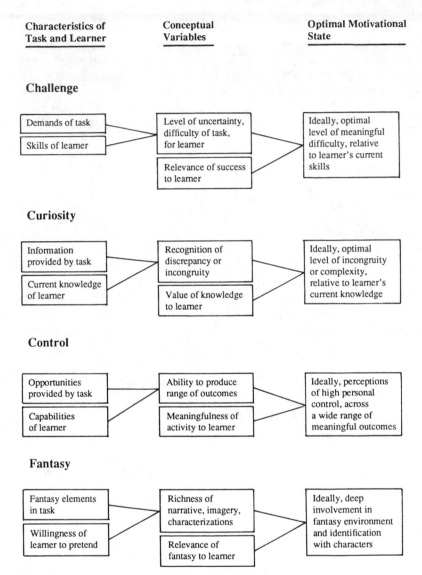

| Characteristics of Task and Learner | Conceptual Variables | Optimal Motivational State |

Challenge

| Demands of task / Skills of learner | Level of uncertainty, difficulty of task, for learner / Relevance of success to learner | Ideally, optimal level of meaningful difficulty, relative to learner's current skills |

Curiosity

| Information provided by task / Current knowledge of learner | Recognition of discrepancy or incongruity / Value of knowledge to learner | Ideally, optimal level of incongruity or complexity, relative to learner's current knowledge |

Control

| Opportunities provided by task / Capabilities of learner | Ability to produce range of outcomes / Meaningfulness of activity to learner | Ideally, perceptions of high personal control, across a wide range of meaningful outcomes |

Fantasy

| Fantasy elements in task / Willingness of learner to pretend | Richness of narrative, imagery, characterizations / Relevance of fantasy to learner | Ideally, deep involvement in fantasy environment and identification with characters |

Figure 2.   Sources of intrinsic motivation.

challenge, a number of theorists have suggested, an activity must present a clear and meaningful goal, or set of goals, whose attainment is uncertain. Optimally challenging activities, therefore, will be those at an intermediate level of difficulty for the student—activities that are neither trivially simple nor impossibly hard. Moreover, in order to remain challenging over time, an activity must be able to vary in its demands on the learner as he or she acquires increased information about, and/or skill at, the task.

Essentially similar ideas have been discussed by previous authors in a variety of contexts. White (1959, 1960), Harter (1978, 1981), and others, for example, have postulated a basic and innate drive toward mastery that has been labeled an "effectance" motive. Kagan's (1972) focus on uncertainty as a motivational force takes a conceptually related position, as do a number of discussions of perceptions of competence (Deci, 1975; Lepper & Greene, 1978c; Weiner, 1980) or self-efficacy (Bandura, 1977; Bandura & Schunk, 1981) as critical determinants of intrinsic motivation. In each case, activities that present a moderate level of difficulty to the student are assumed to be preferred. Similarly, conceptual analyses by Csikszentmihalyi (1975, present volume) have focused on the ways in which activities capable of continuously adjusting the level of challenge they provide, as a function of the progress of the learner, may produce a state of "flow" that is characteristic of behaviors that are highly intrinsically motivating.

In addition, though less widely discussed, the goals toward which activities must be directed must have some meaning for students in order for them to find the challenge of reaching that goal intrinsically motivating (Malone & Lepper, 1987). For instance, for a challenge to be intrinsically motivating, it must engage the learner's sense of self-esteem. The activity must draw on some skill or knowledge of the student, and the student must value that specific skill or knowledge. Under the right conditions, even the most boring activity could be made more challenging by imposing constraints on one's engagement in the activity. Some constraints may prove legitimate and meaningful to individuals or social groups (e.g., standing at a specified distance from the target at an archery context); whereas others may normally be seen as meaningless (e.g., standing on only one foot at the archery contest). Increases in the challenge provided by an activity should have positive effects on the intrinsic motivational appeal of the activity only when constraints are perceived as meaningful.

Curiosity

A second, crucial source of intrinsic motivation that activities may offer involves an appeal to the learner's sense of curiosity. Curiosity will be elicited, a number of authors have argued, by activities that provide students with information or ideas that are surprising, incongruous, or discrepant from their existing beliefs and ideas. Thus, information that suggests to students that their ideas are incomplete, inconsistent, or even unparsimonious should be effective in provoking their curiosity (Malone, 1981). Incongruities instigate information-seeking, disconfirmed expectancies call for explanations, and inconsistencies cry out for resolutions. As was the case with challenge, however, intermediate levels of incongruity or discrepancy are hypothesized to be optimal. Ideas too greatly at variance with existing information and beliefs will tend to be discounted or rejected; ideas too similar to existing knowledge may be assimilated or ignored.

Once again, similar ideas have been discussed by a variety of previous authors. Berlyne (1960, 1965), for instance, focused on the idea of an optimal level of informational complexity and arousal as the major determinant of an individual's level of curiosity and examined at length the factors that contribute to informational complexity. Hunt (1961, 1965), drawing on ideas from Piaget (1951, 1952), provided a conceptually analogous model of curiosity in his discussion of optimal levels of discrepancy or incongruity (relative to current knowledge and expectations) as the wellspring of information-seeking and conceptual change.

Control

A third potential source of intrinsic motivation involves providing the student with a sense of control. From this perspective, empowering, and hence intrinsically motivating, learning environments will be those in which the student's outcomes may vary greatly and as a direct function of his or her own responses. Activities and environments that undermine a learner's sense of control, by contrast, will have detrimental effects on subsequent motivation and interest.

DeCharms (1968), for example, has posited that people have a basic drive to seek out and exert control over their environments—to experience themselves as "Origins," rather than "Pawns." Deci (1975, 1981), likewise, has sought to define intrinsic motivation in terms of a fundamental human drive toward self-determination. As a result, increasing even just the "illusion of control" (Langer, 1975) that activities provide might help to stimulate pupils' intrinsic motivation. Conversely, experiences that decrease perceptions of control can be shown, as in the literature on learned helplessness (e.g., Dweck, 1975; Seligman, 1975), to decrease later intrinsic interest in the activity.

Fantasy

Finally, activities may promote intrinsic motivation through the creation of learning environments that encourage the learner to become involved in a world of fantasy and make-believe. Such fantasy environments can evoke mental images of physical or social situations not actually present and may contribute to intrinsic motivation in several ways. First, the use of fantasy learning environments may serve a variety of motivational or emotional needs. In fantasy, students can experience vicariously, through a process of identification with fictitious characters, a variety of rewards and satisfactions that may not be available to them in real life. In this sense, the use of fantasy may frequently provide one source of meaning for students engaged in otherwise personally irrelevant activities. Also, the introduction of fantasy elements into an activity may help to enhance students' motivation by providing concrete and familiar settings to which the substance of the activity is relevant and to which the material can be related.

The early, psychodynamic literature on fantasy focused heavily on the various emotional needs that fantasy might serve (e.g., Freud, 1950; Murray, 1938). Here, fantasy was taken as a vehicle through which we might identify with characters who achieve levels of fame, fortune, or power that elude us in our daily lives. In contrast, early Piagetian work on fantasy (Piaget, 1951) focused instead on the cognitive structuring and elaboration that fantasy elements added to otherwise more mundane and literal tasks. More recent discussions concerning the antecedents and consequences of fantasy (Fein, 1981; Singer, 1973) have tried to take into account both sorts of processes.

EFFECTS OF MOTIVATIONAL EMBELLISHMENTS

Once one has identified the various sources of intrinsic motivation that may be produced by an activity, one may consider the design principles implied by these factors. In so doing, of course, one is immediately drawn to the question of how one might enhance the motivational appeal of initially uninteresting educational activities through the addition of motivational embellishments of different sorts (Malone, 1980, 1981). Malone and Lepper (1987), for example, present a conceptual analysis of these issues.

Many of the activities children are asked to undertake in school, for example, involve a fairly repetitive and often boring drill-and-practice or study-and-test format. For example, students who have just been taught about the Pythagorean theorem will often be asked in the following days to solve a variety of problems whose solutions involve the use of that theorem in various forms. Given that a certain right triangle has one side of length x and a hypotenuse of length y, what is the length of the other side?

How might such an activity be made more intrinsically interesting? Presumably, one might attempt to enhance the interest value of such an activity by increasing any of the aforementioned sources of intrinsic motivation. If the task appeared too simple for the learner, for example, one might seek to increase the degree of challenge offered by the activity by introducing additional performance contingencies (e.g., a time limit for working on each problem), by adding an element of competition between individuals or groups within the classroom, or by providing inherently more difficult problems.[4]

Alternatively, one might seek to provoke a sense of curiosity on the part of the student, by demonstrating that his or her current knowledge is inaccurate, incomplete, or inelegant. One might describe to the learner, for instance, two children who are trying to figure out the hypotenuse of a right triangle with sides of 90 and 120 feet. As one child begins to apply the relevant formula, taking out a pencil and figuring out 90^2 and 120^2, the other says immediately, "Oh, it's got to be 150." We might ask the learner, "How did this second child get the answer without any calculations?"

Level of student control over the activity might also be varied. Students might be offered choices concerning the time at which, or the order in which, they would attempt various problems. They might be given the option of going ahead to more difficult problems or continuing at the same level of difficulty. Or they might be given the option, at relevant points, of continuing on their own or of requesting assistance.

One particularly interesting case arises, however, when one considers forms of motivational enhancement or embellishment that might be undertaken without any alteration in the fundamental activity itself—cases in which one might be able to examine the effects of motivational embellishments that are independent of instructional content. Here, we might pose the question of the educational consequences of intrinsic motivation in an interesting fashion. If the intrinsic motivational appeal of an educational activity can be increased without concomitant changes in the instructional content of the activity, one may then ask whether children learn any differently when the activity from which they are learning is more fun.

Imagine that one has presented children with a lesson concerning the Pythagorean theorem and now wishes to ask those children to make use of this information in solving relevant problems. Typically, one might

---

[4] Conversely, if the task were initially too difficult for the student, one might seek to provide additional assistance, offer the student hints, or create additional, less-demanding performance goals that would provide a more appropriate level of challenge for that student.

simply present children with a series of problems in which they are asked, in the abstract, to determine the length of one side of a right triangle, given knowledge of the lengths of the other two sides—a quite straightforward activity. Suppose, however, that one were able to embed these same problems requiring the use of the Pythagorean theorem in some larger fantasy context that might be of more inherent interest to the student. For example, the student might need to calculate the distance from point a to point b in order to be able to advise Captain James T. Kirk on how to set the transporter beam on the Federation Starship *Enterprise* in order to pick up the necessary dilithium crystals directly below on the planet's surface, given that Kirk knows only the distances of the ship and the crystals from a third point where his scouting party is stopped.

With this particular sort of motivational embellishment, it becomes especially interesting to ask what the consequences of increasing the motivational appeal of the activity might be—controlling for the instructions, problems, and feedback that students receive and the time that they are allowed to spend with the activity. Do students exposed to these two types of activities show differences in their learning from the activity or their interest in it—both in the initial setting in which the embellishments are provided and in subsequent situations in which they are not (Lepper, 1985)? Such comparisons are of particular theoretical interest both because they speak to classic controversies concerning the role of intrinsic motivation in education and because they simultaneously address current heated policy debates concerning the appropriate role or motivational embellishments in education (Baker, Herman, & Yeh, 1981; Lepper & Chabay, 1985; Lepper & Malone, 1987).

Immediate Effects

Consider, first, the immediate effects (both on motivation and on learning) of such motivational embellishments in terms of students' reactions to otherwise identical educational activities presented with or without such adornments.

Effects on Motivation. The first question about such techniques is obvious: Do these sorts of instructionally incidental embellishments actually enhance students' interest in the activity itself? Somewhat surprisingly, there is little empirical evidence available to answer this question.

Some evidence that these sorts of enhancement procedures can increase students' interest in the activity, however, has been obtained by Lepper and Hodell (1988). This study compared the effects of two parallel versions of a computer-based activity designed to give children experience with, and feedback concerning, the use of Cartesian coordinates. In the basal version, the activity presented children with a series of tasks that involved the use of a coordinate system to pinpoint a randomly chosen target point on the grid; in the embellished version, the same set of problems and exercises was embedded in a fantasy context in which the learner was asked to help a graphics character find a series of hidden treasures. Across several sessions, children were offered a continuous choice between their version of the experimental activity and a common distractor activity. On the average, children working with the embellished version of the activity chose to spend about 50% more time with it than children working with the unembellished version chose to spend with that activity. Other findings by Malone (1981; see also Lepper & Malone, 1987) also suggest that the addition of relatively minor motivational embellishments can have large effects on student interest.

Effects on Learning.   Given that children do seem to find such activities more intrinsically motivating, a second obvious question arises: Do children working with a motivationally enhanced version of an activity learn any more, or any differently, than children working with an unadorned version of that activity? Will motivational embellishments distract children from the educational content of the activity and waste their time on irrelevant frills? Or will motivational adornments of this sort increase children's attention to, and learning of, the underlying content embodied in the program?

Again, recent research suggests that these sorts of embellishments can have positive effects on learning as well—even when the time spent at the activity is controlled, so that differences in learning are not simply the result of children spending more time with activities they find more highly motivating. In three separate studies, involving different basic activities and different fantasy overlays, enhanced learning of the material presented by students exposed to motivationally embellished educational programs has been observed. Unexpectedly, in the first of these studies, this enhancement-of-learning effect occurred only for boys (Lepper & Hodell, 1988). In both of the subsequent studies, however, such effects were equally apparent for both boys and girls (Hodell & Lepper, 1988; Parker & Lepper, 1988), suggesting that this finding is more robust than it had initially appeared.

Subsequent Effects

In addition to these immediate effects on motivation and learning, one may also ask what sorts of long-term effects such motivational embellishments may have on later interest in, or retention of, the material in subsequent situations.

Effects on Motivation. Consider the later motivational consequences of such activities. The important question here is not whether students continue to find the motivationally enhanced activity itself more interesting. Rather, it is whether children come to enjoy more, or less, the material presented via one form of the activity or another. Does the addition of game-like or fantasy elements to an activity designed to present mathematics, for example, lead children to be more or less attentive, or interested, or excited, when they encounter similar mathematical problems or topics elsewhere? Will one find a generalization of positive affect and interest, such that the subject matter becomes more enjoyable, even in the later absence of motivational enhancements? Or, will one find a contrast effect, such that the activity seems even less intrinsically motivating to students, once the added motivational features of the enhanced activity have been withdrawn?

To date, the evidence provides some support for a positive generalization of motivational benefits from the use of motivational embellishments. Hodell and Lepper (1988), in particular, found that students who had worked with a motivationally embellished computer program designed to teach children about Cartesian coordinates subsequently reported more positive attitudes towards graphing and related tasks—in the library, several days later, apart from any computer-based activities—than their peers who had worked with an unembellished version of the same program initially. In other studies, similar but statistically nonsignificant effects were obtained. In no case has there been evidence to support a contrast analysis.

Effects on Learning. Finally, one might also ask about subsequent learning or retention of the material initially learned at the activity. On these measures, the results also suggest a carryover of benefits of motivational-enhancement strategies. For example, in each of the studies demonstrating an effect of motivational adornments on learning, differences between conditions were apparent on paper-and-pencil achievement tests administered 1–2 weeks following the experimental sessions (Hodell & Lepper, 1988; Lepper & Hodell, 1988; Parker &

Lepper, 1988). In one of these studies, there was also evidence of differences in learning that extended beyond the specific tasks explicitly called for by the activity; students also performed better on more difficult generalization tests that built on the skills in which pupils had been instructed (Lepper & Hodell, 1988).

IMPLICATIONS FOR THE CLASSROOM

Taken together, these findings suggest the potential utility of motivational-enrichment strategies in the design of educational activities as one means of combating the problem of declining intrinsic motivation in school (Lepper, 1985; Lepper & Malone, 1987). Not only do such embellishments appear to make the activity itself more interesting and enjoyable for students; they also appear capable, under appropriate circumstances, of enhancing student learning and retention and promoting more positive subsequent attitudes toward the subject matter being presented.

In contemplating the implications of these more recent results for classroom practice, however, two additional considerations should be kept in mind. On the one hand, it seems likely that the foregoing experimental studies actually underestimate the potential benefits of such motivational-enhancement techniques because these studies have all involved an attempt to control for the time that children worked with the experimental activities. In many classroom contexts, however, children may have more freedom to determine the amount of time they spend with different activities. In these circumstances, more powerful and pervasive effects on learning and motivation might be expected if students exposed to motivationally enriched educational materials were to choose to spend more time with the experimental activities than those exposed to their unembellished counterparts.

On the other hand, it is also important that such procedures not be viewed as a motivational panacea. Although such techniques can be shown in the laboratory to produce significant benefits, it seems equally clear that not all motivational embellishments will produce these same positive outcomes. Lepper and Malone (1987), for example, describe a number of educational computer programs that are available in many classrooms today, in which motivational enhancements appear to have negative, rather than positive, effects on children's learning. Indeed, they suggest that it is distressingly easy to design educational programs that may prove highly motivating, but instructionally useless.

One critical distinction between those cases in which added motivational embellishments enhance, and those in which they undermine, student learning involves the extent to which the motivational goals of an educational activity either reinforce, or compete with, the instructional goals of that activity (Lepper & Malone, 1987).[5] In some instructional computer simulations, for example, students are allowed to accumulate winnings (hypothetical dollars or points earned) across an endless series of problems; and in these activities, children will often enter relatively mindless answers, trial after trial, as fast as they can type them in, because this provides a quicker means of accumulating earnings than a more thoughtful consideration of each answer. If these same activities simply limited students to 20 problems at a time, however, then the child could effectively accumulate big scores only by mindful attention to each answer. In the first instance, the goals of winning the game and learning the material appear to compete with each other; in the second instance, motivational goals appear congruent with instructional goals.

Finally, it seems likely that the effects of many types of motivational enrichments may depend on characteristics of the student as well. Clearly, different students may value different sorts of accomplishments (e.g., Malone & Lepper, 1987). Equally clearly, different students are likely to find different fantasy goals or contexts appealing (e.g., Singer, 1973). Hence, it may be important to find methods for matching particular students to particular activities or for offering students choices along these dimensions. Even the general strategy of motivational embellishment itself may have differential appeal to individual students. Perhaps such motivational variables, for example, may have the most effect on precisely those students who are least intrinsically motivated, at first, by the material itself.

CONCLUSIONS

In this chapter we have tried to address two complementary questions concerning the determinants and the consequences of intrinsic motivation in the classroom. In the first instance, we examined the potential significance of children's apparent loss of intrinsic motivation in school as they grow older, in terms of the literature that documents some of the ways in which we may unintentionally undermine intrinsic interest

---

[5] A fuller, more principled discussion of the circumstances in which the addition of motivational embellishments to an educational program is likely either to enhance or to decrease student learning and retention is presented in Lepper and Malone (1987).

through the misapplication of extrinsic rewards and sanctions. In the second, we explored the possibilities for overcoming such effects, in terms of the literature concerned with methods of designing more intrinsically motivating educational activities. Let us consider these two questions in turn.

First: Should we be concerned if children become increasingly extrinsically motivated and decreasingly intrinsically motivated as they progress through school? We think that the answer is yes, for several reasons. On the one hand, of course, one might value intrinsic motivation for its own sake. Helping children to enjoy the activities they undertake in school might be an end in itself.

In addition to its potential inherent value, however, the research literature on the ways in which intrinsic motivation is often undermined suggests that there are a variety of negative consequences that follow when extrinsic motivation supplants intrinsic motivation. On the one hand, extrinsically motivated students will be less likely to approach or choose similar activities in subsequent situations unless they expect further extrinsic rewards or sanctions to be forthcoming. Thus, they will be less likely to continue to pursue the subjects taught outside of the context of specific classroom assignments. On the other hand, the presence of salient extrinsic incentives also seems to have a variety of detrimental effects on learning and performance, both within the situation in which those incentives were offered and in later situations as well.

Second: Can such effects be overcome? We believe that the answer is "yes" once again. Here, the more recent research literature that we have discussed, concerning techniques for designing more intrinsically motivating educational activities, is relevant. It suggests that relatively small motivational embellishments can, under appropriate circumstances, have significant positive effects not only on students' enjoyment of the activity so embellished, but also on students' learning from the activity, their retention of the material learned, and their subsequent attitudes toward the subject matter being presented.

With the usual wisdom of hindsight, such conclusions may seem obvious. Therefore, it is important to be clear that both sets of statements deal with issues that have been highly controversial. In the arena of extrinsic rewards and intrinsic motivation, for example, there has been vociferous debate concerning the possibility that the use of tangible rewards might prove counterproductive (cf. Lepper, 1983a; Lepper & Greene, 1978b). Why shouldn't two rewards prove better than one, promoting enhanced motivation in subsequent settings?

Similarly, discussions concerning the relative merits and drawbacks of the use of motivational embellishments have produced vehement disagreement among educators (cf. Condry & Keith, 1983: Lepper, 1985; Lepper & Chabay, 1985). Proponents of such devices are often met with claims that such techniques distract students and undermine learning. Such techniques are likewise frequently criticized as likely to produce students who will be dependent on these motivational devices and who find the subject matter less inherently interesting in the absence of these gimmicks.

In an earlier era, Sydney Smith, the noted English cleric and essayist, voiced his strong opinion concerning the relationship between students' interests and learning: "Everything which is written is meant either to please or to instruct. The second object is difficult to effect, without attending to the first." If we take seriously the evidence presented in this chapter, we might say the same for most things that go on in schools.

ACKNOWLEDGMENT

Preparation of this chapter was supported, in part, by Research Grant HD-17371 from the National Institute of Child Health and Human Development to the senior author.

REFERENCES

Amabile, T. M. (1979). Effects of external evaluation on artistic creativity. *Journal of Personality and Social Psychology, 37,* 221–233.

Amabile, T. M., Hennessey, B. A., & Grossman, B. S. (1986). Social influences on creativity: The effects of contracted-for reward. *Journal of Personality and Social Psychology, 50,* 11–23.

Atkinson, J. W. (1964). *An introduction to motivation.* Princeton, NJ: Van Nostrand.

Bahrick, H. P. (1954). Incidental learning under two incentive conditions. *Journal of Experimental Psychology, 47,* 170–172.

Bahrick, H. P., Fitts, P. M., & Rankin, R. E. (1952). Effects of incentive upon reactions to peripheral stimuli. *Journal of Experimental Psychology, 44,* 400–406.

Baker, E. L., Herman, J. L., & Yeh, J. P. (1981). Fun and games: Their contribution to basic skills instruction in elementary school. *American Educational Research Journal, 18,* 83–92.

Bandura, A. (1969). *Principles of behavior modification.* New York: Holt, Rinehart and Winston.

Bandura, A. (1977). Self-efficacy: Toward a unifying theory of behavioral change. *Psychological Review, 41,* 191–215.

Bandura, A., & Schunk, D. H. (1981). Cultivating competence, self-efficacy, and intrinsic interest through proximal self-instruction. *Journal of Personality and Social Psychology, 41,* 586–598.

Berlyne, D. E. (1960). *Conflict, arousal, and curiosity.* New York: McGraw-Hill.

Berlyne, D. E. (1965). *Structure and direction in thinking.* New York: McGraw-Hill.

Bruner, J. S. (1962). *On knowing: Essays for the left hand.* Cambridge, MA: Harvard University Press.

Bruner, J. S. (1966). *Toward a theory of instruction.* Cambridge, MA: Harvard University Press.

Calder, B. J., & Staw, B. M. (1975). Self-perception of intrinsic and extrinsic motivation. *Journal of Personality and Social Psychology, 31,* 599–605.

Condry, J. (1977). Enemies of exploration: Self-initiated versus other-initiated learning. *Journal of Personality and Social Psychology, 35,* 459–475.

Condry, J. (1978). The role of incentives in socialization. In M. R. Lepper & D. Greene (Eds.), *The hidden costs of reward* (pp. 179–192). Hillsdale, NJ: Erlbaum.

Condry, J., & Chambers, J. (1978). Intrinsic motivation and the process of learning. In M. R. Lepper & D. Greene (Eds.), *The hidden costs of reward* (pp. 61–84). Hillsdale, NJ: Erlbaum.

Condry, J., & Keith, D. (1983). Educational and recreational uses of computer technology. *Youth and Society, 15,* 87–112.

Csikszentmihalyi, M. (1975). *Beyond boredom and anxiety.* San Francisco: Jossey-Bass.

Cuban, L. (1982). Persistent instruction: The high school classroom, 1900–1980. *Phi Delta Kappan,* 113–118.

DeCharms, R. (1968). *Personal causation.* New York: Academic Press.

Deci, E. L. (1971). Effects of externally mediated rewards on intrinsic motivation. *Journal of Personality and Social Psychology, 18,* 105–155.

Deci, E. L. (1975). *Intrinsic motivation.* New York: Plenum.

Deci, E. L., & Ryan, R. M. (1981). *The psychology of self-determination.* Lexington, MA: Heath.

Deci, E. L., & Ryan, R. M. (1985). *Intrinsic motivation and self-determination in human behavior.* New York: Plenum.

Dewey, J. (1963). *Experience and education.* New York: Collier Books. (Original work published 1938).

Dweck, C. S. (1975). The role of expectations and attributions in the alleviation of learned helplessness. *Journal of Personality and Social Psychology, 31,* 674–685.

Dweck, C. S. (1986). Motivational processes affecting learning. *American Psychologist, 41,* 1040–1048.

Dweck, C. S., & Elliott, E. S. (1983). Achievement motivation. In P. H. Mussen (Gen. Ed.) & E. M. Hetherington (Vol. Ed.), *Handbook of child psychology: Vol. IV. Social and personality development* (pp. 643–691) New York: Wiley.

Easterbrook, J. A. (1959). The effect of emotion on cue utilization and organization of behavior. *Psychological Review, 66,* 183–201.

Fein, G. G. (1981). Pretend play in childhood: An integrative review. *Child Development, 52,* 1095–1118.

Freud, S. (1950). *Beyond the pleasure principle.* New York: Liveright. (Original work published 1920).

Garbarino, J. (1975). The impact of anticipated rewards on cross-age tutoring. *Journal of Personality and Social Psychology, 32,* 421–428.

Ginsberg, H. (1977). *Children's arithmetic: The learning process.* New York: Van Nostrand.

Glucksberg, S. (1962). The influence of strength of drive on functional fixedness and perceptual recognition. *Journal of Experimental Psychology, 63,* 36–41.

Glucksberg, S. (1964). Problem solving: Response competition and the influence of drive. *Psychological Reports, 15,* 939–942.

Greene, D., & Lepper, M. R. (1974). Effects of extrinsic rewards on children's subsequent intrinsic interest. *Child Development, 45*, 1141–1145.

Harackiewicz, J. M., Manderlink, G., & Sansone, C. (in press). Competence processes and achievement motivation: Implications for intrinsic motivation. In A. K. Boggiano & T. S. Pittman (Eds.), *Achievement and motivation: A social-developmental perspective.* Cambridge, England: Cambridge University Press.

Harter, S. (1978). Effectance motivation reconsidered: Toward a developmental model. *Human Development, 1*, 34–64.

Harter, S. (1981). A new self-report scale of intrinsic versus extrinsic orientation in the classroom: Motivational and informational components. *Developmental Psychology, 17*, 300–312.

Hodell, M., & Lepper, M. R. (1988). *The role of fantasy in student motivation and learning.* Unpublished manuscript, Stanford University.

Holt, J. (1964). *How children fail.* New York: Holt, Rinehart and Winston.

Holt, J. (1968). *How children learn.* New York: Dial.

Hunt, J. Mc.V. (1961). *Intelligence and experience.* New York: Ronald Press.

Hunt, J. McV. (1965). Intrinsic motivation and its role in psychological development. In D. Levine (Ed.), *Nebraska symposium on motivation* (Vol. 13, pp. 189–282). Lincoln, NE: University of Nebraska Press.

Jackson, P. W. (1968). *Life in classrooms.* New York: Holt, Rinehart and Winston.

Kagan, J. (1972). Motives and development. *Journal of Personality and Social Psychology, 22*, 51–66.

Kazdin, A. E. (1977). *The token economy.* New York: Plenum.

Kruglanski, A. W. (1978). Endogenous attribution and intrinsic motivation. In M. R. Lepper & D. Greene (Eds.), *The hidden costs of reward* (pp. 85–108). Hillsdale, NJ: Erlbaum.

Kruglanski, A. W., Friedman, I., & Zeevi, G. (1971). The effects of extrinsic incentives on some qualitative aspects of task performance. *Journal of Personality, 39*, 606–617.

Langer, E. J. (1975). The illusion of control. *Journal of Personality and Social Psychology, 32*, 311–328.

Lepper, M. R. (1981). Intrinsic and extrinsic motivation in children: Detrimental effects of superfluous social controls. In W. A. Collins (Ed.), *Minnesota symposium on child psychology* (Vol. 14, pp. 155–214). Hillsdale, NJ: Erlbaum.

Lepper, M. R. (1983a). Extrinsic reward and intrinsic motivation: Implications for the classroom. In J. M. Levine & M. C. Wang (Eds.), *Teacher and student perceptions: Implications for learning* (pp. 281–317). Hillsdale, NJ: Erlbaum.

Lepper, M. R. (1983b). Social control processes and the internalization of social values: An attributional perspective. In E. T. Higgins, D. N. Ruble, & W. W. Hartup (Eds.), *Developmental social cognition: A sociocultural perspective* (pp. 294–330). New York: Cambridge University Press.

Lepper, M. R. (1985). Microcomputers in education: Motivational and social issues. *American Psychologist, 40*, 1–18.

Lepper, M. R., & Chabay, R. W. (1985). Intrinsic motivation and instruction: Conflicting views on the role of motivational processes in computer-based education. *Educational Psychologist, 20*, 217–230.

Lepper, M. R., & Gilovich, T. (1981). The multiple functions of reward: A social-developmental perspective. In S. S. Brehm, S. M. Kassin, & F. X. Gibbons (Eds.), *Developmental social psychology* (pp. 5–31). New York: Oxford University Press.

Lepper, M. R., & Greene, D. (1975). Turning play into work: Effects of adult surveillance and extrinsic rewards on children's intrinsic motivation. *Journal of Personality and Social Psychology, 31,* 479–486.

Lepper, M. R., & Greene, D. (1978a). Divergent approaches to the study of rewards. In M. R. Lepper & D. Greene (Eds.), *The hidden costs of reward* (pp. 217–244). Hillsdale, NJ: Erlbaum.

Lepper, M. R., & Greene, D. (Eds.). (1978b). *The hidden costs of reward.* Hillsdale, NJ: Erlbaum.

Lepper, M. R., & Greene, D. (1978c). Overjustification research and beyond: Toward a means–ends analysis of intrinsic and extrinsic motivation. In M. R. Lepper & D. Greene (Eds.), *The hidden costs of reward* (pp. 109–148). Hillsdale, NJ: Erlbaum.

Lepper, M. R., Greene, D., & Nisbett, R. E. (1973). Undermining children's intrinsic interest with extrinsic rewards: A test of the "overjustification" hypothesis. *Journal of Personality and Social Psychology, 28,* 129–137.

Lepper, M. R., & Hodell, M. (1988). *When learning is fun: Instructional consequences of enhancing students' intrinsic motivation.* Unpublished manuscript, Stanford University.

Lepper, M. R., & Malone, T. W. (1987). Intrinsic motivation and instructional effectiveness in computer-based education. In R. E. Snow & M. J. Farr (Eds.), *Aptitude, learning, and instruction: Vol. III. Conative and affective process analyses.* Hillsdale, NJ: Erlbaum.

Lepper, M. R., Sagotsky, G., Dafoe, J., & Greene, D. (1982). Consequences of superfluous social constraints: Effects of nominal contingencies on children's subsequent intrinsic interest. *Journal of Personality and Social Psychology, 42,* 51–64.

Loveland, K. K., & Olley, J. G. (1979). The effect of external reward on interest and quality of task performance in children of high and low intrinsic motivation. *Child Development, 50,* 1207–1210.

Mahoney, M. J. (1974). *Cognition and behavior modification.* Cambridge, MA: Ballinger Publishing Company.

Malone, T. W. (1980). *What makes things fun to learn: A study of intrinsically motivating computer games.* Unpublished doctoral dissertation, Stanford University.

Malone, T. W. (1981). Toward a theory of intrinsically motivating instruction. *Cognitive Science, 4,* 333–369.

Malone, T. W., & Lepper, M. R. (1987). Making learning fun: A taxonomy of intrinsic motivations for learning. In R. E. Snow & M. J. Farr (Eds.), *Aptitude, learning, and instruction: Vol. III. Conative and affective process analyses.* Hillsdale, NJ: Erlbaum.

McClelland, D. C. (1961). *The achieving society.* Princeton, NJ: Van Nostrand.

McClelland, D. C., Atkinson, J. W., Clark, R. W., & Lowell, E. L. (1953). *The achievement motive.* New York: Appleton-Century-Crofts.

McGraw, K. O. (1978). The detrimental effects of reward on performance: A literature review and a prediction model. In M. R. Lepper & D. Greene (Eds.), *The hidden costs of reward* (pp. 33–60). Hillsdale, NJ: Erlbaum.

McGraw, K. O., & McCullers, J. C. (1979). Evidence of a detrimental effect of extrinsic incentives on breaking a mental set. *Journal of Experimental Social Psychology, 15,* 285–294.

McLoyd, V. C. (1979). The effects of extrinsic rewards of differential value on high and low intrinsic interest. *Child Development, 50,* 1010–1019.

Miller, L. B., & Estes, B. W. (1961). Monetary reward and motivation in discrimination learning. *Journal of Experimental Psychology, 61,* 501–504.

Mischel, W. (1973). Towards a cognitive social learning reconceptualization of personality. *Psychological Review, 80,* 252–283.

Murray, H. A. (1938). *Explorations in personality.* New York: Oxford.

O'Leary, K. D., & Drabman, R. (1971). Token reinforcement programs in the classroom: A review. *Psychological Bulletin, 75,* 379–398.
Parker, L., & Lepper, M. R. (1988). *Intrinsic motivation and learning: Beneficial effects of fantasy involvement.* Unpublished manuscript, Stanford University.
Piaget, J. (1951). *Play, dreams, and imitation in childhood.* New York: Norton.
Piaget, J. (1952). *The origins of intelligence in children.* New York: International University Press.
Pittman, T. S., Emery, J., & Boggiano, A. K. (1982). Intrinsic and extrinsic motivational orientations: Reward-induced changes in preference for complexity. *Journal of Personality and Social Psychology, 42,* 789–797.
Quattrone, G. (1985). On the congruity between internal states and action. *Psychological Bulletin, 98,* 3–40.
Ryan, R. M., Connell, J. P., & Deci, E. L. (1985). A motivational analysis of self-determination in education. In C. Ames & R. E. Ames (Eds.), *Research on motivation in education: Vol. II. The classroom milieu* (pp. 13–51). New York: Academic Press.
Schunk, D. H. (1984). Self-efficacy perspective on achievement behavior. *Educational Psychologist, 19,* 48–58.
Schunk, D. H. (1985). Self-efficacy and classroom learning. *Psychology in the Schools, 22,* 208–223.
Seligman, M. E. P. (1975). *Helplessness: On depression, development, and death.* San Francisco: W. H. Freeman.
Silberman, C. (1970). *Crisis in the classroom.* New York: Random House.
Singer, J. L. (1973). *The child's world of make-believe.* New York: Academic Press.
Sirotnik, K. A. (1983). What you see is what you get— Consistency, persistency, and mediocrity in classrooms. *Harvard Educational Review, 53,* 16–31.
Spence, K. W. (1956). *Behavior theory and conditioning.* New Haven, CT: Yale University.
Terrell, Jr., G., Durkin, K., & Wiesley, M. (1959). Social class and the nature of the incentives in discrimination learning. *Journal of Abnormal and Social Psychology, 59,* 270–272.
Weiner, B. (1974). *Achievement motivation and attribution theory.* Morristown, NJ: General Learning Press
Weiner, B. (1979). A theory of motivation for some classroom experiences. *Journal of Educational Psychology, 71,* 3–25.
Weiner, B. (1980). *Human motivation.* New York: Holt, Rinehart and Winston.
Weiner, B. (1985). An attributional theory of achievement motivation and emotion. *Psychological Review, 92,* 102–107.
White, R. W. (1959). Motivation reconsidered: The concept of competence. *Psychological Review, 66,* 297–333.
White, R. W. (1960). Competence and the psychosexual stages of development. In M. R. Jones (Ed.), *Nebraska symposium on motivation* (Vol. 8, pp. 97–140). Lincoln, NE: University of Nebraska Press.
Winnett, R. A., & Winkler, R. C. (1972). Current behavior modification in the classroom: Be still, be quiet, be docile. *Journal of Applied Behavior Analysis, 5,* 199–504.

4

Social Life as a Goal-Coordination Task

Kenneth A. Dodge
Steven R. Asher
Jennifer T. Parkhurst

INTRODUCTION

We have several goals in writing this chapter, and we hope to accomplish them in a balanced fashion. One goal is to provide an overview of research and thinking about the concept of children's social competence. In this review, we point out that competence has often been defined as the achievement of one's goals in a particular social situation (Ford, 1982). Proceeding from this definition, researchers have studied the social–cognitive and behavioral skills that may be required in order to achieve intended outcomes such as joining a group or making a friend (e.g., Goetz & Dweck, 1980; Gottman, 1983; Gottman, Gonso, & Rasmussen, 1975; Putallaz & Gottman, 1981). Likewise, this definition has been central to the development of intervention programs aimed at teaching skills that lead to being judged as more socially competent (e.g., Ladd, 1981). However, this definition (and a good deal of research) has ignored the importance of the goals themselves. A child may be quite effective at achieving certain goals but be socially deviant because the goals themselves are deviant.

So a second purpose of this chapter is to emphasize the importance of

107

considering the process of goal selection in understanding children's social behavior. Studies have examined developmental and individual differences in children's goals (Ford, 1982; Renshaw & Asher, 1983). Results from these studies support the view that consideration of children's goal selection is essential to understanding children's responses to social situations. This work has broadened our understanding of social behavior, but it has been limited by its assumption that people only pursue one goal at a time. For example, children have been characterized as either relationship oriented or performance oriented, almost as if a child cannot be both. In fact, the child's social world is much more complex and requires consideration of multiple options at a given time.

Consider the following case example:

> Jeremy, age 9 years, is playing in his backyard with his brother, Alex, and a new friend from school, Warren. They are in the middle of an important free-throw shooting contest. Alex is winning, but Warren's last turn is coming up. Jeremy sees Warren cheat by stepping across the line. Warren's shot goes in the basket, and he declares himself the victor. Alex protests about Warren's cheating. They turn to Jeremy for his opinion. At that moment, Jeremy's mother calls to him from the house, telling him to come inside for dinner.

Is there only one socially competent action for Jeremy to take? Jeremy's mother might say that Jeremy should quickly excuse himself and come to dinner. Alex and Warren would have their own opinions. Jeremy's life is complex and is characterized by many goals. He wants to foster his friendship with Warren, who happens to be a popular boy at school. He also wants to be fair to his brother and to win the game himself. Finally, he wants to please his mother. Jeremy's life is a juggling act, and he must learn to coordinate these goals. One socially competent response is not obvious.

A third objective of this chapter, then, is to broaden our perspective of the study of goals by arguing that social competence involves both the ability to coordinate among multiple relevant social goals and the ability to accomplish single goals. Understanding how a child performs this balancing act is a fourth objective. Specifically, we describe how the child's processing of social information can facilitate or undermine the goal coordination task. In this regard, we propose various ways that children can succeed or fail in balancing goals in social interactions. Because this discussion is speculative, a final purpose of our chapter is to propose a program of empirical research into the processes involved in children's goal coordination.

RECENT CONCEPTIONS OF
SOCIAL COMPETENCE

The modern study of social competence gained vigor in the 1950s and 1960s with the findings that measures of social competence were correlated with mental health (Zigler & Phillips, 1961) and that competence indicators were predictive of favorable responses to the treatment of schizophrenia (Zigler & Phillips, 1961). Roff (1961) added to this picture by finding that maladaptive outcomes in adulthood (such as a dishonorable discharge from the military) could be predicted by knowing that an individual was socially incompetent in early and middle childhood. Social incompetence in the early elementary school years was also found to predict later truancy, school discipline problems, and eventual dropout (Gibson & Hanson, 1969; Ullmann, 1957). Through research such as this, researchers became aware of the importance of understanding the phenomenon of social competence in childhood (for a recent review of the long-term risk literature, see Parker & Asher, 1987).

Despite early enthusiasm for studying social competence, theorists were not in agreement as to how to conceptualize social competence or how to measure it. Some theorists defined competence in terms of specific behaviors (White, Kaban, Marmor, & Shapiro, 1972), whereas others focused on underlying abilities (Meichenbaum & Butler, 1980). Some theorists thought of social competence as a trait, whereas others conceptualized competence as a series of acquired skills. A commonly accepted definition of social competence has been the ability to attain personal goals in social situations (O'Malley, 1977), without any reference to the appropriateness of the goals themselves. Such a definition ignores the fact that part of competence involves deciding what goals to pursue in specific situations.

A highly influential paper by Goldfried and d'Zurilla (1969) helped theorists clarify some of these issues. They noted that competence is a judgment made by one person about the performance of another person. This judgment could be about one's behavior in all situations or about behavior in a single situation. Goldfried and d'Zurilla suggested that it is most profitable to consider judgments made about a person in critical, problematic situations, for it is these situations, by definition, that are most closely tied to important social outcomes.

Goldfried and d'Zurilla were concerned with the performance of male college students in social situations, so they asked these students to name situations that were critical for them. They then presented these situations to their subjects in hypothetical format and asked them to describe how they would behave in response to each situation. Other students then rated the performance of these subjects as a measure of the competence of their behavior. An example of one of the situational stimuli used by Goldfried and d'Zurilla follows:

> Although most of your classes are in the afternoon, you have one class that meets at 8 o'clock in the morning. Consequently, after the first few weeks of school, you began attending this class less regularly. This was mostly due to the fact that you often study late and then sleep through the class.
>
> It is now about halfway through the semester and you have missed 2 weeks of your morning class, or six consecutive meetings. You are reluctant to return not only because you will be unfamiliar with the subject matter, but also because you are afraid of the instructor's reaction to your absence.

Responses to this stimulus were rated on a 0–8 scale of increasing competence. For example, a response such as "Drop the course and plan to avoid these situations in the future," was scored as fairly incompetent (a score of 2), whereas a response of "Get missed work from classmates, explain to instructor why absent, look interested in class, put in extra time catching up, rearrange study habits, and get to bed earlier" was scored as highly competent (a score of 8).

The conceptualization by Goldfired and d'Zurilla led others to generate taxonomies of important social situations for specific populations and to assess the social competencies of individuals within these populations. For example, Freedman, Rosenthal, Donahoe, Schlundt, and McFall (1978) generated a taxonomy of problematic situations for adolescent males. Their assessments of response patterns in these situations led them to conclude that juvenile delinquent males behave in ways that are judged as relatively incompetent in comparison to the behavior of nondelinquent males. This was an important finding, for it suggested that remedial intervention programs might be designed for delinquent males to increase their social competence.

This focus on specific situations quickly led other researchers to examine the social knowledge involved in competent performance of various social tasks. For example, Spivack, Platt, and Shure (1976) found that socially competent children generated more solutions and more-effective solutions to hypothetical interpersonal problems than did incompetent children. Gottman et al. (1975) and Ladd and Oden (1979) found that knowledge of how to perform certain tasks such as making a new friend or helping a peer in need is predictive of status in the peer group. Finally, Asher and Renshaw (1981) found that popular children had more effective and more relationship-enhancing strategies than did unpopular children in response to hypothetical situations involving initiation of relationships, maintenance of relationships, or conflict resolution. These studies were promising in that they suggested that socially incompetent children might be able to achieve more favorable social outcomes if they could be taught social knowledge.

Implicit in Goldfried and d'Zurilla's conceptualizations and those of subsequent social–cognitive researchers was the assumption that be defining a situational stimulus to a child, the expected goal of the respondent in that situation was also defined. For example, in response to the situational stimulus about missing classes described earlier, it was assumed that the respondent would recognize and accept that the goal in responding would be, and should be, to stick with the class in order to earn as high a grade as possible. This is an assumption that may be challenged, however. A reasonable alternative goal might be to relieve one's anxiety and to maintain one's sense of competence (rather than risk it) by dropping the course and starting over next semester.

Consider another example, taken from the taxonomy generated by research on adolescent females by Gaffney and McFall (1981).

> You're on a bike hike with five of your friends. One of the girls, who just moved into your neighborhood, is very slow and is holding the group up. The other girls you are with are all yelling at her and threatening to leave her behind.

Given this situation, one girl might perceive that her goal is to maintain her old friendships because the other girls might make fun of her if she sides with the new girl. In this case, she might not say anything and might just keep siding with her friends. Another girl might perceive that it is more important to be kind to the new girl, even at the risk of her old friendships. This girl might tell her friends to slow down and stop yelling at the new girl. Which response is more competent? Because competence is a judgment made by another person, presumably the competence rating will be made in reference to this other person's perception of what the goal ought to be in this situation. If the rater endorses goals similar to those of the first girl, her behavior would probably be judged by this rater as more competent than the behavior of the second girl. In this particular situation, the consensus of the girls in the Gaffney and McFall study was to endorse the goals and behaviors of the second girl. They rated the response of the first girl as highly incompetent.

One way to deal with this problem is to present to the child not only a situation but a particular goal as well. This was the tack taken by

Gottman et al., (1975) and subsequent researchers as well (e.g., Goetz & Dweck, 1980; Ladd & Oden, 1979). For example, Gottman et al. (1975) asked children to role-play making a new friend. By specifying both the situation *and* the goal to the child, they were not confronted with the potential problem that a child might not *want* to become friends with a particular person. By their directive, they assumed that all children accepted the goal that they defined.

Even though the strategy of defining the goal may be effective for the study of specific social skills, it does not obviate the need to study goal selection. For example, under natural conditions, children are not usually told by an adult to initiate a friendship with a particular child or group of peers. Instead, as they encounter peers in their classroom, on the playground, and in their neighborhoods, it is up to them to decide whether to initiate relationships, when, with whom, and for what purposes. Studying the processes involved in children's social interactions involves contending with the problem of goals.

Interestingly, researchers who studied processing of information and performance in cognitive tasks also avoided the problem of goals for a long time. Miller, Galanter, and Pribram (1960), in their classic work, *Plans and the Structure of Behavior,* vividly described the paths and actions involved in the processing of information to achieve a specified goal or solve a particular problem. All of these paths, however, *assumed* the prior existence of a goal. Similarly, Newell and Simon (1972) and Hayes (1981) used a computer metaphor to describe the processing of information in solving a problem. Both perspectives start at the point of a specified goal. It is clear that a fundamental difference between the action of a computer and the behavior of children is that computers are not self-directed or motivated, whereas children are constantly setting goals and learning to direct their own behavior. As important a problem as this is for the cognitive problem-solving researchers, it is an even greater problem for students of social behavior. In contrast to cognitive problems, which are usually clearly defined, social interactions are almost always ill defined (Greene, 1976). As such, they are open to multiple construals and multiple goal possibilities.

These problems led Renshaw and Asher (1982) to advance two hypotheses that have broad ramifications for research in social competence. The first hypothesis was that many past findings concerning the behavioral deficits of socially incompetent children (relative to competent children) might be better explained as differences in goal construals than as differences in skills. The findings of Coie and Kupersmidt (1983), in a study of the behavior of popular and rejected boys upon entering a group of unacquainted peers, serve as a good example. In that study, rejected boys were observed to bully peers and to be more forceful during their initial interactions with peers, whereas popular boys held back, sized things up, and accommodated to others. One interpretation of these findings is that rejected boys lack knowledge of how to get peers to like them. Renshaw and Asher suggested, instead, that the rejected boys may have been operating with a different goal in mind. Their goal may have been to maximize their influence and control over others, in contrast to the goal among popular boys to become liked by peers.

As another example, consider the findings by Richard and Dodge (1982) concerning the solution-generating skills of popular and aggressive boys. They found that in response to hypothetical conflict situations, aggressive boys were more likely to generate coercive, aggressive solutions than were popular boys. Instead of interpreting this difference as a skill deficit among aggressive boys, Renshaw and Asher would suggest that the aggressive boys may primarily have been pursuing goals of self-protection and retaliation, in contrast to popular boys, who may have been pursuing a goal of becoming well liked. Goals of self-protection and getting even would lead a child to respond to ambiguous provocations with anger and retaliation rather than with actions that leave open the possibility of a more positive social relationship.

The second hypothesis by Renshaw and Asher was that systematic assessments of children's goal orientations would reveal significant differences between popular and rejected children. To assess children's goals in social situations, Renshaw and Asher (1983) presented popular and unpopular children with hypothetical problems, such as being rebuffed by a group of peers at play. In addition to asking children what they would do in response to these problems (in the tradition of Spivack, Platt, & Shure, 1976), Renshaw and Asher asked children why they would act in a particular way and what they were trying to accomplish with a particular action. They found that children's goals varied widely, and that unpopular children's actions were less apt to be in the service of positive social goals than was true of popular children. Similar supportive evidence has been provided by Ford (1982), who asked high school students to rank order the personal importance of various goals, such as having close friends, getting good grades, and learning new skills. He found that students who had been independently rated as highly socially competent tended to endorse interpersonal goals over nonsocial goals, in contrast to incompetent students, who demonstrated a reverse pattern.

The focus on children's goals in their social interactions is an advance over previously held notions that social competence is the display of particular social behaviors or the ability to attain particular outcomes. This newer focus emphasizes the importance of children's construals of situations and their selection of priorities in outcomes. This perspective helps make sense of empirical differences between competent and incompetent children and suggests that interventions with incompetent children might include a focus on changing children's goals as well as improving social knowledge and skills.

Even as promising as this perspective and the corresponding data are, several findings have tempered enthusiasm. For example, Renshaw and Asher (1983) found that even though popular children's suggested strategies were more often in service of positive social goals than was true of unpopular children, the two groups did not differ in how often they chose to pursue hostile and avoidant goals. Likewise, in more recent work, Taylor and Asher (1987) found that although popular children gave greater importance to relationship goals than rejected children, this difference was not consistently significant across studies. Indeed, both popular and rejected children regard relationship goals as extremely important.

GOAL COORDINATION AS A SOCIAL TASK

In retrospect, the focus on children's goals is certainly an important conceptual step forward, but the relation between children's goals and their behavior may be more complicated than initially hypothesized. It is not simply that conpetent functioning involves endorsing prosocial goals whereas incompetent functioning involves endorsing hostile, avoidant, or self-protective goals. Our hypothesis is that differences between competence and incompetence are less likely to be found in the differential endorsement of single goals, and more likely to be found in how successfully children manage goal conflicts and integrate their various goals in a particular situation.

The notion that social life requires the reconciliation of goal conflicts can be found in earlier theoretical writing. Several theorists have pointed out that people usually have more than one goal and that a major task is the resolution of conflicts among their goals. The id versus superego conflict described by Freud is one major example. Freud described the essential nature of human life as a conflict between the unconscious goals (motives, drives, wishes) of the individual for self-gratification and the desire to meet societal expectations. Effective goal coordination consists of meeting both of these needs.

More recently, Ford (1984) considered the kinds of goal conflicts that individuals face in relation to certain core issues. One arena of conflict is *identity,* in which one chooses between the goal of individuality and the goal of belongingness. Another concern is *social comparison,* in which individuals choose between superiority and equity in their relationships with others. On the matter of *control,* individuals choose between self-determinism and social responsibility. It is short-sighted to conclude that social competence consists of choosing the most desirable single goal in each arena of conflict. Rather, competence involves the appropriate coordination of various goals according to the particular context.

Argyle, Furnham, and Graham (1981) also highlighted the importance of context in relation to goals. Their work focused on the goals that people are likely to have in specific situations, and on the ways in which people's goals in a given situation may be compatible or incompatible with one another and with those of other people. These authors described various kinds of relationships between goals, the most basic being *independence* (pursuing each goal neither helps nor hinders the other), *instrumentality* (pursuit of one goal helps the other), and *interference* (pursuit of one goal interferes with the other). Based on these ideas, Argyle et al. did interesting research on adults' knowledge concerning compatibilities and incompatibilities between combinations of goals in specific social situations. Argyle et al. also suggested that social skillfulness involves techniques for overcoming conflicts between goals within situations.

Conceptualizing social competence as requiring the reconciliation of multiple goals makes us appreciate the enormous complexity of everyday social life. In the next sections of this chapter, we suggest some ways in which people actually engage in the process of coordinating multiple goals. We also describe various ways in which breakdowns can occur in the goal-coordination task.

FEATURES OF THE GOAL-COORDINATION TASK

The task that children face in trying to pursue their various goals can be made more or less complicated, depending on the particular requirements of each goal. Some goals are highly specific whereas others are not. A highly specific goal has a limited time frame for accomplishment (e.g., "have fun with Joan *today*") or must be met in a highly specific way (e.g., "have fun with Bill playing video games"). Goals that are less specific can be met within a more flexible time frame (e.g., "see Tom sometime soon") or can be met in a variety of ways (e.g., "have fun with

Joe by going to a movie, 'hanging out,' or going for a soda together"). When a highly specific goal conflicts with other goals, especially other highly specific goals, the goal coordination task is much more demanding and less likely to be satisfactorily resolved. For example, suppose a child has two goals for the evening: (1) to appease his mother, who wants him to babysit for his younger sister while the mother goes out, and (2) to have fun tonight with his best friend. Reconciling these will be easier if "having fun" can be satisfied by a wide range of activities, including watching television or playing a game. However, if "having fun" means only going out to the movies, reconciling these goals will be a nearly impossible task.

The complexity of the goal-coordination task also depends on how much time and energy is required to pursue each goal and how much of one's interactions will be influenced by a particular goal. For example, building a new friendship may be a more consuming activity than getting along amicably with an acquaintance, and so the friendship-making goal has a greater potential for conflicting with other goals.

The task of trying to meet all of one's goals is also complicated by the fact that attaining certain goals requires pursuit of many subtasks which themselves become goals. There are often limits on the order in which these can be met, because pursuit of each is dependent on completion of others (Schank & Abelson, 1977). For instance, having a successful birthday party requires a child (1) to obtain parental permission, (2) to decide who to invite, and (3) to extend the invitations. As another example, consider the task of making a new friend. This could involve getting introduced, finding a way to spend some time together, discovering common interests, and ultimately engaging in some degree of intimate self-disclosure.

Furthermore, goal coordination is not simply a matter of coordinating one's own goals, but also involves taking account of other people's needs and interests. Both Freud, Argyle, and Ford's analyses all imply that a fundamental source of goal reconciliation problems is the conflict of needs or interests that arises between people in their everyday social lives. Maintaining good relationships and successfully pursuing one's own goals often require taking account of or serving other people's needs and goals. An important task of social life is to find ways of reconciling one's own and others' interests. For example, literature on children's discourse provides many instances of the ways in which competent interaction requires that children take into account how their goals may conflict with the goals or interests of others (Brown & Levinson, 1978; O'Keefe & Delia, 1981; Parkhurst & Gottman, 1987).

GOAL COORDINATION FROM AN
INFORMATION-PROCESSING PERSPECTIVE

The task of coordinating goals can be productively viewed from an information-processing perspective. Information-processing models of interpersonal competence (Dodge, 1986; McFall & Dodge, 1982; Rubin & Krasnor, 1986) focus on the processing of social cues and social knowledge during interaction with others. Next, we describe the ways in which goal-coordination processes occur within an information processing framework.

According to Dodge's (1986) information-processing formulation, a child's behavior in social situations occurs as a function of how he or she perceives and interprets cues and generates potential responses to those cues. Dodge has proposed that this processing occurs in several sequential steps that take place very rapidly, and often without conscious thought. Five sequential steps of processing have been proposed, including (1) encoding social cues, (2) interpreting those cues, (3) generating possible responses to the cues, (4) evaluating the potential consequences of each response and the selecting a response believed to lead to optimal consequences, and (5) enacting and monitoring the chosen response.

Encode. The first step of processing for a child is to encode the cues that are present in the social environment. This step involves processes of attention to cues, sensation, and perception. Because there are literally thousands of cues upon which a child might focus, the child selectively attends to certain cues at the cost of attention to other cues. For example, consider a child who is playing a game of baseball with peers. That child might focus his or her attention on the action of the game itself, such as the score or important plays. The child might also focus on the social interactions among the players. Or the child could focus on how each participant is doing at the game. Depending on the child's goals, it may be necessary to focus on several aspects of the game context. Indeed, in most games, children commonly have multiple goals, including the desire to succeed at competition, to show off their skills, to maintain their friendships, and to have fun. In order to pursue all of these goals, the child must attend to cues relevant to each.

Interpret. Once cues are encoded, the next processing step for a child is to interpret the encoded cues in an accurate or nonbiased way. Because many socially encoded cues are ambiguous, the opportunity for motivational processes to bias the interpretation process is great. It is important for children to be objective and not to misinterpret another's actions. Take the important matter of deciding whether someone means to hurt you versus the possibility that an action was accidental. For example, in a baseball game, when a pitcher hits a batter with the pitch or when a base runner crashes into an infielder, it is important to judge accurately whether the action was intentional. Children who are consistently biased in their interpretations of such events will face difficulties. Dodge (1980; Dodge & Frame, 1982) found that children who are disliked by their peers for unduly aggressive behavior display a bias toward interpreting peers' aversive behavior as hostile and intended to harm. In contrast, children who are prosocial and better liked are more likely to give others the benefit of the doubt.

Generate Possible Responses. The third step of information processing is to access or generate one or more possible behavioral responses to the encoded and interpreted cues. The child with multiple goals in a situation is faced with the task of generating behavioral responses that will facilitate multiple goals simultaneously, or at least responses that will facilitate some goals without interfering with others. For example, consider the child who is playing a dart board game and is asked to relinquish his turn. Most children have multiple goals in such a situation. Perhaps the child wants both to maintain a friendship and to finish his turn. Faced with these competing goals, the child is challenged to generate a response that serves both goals at once, such as politely proposing that the other child serve as a judge and official scorer and then join the next game. The next section of this chapter, "Ways of Coping with Multiple Goals," more fully considers particular enactment strategies that are commonly adopted in response to the goal-coordination task.

Evaluate and Select Responses. The fourth step of processing is to represent mentally the consequences of each response that has been accessed in order to select the best available response. The child considers the probable outcomes of a given response and decides whether those outcomes are desirable. For example, in response to the girls' bike-hike vignette, described in Gaffney and McFall's research, someone could generate a response of slowing down to be with the new girl. At this fourth step of processing, the child evaluates the probable consequences of this response to determine whether to choose it for enactment. She may determine that if she were to slow down, the new girl would like her, but that the other girls would call her names. If several goals are to be coordinated satisfactorily, the evaluation of a particular response must be made with reference to each. Success at selecting the best available responses also requires that the child choose a response he or she is capable of carrying out successfully.

Enact and Monitor Response. The final step of social information processing involves the enactment and monitoring of the response that has been selected. Transforming a strategy successfully into a specific response draws on the child's verbal and motor skills, as well as on the child's knowledge of script-like interactional strategies. It is often quite challenging to carry out strategies or plans aimed at fulfilling multiple goals. Indeed, children often do not have the resources necessary to pursue multiple goals or monitor the effects of their actions on both goals. For example, a child who tries to watch his favorite television program while carrying on a conversation with his friend may find it impossible to pay adequate attention to both. As a result, the child may appear impatient or distracted.

As another example, consider a teenage boy who has a date for Saturday night but whose socially inept cousin has just arrived in town. The host's goals are to keep his date and at the same time manage to include and entertain his cousin. The boy's plan is to find a date for the cousin and take his cousin along. However, finding a date for this awkward cousin is not easy, given the other goal of remaining on good terms with the girl who might be invited along. Because people often must monitor the enactment process in relationship to multiple goals, it is critical, in this example, that our protagonist pay attention not only to his own evening's pleasure but to the social experiences of his cousin and the blind date.

WAYS OF COPING WITH MULTIPLE GOALS

The previous discussion of goal coordination from an information-processing perspective serves to communicate the complexity of the child's task. Even if children are attentive to a variety of cues, unbiased in their interpretations, and careful in their evaluation and monitoring of potential and actual responses, they could fail to cope with multiple goals due to lack of knowledge of effective strategies. In this section, we discuss various general approaches to the task of coordinating multiple goals.

Single, Integrative Strategy. When faced with multiple goals, the most efficient solution is often for the child to employ a single strategy that will satisfy several goals simultaneously. This approach allows the child to pursue all of his or her goals without modifying or abandoning any of them. For example, consider the case of Jeremy whose new friend Warren won the free-throw shooting contest by cheating and stepping over the line. If Jeremy seeks both to foster the friendship and to make sure the game is won fairly, one solution is for Jeremy to suggest tactfully that Warren accidentally stepped over the line and propose that Warren take his turn over. In so doing, Jeremy retains the path toward a friendship while not relinquishing his goal that the game be a fair test of skill. Jeremy has succeeded in coordinating his goals with a single strategy.

But sometimes there is no feasible way even for highly competent individuals to attain multiple goals with a single strategy. Some goals are so incompatible that it is best not to try to reconcile them. For example, children are commonly faced with the situation in which two different people make opposing demands, which cannot both be satisfied at the same time.

Furthermore, an individual may not have the sophistication or finesse to employ successfully an integrative strategy in certain situations. Consider the challenge that faces our adolescent protagonist whose awkward cousin is coming to town. The single strategy of finding a blind date contains several potential pitfalls, and it will take both great skill and some luck for everything to work out. Indeed, in this case, it may not even turn out to be an economical strategy for the adolescent to spend a lot of time and energy finding the right blind date.

Multiple Simultaneous Strategies. Another approach to achieving multiple goals is to employ several strategies more or less simultaneously in order to pursue multiple goals in the same situation. This is the path taken by a child who sorts laundry for her mother while talking with her friend on the phone. Everyday life, especially adult life, is filled with this approach to handling multiple goals. It is a highly practical way of dealing with complexity, particularly when one or more activities are so routine that attention need only be directed to one.

However, when more than one strategy requires active attention, difficulties may arise. Indeed, children in particular have problems here because fewer of their behavioral routines are well established. In addition, children sometimes lack knowledge that certain strategies may be incompatible in a situation. Consider the adolescent boy who needs to finish studying for a test and wants to further a new relationship with a girl at his church's youth group picnic. Suppose he goes to the picnic taking his books. A likely result is that he will not be able to study effectively at the picnic and that if he tries, he will also not have much success with the girl.

Deferring Goals. Thus far, we have been discussing goal-coordination strategies that enable someone to pursue all of their goals in the same situation without deferring or changing any of their goals. Although it is certainly an enticing prospect to "have it all," reality does have a way of intruding. Accordingly, other approaches deserve consideration. One approach is to pursue one goal at a time by focusing on one immediate goal and deferring others. Meeting diverse needs can be accomplished through creative scheduling, and it may be better in some cases to set some short-term priorities rather than trying to accomplish everything simultaneously. For example, the adolescent with a visiting cousin might consider the strategy of explaining his situation to his girlfriend and postponing their date.

Inducing people, especially children, to set priorities is not always easy. Indeed, children, in particular, have difficulty deferring an attractive goal (Mischel & Patterson, 1978; Patterson & Mischel, 1976). As a result, they may try to pursue several goals at the same time even when it is inappropriate.

Even when children do defer a goal, problems can arise. Successful coordination through setting priorities often requires more than simply putting off one of the goals. Instead, it requires careful scheduling to ensure that all goals can be achieved. It also may require that at least some continuing attention be paid to the secondary goal. For example, the student who decides to put priority on schoolwork for a semester and to defer an active social life will still need to engage in a certain degree of friendship maintenance to ensure that good friends are not lost in the meantime. The problem for children is that they often simply pursue the goal of greatest concern at the moment to the detriment of other goals. This tendency is exemplified by the child who drops her chores when asked by a friend to play but later is quite upset when she realizes she no longer has time to get them done.

Modifying Goals. A final approach to goal coordination is to reconcile goals by modifying one or more of them. This may mean altering one's criteria for considering them satisfied. For example, a student with high academic standards who also wants to play on the basketball team may need to redefine what "doing well in school" means, to include the possibility of an occasional "B." Sometimes goal criteria include the amount of time to be devoted to a particular activity (e.g., practicing the piano four times per week), and it may be necessary to adjust these criteria in light of other goal demands.

Generalizing from Specific Subgoals. In some cases, altering criteria simply will not work either because incompatibility with other goals will still remain or because the original goal is a highly specific one (e.g., to see a particular movie). One solution is to identify the higher-order needs that the goal was intended to serve and to find another goal serving the same purposes. The challenge is to find a new goal that is compatible with the child's higher-order needs. Consider the boy who is frustrated because he wants to go to the movies with his friend the same evening his mother wants him to babysit. One solution is to identify the higher-order goal (to have fun with his friend) and to ask his mother if he can invite the friend over to play cards while he is babysitting.

This general approach to goal coordination requires a kind of flexibility that people can find difficult. Nonetheless, resistance to modifying one's criteria for goal fulfillment can lead to negative consequences, including fatigue and failure to accomplish one or more of the goals. Inflexibility can also lead to poor interpersonal relationships. The person who refuses to modify any of his or her goals is likely to be seen as stubborn, selfish, or indifferent to others' concerns.

The preceding comments should not be taken to mean that extreme readiness to be flexible is the most competent approach. Certain needs can only be met through certain goals, and certain goals are inextricably linked to particular criteria for their fulfillment. In these cases, modifying a goal may leave the individual in a state of serious dissatisfaction or frustration. The wise person knows how far he or she can modify a goal without experiencing serious loss. In this way, knowledge of self lies at the heart of social competence.

Summary.   Social competence should not be viewed as identical with uniform success in reaching one's original goals. Often, environmental and personal constraints prevent the accomplishment of multiple goals. Priorities must be evaluated and compromises must be reached. Even important goals must be sacrificed occasionally. Competence in goal coordination might be defined as the greatest possible satisfaction of needs and desires, given the circumstances.

BREAKDOWNS IN THE GOAL-COORDINATION PROCESS

The preceding sections contain many implications for ways in which the goal-coordination process can go awry. As implied by our earlier discussion of information processing, breakdowns can occur due to (1) failure to attend to those cues that are related to all of one's goals in a situation, (2) a distorted interpretation of those cues, (3) failure to interpret situations in relation to others' needs and interests, (4) failure to access strategies allowing coordination of goals, and/or (5) failure to pay attention either to the potential or to the actual consequences of actions in relation to all relevant goals.

Breakdowns can also occur due to lack of certain kinds of knowledge or expertise. Children need to know various things, for example: (1) what cues in social situations are likely to mean, (2) specific integrative strategies, (3) the likely consequences of various strategies, (4) how to implement various strategies, and (5) sufficient knowledge of their own needs to know how far they can modify a goal without experiencing serious loss.

A variety of motivational and emotional factors are also capable of having adverse effects on children's coordination of goals. First, competent functioning can be undermined by impulsivity, inflexibility, or other personal characteristics. Second, certain more transient emotional states can interfere with competent information processing. These include fatigue, depression, and anger. These internal states are known to interfere both with problem solving (Masters, Felleman, & Barden, 1981) and with the accurate interpretation of others' intentions (Dodge & Somberg, 1987). Indeed, some children may be more susceptible to the debilitating effects of emotion than other children (Dodge & Somberg, 1987). Masters et al. (1981) call these children "emotionally vulnerable."

A major effect of emotional states is to alter the relative pursuit of various goals. Ford (1985) notes that in some circumstances the effect of emotional states is adaptive. For example, anger may energize behavior so that obstacles to goal achievement may be overcome, and depression may inhibit activity so that unattainable goals are no longer pursued. The more common effect of emotional states, however, may be to disrupt goal coordination. Strong emotional states may disrupt the ability of a child to keep in mind multiple perspectives and multiple roles. Strong emotional states may also lead to the pursuit of single goals and the neglect of peripheral goals. The goal selected may be the one most closely related to the emotional state, not the one that would otherwise be selected by the child (see Parkhurst & Asher, 1985). Because goal coordination is a particularly difficult cognitive task for a child, it may be one of the first to be disrupted by temporary emotional states.

Finally, goal coordination does not occur at all when goal conflicts are dealt with by abandoning one or more goals. Although sometimes abandoning a goal may be necessary and even wise, there are many situations in which abandoning pursuit of goals is maladaptive. This is especially the case when achieving the goal would meet a major need and no other substitute goal exists that would serve the same function. This type of situation can lead to unresolved needs and to the adoption of maladaptive defensive processes. Indeed, the defense mechanisms were postulated by Freud as ways of coping with goal conflicts. The simplest coping mechanism that he described was *repression*, which in the present context would mean pursuing one of the conflicting goals, abandoning the other, and dealing with one's unresolved needs by keeping them out of consciousness. This strategy, as Freud and many others have noted, is often an ineffective way of coping with basic human conflicts.

GOAL COORDINATION AND THE PROBLEM OF SINGLE-MINDEDNESS

It should be clear from many of our illustrations in this chapter that we expect children to have broad goals in many domains, such as for their academic performance, their relationships with others, their participation and performance in games and sports, and their physical well-being. We have proceeded on the assumption that the child should seek to coordinate these goals, both in specific situations and in life more generally. As researchers concerned with social competence, we clearly believe that goals for friendship and good relations with others are particularly important.

However, we want to acknowledge that individuals may be faced with deciding whether pursuing goals in a wide range of domains is always the best thing to do. For instance, many adults think it better to focus virtually all of their attention on a central achievement goal, even when that has meant sacrificing goals in many other domains. American society certainly has encouraged the single-minded pursuit of central achievement goals. Some of the greatest accomplishments occur when an individual devotes virtually exclusive attention to pursuit of a single goal. Society often has great rewards for the budding gymnast who trains rigorously 8 hours a day for years, or the scientist who spends virtually his or her entire life in the laboratory. Such dedication is valued highly and admired.

For the adult facing this choice, there is no simple solution to this problem of single-mindedness. Certainly the unrelenting pursuit of a single central goal is a risky business. It allows high levels of attainment, and when the individual is successful, that individual is honored and rewarded and derives great satisfaction from the outcome. But when it leads to failure, the individual has little else to serve as a source of meaning or satisfaction. The result may be dejection, despair, and even suicide. Pursuing many kinds of goals, on the other hand, is more compatible with moderate attainments. The glory of great attainments is unlikely, but so too is despair, because the individual has many supports.

It is impossible to say with certainty what the most competent path is for an adult. Even the successful attainment of a single difficult goal may leave an individual with feelings of emptiness, whereas the pursuit of many less-challenging goals may lead to feelings of mediocrity. Each person must learn to evaluate his or her own capabilities and to select goals (and strategies for coordinating them) that fit his or her talents and circumstances.

In the case of children, however, it could be hypothesized that the costs of single-mindedness are much higher. Parents may be tempted to encourage their talented child to focus every effort on becoming a great violinist, tennis player, or mathematician. They may feel that social goals are relatively unimportant. Such single-mindedness may result in the child failing not only to have other immediate sources of satisfaction, but also to develop other skills, especially social skills, which most individuals develop in childhood. Many of these skills may, in fact, contribute instrumentally to children's ability to attain their central goals in adulthood.

If children acquire social competencies but become single-minded in adulthood, they have resources to draw on, not only in pursuing whatever goals they choose to focus on, but also in putting together another life if they do not achieve their primary goal. If someone is single-minded in childhood, however, he or she may lack those resources. We are aware of no research addressing this important life-span problem of the long-term consequences of single-mindedness in childhood.

DEVELOPMENTAL PERSPECTIVES ON THE GOAL-COORDINATION TASK

From earlier sections, it is clear that social goal coordination tasks are complex indeed and that there are many potential pitfalls. For the very young child, these pitfalls are skillfully avoided, not primarily through the child's own actions but through the mediating actions of parents or other adults. In infancy and throughout early childhood, coordination of goals is often facilitated at each step of information processing by such mediation. Adults assist children by pointing to other relevant cues in the environment, helping children interpret those cues, helping formulate alternative strategies, and focusing children's attention on the consequences of their behavior.

At the first step of information processing (attention to cues), adults often help a child focus attention on aspects of multiple-goal situations that have been neglected by the child. Consider the toddler who is watching her pet dog frolic but fails to notice an older sibling's recently completed jigsaw puzzle which is lying in her way. A parent of this toddler might tell her to "watch out for the puzzle" to ensure that this important cue does not go undetected.

With regard to the interpretation step, parents regularly try to give meaning to social information that has been detected but not fully appreciated: "When you mess up your brother's puzzle, it upsets him," "Maybe your friend ignored you because he is mad about something," "Maybe John didn't mean it when he bumped into you."

Considerable parental effort also goes into generating alternative strategies for coordinating diverse goals: "Try asking him nicely instead of yelling at him," "Why don't you two girls take turns?" "How about turning off the TV set so you can pay attention?"

At the response-evaluation stage, parents can point out ways in which a child's behavior might lead to the neglect of one goal even though the behavior serves another goal: "If you spend all of your money on ice cream you won't have any left for the movies;" "If you play outside now before dinner time, then you'll have to do your homework during your favorite television show."

And, finally, there is considerable assistance at the enactment stage. Consider, once again, the example of having a birthday party. Clearly, the parent of a young child takes major responsibility for monitoring implementation. This extends to the party itself, when the parents pay attention to whether everyone is included and is having a good time.

As children get older, more and more of the information-processing work is assumed by the child. Along the way, the adult's task is to help the child successfully coordinate goals without being unduly interfering.

All this mediational work by adults points to the fact that young children need help with the goal-coordination task. Indeed, the development of the capacity to coordinate multiple goals follows a complex path. In early childhood, children become able to match a specific goal with a particular setting, but typically only consider one goal at a time. At some point, the child recognizes that there are multiple goals in many situations and that these goals may be in conflict. The child eventually learns to cope with these conflicts by coordinating goals. As the child matures, his or her ability to consider multiple goals and to coordinate multiple responses increases. For example, there is clear evidence that children's performance on two simultaneous tasks improves over age (Maccoby, 1969; Manis, Keating, & Morrison, 1980).

Relatively little research has been done on developmental changes in goal coordination. However, important beginning work has been done by Clark, Delia, and their co-workers in the area of speech communication (e.g., Clark & Delia, 1976; Clark, O'Dell, & Willihnganz, 1985; Delia, Kline, & Burleson, 1979). These studies have focused on developmental changes in children's attempts to persuade others to do something. Specifically, this research group has been interested in the degree to which children's persuasive strategies (1) implicitly recognize that others have their own agendas that may affect the success of a request, (2) attempt to address others' agendas, and (3) effectively integrate their own agendas with those of the person they are trying to persuade (Clark & Delia, 1976; Delia et al., 1979).

Clark and Delia (1976) and Delia et al. (1979) showed (1) that by age 7 years, most children recognize that others have their own motivational agendas, and they try to justify their requests accordingly, (2) that by age 11, most children anticipate the other's objections and counter-arguments and forestall these in their arguments, and (3) that by 14 or 15 most children use arguments in which they emphasize the ways in which it is in the other person's interest to do what the child wants.

O'Keefe and Delia (1985) proposed that this sequence should be interpreted in terms of an increasing general ability to recognize and integrate multiple goals. To test this proposition, Clark, O'Dell, and Willinganz (1985) examined developmental changes in children's resort to compromise when confronted by conflicts between their own and others' wishes. These authors considered a compromise to be any proposed plan that would allow at least partial satisfaction of each person's aims. They found that between third and sixth grades, children were increasingly able to propose compromises when prompted to do so, and that they also tended increasingly to propose such compromises spontaneously.

This work suggests that developmental research into goal coordination will prove fruitful. In the next section, we describe several methods that could be used in a broad program of research in this area.

ASSESSING CHILDREN'S GOAL-COORDINATION PROCESSES

Given how little research has been addressed to children's goal-coordination processes, there is a need for reliable and valid methods for assessing goal coordination. Two possible methods are suggested by previous research on children's social problem-solving and communication skills: interviews regarding hypothetical situations and observational studies. These methods could be both used in both longitudinal and cross-sectional developmental research. They could also be used to examine the goal-coordination processes of children of different status in the peer group.

HYPOTHETICAL SITUATIONS

The first consists of presenting a child with a hypothetical interpersonal dilemma involving multiple goals, and soliciting from the child one or more possible responses or strategies for dealing with the goal conflict. This procedure has been used frequently in studies of social problem solving (Asher & Renshaw, 1981; Richard & Dodge, 1982; Rubin & Krasnor, 1986; Spivack et al., 1976). A typical stimulus story for boys aged 8–10 years might consist of the following:

> Imagine that you invited a boy from your school over to your home to play a game. This is a boy that you like a lot, and you hope that he will like you, too. You are playing a game with him, and you would really like to win. Just as you are about to take the last turn, he moves his marker ahead several spaces so that he wins the game. What would you say or do? Why would you act that way?

The responses by the child could be scored in the traditional ways—according to quantity and quality of solutions. But the response pattern could also be scored according to the level at which the child is coordinating the multiple goals in this situation (securing a friendship, winning the game, and playing fairly). Because goal-coordination efforts may not be obvious, the child's rationale for his or her response (answer to why he or she responded in a certain way) could be used to score goal coordination. For example, a response of "I would cry because I lost" would be scored as the lowest level because it indicates little clearly goal-directed activity at all. A response of "I would hit his hand so I could win" would be scored at the next level because it indicates the pursuit of a single goal. A response combination of "I would hit his hand so I could win and I would ask him to play another game" would be scored at a higher level because it indicates the pursuit of multiple but isolated goals. Finally, a response of "I would ask him if maybe he made a mistake because it's supposed to be my turn" would be scored at the highest level because it indicates the pursuit of multiple goals through a single integrative strategy. The hypothetical-situations technique allows for strict control over social stimuli and enables the researcher to assess many goal conflict responses in a short period of time.

Clark and Delia and their colleagues have made creative use of the hypothetical-situations method for studying goal coordination. For example, in one study, "children were asked to pretend that they had found a lost puppy and gone to the nearest house and asked the woman who lived there is she would keep the puppy" (Clark & Delia, 1976, p. 1099). Following this, subjects have been asked to tell the interviewer exactly what they would say to obtain agreement. Subjects' answers were then recorded, transcribed, and their different tactics counted and coded according to the developmental level represented.

An interesting modification of this approach was used by Clark (1979), who examined the effects of changing the nature or strength of the goals that subjects were told they had in a particular situation. She asked college students to imagine situations in which it was their task to persuade someone to do something. She varied the importance of obtaining compliance and of maintaining good relations with the other person. If subjects were told they had no interest in maintaining good relations with the other person and held the other in contempt, they were more likely to say things designed to promote a negative relationship with the other, to make direct or implied threats, and to use guilt- or shame-inducing tactics.

Given the same situation, those told that they liked and had an interest in dating that person were more likely to use such strategies as conveying their request by implication, emphasizing the advantages to the other of doing as desired, offering rewards for compliance, sweetening the request with compliments, minimizing the request, and expressing regret at making demands. Tactics used in the latter situation included many previously identified by Brown and Levinson (1978) as means of reconciling socially threatening personal goals with goals of avoiding offense and promoting others' goodwill. When Clark made it both highly important to obtain the other's compliance and to avoid offending the other person, subjects simultaneously both used more forceful tactics and employed strategies designed to neutralize the other's resentment, such as making explicit statements of liking and concern for the other, acknowledgments that the other might resent the interference, and justification of their use of authority. These findings show that it is possible to manipulate goals experimentally within a hypothetical-situations paradigm.

Prior to designing stories in which children are provided with a situation and with goals, it would be of value to identify the kinds of goals that children are likely to have in specific situations. One approach to identifying goals is to interview children about what they would do in various situations and then to ask them why (Renshaw & Asher, 1983).

Another approach is to ask children to rate the degree to which they consider each of various possibilities to be goals in particular situations (Argyle et al., 1981).

One problem with the sole use of the hypothetical story format for assessment is that children's actual social behavior in goal conflict situations is not assessed. Observation of children's playground (or specially formed play group) constitutes a procedure for assessing children's coordination of goals in actual interaction. Rubin and Krasnor (1986) have studied children's problem-solving behavior in natural contexts. Their coding procedures might be adopted for the observation of responses to goal-conflict situations. This procedure could be used to determine how children actually behave when confronted with naturally occurring goal conflicts.

Furthermore, it is possible to manipulate goals experimentally in an observational context. For example, the experimenter could instruct a child to try to initiate a friendship with a peer while playing a game with that peer. At the same time, the experimenter could set up the game so that the child would earn points (or some other reward) for defeating the other child. How the child responds to this goal conflict could be observed and analyzed. This procedure also enables researchers to study the child's flexibility in taking on different goals. For example, the experimenter could introduce various goals in different sequences and observe how the child copes with a changing goal-coordination task.

Observation of a child's actual responses to goal conflict enables researchers to study conflict resolution, but the child's goals can only be inferred from the behavior. A supplement to this procedure might be to interview children about their goals soon after a conflict episode (see Eisenberg-Berg & Neal, 1979). Showing children a videotape of their interactions may assist the interview process.

THE NEED FOR INTERVENTION RESEARCH

One effective way of testing the role of goal-coordination processes in children's social relationships is to intervene by training children in goal-coordination processing and observing the effects of this intervention on subsequent social functioning. Certainly the need exists for effective interventions for children having peer-relationship problems.

Extensive research over several decades reveals that a considerable number of children lack friends in school and are quite rejected by their peers (Asher & Hymel, 1981; Coie, Dodge, & Coppotelli, 1982; Gronlund, 1959). These children are more likely to experience strong feelings of loneliness and social dissatisfaction (Asher & Wheeler, 1985; Parkhurst & Asher, 1987; Williams & Asher, 1987). They are also more likely to have serious later adjustment problems, especially elevated school drop-out rates (Parker & Asher, 1987). This pattern of evidence has motivated considerable intervention research, much of it from a social-skills-training perspective (see Coie & Koeppl, in press; Ladd & Asher, 1985, for reviews). Although results from several studies (e.g., Bierman, 1986; Gresham and Nagle, 1980; Ladd, 1981; Oden & Asher, 1977) are quite encouraging, not all studies have been successful, and even within successful studies, not all children benefit. Our view is that attending to how children coordinate goals in problematic social situations may enhance the effectiveness of existing interventions.

Children who have been determined to be lagging or deficient in goal coordination could be trained systematically to coordinate goals. This training could take the form of coaching or direct instruction. Clark, Willihnganz, and O'Dell (1985) have used such an approach in a promising attempt to increase fourth-grade children's ability to generate strategies for integrating multiple goals. The intervention consisted of instruction during two 45-minute sessions, one on compromise strategies and one on persuasive strategies that integrate one's own and another's interest. Each session included rationales concerning the importance of mastering these strategies, descriptions and illustrations of the strategies, practice in generating examples of each strategy, and a worksheet to complete at home, which required children to continue practicing application of the strategies to various situations. Effects of the intervention were assessed using hypothetical situation interviews. Between pretest and posttest, there were significant increases in children's spontaneous and prompted integrative persuasive arguments. Interventions such as these could be used to test whether instruction in goal coordination facilitates the social adjustment of poorly accepted children.

SUMMARY

This chapter began with a historical review of conceptions of children's social competence. We noted a progression toward the systematic analysis of children's goals in social situations. Most research on children's goals has emphasized children's preference for one type of goal over another type within particular situations. This research has yielded small developmental and status differences in children's goal preferences. We have proposed in this chapter that social outcomes are more a function of how children coordinate multiple goals than of the goal preferences themselves. The coordination of multiple goals was viewed in the context of children's processing of social information, and it became apparent that goal coordination requires skillful responding at all stages of processing. We discussed the various basic approaches that the child can take toward coordinating goals and noted the various ways that breakdowns in coordination might occur. We offered a developmental perspective on the acquisition of goal-coordinated social behavior and made proposals concerning methods for assessing children's goal coordination. Finally, we have suggested that interventions focused on goal coordination will help children who have serious social relationship problems.

REFERENCES

Argyle, M., Furnham, A., & Graham, J. A. (1981). *Social situations*. New York: Cambridge University Press.

Asher, S. R., & Hymel, S. (1981). Children's social competence in peer relations: Sociometric and behavioral assessment. In J. D. Wine & M. D. Smye (Eds.), *Social competence* (pp. 125–157). New York: Guilford.

Asher, S. R., & Renshaw, P. D. (1981). Children without friends: Social knowledge and social skill training. In S. R. Ahser & J. M. Gottman (Eds.), *The development of children's friendships* (pp. 273–296). New York: Cambridge University Press.

Asher, S. R., & Wheeler, V. A. (1985). Children's loneliness: A comparison of rejected and neglected peer status. *Journal of Counseling and Clinical Psychology, 53*, 500–505.

Bierman, K. L. (1986). Process of change during social skills training with preadolescents and its relation to treatment outcome. *Child Development, 57*(1), 230–240.

Brown, P., & Levinson, S. (1978). Universals in language usage: Politeness phenomena. In E. N. Goody (Ed.), *Questions and politeness: Strategies in social interactions* (pp. 56–289). New York: Cambridge University Press.

Clark, R. A. (1979). The impact of self-interest and desire for liking on the selection of communication strategies. *Communication Monographs, 46*(4), 257–273.

Clark, R. A., & Delia, J. G. (1976). The development of functional persuasive skills in childhood and early adolescence. *Child Development, 47*, 1008–1014.

Clark, R. A., O'Dell, L. L., & Willihnganz, S. (1985). Training fourth-graders in compromising and persuasive strategies. *Communication Education, 37*, 331–342.

Clark, R. A., Willihnganz, S., & O'Dell, L. L. (1985). *The development of compromising as an alternative to persuasion*. Unpublished manuscript, University of Illinois, Urbana-Champaign.

Coie, J. D., Dodge, K. A., & Coppotelli, H. (1982). Dimensions and types of status: A cross-age perspective. *Developmental Psychology, 18*, 557–570.

Coie, J. D., & Koeppl, G. K. (in press). Adapting intervention to the problems of aggressive and disruptive rejected children. In S. R. Asher & J. D. Coie (Eds.), *Peer rejection in Childhood*. New York: Cambridge University Press.

Coie, J. D., & Kupersmidt, J. B. (1983). A behavioral analysis of emerging social status in boys' groups. *Child Development, 54*, 1400–1416.

Delia, J. G., Kline, S. L., & Burleson, B. R. (1979). The development of persuasive strategies in kindergartners through twelfth-graders. *Communication Monographs, 46*(4), 241–256.

Dodge, K. A. (1980). Social cognition and children's aggressive behavior. *Child Development, 51*, 162–170.

Dodge, K. A. (1986). A social information processing model of social competence in children. In M. Perlmutter (Ed.), *Minnesota symposium on child psychology* (Vol. 18, pp. 77–126). Hillsdale, NJ: Erlbaum.

Dodge, K. A., & Frame, C. L. (1982). Social cognitive biases and deficits in aggressive boys. *Child Development, 53*, 620–635.

Dodge, K. A., & Somberg, D. R. (1987). Hostile attributional biases among aggressive boys are exacerbated under conditions of threats to the self. *Child Development, 58*, 213–224.

Eisenberg-Berg, N., & Neal, C. (1979). Children's moral reasoning about their own spontaneous prosocial behavior. *Developmental Psychology, 15*, 228–229.

Ford, M. E. (1982). Social cognition and social competence in adolescence. *Developmental Psychology, 18*, 323–340.

Ford, M. E. (1984). Linking social–cognitive processes with effective social behavior: A living systems approach. In P. C. Kendall (Ed.), *Advances in cognitive-behavioral research and therapy* (Vol. 3). New York: Academic Press.

Ford, M. E. (1985). A living systems conceptualization of social intelligence: Outcomes, processes, and developmental change. In R. J. Sternberg (Ed.), *Advances in the psychology of human intelligence* (Vol. 3, pp. 119–171). Hillsdale, NJ: Erlbaum.

Freedman, B. J., Rosenthal, L., Donahoe, C. P., Jr., Schlundt, D. G., & McFall, R. M. (1978). A social-behavioral analysis of skill deficits in delinquent and non-delinquent adolescent boys. *Journal of Consulting and Clinical Psychology, 46*, 1448–1462.

Gaffney, L. R., & McFall, R. M. (1981). A comparison of social skills in delinquent and non-delinquent girls using a behavioral role-playing inventory. *Journal of Consulting and Clinical Psychology, 49*, 959–967.

Gibson, H. B., & Hanson, R. (1969). Peer ratings as predictors of school behaviors and delinquency. *British Journal of Social and Clinical Psychology, 8*, 313–322.

Goetz, T. E., & Dweck, C. S. (1980). Learned helplessness in social situations. *Journal of Personality and Social Psychology, 39*, 246–255.

Goldfried, M. R., & d'Zurilla, T. J. (1969). A behavioral-analytic model for assessing competence. In C. D. Spielberger (Ed.), *Current topics in clinical and community psychology* (Vol. 1, pp. 151–196). New York: Academic Press.

Gottman, J. M. (1983). How children become friends. *Monographs of the Society for Research in Child Development, 48*(3, Serial No. 201).

Gottman, J. M., Gonso, J., & Rasmussen, B. (1975). Social interaction, social competence, and friendship in children. *Child Development, 46*, 709–718.

Greene, D. (1976). Social perception as problem solving. In J. S. Carroll & J. W. Payne (Eds.), *Cognition and social behavior* (pp. 155–161). Hillsdale, NJ: Erlbaum.

Gresham, F. M., & Nagle, R. J. (1980). Social skills training with children: Responsiveness to modeling and coaching as a function of peer orientation. *Journal of Consulting and Clinical Psychology, 18*, 718–729.

Gronlund, N. E. (1959). *Sociometry in the classroom*. New York: Harper.

Hayes, J. R. (1981). *The complete problem solver.* Philadelphia: The Franklin Institute Press.

Ladd, G. W. (1981). Effectiveness of a social learning method for enhancing children's social interaction and peer acceptance. *Child Development, 52,* 171–178.

Ladd, G. W., & Asher, S. R. (1985). Social skill training and children's peer relations. In L. L'Abate & M. A. Milan (Eds.), *Handbook of social skills training and research* (pp. 219–244). New York: Wiley.

Ladd, G. W., & Oden, S. L. (1979). The relationship between peer acceptance and children's ideas about helpfulness. *Child Development, 50,* 402–408.

Maccoby, E. E. (1969). The development of stimulus selection. In J. P. Hill (Ed.), *Minnesota symposium on child psychology* (Vol. 3, pp. 68–96). Minneapolis: University of Minnesota.

Manis, F. R., Keating, D. P., & Morrison, F. J. (1980). Developmental differences in the allocation of processing capacity. *Journal of Experimental Child Psychology, 29,* 156–169.

Masters, J. C., Felleman, E. S., & Barden, R. C. (1981). Experimental studies of affective states in children. In B. B. Lahey & A. E. Kazdin (Eds.), *Advances in clinical child psychology* (Vol. 4, pp. 91–118). New York: Plenum.

McFall, R. M., & Dodge, K. A. (1982). Self-management and interpersonal skills learning. In P. Karoly & F. H. Kanfer (Eds.), *Self-management and behavior change: From theory to practice.* New York: Pergamon.

Meichenbaum, D., & Butler, L. (1980). Cognitive ethology: Assessing the streams of cognition and emotion. In K. Blankenstein, P. Pliner, & J. Polivy (Eds.), *Advances in the study of communication and affect: Assessment and modification of emotional behavior* (Vol. 6, pp. 139–163). New York: Plenum.

Miller, G. A., Galanter, E., & Pribram, K. H. (1960). *Plans and the structure of behavior.* New York: Holt, Rinehart and Winston.

Mischel, W., & Patterson, C. J. (1978). Effective plans for self-control in children. In W. A. Collins (Ed.), *Minnesota symposium on child psychology* (Vol. 11). Hillsdale, NJ: Erlbaum.

Newell, A., & Simon, H. (1972). *Human problem solving.* Englewood Cliffs, NJ: Prentice-Hall.

Oden, S., & Asher, S. R. (1977). Coaching children in social skills for friendship making. *Child Development, 48,* 495–506.

O'Keefe, B. J., & Delia, J. G. (1981). Impression formation processes and message production. *Journal of Personality and Social Psychology, 40*(5), 945–960.

O'Keefe, B. J., & Delia, J. G. (1985). Psychological and interactional dimensions of communicative development. In A. Giles & R. St. Clair (Eds.), *Recent advances in language, communication, and social psychology* (pp. 41–85). London: Erlbaum.

O'Malley, J. (1977). Research perspective on social competence. *Merrill-Palmer Quarterly, 23,* 29–44.

Parker, J. G., & Asher, S. R. (1987). Peer relations and later personal adjustment: Are low-accepted children at risk? *Psychological Bulletin, 102,* 357–389.

Parkhurst, J. T., & Asher, S. R. (1985). Goals and concerns: Implications for the study of children's social competence. In B. B. Lahey & A. E. Kazdin (Eds.), *Advances in clinical child psychology* (Vol. 8, pp. 199–228). New York: Plenum.

Parkhurst, J. T., & Asher, S. R. (1987, April). The social concerns of aggressive-rejected children. In J. D. Coie (Chair), *Types of aggression and peer status: The social functions and consequences of children's aggression.* Symposium conducted at the biennial meeting of the Society for Research in Child Development, Baltimore.

Parkhurst, J. T., & Gottman, J. M. (1987). How young children get what they want. In J. M. Gottman & J. G. Parker (Eds.), *Conversations of friends: Speculations on affective development.* (pp. 315–345). New York: Cambridge University Press.

Patterson, C. J., & Mischel, W. (1976). Effects of temptation-inhibiting and task-facilitating plans on self-control. *Journal of Personality and Social Psychology, 33,* 209–217.

Putallaz, M., & Gottman, J. M. (1981). An interactional model of children's entry into peer groups. *Child Development, 52,* 286–294.

Renshaw, P. D., & Asher, S. R. (1982). Social competence and peer status: The distinction between goals and strategies. In K. H. Rubin & H. S. Ross (Eds.), *Peer relationships and social skills in childhood* (pp. 375–395). New York: Springer-Verlag.

Renshaw, P. D., & Asher, S. R. (1983). Children's goals and strategies for social interaction. *Merrill-Palmer Quarterly, 29,* 353–374.

Richard, B. A., & Dodge, K. A. (1982). Social maladjustment and problem-solving in school-aged children. *Journal of Consulting and Clinical Psychology, 50,* 226–233.

Roff, M. (1961). Childhood social interactions and young adult bad conduct. *Journal of Abnormal and Social Psychology, 63,* 333–337.

Rubin, K. H., & Krasnor, L. R. (1986). Social cognitive and social behavioral prospectives on problem-solving. In M. Perlmutter (Ed.), *Minnesota symposium on child psychology* (Vol. 18, pp. 1–68). Hillsdale, NJ: Erlbaum.

Schank, R. E., & Abelson, R. P. (1977). *Scripts, plans, goals and understanding.* Hillsdale, NJ: Erlbaum.

Spivack, G., Platt, J. J., & Shure, M. B. (1976). *The problem-solving approach to adjustment.* San Francisco: Jossey-Bass.

Taylor, A. R., & Asher, S. R. (1987). *Children's goals in game situations: Effects of gender, grade level, and sociometric status.* Unpublished manuscript, University of Illinois, Urbana-Champaign.

Ullmann, C. A. (1957). Teachers, peers, and tests as predictors of adjustment. *Journal of Educational Psychology, 48,* 257–267.

White, B., Kaban, B., Marmor, J., & Shapiro, B. (1972). *Child rearing practices and the development of competence.* Cambridge, MA: Laboratory of Human Development, Harvard University.

Williams, G. A., & Asher, S. R. (1987, April). *Peer- and self-perceptions of peer rejected children: Issues in classification and subgrouping.* Paper presented at the biennial meeting of the Society for Research in Child Development, Baltimore.

Zigler, E., & Phillips, L. (1961). Social competence and outcome in psychiatric disorder. *Journal of Abnormal and Social Psychology, 63,* 264–271.

PART II

The Classroom and School Contexts

5

Stage–Environment Fit: Developmentally Appropriate Classrooms for Young Adolescents

Jacquelynne S. Eccles
Carol Midgley

> *It has been clear for some time that the entry into junior high school probably represents the most abrupt and demanding transition of an individual's entire educational career. This is a crisis period that has important educational as well as personal consequences.*
>
> Hamburg, 1974

> *The junior high school, by almost unanimous agreement, is the wasteland—one is tempted to say cesspool—of American education.*
>
> Silberman, 1970

> *There is considerable lack of fit between what we know about young adolescents and what we do to them five days a week in school.*
>
> Lipsitz, 1977

INTRODUCTION

Recently, there has been considerable interest in the effect of the transition from elementary to middle or junior high school on early adolescent development. Some investigators have suggested that the transition may be causally related to changes in young adolescents' motives, beliefs, values, and behaviors (Blyth, Simmons, & Carlton-Ford, 1983; Eccles, Midgley, & Adler, 1984; Simmons & Blyth, 1987). Several important questions have been raised. Does the transition have a negative impact on early adolescent development? What are the mediators between the transition and changes in beliefs and behaviors? Which young adolescents are most vulnerable to transition effects? What are the long-term consequences of the transition effects? Is a school transition at this stage of life inevitably detrimental for some groups of children? Simmons and her colleagues have argued that the *timing* of the transition to junior high school results in more disruption to the individual than would a similar transition a few years later "after the individual has developed a more mature sense of who he or she is" (Blyth et al., 1983, p. 106). While this may be true, Eccles et al. (1984) have argued that the *nature* of the transition is also critical. Transition to a more facilitative environment, even at a vulnerable age, should have a positive impact on children's perceptions of themselves and their educational environment. Both of these perspectives are probably accurate and need to be considered as we try to determine the optimal environment for young adolescents. In fact, as both Simmons and Blyth (1987) and Eccles et al. (1984) argue, it may be the coincidence of the type of transition and the timing that makes the junior school transition especially problematic for some children.

In this chapter, we argue that changes in a cluster of classroom organizational, instructional, and climate variables, including task structure, task complexity, grouping practices, evaluation techniques, motivational strategies, locus of responsibility for learning, and quality of teacher–student and student–student relationships may contribute to the change in students' motivation and achievement-related beliefs assumed to coincide with the transition into junior high school.

Evidence suggests that many young adolescents experience increases in the following as they move from elementary school to junior high school: the size of the school and the student body, the extent of both departmentalization and ability grouping, use of competitive motivational strategies, rigor in grading and a focus on normative grading standards, teacher control, and whole class instruction. Many also experience decreases in teacher trust of students, opportunities for student autonomy, teachers' sense of efficacy, and continuous, close, personalized contact between teachers and students and between students and their peers. Finally, contrary to what one might expect, some evidence suggests that some junior high school teachers provide students with fewer opportunities for higher-level cognitive problem solving than they received in upper elementary school.

We believe that these changes are *particularly* harmful at early adolescence in that they emphasize competition, social comparison, and ability self-assessment at a time of heightened self-focus; they decrease decision making and choice at a time when the desire for control is growing; they emphasize lower-level cognitive strategies at a time when the ability to use higher-level strategies is increasing; and they disrupt social networks at a time when adolescents are especially concerned with peer relationships and may be in special need of close adult friendships. We also believe that these environmental changes, coupled with the normal course of individual development, result in a developmental mismatch in which the fit between the young adolescent and the classroom environment is particularly poor, increasing the risk of negative motivational outcomes (see Fraser & Fisher, 1983; Hunt, 1975; Lewin, 1935; Mitchell, 1969 for general discussion of person–environment fit theory).

To make these arguments, we have organized the chapter in the following way: First, we review the evidence regarding changes in early adolescent beliefs and behaviors, with an emphasis on changes associated with the transition to junior high school. Second, we review the studies assessing changes in the classroom environment associated with the transition to junior high school. Finally, we discuss the possible link between these two literatures.

CHANGES IN YOUNG ADOLESCENTS' BELIEFS AND BEHAVIORS

Both Higgins and Parsons (1983) and Eccles *et al.* (1984) argued that changes in children's motivation and their achievement related beliefs and cognitions could be explained, in part, by systematic changes in the social environments to which they are exposed. In their chapter, Eccles et al. (1984) reviewed the nature of the changes in children's beliefs and motivation, concluding that (1) children's attitudes toward school and toward their own academic competence decline with age until the late high school years; (2) the decline is most marked when children first enter school and again when they move into junior high school; and (3) the decline varies across subject areas and activity domains.

Because many of the studies reviewed by Eccles et al. (1984) were not explicitly designed to look at transition effects, they typically confounded age, grade level, and school structure change, and often used a cross-sectional design, making it difficult to interpret the likely ante-cedents of developmental differences. Three major changes character-ize the literature since 1983: (1) There are more direct comparisons of different types of school structure, allowing one to unconfound the effects of age, grade level, and school structure in looking at develop-mental change. (2) More attention has been paid to assessing individual differences in young adolescents' reaction to both school transitions and to various types of posttransition school environments. (3) Studies have included more refined assessments of the nature of the classroom and school environments the children are moving from and into. Each of these advances has increased our ability to evaluate various causal explanations for developmental change in early adolescents' self-perceptions and school-related motivation. In this section we expand on the Eccles et al. (1984) review, focusing particularly on studies that assess longitudinal change linked directly to the junior high or middle school transition. Studies focused on the nature of the school environment before and after the transition are discussed in a later section.

Studies of change in beliefs and behaviors have made two kinds of age and/or across-grade-level comparisons: (1) mean grade-level differences on various indicators of performance, motivation, interest, and self-perceptions, and (2) differences in the patterns of associations among these variables. Studies have also distinguished between attitudes toward school and school subjects and more self-focused perceptions and motivation. Our review is organized around these distinctions. Within each section, we begin with the simplest designs and then move to studies with more refined dependent measures, comparisons of various patterns of school organization, and analyses of individual differences.

ATTITUDES TOWARD SCHOOL AND SCHOOL SUBJECTS

In general, as concluded by Eccles et al. (1984), there is a gradual decline in students' general attitudes toward school and academic subjects with advancing age and grade level (Epstein & McPartland, 1976; Haladyna & Thomas, 1979; Lee, 1979; Neale & Proshek, 1967; O'Connor, 1978; Thompson, 1982; Trebilco, Atkinson, & Atkinson, 1977; Yamamoto, Thomas, & Karns, 1969). For example, Larson (1982, 1983) found a decline in students' satisfaction with their school and teachers across grades six to eight. Similarly, in our study of Transitions at Early Adolescence (being conducted by Eccles, Midgley, Feldlaufer,

Reuman, Wigfield, Mac Iver, Flanagan, Jacobs, Miller, and Yee), students increased the relative importance they attached to the stem "because I have to" as a reason for attending school as they moved from elementary school into a traditional junior high school (Eccles, Wigfield, Reuman, & Mac Iver, 1987). The differences, however, vary in magnitude across and within these studies depending on the particular subject area being rated (Brush, 1980; Eccles et al., 1984; Gottfried, 1981) and the type of school and/or instructional format (Berndt, 1987; Berndt & Hawkins, 1987; Larson, 1982, 1983; Moore, 1983; Power, 1981), suggesting that the age–grade differences in attitudes toward one's school are influenced by the *nature* of the school environment one is in. In particular, when comparisons are made, the declines are more extreme for students moving into traditional junior high schools than for children moving into or through either a nontraditional junior high school or a middle school, or staying in a K–8 school (Berndt & Hawkins, 1987; Larson 1982, 1983; Moore, 1983).

While only a few studies have tried to unconfound age, grade, and transition effects on students attitudes toward school, the results are quite consistent: Transition appears to have a greater impact on change in attitudes toward school than do either age or grade changes by themselves (Jennings & Hargreaves, 1981; Simmons & Blyth, 1987; Simmons, Blyth, Van Cleave, & Bush, 1979; Thornburg & Glider, 1984). Furthermore, as one would expect, the nature of the transition has a substantial impact on the changes obtained in young adolescents' attitudes toward school, with transition into a more traditional junior high school environment, especially in large urban setting, leading to more negative change (Berndt, 1987; Berndt & Hawkins, 1987; Larson, 1982, 1983; Moore, 1983; Power, 1981; Simmons & Blyth, 1987; Trebilco et al., 1977; Warburton, Jenkins, & Coxhead, 1983). This pattern is true for some of the more subtle indicators of students' attitudes toward school, such as their feelings of anonymity (Blyth et al., 1983; Thornburg, 1985), their participation in extracurricular activities (Blyth et al., 1983), and truancy (Nielsen & Gerber, 1979), as well as for the more direct attitudinal measures mentioned earlier.

SELF-PERCEPTIONS: SELF-ESTEEM AND SELF-CONCEPT

Findings regarding self-perceptions are both more interesting and less consistent. In their classic study in Baltimore, Simmons, Rosenberg, and Rosenberg (1973) found that young adolescents, compared to children in grades three to six, exhibited heightened self-consciousness, instability of self-image, lower confidence in their academic ability, slightly lower global self-esteem, and more frequent depressive affect. Furthermore, and most importantly for this chapter, the 12-year-olds in a seventh-grade junior high school evidenced greater disturbance in self-image and confidence than the 12-year-olds in a sixth-grade elementary school, suggesting that the developmental differences are influenced by the educational environments experienced by the young adolescents, independent of, or at least in addition to, age.

Subsequent studies assessing change in self-perceptions have yielded a mixed pattern of results (see Table 1). Some studies report definite transition effects on self-perceptions. For example, Eccles, Adler, Futterman, Goff, Kaczala, Meece, and Midgley (1983) found a decline in children's confidence in their math abilities across grades 6–12 that was especially marked at the junior high school transition. Similarly, in The Transitions at Early Adolescence Study, Eccles et al. (1987) found a decline in general self-esteem between grades 6 and 7 when the children moved from elementary school to junior high school. And finally, Simmons and Blyth (1987) reported that the relative advantages experienced by sixth-grade children in a K–6 and 7–9 system disappeared after they made the transition to junior high school. Initially, the sixth-grade children in a K–6 school had higher self-ratings of their looks, sports ability, schoolwork ability, intelligence, and popularity than did their peers in the K–8 system in Year 1 of their study. But the next year, after the K–6 students had moved to junior high, these advantages disappeared. In contrast, other studies report little evidence of transition effects. For example, Thornburg and Jones (1982) found a decline in general self-esteem across ages 9–14 that was associated more strongly with age than with either grade level or school transitions, and Harter, Whitesell, and Kowalski (1987) found a decline in perceived cognitive competence between sixth and seventh grade for all children whether or not they made a school transition. Finally, several investigators have failed to find either grade-level differences or transition effects either in children's general self-esteem/confidence or in children's confidence in their abilities in specific domains even when they used the same measures as in the aforementioned studies (Connell, 1980; Connell & Tero, 1982; Dusek & Flaherty, 1981; Eccles, Wigfield, & Kaczala, 1988; Fenzel & Blyth, 1986; Greene, 1985; Harter, 1982; Jones, 1984; Prawat, Grissom, & Parish, 1979; Wigfield, 1984). Consequently, it appears that both the grade-related decline found by Eccles et al. (1984) and the school-structure-related decline found by Simmons et al. (1979) are not universal.

TABLE 1

Summary of Studies Related to School Transitions during Early Adolescence

Authors	Measures	Subjects	Developmental pattern
		AGE–GRADE COMPARISONS	
Cross-sectional studies			
Buhrmester (1980)	School fears and anxieties	Grades 3–9; school transition at grade 7	Increase from grades 6 to 7.
Connell (1980)	Perceptions of control over outcomes	Grades 3–9; school transition at grade 7	Increase in known vs. unknown source of control until grade 6; dramatic decrease at grade 7; subsequent increase.
Eccles, Adler, Futterman, Goff, Kaczala, Meece, & Midgley (1983); Eccles, Midgley, & Adler (1984)	Ability self-concept for math and English, perception of task difficulty for math and English, and perceived value of math and English	Grades 5–12; school transition at grade 7	Decline in attitudes toward math; marked drop from grades 6 to 7. No drop for English.
Epstein & McPartland (1976)	Attitudes toward school in general, commitment to schoolwork, and attitudes toward teachers	Grades 5–12; school transition at grade 6	Decline in commitment to schoolwork over the grades.
Gottfried (1981)	Academic intrinsic motivation for reading, math, social studies, and science	Grades 4–7; no school transition	Decline in intrinsic motivation at 7th grade for all subjects, but especially for reading and science.

(continued)

TABLE 1 (*Continued*)

Authors	Measures	Subjects	Developmental pattern
Haladyna & Thomas (1979)	Attitudes toward school in general and toward seven primary subject areas	Grades 1–8; school transition at grade 7	Decline in attitudes toward school and toward math, physical education, art, music, and science. Drop most marked from grades 6 to 7 for subjects, and from grades 4 to 5 for school in general.
Harter (1980), (1981)	Classroom Motivation Orientation (intrinsic–extrinsic)	Grades 3–9; school transition at grade 7	General decline; three scales of the motivational component show a marked drop from grades 6 to 7
Harter (1982)	Perceived Competence Scale (four scales: cognitive, social, physical, and general), achievement test scores	Grades 3–9; school transition at grade 7	No shift in absolute levels. Decline in relation between perceived cognitive competence and achievement test scores at grade 7.
O'Connor (1978)	Perceptions of self, ideal self, and teachers' feelings	Grades 4–6; school transition at grade 6	6th graders had largest self-ideal discrepancy and perceived teachers as being most negative about them.
Prawat, Grissom, & Parish (1979)	Locus of control, achievement motivation, and global self-esteem	Grades 3–12; grades 6–8 in middle school	Drop in achievement motivation only during middle school years.
Thornburg (1985)	Simmons & Rosenberg's Self-Esteem Scale, perceived anonymity, and victimization	Ages 11–13; grades 6–8 (in middle school)	Decline in feelings of anonymity and victimization. Decline in girls' self-esteem.
Wigfield (1984); Eccles, Wigfield, & Kaczala (1988)	Self-concept of ability and interest in English and math	Grades 5–12; school transition at grade 7	Decline in self-concept and interest in math but not English.

Wigfield & Meece (1987)	Math anxiety and math worries	Grades 6–12; school transition at grade 7	No consistent developmental trends; lowest in grade 6, highest in grade 9.
Longitudinal and cross-sequential studies			
Schulenberg, Asp, & Petersen (1984)	Self-Image Questionnaire for Young Adolescents, school grades	3 waves: 1 each school year; initial sample in grade 6; most but not all of the sample made a school transition at grade 7	Self-image increase from grades 6 to 8. School grades decline, especially between grades 6 and 7. Decline of popularity of math in grade 7.

SCHOOL TRANSITION COMPARISONS

Cross-sectional studies			
Thompson (1982)	School climate with respect to home–school relations, child communication patterns, and alienated–deviant behaviors	Grades 5–8; school transition at grade 7	Sharp decline in home–school relations, student perceptions of power and control at school, and increase in alienated deviant behavior. Changes occur primarily between grades 6 and 7.
Longitudinal studies			
Berndt (1987); Berndt & Hawkins (1987)	Harter's Perceived Competence Scale; Classroom Environment Scale: involvement, affiliation, and teacher support	3 waves: spring grade 6, fall and spring grade 7; school transition at grade 7	Decline in perceived competence. Students' rating of teacher support declined for students moving into a traditional school but remained stable for students moving into a school with small-teams approach.

(continued)

TABLE 1 (*Continued*)

Authors	Measures	Subjects	Developmental pattern
Connell & Tero (1982)	Harter's Perceived Competence Scale for Children, children's perception of control, and the Iowa Test of Basic Skills	Wave 1: April, grades 3, 4, 6, & 7; Wave 2: longitudinal follow-up Oct., grades 5, 6, & 8; school transition at grades 4 & 7	Increase in mean level of unknown perceptions of control after the transition to junior high school; no change with movement from grade 3 to 4. No change in competence evaluation or affect associated with either transition.
Eccles, Wigfield, Reuman, & Mac Iver (1987)	Self-concept of ability in math, English, sports, & social; general self-esteem; reasons for coming to school	4 waves; fall and spring of grade 6, fall and spring of grade 7; school transition at grade 7	Decline in self-concept, especially marked for social and general self-esteem. Increase in "because I have to" as reason to attend school.
Greene (1985)	Self-reported moods and activities, Simmons & Rosenberg's Self-Esteem Scale, activity participation	3 waves over 9 months: spring year 1, fall and winter year 2; grades 5 & 6; school transition at grade 7	No differences in self-esteem. Transition students were more variable in mood than nontransition students and more variable after the transition than before. Activity preferences differ for transition and nontransition students.
Nottelmann (1982, 1987)	Harter's Perceived Competence Scale, teachers' rating scale of child's actual competence, and pubertal index	3 waves: May school year 1, November and May school year 2:	Children's perception of competence weakly affected by transition: Transition students had slightly higher estimates of their general competence than nontransition students. Absolute

	initial sample in grades 5 & 6 in K–5/6–8 or K–6/7–9 systems		differences between children's self-assessments and teachers' ratings greater before than after transition.
Petersen & Crockett (1985)	Pubertal development, body image, impulse control, psychopathology, course grades, and family relations	3 waves: 1 each school year for 3 years; initial sample in grade 6; school transition for most children at grade 7	Body image declined, school grades declined, perceptions of family relations declined, perception of peer relations improved from grades 6 to 7.
Power (1981)	Attitudes toward science (semantic differential scale), Learning Environment Inventory, and Classroom Activities Questionnaire	4 waves: March and November in 2 sequential years; initial sample in grade 7; school transition at grade 8	Students making a transition to traditional classrooms declined in attitudes toward science, while students moving into open-area classrooms improved in attitudes. Student perceptions of the environment not strongly associated with attitudes.
Reuman, Mac Iver, Eccles, & Wigfield (1987)	Self-concept of ability in math, anxieties in math, interest in math, teacher's ratings of child's natural math talent	4 waves, fall and spring of grade 6, fall and spring of grade 7; school transition at grade 7	Slight decline in self-concept depending on ability level of 7th grade class. Decrease in teachers' ratings of children's natural talent.

(continued)

149

TABLE 1 (*Continued*)

Authors	Measures	Subjects	Developmental pattern
Rubenfeld & Schumer (1986)	Self-image, puberty assessments, extracurricular activities, anonymity, locus of control, standardized tests, and grades	2 waves: May school year 1, November school year 2; initial sample grade 6; school transition at grade 7 (girls only)	Sharp decline in self-image, primarily due to drop in perceived appearance. Drop in participation in extracurricular activities. Increase in anonymity.
Schwarzer, Jerusalem, & Lange (1982) (Germany)	Self-esteem, self-concept of ability, self-efficacy, and latent self-concept	2 waves: September and January of first year in secondary school; ages 10–11 years	Academic self-concept of low-ability children positively affected by entrance into lower ability tracked institution.
Youngman (1978) (England)	Self-concept, attitudes toward school, and standardized tests	2 waves: May school year 1, spring school year 2; initial sample: last year of primary school	Pattern of change dependent on type of school, rural versus urban setting, and initial personality characteristics of the children. Some children more at risk (children with initially poor self-concepts and disenchanted children) for the negative changes associated with transition into secondary school than others.

SCHOOL ORGANIZATIONAL COMPARISONS

Cross-sectional studies

Study	Measures	Grades/ages	Findings
Moore (1983)	Attitude toward school, self-esteem, pupil control behavior, reading test scores, and attendance	Grades 7–8 in K–8 and in traditional junior high school	Students in K–8 school had more favorable responses on all scales than did students in junior high schools.
Simmons, Rosenberg, & Rosenberg (1973)	Specific and global self-esteem scales, perception of opinions of others, and self-consciousness	Ages 8–18 in K–6, 7–9, & 10–12 systems	Decline in self-esteem; marked drop between grades 6 and 7. 12-year-olds in 7th grade in junior high school had lower self-esteem than 12-year-olds in 6th grade in elementary school.
Thornburg & Glider (1984)	Simmons & Rosenberg's Self-Esteem Scale; anonymity and victimization	Grades 6–7 in two K–6 schools and one 6–8 school	Age produced more significant effects than either school configuration or grade. Minimal changes in social characteristics and perception due to school transition or grade changes, and these depended on grade level of transition.
Thornburg & Jones (1982)	Simmons & Rosenberg's Self-Esteem Scale; anonymity and victimization	Grades 4–9 in four different school configurations: K–8, 5–8, 6–8, & 7–9	General decline in self-esteem. Transition at 6th grade lowered self-esteem while transition at 7th grade did not. 14-year-olds in 8th grade did not differ from 14-year-olds in 9th grade on any subscale.
Warburton, Jenkins, & Coxhead (1983) (England)	Attitudes toward science, science achievement tests	Age 14, transferred into secondary schools at ages 11, 12, or 13	Pupils transferring at age 13 scored higher on science achievement tests than those transferring at ages 11 or 12. Students transferring at age 12 scored lower on attitudes toward science tests than those transferring at either 11 or 12.

(continued)

TABLE 1 (*Continued*)

Authors	Measures	Subjects	Developmental pattern
Longitudinal and cross-sequential studies			
Blyth, Simmons, & Bush (1978); Simmons & Blyth (1987); Simmons, Blyth, Van Cleave, & Bush (1979)	Self-image, Simmons & Rosenberg's Self-Esteem Scale, perception of other's expectations, personal characteristics, attitudes toward school, extracurricular activities	2 waves, 1 year apart; initial sample in grade 6 in K–8/9–12 or K–6/7–9/10–12 systems	Decline in self-esteem for 7th grade girls making the transition to a junior high school, especially if they had begun dating. No such decline for other groups. Perceptions of anonymity increase with transitions to junior high but not for students in K–8 system. Lower participation in extracurricular activities for 7th graders in junior high school than in K–8 school. Boys moving into junior high report increased victimization while boys in K–8 report a decline.
Blyth, Simmons, & Carlton-Ford (1983); Simmons & Blyth (1987)	Simmons & Rosenberg's Self-Esteem Scale, grade-point average (GPA), tests, physical measurements	4 waves, one in each grade 6, 7, 9, & 10; initial sample in grade 6 in K–8/9–12 or K–6/7–9/10–12 systems	Greater decline in self-esteem of those transferring at 7th grade than those transferring from a K–8 school to the 9th-grade in high school, especially among females. Greater decline in girls' self-esteem from grades 6 to 7 in those girls making junior high transition than for girls staying in K–8 system. Girls making junior high transition show additional decline when they move into high school. Decline in boys' GPA when moving into junior high school. Decline in girls' GPA when they move into high school.

Harter, Whitesell, & Kowalski (1987)	Affective reaction to schoolwork, perceived academic competence, intrinsic vs. extrinsic motivational orientation, schoolwork performance concerns	2 waves: May school year 1, December school year 2; initial sample: grades 5–7 in either K–5/6–8 or a K–6/7–9 system	No change in perceived academic competence for children moving to middle school at grade 6, decrease with movement to 7th grade—both within a middle school and in association with transition to junior high. Students showing increases in perceived competence increased in intrinsic motivation. Affective reaction declined with school transition independent of grade.
Jennings & Hargreaves (1981) (England)	Academic self-image and attitude toward various aspects of school life	2 waves: spring grade 6, fall grade 7; initial sample: ages 10–11 in traditional feeder comprehensive school system or in feeder–middle-school program in same building	Students moving from a feeder school to a comprehensive school scored lower on 7 of 10 subscales, whereas those whose school was reorganized as a middle school that remained in the same building scored higher on 9 of 10 scales.
Jones (1984)	Nine self-image measures, self-consciousness, Simmons & Rosenberg's Self-Esteem Scale; victimization and anonymity.	5 waves: 1 in spring of school year 1; 4 in first quarter of school year 2; initial sample	Self-consciousness decreased after transition and perceived victimization and anonymity increased. Transition effects disappeared after 9 weeks.

(continued)

153

TABLE 1 (*Continued*)

Authors	Measures	Subjects	Developmental pattern
		in grades 5 & 6 in K–5, K–6, and 6–8 systems	
Jones & Thornberg (1985)	Simmons & Rosenberg's Self-Esteem Scale; anonymity, victimization, and generational differences	2 waves: wave 1—late spring school year 1; Wave 2—early fall school year 2; Initial sample—grades 5 & 6 in K–5/6–8 or K–6/7–9 systems	Reports of previous change mediated transition effects on anonymity and self-consciousness measures but had little effect on victimization and self-esteem measures. School transitions lead to increase in anonymity but have no effect on self-esteem, feeling of victimization or self-consciousness.
Larson (1982, 1983)	Self-assessment of school experience, locus of control, self-image Quality of School Life Scale (QSL), and Piers & Harris's Self-Concept Scale	4 waves: November and May of 6th grade, May grade '7, May grade 8; initial sample in grade 6 of 6–8 middle school	General increase in self-esteem in 6th grade. Only minor differences among different school structures. Scores for 6th graders in elementary school increased more than 6th graders in middle school. By the end of the 8th grade, scores the same. 7th and 8th graders feel better about themselves when 9th graders are not present. 6th graders prefer middle schools more than elementary schools. Scores on the QSL declined with grade; magnitude of decline greater in the junior high school than in middle school.

Mixed patterns of results also emerge for general measures of self-esteem and confidence in studies that assess specific domains. For example, we have found different patterns of change associated with children's estimates of their competence in various domains: The longitudinal declines at the transition to junior high school were the most extreme for children's ratings of their social and physical competence and their general self-esteem (Eccles et al., 1987). In contrast, Petersen and her colleagues found the largest declines associated with body image and general psychological adjustment rather than with social confidence (Petersen & Crockett, 1985; Schulenberg, Camarena, Sarigiani, & Ebata, 1986).

Longitudinal changes on more specific measures of perceived competence in particular academic domains are even less extreme and more variable; and they appear to depend on several additional variables such as the initial ability and motivational levels of the child, the ability grouping and general teaching practices experienced by the child in each grade, and the type of school structure and transition (Eccles et al., 1987; Reuman, Mac Iver, Eccles, & Wigfield, 1987; Schwarzer, Jerusalem, & Lange, 1982; Youngman, 1978). The general patterns of these changes make sense given these mediating and moderating variables. For example, as one would predict from social comparison theory, movement into between-class or between-school ability-tracked environments appears to induce an increase in the academic self-concepts of low-ability children and a decrease (or no change) in the academic self-concepts of high-ability children (Reuman et al., 1987; Schwarzer et al., 1982).

Both sex and pubertal status have also emerged as significant influences on the nature of change in early adolescents' self-perceptions, suggesting that some children are more vulnerable to the negative effects of the junior high school environment than others. For example, Simmons and her colleagues, in their longitudinal study of children in grades 6 to 10 in Milwaukee, report that girls who move into a junior high school at seventh grade evidence a decline in their self-esteem that is not matched by either girls moving from sixth to seventh grade in a K–8 school or by boys making either transition (Blyth, Simmons, & Bush, 1978; Blyth et al., 1983; Simmons & Blyth, 1987; Simmons et al., 1979). Although not consistent across all studies, a similar pattern of gender differences in the response to the junior high school transition has been reported in several studies (e.g., Larson, 1982, 1983; Simmons et al., 1973). When reported, these gender differences appear to reflect the greater vulnerability of relatively more mature girls, particularly on measures assessing physical or social self-concept and/or general self-esteem (at this age, more mature means showing signs of pubertal development and initial interest in dating) (Blyth, Simmons, Zakin, & Murry, 1982; Nottelmann, 1982; Simmons et al., 1973). It should be noted, however, that several longitudinal studies report neither consistent gender effects nor consistent pubertal status effects (e.g., Berndt & Hawkins, 1987; Harter et al., 1987; Petersen & Crockett, 1985) or report even more complex patterns of interactions involving both gender and academic ability level as well as the type of transition being made and the age of the children (Eccles et al., 1987).

Other child characteristics that have been suggested as moderators of the impact of school transition include the stability of one's friendship network, one's pretransition levels of self-esteem and domain-specific confidence, physical appearance, ethnic group, and family relationships and structure (Barber, 1987; Berndt, 1987; Flanagan, 1987; Nisbet & Entwistle, 1969; Simmons & Blyth, 1987; Simmons, Carlton-Ford, & Blyth, 1987). Although these suggestions are just beginning to be studied, some support has emerged for the importance of each of these variables.

The comparisons of most relevance to this chapter are those that assess developmental change longitudinally over the transition to either middle or junior high school, and those that compare children of the same age and grade level making different types of school-level changes. Stimulated by the seminal work of Simmons and her colleagues, there are now several such studies focusing on self-perception, self-concept, and self-esteem. The results, however, are not consistent across studies. The subsequent longitudinal studies by Simmons, Blyth, and their colleagues comparing children moving from sixth to seventh grade in a K–8 school, with children moving from a K–6 elementary school into a traditional 7–9 junior high school yield the pattern already discussed: Girls, especially early maturers who have also started dating, evidence a decline in their self-esteem when they move into a junior high school at seventh grade. Similar patterns of school-related change were reported by Larson (1982, 1983) for girls and by Moore (1983) for both sexes; in both cases, students making the transition into a junior high school evidenced a greater decline in their self-perceptions than students making other types of sixth- to seventh-grade transitions. The other major studies that either compare fifth to ninth graders undergoing different types of school–grade transitions (both within a school and between schools), or follow children of this age range longitudinally as they make the transition into a middle or junior high school, have yielded quite mixed results with no clear pattern even when similar or identical measures of self-perceptions are used (Clark & Clark, 1982;

Eccles et al., 1988; Harter, et al., 1987; Jones & Thornburg, 1985; Nottelmann, 1982, 1987; Thornburg & Glider, 1984; Thornburg & Jones, 1982; see Table 1).

Although less common, studies assessing the relationship of self-perception to other variables have yielded a more consistent pattern. For example, even though there were no significant grade-level differences in the level of perceived competence, Harter (1982) found the lowest correlation between school performance and perceived academic competence among seventh graders (most of whom were in their first year of junior high school). Similarly, O'Connor (1978) found the greatest discrepancy between children's real and ideal self images among sixth graders who had just made the transition to a middle school. These results suggest that children's standards for self-evaluation may be disrupted when they move to a new school environment. Longitudinal studies offer some support for this hypothesis. For example, Harter et al. (1987) found the strongest negative relationship of anxiety to perceived intellectual competence and to intrinsic motivation among early adolescent children who had just undergone a school transition into either a middle school or a junior high school. Similarly, the across-time correlations between children's ratings of their math competence in our Transitions at Early Adolescence study are much lower across the 6-month period marking the transition from a K–6 elementary school to a 7–8 or 7–9 junior high school than across the 6-month period within each school year (Reuman et al., 1987). Whether these changes reflect changing grade level or changing school remains to be determined.

SELF-RELATED AFFECTIVE REACTIONS: ANXIETY,
WORRY, AND AFFECTIVE RESPONSE TO PERFORMANCE

Several investigators have assessed developmental changes in early adolescents' affective reactions to school. Although there are fewer studies of these changes than of changes in self-perceptions, the findings are rather consistent for global measures. In cross-sectional studies of upper elementary and junior high school age children, older children report higher levels of test anxiety, more self-consciousness, and more extreme worries about their performance (Buhrmester, 1980; Harter et al., 1987; Hill, 1980). The one study that focused directly on school transition effects suggests that transitions, rather than grade level changes, may be responsible for these increases in worry and anxiety, as well as for a decline in young adolescents' positive response to their academic performance (Harter et al., 1987). But given the mixed pattern that has emerged as more studies have been done on self-perceptions, we need to be cautious in generalizing these results until more work is done on these outcome measures.

Studies looking at math anxiety in particular have yielded a different picture. Although only a few studies have been done, they do not report a consistent developmental decline across the early adolescent years (Reuman et al., 1987; Wigfield & Meece, 1987). As was true for subject-matter-specific self-concepts, the developmental changes in math anxiety seem more sensitive to the specific instructional environment the children move into than to school transitions per se.

MOTIVATIONAL ORIENTATION

The final set of achievement-related beliefs are all associated with motivational orientation. Three different sets of constructs have been investigated: (1) general achievement motivation, (2) intrinsic versus extrinsic motivation, and (3) locus of control–knowledge of control. The results across all three constructs are fairly consistent and, for the most part, seem to be linked quite directly to the middle-school–junior-high school transition when these transitional effects are tested. In general, young adolescents, following a transition into either a middle school or a junior high school, (1) report lower achievement motivation (Prawat et al., 1979), (2) appear more extrinsically motivated and less intrinsically motivated (Harter, 1982; Harter et al., 1987), and (3) are more likely to report than they do not understand the causes of their outcomes (Connell, 1980; Connell & Tero, 1982). This last result is especially interesting given that it represents a reversal of the general developmental trend toward increasing understanding of the causes of one's academic outcomes with advancing age and grade level. However, although it is interesting, it is not surprising. Just as perceptions of anonymity increase when students move to a new school, the degree to which students are unsure of the reasons for outcomes in the academic domain might be expected to increase when they move to a new environment, at least temporarily, until they can reassess the criteria being used by teachers for performance evaluation in this new setting.

Most important for our argument, the downward shifts in motivational orientation appear to be linked to the decline in children's perceived competence associated with the transition to a new grade level. They are also related to children's perception of the changes in their educational environments: Children who perceive that their new environment is more externally controlled in terms of increased external emphasis on getting good grades, increased scholastic competition, and increased teacher control also report higher levels of intrinsic motivation (Harter et al., 1987). As we discuss more fully later in this chapter, these are the types of changes that often characterize the differences between elementary school and junior high school environments.

It should be noted that two studies find declines in intrinsic motivation associated with grade changes independent of transition effects (deCharms, 1980; Gottfried, 1981). Therefore, as is true for self-perceptions, both grade-related changes and transition effects may depend on the educational environments the students move out of and into.

SUMMARY

There is some evidence in a number of studies that the transition from elementary school to middle or junior high school is associated with negative changes in young adolescents' motives, beliefs, values, and behaviors; yet other studies, sometimes using similar measures, fail to replicate these findings. Why are the findings inconsistent? One reason may be the failure to specify what the transition actually represents— a transition from what to what? In most cases, researchers assume that the transition to junior high school represents a shift from a smaller, more personal elementary school environment in which students experience one teacher and a stable peer group, to a larger, departmentalized school; changes at the school or classroom level are rarely measured. Although there may be systematic changes in the classroom environment across the transition in *most* cases, one cannot assume that is true for *all* cases. Indeed, classroom practices that have little to do with the departmentalized organization or size of the junior high school may change after the transition in many schools and may have a particularly powerful influence on student beliefs and behaviors. The fact that students' attitudes toward mathematics and English show different patterns of changes during the transition supports this suggestion (Eccles et al., 1983). Similarly, the fact that changes vary across schools with different organizational structures (Simmons & Blyth, 1987) suggests that variations at the school level are also important. As has been concluded from the voluminous and often inconsistent literature on ability grouping and open versus traditional classrooms, it is extremely important to specify what is meant by terms and to document exactly what is going on at both the classroom and the school level (Marshall, 1981; Passow, 1966).

In fact, the studies just reviewed support the hypothesis that transition effects are mediated by changes in the school and classroom environment. For example, the transition differentially affected students in the following situations: (1) students who moved into a junior high school that was organized into small teams responded differently than students who moved into a traditional junior high school (Berndt & Hawkins, 1987); (2) students who moved into open-area science classrooms responded differently than those who moved into traditional science classrooms (Power, 1981); and (3) students who moved into a comprehensive secondary school responded differently than those who moved into a technical school (Trebilco et al., 1977). Even in these studies, it would be more enlightening to have information about specific organizational, instructional, and climate variables in order to assess directly whether the changes in students' beliefs and self-perceptions are related to changes in those characteristics of the school environment outlined earlier: namely, (1) practices linked to increased incidence of self-evaluation and social comparison such as competitive motivational structures, ability grouping, whole-class instruction, and normative grading coupled with tougher grading standards; (2) practices linked to decreased student autonomy and increased teacher control; and (3) practices linked to decreased personal contact and increased bureaucratization. Eccles et al. (1984) documented the association of these school and classroom characteristics to lower self-perceptions and motivation, less interest in the subject matter, and more negative attitudes toward the environment. Thus, it seems likely that such changes could contribute to the declines summarized here. The evidence that such changes often characterize the transition to junior high school is reviewed in the next section.

What do the studies reviewed in this section tell us about other influences on the relationship between the transition and student belief systems? Gender has emerged as important in several studies. While the results are not entirely consistent, typically, when gender differences are found, females seem to experience more negative change in their self-esteem than males. What can account for the discrepant studies? Jones (1981) suggests that the age of transition and the type of postelementary school environment might be critical. In particular, he suggests that the nature of the middle school, with its de-emphasis on events such as interscholastic sports and extracurricular activities, which have traditionally brought prestige to the male, coupled with the fact that transition into middle school typically occurs at the sixth rather than the seventh grade when girls are more likely to be prepubertal, may result in less self-enhancement for males and less conflict for females.

The role of race, ethnic group, and social class as moderator variables has not been given adequate attention. Simmons' work, however, suggests that the transition may affect black and white girls differently (Simmons & Blyth, 1987) and there are certainly good reasons to predict that each of these population characteristics will be important.

Pubertal timing has also been suggested as important but there does not appear to be a strong direct association between pubertal timing or status and early adolescent adjustment, or a strong interactive effect of pubertal timing and school transition (Petersen & Crockett, 1985). When there is an effect, pubertal status appears most related to variables associated with the physical aspects of puberty such as feelings of attractiveness and body image, and to general self-esteem rather than to more academic achievement-related beliefs. There is also some evidence suggesting that girls who experience simultaneous pubertal, social (such as dating), and school changes are especially vulnerable to negative transition effects (Blyth et al., 1983; Nottelmann, 1982; Simmons & Blyth, 1987). In light of the conflicting results, Petersen concluded that "the belief in pubertal development as the primary influence on adjustment must be modified" (Petersen & Crockett, 1985, p. 203) and suggested that stereotypical "pubertal behavior" is likely to characterize particular populations of adolescents when the majority of its members become "mid-pubertal" regardless of the pubertal status of specific individuals within the population. Grouping populations of early adolescents together in an isolated setting like a junior high school may exacerbate this process, leading us to attribute, mistakenly, early adolescent behavioral changes primarily to pubertal status rather than to environmental influences in interaction with pubertal development.

Age at transition and grade at transition are confounded, and both, in turn, are confounded with transition to middle versus junior high school. Most junior high schools begin at the seventh grade, whereas most middle schools begin at fifth or sixth grade. The middle school philosophy is also different from the junior high school philosophy in ways that ought to yield less negative transition effects. In fact, several of the studies comparing transition to middle and junior high schools find somewhat more positive effects associated with middle school attendance (Larson, 1982, 1983; Warburton, Jenkins, & Coxhead, 1983). However, the differences in practices between middle and junior high schools can not be inferred; there is evidence that many middle schools in actual practice do not differ markedly from junior high schools (Erb,

1981; Lipsitz, 1977; Ward, Mergendoller, & Mitman, 1982). For example, in Larson's study (1982, 1983) the incidence of interdisciplinary teams and heterogeneous ability grouping was much greater at the middle than the junior high schools, but other instructional practices did not differ.

Grade configuration has been studied extensively, particularly by Thornburg and his colleagues. The findings regarding the superiority of the K–8 system for young adolescents appear to be consistent, though the reasons for this superiority have still not been carefully researched. In comparisons of different schools that house only young adolescents, there is not yet strong evidence that one grade organization is superior to another. As Lipsitz (1977) and others have pointed out, the effects of grade organization are best assessed in systems that differ only on that variable. "Given a school environment that matches young adolescents in their vitality, creativity, and sensitivity to changes . . . any organization will look beautiful. But given two schools equally open to the variability and energies of this age group, school organization based on differing choices about age-integration and the implications of adolescent development should produce some differing outcomes. We don't know what these will be" (p. 97).

Simmons has proposed that size and location (urban or suburban) of the junior high school may be important variables to consider (Simmons & Blyth, 1987; Simmons et al., 1987). Using data from a 5-year longitudinal study, the effects of school size, ethnic heterogeneity, and group or individual movement from class to class were examined. The nine junior high schools in this sample were departmentalized, but in some of them, the children moved as a group from class to class, while in others, the children moved independently among classes. In general, larger school size and greater ethnic heterogeneity were associated with some negative effects including loss of self-esteem, decreased involvement with school activities, and increased feelings of victimization and anonymity. These results are consistent with some of the findings from the small-school–big-school literature (Barker & Gump, 1964), suggesting that large schools may provide less positive environments, especially for vulnerable or marginal children. Although Simmons' studies were conducted in large, urban areas, a number of studies have been conducted with suburban middle- and upper-middle-class samples (Nottelmann, 1982, 1987; Schulenberg, Asp, & Petersen, 1984), and these studies yield less clear-cut results. Thus, until more studies are conducted with contrasting and carefully specified samples, it will not be possible to determine the extent to which size and location of school are important mediators of transition effects.

The evidence of negative changes in the belief systems of young adolescents as they move from elementary school to junior high school must be taken seriously. The studies that show positive effects for students moving into certain programs are encouraging. Although some people believe that the physiological changes associated with puberty make it difficult for most children to maintain a healthy self-image and an academic orientation at this stage of life, a more detailed understanding of the effect of specific changes in the school and classroom environments on these developing children is needed. Furthermore, studies are needed that assess the impact of different environmental characteristics on different components of young adolescents' beliefs, self-perceptions, motivations, and interest patterns. General school characteristics, such as size and formality, are probably more likely to influence general self-esteem, feelings of anonymity and victimization, self-concepts in domains other than the academic, and other indices of general mental health. In contrast, classroom and teacher characteristics are more likely to influence subject-matter-specific beliefs and both general and specific academic motivational orientations. But until studies provide us with more specific information, it is helpful to know what the literature now suggests regarding systematic changes in the school or classroom environment as children move into middle and junior high schools. The next section of this chapter undertakes such a review.

CHANGES IN THE ACADEMIC ENVIRONMENT

What do we know about systematic changes in the school or classroom environment in association with the transition from elementary school to middle or junior high school? We know that, in most cases, students move to a larger school, and they shift from being in the oldest to the youngest class; in addition, these students are more likely to be assigned to classrooms on the basis of their ability and to receive letter grades on classwork and report cards than was the case in elementary school. The self-contained classroom with one teacher and a stable peer group is typical of many elementary schools, whereas departmentalization of subject matter characterizes most junior high schools, so that students have a different teacher for each subject matter area, and their classroom composition changes across the school day.

In this section, we describe several empirical studies that compare the elementary school environment to the junior high school environment.

(In some cases, the comparison is actually made with middle schools or secondary schools.) Given the concern with junior high schools, remarkably few studies have focused on differences in the classroom or school environment across grades or levels. Therefore, we have drawn together information from a variety of sources, looking for converging evidence on which to base our description of classrooms before and after the transition to junior high school. A few of the transition studies described in the first section included environmental variables; researchers in the United Kingdom and Australia, in particular, have stressed the importance of including environmental measures in studies looking at transition effects. In The Transitions at Early Adolescence Study, we have measured the math classroom environment before and after the transition to junior high school, using student, teacher, and observer perceptions. Other studies have compared classrooms across grades or school levels without focusing on the transition. Recently, a few studies have directly compared different school structures for young adolescents (middle versus junior high school, team approach versus departmentalized approach, K–8 grade organization versus 7–9). These studies use a number of different high- and low-inference observation systems and self-report measures and a variety of informants, including teachers, students, and trained observers. Nonetheless, we have done our best to integrate the findings into a coherent composite picture. It should be noted, however, as we argued earlier, that there is variation across schools on all these indicators and that it is crucial to find studies that measure both the environmental characteristics of pre- and posttransition schools and students beliefs and attitudes.

Looking at the relatively few studies that have been conducted, four patterns emerge. First, junior high school classrooms, as compared to elementary school classrooms, are characterized by a greater emphasis on teacher control and discipline, a less personal and positive teacher–student relationship, and fewer opportunities for student decision-making and self-management. Second, the shift to junior high school is associated with an increase in practices such as whole class task organization, between classroom ability grouping, and public evaluation of the correctness of work; each of which may encourage the use of social comparison and ability self-assessment. Third, there is evidence that classwork, especially in mathematics, during the first year of junior high school requires lower-level cognitive skills than classwork at the elementary level. Finally, junior high school teachers appear to use a higher standard in judging students' competence and in grading their performance than do elementary school teachers.

TEACHER TRUST, DISCIPLINE, AND CONTROL:
TEACHER—STUDENT RELATIONSHIPS

In Eccles et al. (1984), we argued that declining opportunities for autonomy and choice, in concert with increasing levels of teacher control, could undermine students' academic interest and motivation. If young adolescents experience these types of changes as they move into junior high schools, then we would expect their interest and intrinsic motivation to decline.

Brophy, Evertson, and their colleagues have found consistent evidence that junior high school teachers spend more time maintaining order and less time teaching than elementary school teachers (Brophy & Evertson, 1978). Other researchers have also found that junior high school classrooms are characterized by high levels of teacher control and discipline (e.g., Moos, 1979). Willower, Hoy, Helsel, and their colleagues have conducted a large number of studies assessing educators' orientation to controlling, disciplining, and trusting students. Based on both student and teacher perceptions, elementary school educators consistently emerge as less oriented to control and discipline than secondary school educators (Hoy, 1968; Pritchett & Willower, 1975; Sweeting, Willower, & Helsel, 1978; Willower, Eidell, & Hoy, 1967; Willower & Jones, 1967; Willower & Lawrence, 1979; Yuskiewicz & Willower, 1973). Brooks (1977) found that junior high school teachers had a more custodial orientation than senior high school teachers. In addition, teachers in junior high schools were found to be more custodial than their middle school counterparts (Hedberg, 1973; Highberger, 1976), and seventh- and eighth-grade students in K–8 schools rated their teachers as less controlling and more humanistic than seventh-grade students in traditional high schools (Moore, 1983). In The Transitions at Early Adolescence Study, sixth-grade elementary-school math teachers trusted students more and believed that students needed to be controlled and disciplined less than did junior high school math teachers (Midgley, Feldlaufer, & Eccles, in press).

Several studies also point to a change in the teacher—student relationship after the transition to junior high school. In the Trebilco et al. study (1977), for example, students reported less-favorable interpersonal relationships with their teachers after their transition to secondary school. In The Transitions at Early Adolescence Study, both students and observers rated junior high school mathematics teachers as less friendly, less supportive, and less caring than the teachers who taught the students mathematics the previous year, in elementary school (Feldlaufer, Midgley, & Eccles, in press). Finally, Hawkins and Berndt

(1985) reported a decline in students' ratings of both affiliation with other students and support from teachers following the transition. They also found that these declines were more marked for the group of students who moved into a traditional junior high school than for the group who moved into a junior high school with a small-teams approach. This latter group actually perceived an increase in teacher support in conjunction with the transition. The authors conclude that "school structures that encourage close, supportive contact between students, and among teachers and students, contribute to positive self-concept and attitudes toward school following the transition to junior high" (Hawkins & Berndt, 1985, p. 16).

Taken together, these various studies suggest that many young adolescents experience an increase in teacher control and a decrease in the quality of their affective relationships with their teacher as they move into traditional junior high schools—both of which could precipitate a decline in student interest and motivation.

STUDENT SELF-MANAGEMENT AND CHOICE

It seems unlikely that teachers who distrust students and feel the need to control students' behavior will offer their students opportunities for self-management and choice. Consequently, as predicted by Eccles et al. (1984), it is quite possible that students will, in fact, have fewer such opportunities in junior high school than they had in elementary school despite their increasing age. Several studies provide support for this hypothesis. A study of particular importance is the Junior High School Transition Study (Ward, Mergendoller, Tikunoff, Rounds, Dadey, & Mitman, 1982). The study followed students from 13 sixth-grade classrooms in four feeder elementary schools to 11 seventh-grade classrooms in one 7–8 junior high school. Using classroom observations and teacher interviews, they found that sixth graders were given more opportunities to take responsibility for various aspects of their school-work and were given more choices than were seventh graders.

In an elementary-school study that has implications for the junior high school, Lee (1979) interviewed second-, fourth-, and sixth-grade students and teachers regarding perceived constraints and prerogatives in schools and those they thought students ought to have. Children saw much less congruence between the actual school environment and their assessment of what should be than did the teachers. Children's perceptions of their status changed significantly over grade level but teacher perceptions showed little variation with grade. Although students felt significantly less constrained over the grades, particularly between the second and fourth grade, there was a grade-related decrease in student's congruence due to a greater increase in their perceptions of what they should be able to do than of what they actually perceived they could do. Lee suggests that this pattern of decreasing congruency may be a precursor to student alienation in the secondary school. Using some of Lee's measures, The Transitions at Early Adolescence Study has assessed student and teacher perceptions of actual and preferred decision-making opportunities in mathematics classrooms before and after the transition to junior high school. Both students and teachers perceived fewer actual decision-making opportunities after the transition. In addition, while students expressed a desire for more input after the transition, their junior high school teachers actually believed they should have fewer decision-making opportunities than did their elementary teachers (Midgley & Feldlaufer, 1986).

TASK ORGANIZATION

Although there has been an increase in interest in the effects of task differentiation, competition, and evaluation practices in the classroom on student motivation and ability perceptions (e.g., Ames & Ames, in press; Covington, 1984; Eccles et al., 1984; Maehr, 1984; Marshall & Weinstein, 1984; Rosenholtz & Simpson, 1984), few empirical studies have traced changes in these variables across grade levels or school levels. In the Junior High School Transition Study, whole-group instruction was the norm in the seventh grade, small-group instruction was rare, and individualized instruction was not observed at all. In contrast, sixth-grade teachers mixed whole- and small-group instruction within and across subject areas (Rounds & Osaki, 1982). Changes in task organization after the transition to junior high school were also found in The Transitions at Early Adolescence Study: Both teachers and observers reported an increase in whole-class task organization after the transition with most students working on the same assignment at the same time, using the same textbooks, and receiving the same homework assignment (Feldlaufer et al., in press).

Changes such as these are likely to increase social comparison, concerns about evaluation, and competitiveness. They may also increase the likelihood that teachers will use normative grading criteria and more public forms of evaluation, both of which may impact negatively on some children's self-perceptions and motivation. These changes may also make aptitude differences more salient to both teachers and students, leading to increased teacher expectancy effects and decreased feelings of efficacy among teachers.

ABILITY GROUPING

We originally proposed that assigning students to classrooms on the basis of their ability would be another practice that could account for the decline in young adolescents' self-perceptions and academic motivation, particularly in mathematics and particularly for low-skill-level children (Eccles et al., 1984). We suggested that between-classroom grouping by ability might increase the likelihood of whole-class instruction, might make ability assessments seem more stable and unmodifiable to both teachers and students, and might create a stigma for low-skill students (see Eccles & Wigfield, 1985, for further discussion). There is evidence that assigning students to classes on the basis of their ability becomes more frequent after the transition to junior high school (Coldiron & McDill, 1987; Oakes, 1981). In addition, in junior high schools that do not use this practice, there is some evidence that within-classroom grouping by ability rather than by student interests increases after the transition (Rounds & Osaki, 1982).

The consequences of these changes appear more complex than we had originally speculated. Evidence from The Transitions at Early Adolescence Study suggests that changes in ability grouping practices at the transition to junior high school are related to changes in students' beliefs, values, and motivation (Reuman et al., 1987). But as reviewed earlier, the effects on these motivational constructs seem to be more a consequence of shifts in one's social comparison group than to the preceding factors: Students moving into high-math-ability classrooms suffer a decline in their self-perceptions and an increase in their anxiety while students moving into low-math-ability classrooms experience an increase in their self-perceptions and a decline in their anxiety. Thus, in terms of short-term motivational outcomes, the increase in the practice of assigning students to classrooms on the basis of their ability, common at junior high school, appears to have its most negative impact on students in high-ability classrooms. Whether the effects on long-term motivation, on teacher beliefs, and on school achievement coincide with our original predictions remains to be seen.

EVALUATION PRACTICES

Just as whole-group instruction and ability-grouping practices influence students' confidence and interest by inducing increased self-focus and competition, a greater emphasis on public evaluation can also undermine confidence and motivation by arousing anxiety, self-focus, and competitiveness (see Eccles et al., 1984, for discussion). The data on changes in the nature of evaluation are less consistent, however, than the findings on whole-class instruction. In the Junior High School Transition Study, the evaluation practices of the sixth- and seventh-grade teachers did not differ (Rounds & Osaki, 1982). Likewise, in The Transitions at Early Adolescence Study, there was no evidence of a change in the frequency of giving grades on math classwork or homework assignments after the move to junior high school (Feldlaufer et al., in press).

These findings contrast with reports from other researchers who have found that as children progress through school, evaluation becomes more formal and more frequent (Gullickson, 1985; Hill & Wigfield, 1984). Surveying elementary, junior high school, and senior high school teachers regarding their evaluation practices, Gullickson (1985) found substantial differences across grades. Elementary teachers relied on a diversity of techniques; evaluations based on class discussions, papers, and behavior were emphasized more than objective tests. In junior high school, the use of objective tests as a basis for evaluation became much more common, and there was less variety in evaluation techniques. Harter et al. (1987) also found changes across grade levels. Sixth, seventh, and eighth graders in a middle school were asked questions about the emphasis on, and the frequency of, external evaluation of their academic performance, and about the saliency of social comparison for the current year and the previous year. At all three grade levels, students reported that in the current year, the environment was more evaluative and the social comparison was more salient than in the previous year. Eighth graders perceived the most difference between the former and current year.

ASSESSMENT OF COMPETENCE AND STANDARDS
FOR EVALUATION

No predictors are as highly correlated with students' self-confidence and expectations as the grades they receive and their teachers' perceptions of their competence. If these change, or if the criterion on which they are based changes when students move into junior high school, then we would expect to see a shift in both the absolute levels of students' confidence in their academic abilities and the initial relationship of grades and teacher ratings of competence to students' self-perceptions.

There is evidence that junior high school teachers may use a stricter standard than elementary school teachers to assess student competency and to evaluate student performance. In Nottelmann's transition study (1982, 1987), the elementary school teachers gave higher ratings of competency to students than the middle or junior high school teachers gave these same students. Similar results are emerging in The Transitions at Early Adolescence Study for sixth-grade elementary school teachers' and seventh-grade junior high school teachers' ratings of the same children's natural mathematical talent (Reuman et al., 1987).

There is even stronger evidence that children receive lower grades after the transition to junior high school than before. Armstrong (1964, as cited in Finger & Silverman, 1966) reviewed the school records of a large number of students in New York State schools. Approximately 45% of students with good elementary grades received fair or poor grades in junior high school. Finger and Silverman (1966) examined student reports of the grades they received the first marking period in junior high school and those received the previous year, in elementary school. Dividing students into groups based on whether their seventh grade marks were higher, the same, lower, or much lower than their sixth grade marks, higher grades in junior high school were received by 16% of the students, 30% stayed the same, and 54% received lower or much lower grades than they had received in elementary school. Similarly, in the Simmons and Blyth study (1987), students entering the junior high school at the seventh grade experienced a significant drop in mean grade point average when compared to students who moved to seventh grade in the K–8 setting.

Several authors interpret this decline as reflecting changes in performance, suggesting that the drop in performance might be accounted for by the increased cognitive and social demands on students in the junior high school. There is evidence, however, that challenges this suggestion. For example, in the Early Adolescence Study conducted by Petersen and her colleagues, final course grades in five subject matter areas declined significantly for both boys and girls between sixth and seventh grade despite the fact that there was no evidence of a parallel decrement in IQ, achievement test, or cognitive test scores (Kavrell & Petersen, 1984; Schulenberg et al., 1984). "Since cognition and achievement generally improve over early adolescence, the most probable explanation for the decline seen in academic performance is that teachers are grading harder over time" (Kavrell & Petersen, 1984, p.27). In support of this suggestion, Felner, Primavera, and Cauce (1981) found that moving to a new elementary school in grades one through eight did not have a significant impact on school performance; in contrast, the transition from elementary school to high school was associated with a drop in grades in English, mathematics, science, and social studies. Overall, students' GPA decreased by more than one-half letter grade after the transition.

The findings regarding differences in teachers' perceptions of students' competency and evaluation of performance before and after the transition are consistent and compelling. Further work needs to be undertaken to determine whether these differences reflect true changes in performance, differences in teacher standards, or both.

COMPLEXITY OF CLASSWORK

One rationale often given for the large, departmentalized junior high school system is its efficiency in providing children with higher level academic work and more varied academic courses taught by specialists in the field. It is argued that the children are ready for more formal instruction in the various subject areas. Two assumptions are implicit in this argument. First, it is assumed that more formal, departmentalized teaching is conducive to the learning of higher-order cognitive processes. Second, it is assumed that children in junior high school are undertaking higher-order learning tasks in their departmentalized courses. Both of these assumptions are being questioned. There is growing evidence that although students may anticipate that junior high school will be more difficult and require higher level skills and understanding than elementary school, this may not reflect the actual situation. In an observational study of 11 junior high science classes, only a very small proportion of tasks required higher-level creative or expressive skills (Mitman, Mergendoller, Packer, & Marchman, 1984). Of the 31 laboratory activities that were observed, 30 were low level. Worksheets that generally required only copying of answers were the most frequent task type. Although this study did not contrast elementary and junior high school classrooms, it does provide evidence of the level of cognitive complexity required in junior high school science classrooms. Similarly, Sanford (1985), selecting well-organized teachers who were known to use a variety of tasks in their classrooms, observed six seventh- through tenth-grade science, social studies, and English classes. Two mathematics classrooms that were originally chosen for the study were not included because of the great predominance of routine tasks and use of algorithms in these classes! Even in this highly selective sample, teachers were not equally or consistently successful in engaging their students in work requiring high-level thinking.

In a study that provides information about the complexity of tasks before and after a school transition, Walberg, House, and Steele (1973) asked a cross-sectional sample of students in grades 6 through 12 about the general kinds of activities that characterized their classrooms. Activities were classified according to Bloom's taxonomy of educational objectives. Lower-level cognitive processes such as memorizing and knowing the best answer were emphasized more in the higher grades, while higher level processes such as application, comprehension, finding consequences, and discovering solutions were more prominent in the lower grades. The transition from elementary school to high school occurred after the eighth grade; lower-level processes reached a peak in the ninth and tenth grades, after the transition.

Using classroom observations, a similar pattern was identified in the Junior High School Transition Study. Sixth graders were expected to respond to diverse instructional and interactional demands. In contrast, recitation, memorization, recall, recognition, and teacher-assigned seat-work was the norm for the seventh-grade classes (Rounds & Osaki, 1982). The authors noted in particular that the sixth-grade math curriculum better provided for the students' needs and abilities than did the seventh-grade program, which was mainly a review of the sixth-grade syllabus.

These studies suggest that actual cognitive demands may not be increasing as children move into junior high school. Thus we may, in fact, have a situation where the cognitive level actually decreases after the transition and yet many children find themselves with lower grades.

LESS-TRADITIONAL PROGRAMS

Many of the characteristics we have been discussing relate to the general distinction between open or alternative or less traditional programs and the traditional junior high school classroom. Less traditional programs often aim to provide students with more control over the learning environment, to increase cooperative learning and decrease competition and social comparison, and to replace rote memory tasks and worksheets with a more problem-centered orientation to curriculum. That there are fewer open classrooms and alternative programs at the junior high school level than at any other level provides further documentation of the environmental changes suggested so far (Lipsitz, 1977; Mergendoller, 1982).

Some educators suggest that these less traditional programs, or some aspects of these programs, are more appropriate as children approach early adolescence than for younger children (Brophy & Evertson, 1976) and that the increase in traditional styles of instruction at junior high

school may be one of the factors that undermines young adolescents'
motivation and self-perceptions (Eccles et al., 1984; Lee, 1979; Mergendoller, 1982). Across the first through eighth grades, Arlin (1976) found
a significant interaction effect of open or traditional educational philosophy and grade level on student academic attitudes. In general, the
younger students preferred a traditional learning environment and the
older children preferred a more open style. For attitudes toward
teachers, learning processes, and language, the students in the lower
grades had more positive attitudes in traditional than in open
classrooms. By the upper grades, the attitudes of students in the open
classrooms caught up to or surpassed the attitudes of students in
traditional classrooms. Girls, in particular, seemed to enjoy less traditional practices as they became older. The suggestion that the impact of
classroom environments on student attitudes may vary across grade
levels and that self-management may be even more critical at the upper
elementary grades and in junior high school is supported by a study of
the effects of openness of school structure and teacher management
skills on students' academic attitudes in grades one and five (Blumenfeld, Hamilton, Bossert, Wessels, & Meece, 1982). First graders' attitudes
were unaffected by the type of structure. In contrast, the students with
the most positive attitudes were the fifth graders in well-managed, open
classrooms.

SUMMARY

The findings from these diverse studies are both surprising and
disturbing. The changes in the academic environment that children
experience when they move to junior high school would predict lower
motivation to achieve and more negative self-perceptions at any age
(Eccles et al., 1984), but we believe that these changes are particularly
detrimental for this age group. As children move through early adolescence, they are becoming more knowledgeable and skillful and are
developing cognitively. They are able to use critical thinking to explore
open-ended questions or moral dilemmas rather than dealing primarily
with rote, right answer, memorization. They develop a more differentiated ability concept, moving from equating ability and effort to perceiving ability or intellectual capacity as relatively stable (Nicholls, 1986).
They typically express a desire for more control over their lives (Lee,
1979). At the same time many children are experiencing the changes
associated with puberty. They become increasingly self-focused, self-
conscious, and concerned about themselves in comparison to others

(Elkind & Bowen, 1979; Simmons et al., 1973). Relationships with friends and extraparental adults become especially important (Miller, 1974). Does it make sense to put these developing children in a classroom environment that is less demanding cognitively, that promotes ability evaluation and social comparison, that decreases opportunities for student self-management and choice, and that is more formal and impersonal? We suggest that there is a developmental mismatch resulting from changes in the classroom environment that are at odds with physiological, psychological, and cognitive changes in the young adolescent.

The next section of this chapter focuses on the relation between the changes in young adolescents' beliefs and behaviors and the lack of fit between children at this stage of life and the classroom environments they experience.

STAGE–ENVIRONMENT FIT

This chapter began with a discussion of the impact of the transition from elementary to middle or junior high school on early adolescent development. It has been proposed that simultaneous physiological and environmental changes at this stage of life are disruptive (Blyth et al., 1983; Nottelmann, 1982, 1987). Does that mean that a transition should be avoided or postponed? A transition to a less facilitative environment is certainly to be avoided. We have suggested that the nature of the environmental change, as well as the timing, must be considered. Our review of changes in the classroom environment in association with the transition is an attempt to understand the nature of environmental change during this period. This research leads us to believe that there may be a developmental mismatch between young adolescents and the environments they experience at this stage of life. We suggest that this mismatch may be causally related to the decline in self- and achievement-related beliefs reviewed in the first section. We also propose that a transition to a developmentally appropriate learning environment, even at this vulnerable age, could have a facilitative effect on young adolescents' beliefs and behaviors.

This hypothesis is akin to person–environment fit theory, which states that an individual's behavior is jointly determined by characteristics of the person and properties of the immediate environment. When the needs or goals of the individual are congruent with opportunities afforded by the environment, then favorable affective, cognitive, and behavioral outcomes should result for that individual. Conversely, when a discrepancy exists between the needs of the individual and the opportunities available in that individual's environment, unfavorable outcomes should result (Hunt, 1975; Lewin, 1935; Murray, 1938). Hunt distinguishes between a contemporaneous and a developmental view of person–environment fit. He suggests that developmental change in the person is an interactive function of the person's stage of life and the environment s/he experiences. He points out the implications of this approach for educators. "Maintaining a developmental perspective becomes very important in implementing person–environment matching because a teacher should not only take account of a student's contemporaneous needs by providing whatever structure he presently requires, but also view his present need for structure on a developmental continuum along which growth toward independence and less need for structure is the long-term objective" (p.221).

Epstein (1983) stresses that research that focuses only on the match or fit of students in learning environments misses the potential importance of disequilibrium and mismatched conditions to spur development. She points out the importance of opportunities for self-direction at school during preadolescence and adolescence to compensate for the lack of opportunities in families where the child's abilities in self-direction may be changing faster than families recognize. She believes that, on the average, students gain from having decision-making opportunities at this stage of life, and although some students benefit more than others, classrooms that recognize this need help certain students without hurting others. Similarly, Parsons and Bryan (1987) have pointed out the importance of ideologically challenging environments at early adolescence for continued growth toward gender-role androgyny.

Others have taken a similar perspective, sometimes using different terms and a different framework. Petersen (1980) articulates a bio psychosocial model. Lerner (1982) endorses a life-span view of human development, stating that successful adaptation always involves appropriate coordination between our changing selves and our changing contexts, and that in early adolescence "such adaptational stresses may be most critical, due to their simultaneity and multidimensionality (Lerner, 1982, p.361). Power (1981) takes a "developmental interactionist" view, stating that changes in students' attitudes are not only a function of the characteristics of the person, but also of changes in learning environments across time and of interactions of matches and mismatches between persons and environments. Sprinthall (1985) calls for a "cognitive developmental" approach to education and warns that the lack of growth-enhancing activities for young adolescents who, because of their stage of life, are particularly vulnerable is a very serious problem. "By providing almost no good examples of formal or informal growth enhancing activities, we apparently think that young teenagers will somehow unfold magically. What the adult forgets or refuses to accept is that if we abdicate our responsibilities for effective education, other groups . . . will fill the vacuum" (p.543). Miller (1978) discusses the developmental implications of the work of Piaget, Kohlberg, and Erikson for secondary education and the importance of stimulating higher stages of cognitive, ego, and moral development. "In my view the secondary school curriculum can often be incongruent with the developmental needs of adolescence and thus should be reexamined to take developmental considerations into account" (p.237). Mergendoller (1982) also talks about the deleterious effect the typical comprehensive secondary school can have on adolescent development, but stresses that schools also have the potential to facilitate adolescent growth.

In the rest of this chapter, we consider several questions: From the studies reviewed, what do we know about the links between these environmental changes and children's beliefs at this stage of life? What kinds of studies still need to be done to broaden our knowledge of this relationship? Is there a causal relationship? Can anything be done to improve the situation?

As we have discussed, in several studies that have looked at changes in student beliefs in conjunction with the transition, differences between the elementary and junior high school environment are inferred; they are not measured directly. Thus, age and grade are confounded; changes in belief systems might be the result of age maturation alone. It has been the magnitude of change in concert with the transition that has led these researchers to suggest the relationship. Comparing the effects of the transition at two different ages (fifth to sixth grade versus sixth to seventh grade) is an attempt to separate the age and grade effects, but these studies have not measured the environment directly and do not provide a clear-cut answer (Harter et al., 1987; Jones, 1981; Nottelmann, 1982, 1987; Petersen & Ebata, 1987; Thornburg & Jones, 1982). Comparing seventh-grade students in K–8 schools to similar-age students in junior high school, without assessing environmental differences, can lead to the conclusion that the timing of the transition may be the critical factor, particularly when the transition to high school does not produce a similar effect (Blyth et al., 1983). But since K–8 schools are smaller and typically more personal than junior high schools, these variables may be responsible for the differences rather than the timing per se. And, as Simmons and Blyth (1987) argue, pubertal girls may be particularly sensitive to these conditions.

We also gain information from studies that follow children into different educational environments at the same age (Berndt & Hawkins, 1987), especially when there is some attempt to specify the nature of the differences. Studies that compare children moving into middle school programs versus junior high school programs are usually confounded with age; middle school programs typically begin at grade five or six; junior high schools at grade seven. One cannot assume that a middle school philosophy is necessarily being implemented or that the junior high school is a typical junior high school if the environment is not measured. Studies also suffer from the lack of variation in existing school programs for young adolescents, limiting our knowledge of the effects of environmental change on belief systems to what is common and giving us little insight into what could be (McPartland & Karweit, 1979). Innovative programs are often self-selected, which makes studies of them suspect in terms of generalizability.

Although virtually no researchers have assessed the causal link between shifts in the academic environment and children's belief systems, Eccles et al. (1984) outlined reasons to believe they are related. The changes in task structure, task complexity, grouping practices, evaluation techniques, locus of responsibility for learning, and quality of teacher–student relationships should result in an increased focus on ability assessments, increased salience of a stable conceptualization of ability, increased anxiety over one's relative ability and performance levels, and a decreased sense of control and intellectual challenge. Similarly, changes in school size, stability of friendship networks, the personalized versus bureaucratic tone of the environment, and in the students' opportunity for choice and autonomy should result in increased feelings of anonymity and victimization, increased concern or worry over one's social and academic standing, and decreased interest in, and valuing of, the academic components of school. Each of these consequences, in turn, should have a negative effect on some children's beliefs about themselves and attitudes toward school and learning, especially in students who are not highly able, or who do not perceive themselves as highly able, and students who are marginal or at risk for other reasons.

Longitudinal studies are needed that follow large groups of representative children from elementary school to junior high school in carefully measured contrasting environments. Ideally, these studies would extend at least from the last year of elementary school to the first year of high school. We are currently conducting a large-scale study assessing the effects of systematic changes in the classroom environment across the transition from elementary school to junior high school on students' achievement-related motives, beliefs, values, and behaviors. The Transitions at Early Adolescence Study has a 2-year, four-wave, longitudinal, quasi-experimental design. The sample was drawn from 12 school districts in southeastern Michigan. School districts were selected to maximize variation on classroom environment variables such as between- and within-class ability grouping, grading practices, and task organization. Questionnaire data were gathered from over 3000 students, their math teachers, and their parents in the fall and spring of the last year of elementary school (1983–1984) and again in the fall and spring of the first year of junior high school (1984–1985). In addition, 135 pretransition classrooms and 81 posttransition classrooms were observed for 1 week during mathematics instruction in the fall of each year. Student school records, including final grades in mathematics and English, scores on two achievement tests, and information about absenteeism were collected each year.

We have described some of the preliminary findings on changes in students' attitudes and values and differences between the pre- and posttransition classroom environments in the first two sections of this chapter. In general, we have found evidence of both the declines in students' self-perceptions and the changes in the classroom environment discussed thus far in this chapter. We also have strong evidence of a decline in perceived person–environment fit across the junior high school transition. The discrepancy between students' perceptions of actual decision-making opportunities in the classroom and those they would prefer to have increases after the transition (Midgley & Feldlaufer, 1986). Most importantly, initial studies provide evidence of a causal relationship between changes in children's belief systems and changes in instructional practices during the transition from elementary school to junior high school (Reuman et al., 1987). Many more studies are underway.

If there is a causal relationship, can anything be done to change the junior high school classroom environment? Educators and psychologists have long recognized the need for a more personal, student-managed, task-focused learning environment for young adolescents. That recognition led to the establishment of the junior high school and more recently, the middle school. Unfortunately, many of these intermediate schools reflect a change in grade organization and little more; it has been difficult to translate theory into practice. As we continue to analyze the data from our study, we will be in a position to identify specific classroom practices that facilitate or retard early adolescent development. With growing interest in this age group and increasing empirical evidence to support the theory, the time may be ripe to design and implement developmentally appropriate classrooms for this age group.

We believe that movement into a more facilitative environment at early adolescence can have a positive effect. Clinical and developmental psychologists have suggested that early adolescence is a time of increased plasticity and openness to positive influences (Lerner, 1982; Lipsitz, 1981; Miller, 1974). "The foundation stones of personality development are laid in childhood, but adolescence is a second change for mature development. In the psychological and social turmoil of puberty and adolescence the plasticity of the human personality makes new perceptions of the world possible" (Miller, 1974, p.436). Likewise Felner and his colleagues point to transition points as periods of psychological disequilibrium with the potential for either psychological disturbance or growth (Felner, Farber, & Primavera, 1980).

At the same time, in order to maximize the possibility of effective change, it is important to put more research effort into understanding why the junior high school is the way it is in spite of the theory that suggests it should be otherwise. Are junior high school educators inherently different from elementary school educators? Are there differences in training and experience that influence elementary and junior high school teachers' beliefs and practices? Does the departmentalized organization automatically preclude a developmentally appropriate environment? We doubt it, but that does not mean that this organization should not be open to scrutiny to see whether the detrimental effects of departmentalization outweigh the benefits. Does the larger size of the junior high school contribute to its deficiencies? Does isolating young adolescents and their teachers create an environment in which stereotypes flourish? Is there a "zookeeper" ethic (Leet, 1974; Midgley, Feldlaufer, & Eccles, in press) in schools for young adolescents that socializes teachers to believe that young adolescents are difficult to control and to teach?

Until recently, early adolescence as a stage of life was largely ignored and understudied (Hamburg, 1974; Lipsitz, 1977). This is no longer true. Since the mid-1970s, a large number of important research studies have been undertaken focusing on this age group, and interest appears to be growing. As Sprinthall (1985) points out, however, "the major socializing agencies of our culture have basically ignored this information" (p.546). Let us hope that the future will see the marriage of theory and practice and that our young adolescents will have the benefit of developmentally appropriate classrooms.

REFERENCES

Ames, R., & Ames, C. (in press). Adolescent motivation and achievement. In J. Worell & F. Danner (Eds.), *Adolescent development: Issues for education.* New York: Academic Press.

Arlin, M. (1976). Open education and pupils' attitudes. *Elementary School Journal, 76,* 219–228.

Armstrong, C. M. (1964). *Patterns of achievement in selected New York state schools.* Albany, NY: New York State Education Department. (mimeographed).

Barber, B. (1987, April). *Family structural effects: Importance and assessment.* Paper presented at the biennial meeting of the Society for Research in Child Development, Baltimore.

Barker, R., & Gump, P. (1964). *Big school, small school: High school size and student behavior.* Stanford, CA: Stanford University Press.

Berndt, T. J. (1987, April). *Changes in friendship and school adjustment after the transition to junior high school.* Paper presented at the biennial meeting of the Society for Research in Child Development, Baltimore.

Berndt, T. J., & Hawkins, J. A. (in press). Adjustment following the transition to junior high school. *Monographs in Child Development.*

Blumenfeld, P. C., Hamilton, V. I., Bossert, S. T., Wessels, K., & Meece, J. (1982). Teacher talk and student thought: Socialization into the student role. In J. M. Levine & M. C. Wang (Eds.), *Teacher and student perceptions: Implications for teaching.* Hillsdale, NJ: Erlbaum.

Blyth, D. A., Simmons, R. G., & Bush, D. (1978). The transition into early adolescence: A longitudinal comparison of youth in two educational contexts. *Sociology of Education, 51,* 149–162.

Blyth, D. A., Simmons, R. G., & Carlton-Ford, S. (1983). The adjustment of early adolescents to school transitions. *Journal of Early Adolescence, 3,* 105–120.

Blyth, D. A., Simmons, R. G., Zakin, D. F., & Murry, R. A. (1982, March). *The influence of physical maturity on early adolescents' adjustment to school transitions.* Paper presented at the annual meeting of the American Educational Research Association, New York.

Brooks, R. C. (1977). A study to establish behavioral and other correlates of the Pupil Control Ideology form at the junior and senior high school level. *Dissertation Abstracts International, 38,* 1762A–1763A.

Brophy, J. E., & Evertson, C. M. (1976). *Learning from teaching: A developmental perspective.* Boston, MA: Allyn and Bacon.

Brophy, J. E., & Evertson, C. M. (1978). Context variables in teaching. *Educational Psychologist, 12,* 310–316.

Brush, L. (1980). *Encouraging girls in mathematics: The problem and the solution.* Cambridge, MA: Abt Books.

Buhrmester, D. (1980). *Assessing elementary-aged children's anxieties: Rationale, development, and correlates of the School Concerns Scale.* Unpublished masters thesis, Denver, CO: University of Denver.

Clark, S. N., & Clark, D. C. (1982). School structure: Does it make any difference? *Journal of Early Adolescence, 2,* 241–246.

Coldiron, R. J., & McDill, E. L. (1987, April). *Variations in how teachers and students are brought together for instruction in the middle grades: Staffing, grouping, and scheduling practices in different grades and grade-spans.* Paper presented at the annual meeting of the American Educational Research Association, Washington, DC.

Connell, J. P. (1980). *A multidimensional measure of children's perceptions of control.* Unpublished manuscript, University of Denver.

Connell, J. P., & Tero, P. F. (1982). *Aspects of continuity and change in children's self-regulated cognitions and affects within the academic domain.* Unpublished manuscript, University of Rochester, Rochester, NY.

Covington, M. (1984). The motive for self-worth. In R. E. Ames & C. Ames (Eds.), *Research on motivation in education* (Vol. 1) NY: Academic Press.

deCharms, R. (1980). The origins of competence and achievement motivation in personal causation. In L. J. Fyans, Jr. (Ed.), *Achievement motivation: Recent trends in theory and research.* NY: Plenum.

Dusek, J. B., & Flaherty, J. F. (1981). The development of the self-concept during the adolescent years. *Monographs of the Society for Research in Child Development, 46* (4, Serial No. 191).

Eccles, J., Adler, T. F., Futterman, R., Goff, S. B., Kaczala, C. M., Meece, J. L., & Midgley, C. (1983). Expectancies, values, and academic behaviors. In J. T. Spence (Ed.), *Achievement and achievement motivation.* San Francisco, CA: W. H. Freeman.

Eccles (Parsons), J., Midgley, C., & Adler, T. F. (1984). Grade-related changes in the school environment: Effects on achievement motivation. In J. G. Nicholls (Ed.), *Advances in motivation and achievement* (pp.283–331). Greenwich, CT: JAI Press.

Eccles, J., & Wigfield, A. (1985). Teacher expectations and student motivation. In J. Dusek (Ed.), *Teacher expectancies* (pp.185–217). Hillsdale, NJ: Erlbaum.

Eccles, J., Wigfield, A., & Kaczala, C. (1988). *Ontogeny of achievement-related self and task beliefs.* Unpublished manuscript, University of Michigan, Ann Arbor.

Eccles, J. S., Wigfield, A., Reuman, D., & Mac Iver, D. (1987, April). *Changes in students' beliefs about four activity domains: The influence of the transition to junior high school.* Paper presented at the annual meeting of the American Educational Research Association, Washington, DC.

Elkind, D., & Bowen, R. (1979). Imaginary audience behavior in children and adolescents. *Developmental Psychology, 15,* 38–44.

Epstein, J. L. (1983). Longitudinal effects of family school–person interactions on student outcomes. In A. Kerckhoff (Ed.), *Research in sociology of education and socialization* (Vol. 4, pp.101–127). Greenwich, CT: JAI Press.

Epstein, J. L., & McPartland, J. M. (1976). The concept and measurement of the quality of school life. *American Educational Research Journal, 13,* 15–30.

Erb, T. O. (1981). Eighth grade classrooms in theory and practice: The gap persists. *Journal of Early Adolescence, 1,* 11–25.

Feldlaufer, H., Midgley, C., & Eccles, J. S. (in press). Student, teacher, and observer perceptions of the classroom environment before and after the transition to junior high school. *Journal of Early Adolescence.*

Felner, R. D., Farber, S. S., & Primavera, J. (1980). Children of divorce, stressful life events, and transitions: A framework for preventive efforts. In R. H. Price, J. Monahan, B. C. Bader, & R. F. Ketterer (Eds.), *Prevention in mental health: Research, policy, and practice.* Beverly Hills, CA: Sage.

Felner, R. D., Primavera, J., & Cauce, A. M. (1981). The impact of school transitions: A focus for preventive efforts. *American Journal of Community Psychology, 9,* 449–459.

Fenzel, L. F., & Blyth, D. A. (1986). *Individual adjustment to school transitions: An exploration of the role of supportive peer relations.* Unpublished manuscript.

Finger, J. A., & Silverman, M. (1966). Changes in academic performance in the junior high school. *Personnel and Guidance Journal, 45,* 157–164.

Flanagan, C. (1987, April). *Change in parent life—What does it mean for children?* Paper presented at the biennial meeting of the Society for Research in Child Development, Baltimore.

Fraser, B., & Fisher, D. (1983). Student achievement as a function of person–environment fit: A regression surface analysis. *British Journal of Educational Psychology, 53,* 89–99.

Gottfried, E. (1981, April). *Grade, sex, and race differences in academic intrinsic motivation.* Paper presented at the annual meeting of the American Educational Research Association, Los Angeles.

Greene, A. L. (1985, April). *Self-concept and life transitions in early adolescence.* Paper presented at the biennial meeting of the Society for Research in Child Development, Toronto.

Gullickson, A. R. (1985). Student evaluation techniques and their relationship to grade and curriculum. *Journal of Educational Research, 79,* 96–100.

Haladyna, T., & Thomas, G. (1979). The attitudes of elementary school children toward school and subject matters. *Journal of Experimental Education, 48,* 18–23.

Hamburg, B. A. (1974). Early adolescence: A specific and stressful stage of the life cycle. In G. V. Coelho, B. A. Hamburg, & J. E. Adams (Eds.), *Coping and adaptation.* NY: Basic Books.

Harter, S. (1980). A model of intrinsic mastery motivation in children: Individual differences and developmental change. In W. A. Collins (Ed.), *Minnesota symposium on child psychology* (Vol. 14). Hillsdale, NJ: Erlbaum.

Harter, S. (1981). A new self-report scale of intrinsic versus extrinsic orientation in the classroom: Motivational and information components. *Developmental Psychology, 17,* 300–312.

Harter, S. (1982). The Perceived Competence Scale for Children. *Child Development, 53,* 87–97.

Harter, S., Whitesell, N., & Kowalski, P. (1987). *The effects of educational transitions on children's perceptions of competence and motivational orientation.* Unpublished manuscript, University of Denver.

Hawkins, J. A., & Berndt, T. J. (1985, April). *Adjustment following the transition to junior high school.* Paper presented at the biennial meeting of the Society for Research in Child Development, Toronto.

Hedberg, J. D. (1973). Pupil control ideology of middle school teachers and its relationship to student alienation and to selected organizational and teacher variables. *Dissertation Abstracts International, 34,* 1024A–1025A.

Highberger, J. H. (1976). Attitude toward student control and school climate in middle schools and junior high schools. *Dissertation Abstract International, 37,* 2537A–2538A.

Higgins, E. T., & Parsons, J. E. (1983). Social cognition and the social life of the child: Stages as subcultures. In E. T. Higgins, D. W. Ruble, & W. W. Hartup (Eds.), *Social cognition and social behavior: Developmental issues.* NY: Cambridge University Press.

Hill, K. T. (1980). Motivation, evaluation, and educational test policy. In L. J. Fyans (Ed.), *Achievement motivation: Recent trends in theory and research.* NY: Plenum.

Hill, K. T., & Wigfield, A. (1984). Test anxiety: A major educational problem and what can be done about it. *The Elementary School Journal, 85,* 105–126.

Hoy, W. K. (1968). The influence of experience on the beginning teacher. *The School Review, 76,* 312–323.

Hunt, D. E. (1975). Person–environment interactions: A challenge found wanting before it was tried. *Review of Educational Research, 45,* 209–230.

Jennings, K., & Hargreaves, D. J. (1981). Children's attitudes to secondary school transfer. *Educational Studies, 7,* 35–39.

Jones, R. M. (1981). Social characteristics of early adolescents upon entering a middle school. *Journal of Early Adolescence, 1,* 283–291.

Jones, R. M. (1984). Easing the transition from elementary to middle level education. *Dissertation Abstracts International, 45,* 463A.

Jones, R. M., & Thornburg, H. D. (1985). The experience of school-transfer: Does previous relocation facilitate the transition from elementary- to middle-level educational environments? *Journal of Early Adolescence, 2,* 229–237.

Kavrell, S. M., & Petersen, A. C. (1984). Patterns of achievement in early adolescence. In M. L. Maehr (Ed.), *Advances in motivation and achievement* (pp.1–35). Greenwich, CT: JAI Press.

Larson, J. C. (1982). *Middle schools evaluation.* Rockville, MD: Montgomery County Public Schools.

Larson, J. C. (1983). *Middle school evaluation: Final report, technical appendix.* Rockville, MD: Montgomery County Public Schools.

Lee, P. (1979). *A developmental study of children's prerogatives and constraints in several domains of school experience.* Report to the National Institute of Education, Washington, DC.

Leet, P. M. (1974, April). *Socialization, schooling, and society.* Paper presented at the annual meeting of the American Educational Research Association, Chicago.

Lerner, R. M. (1982). Children and adolescents as producers of their own development. *Developmental Review, 2,* 342–370.

Lewin, K. (1935). *A dynamic theory of personality.* NY: McGraw-Hill.

Lipsitz, J. (1977). *Growing up forgotten: A review of research and program concerning early adolescence.* Lexington, MA: Heath.

Maehr, M. L. (1984). Meaning and motivation: Toward a theory of personal investment. In R. E. Ames & C. Ames (Eds.), *Research on motivation in education* (Vol. 1). NY: Academic Press.

Marshall, H. H. (1981). Open classrooms: Has the term outlived its usefulness? *Review of Educational Research, 51,* 181–192.

Marshall, H. H., & Weinstein, R. S. (1984). Classroom factors affecting students' self-evaluations: An interactional model. *Review of Educational Research, 54,* 301–325.

McPartland, J. M., & Karweit, N. (1979). Research on educational effects. In H. L. Walberg (Ed.), *Educational environments and effects.* Berkeley, CA: McCutchan.

Mergendoller, J. R. (1982, April). *To facilitate or impede? The impact of selected organizational features of secondary schools on adolescent development.* Paper presented at the annual meeting of the American Educational Research Association, New York.

Midgley, C., & Feldlaufer, H. (1986, April). *Students' and teachers' decision-making fit before and after the transition to junior high school.* Paper presented at the annual meeting of the American Educational Research Association, San Francisco.

Midgley, C., Feldlaufer, H., & Eccles, J. S. (in press). The transition to junior high school: Beliefs of pre- and post-transition teachers. *Journal of Youth and Adolescence.*

Miller, D. (1974). *Adolescence: Psychology, psychopathology and psychotherapy.* NY: Jason Aronson.

Miller, J. P. (1978). Piaget, Kohlberg, and Erikson: Developmental implications for secondary education. *Adolescence, 50,* 237–250.

Mitchell, J. V. (1969). Education's challenge to psychology: The prediction of behavior from person–environment interactions. *Review of Educational Research, 39,* 695–721.

Mitman, A. L., Mergendoller, J. R., Packer, M. J., & Marchman, V. A. (1984). *Scientific literacy in seventh-grade life science: A study of instructional process, task completion, student perceptions and learning outcomes: Final report.* San Francisco, CA: Far West Laboratory.

Moore, D. W. (1983, April). *Impact of school grade-organization patterns on seventh and eighth grade students in K–8 and junior high school.* Paper presented at the annual meeting of the New England Research Association, Rockport, ME.

Moos, R. H. (1979). *Evaluating educational environments.* San Francisco, CA: Jossey-Bass.

Murray, H. A. (1938). *Explorations in personality.* NY: Oxford University Press.

Neale, D. C., & Proshek, J. M. (1967). School-related attitudes of culturally disadvantaged elementary school children. *Journal of Educational Psychology, 58,* 238–244.

Nicholls, J. G. (1986, April). *Adolescents' conceptions of ability and intelligence.* Paper presented at the annual meeting of the American Educational Research Association, San Francisco.

Nielsen, A., & Gerber, D. (1979). Psychosocial aspects of truancy in early adolescence. *Adolescence, 14,* 313–326.

Nisbet, J. D., & Entwisle, N. J. (1969). *The transition to secondary education.* London: University of London.

Nottelmann, E. D. (1982, March). *Children's adjustment in school: The interaction of physical maturity and school transition.* Paper presented at the annual meeting of the American Educational Research Association, New York.

Nottelmann, E. D. (1987). Competence and self-esteem during the transition from childhood to adolescence. *Developmental Psychology, 23,* 441–450.

Oakes, J. (1981). Tracking policies and practices: School by school summaries. *A study of schooling* (Tech. Rep. No. 25). Los Angeles, CA: University of California Graduate School of Education.

O'Connor, J. L. (1978). Perceptions of self, ideal self, and teacher feelings in preadolescent children. *Elementary School Guidance and Counseling, 13,* 88–92.

Parsons, J. E., & Bryan, J. (1987). Adolescence: Gateway to androgyny. In B. Carter (Ed.), *Psychology of gender roles.* Hillsdale, NJ: Erlbaum.

Passow, H. A. (1966). The maze of the research on ability grouping. In A. Yates (Ed.), *Grouping in education* (pp.161–169). NY: Wiley.

Petersen, A. C. (1980). Biopsychosocial processes in the development of sex-related differences. In J. E. Parsons (Ed.), *The psychobiology of sex differences and sex roles.* Washington, DC: Hemisphere.

Petersen, A. C., & Crockett, L. (1985). Pubertal timing and grade effects on adjustment. *Journal of Youth and Adolescence, 14,* 191–206.

Petersen, A. C., & Ebata, A. (1987, April) *Responses to developmental and family changes in early adolescence.* Paper presented at the annual meeting of the American Educational Research Association, Washington, DC.

Power, C. (1981). Changes in students' attitudes toward science in the transition between Australian elementary and secondary schools. *Journal of Research in Science Teaching, 18,* 33–39.

Prawat, R. S., Grissom, S., & Parish, T. (1979). Affective development in children, grades 3 through 12. *The Journal of Genetic Psychology, 135,* 37–49.

Pritchett, W., & Willower, D. J. (1975). Student perceptions of teacher pupil control behavior and student attitudes toward high school. *Alberta Journal of Educational Research, 21,* 110–115.

Reuman, D., Mac Iver, D., Eccles, J., & Wigfield, A. (1987, April). *Change in students' mathematics motivation and behavior at the transition to junior high school.* Paper presented at the annual meeting of the American Educational Association, Washington, DC.

Rosenholtz, S. J., & Simpson, C. (1984). The formation of ability conceptions: Developmental trend or social construction? *Review of Educational Research, 54,* 301–325.

Rounds, T. S., & Osaki, S. Y. (1982). *The social organization of classrooms: An analysis of sixth- and seventh-grade activity structures* (Report EPSSP-82-5). San Francisco: Far West Laboratory.

Rubenfeld, L. A., & Schumer, H. (1986, April). *Females at risk: Transition from elementary to junior high school.* Paper presented at the annual meeting of the American Educational Research Association, San Francisco.

Sanford, J. P. (1985). *Comprehension-level tasks in secondary classrooms* (R&D Rep. No. 6199). Austin, TX: Research and Development Center for Teacher Education, University of Texas at Austin.

Schulenberg, J. E., Asp, C. E., & Petersen, A. C. (1984). School from the young adolescent's perspective: A descriptive report. *Journal of Early Adolescence, 4,* 107–130.

Schulenberg, J. E., Camarena, P. M., Sarigiani, P. A., & Ebata, A. T. (1986). *Patterns of gender differences in self-image during early adolescence.* Paper presented at the biennial meeting of the Society for Research on Adolescence, Madison, WI.

Schwarzer, R., Jerusalem, M., & Lange, B. (1982). *The development of academic self-concept with respect to reference groups in school.* Unpublished manuscript.

Silberman, C. E. (1970). *Crisis in the classroom.* NY: Random House.

Simmons, R. G., & Blyth, D. A. (1987). *Moving into adolescence: The impact of pubertal change and school context.* Hawthorn, NY: Aldine de Gruyler.

Simmons, R. G., Blyth D. A., Van Cleave, E. F., & Bush, D. (1979). Entry into early adolescence: The impact of school structure, puberty, and early dating on self-esteem. *American Sociological Review, 44,* 948–967.

Simmons, R. G., Carlton-Ford, S. L., & Blyth, D. A. (1987). Predicting how a child will cope with the transition to junior high school. In R. M. Lerner & T. T. Foch (Eds.), *Biological–psychosocial interactions in early adolescence: A life span perspective.* Hillsdale, NJ: Erlbaum.

Simmons, R. G., Rosenberg, F., & Rosenberg, M. (1973). Disturbance in the self-image at adolescence. *American Sociological Review, 38,* 553–568.

Sprinthall, N. A. (1985). Early adolescents and opportunities for growth in the 1980s: Ships passing in the night, again. *Journal of Early Adolescence, 5,* 533–547.

Sweeting, L. M., Willower, D. J., & Helsel, A. R. (1978). Teacher–pupil relationships: Black students' perceptions of actual and ideal teacher/pupil control behavior and attitudes toward teachers and school. *Urban Education, 13,* 71–81.

Thompson, A. (1982, March). *A social climate perspective on early secondary school effects on student behaviors.* A paper presented at the annual meeting of the American Education Research Association, New York.

Thornburg, H. D. (1985, April). *Early adolescent social characteristics: Developmental and school determinants.* Paper presented at the biennial meeting of the Society for Research in Child Development, Toronto.

Thornburg, H. D., & Glider, P. (1984). Dimensions of early adolescent social perceptions and preferences. *Journal of Early Adolescence, 4,* 387–406.

Thornburg, H. D., & Jones, R. M. (1982). Social characteristics of early adolescents: Age versus grade. *Journal of Early Adolescence, 2,* 229–239.

Trebilco, G. R., Atkinson, E. P., & Atkinson, J. M. (1977, November). *The transition of students from primary to secondary school.* Paper presented at the annual conference of the Australian Association for Research in Education, Canberra.

Walberg, H. J., House, E. R., & Steele, J. M. (1973). Grade level, cognition, and affect: A cross-section of classroom perceptions. *Journal of Educational Psychology, 64,* 142–146.

Warburton, S. J., Jenkins, W. L., Coxhead, P. (1983). Science achievement and attitudes and the age of transfer to secondary school. *Educational Research, 25,* 177–183.

Ward, B. A., Mergendoller, J. R., & Mitman, A. L. (1982). *The years between elementary school and high school: What schooling experiences do students have?* (Rep. EPSSP-82-1). San Francisco: Far West Laboratory.

Ward, B. A., Mergendoller, J. R., Tikunoff, W. J., Rounds, T. S., Dadey, G. J., & Mitman, A. L. (1982). *Junior High School Transition Study: Executive summary.* San Francisco, CA: Far West Laboratory.

Wigfield, A. (1984, April). *Relationships between ability perceptions, other achievement-related beliefs, and school performance*. Paper presented at the annual meeting of the American Educational Research Association, New Orleans.

Wigfield, A., & Meece, J. (1987). *Math anxiety in elementary and secondary school students*. Manuscript submitted for publication.

Willower, D. J., Eidell, T. L., & Hoy, W. K. (1967). The school and pupil control ideology. *Pennsylvania State Studies Monograph* (No. 24). University Park, PA: Pennsylvania State University Press.

Willower, D. J., & Jones, R. G. (1967). Control in an educational organization. In J. D. Rath, J. Pancella, & J. VanNess (Eds.), *Studying teaching*. Engelwood Cliffs, NJ: Prentice-Hall.

Willower, D. J., & Lawrence, J. D. (1979). Teachers' perceptions of student threat to teacher status and teacher pupil control ideology. *Psychology in the Schools, 16,* 586–590.

Yamamoto, K., Thomas, E. C., & Karns, E. A. (1969). School-related attitudes in middle-age students. *American Educational Research Journal, 6,* 191–206.

Youngman, M. B. (1978). Six reactions to school transfer. *British Journal of Educational Psychology, 48,* 280–289.

Yuskiewicz, V. D., & Willower, D. J. (1973). Perceived pupil control ideology consensus and teacher job satisfaction. *Urban Education, 8,* 231–238.

6

Perceptions of Classroom Processes and Student Motivation: Children's Views of Self-fulfilling Prophecies

Rhona S. Weinstein

INTRODUCTION

What makes some children love school, become excited about learning, try hard, and persist despite a difficult task? As one fourth grader described this motivational pattern: "an' um you get excited and start doin' your work . . . then you start doin' it better an' better until you get a good report card." What makes other children tune out, turn off, avoid schoolwork, and exhibit lack of interest, is illustrated by this fourth grader's description: "They just sit around. They don't do nothing. And that's why they   they say 'I can't do this' and that means that they just don't want to do it and you tell yourself that you can't. So you just give up on it and you can't do it."

According to another fourth grader, a key to understanding the roots of student motivation lies with the teacher. This student shares that "sometimes my teacher can make you feel very happy because um the teacher really wants you to learn an' stuff."

How can we account for different motivational patterns in children's approaches to school learning? What contributes to feelings of "can do" and "want to do" in children's minds? What roles can and do teachers play?

The motivation to learn is not simply a function of individual differences among learners—that is, a capacity for interest and persistence that children bring with them when they come to school. Motivation to learn is also fostered by daily experiences with learning in the classroom and at school. In the course of such experiences, children develop expectations that they can and will learn and with such expectations, they persist longer at difficult tasks, choose more challenging material, and engage in more task-appropriate behaviors (Eccles & Wigfield, 1985). As one source of influence, the *expectations of teachers* has been found to be a critical variable in the development of children's expectations for their own learning.

That teachers' expectations can become self-fulfilling in the classroom has been long acclaimed since the famous Rosenthal and Jacobson study (1968) as a potent social influence process on student motivation and learning. This chapter examines and integrates findings from our program of research concerned with the *student mediation* of such prophecies in the classroom—that is, how children are affected by and respond to the expression of teacher expectations in the classroom. The goal here is to utilize the student rather than the researcher perspective to characterize the nature of classroom processes that play a pivotal role in differentiating the opportunities available for children to become motivated learners.

In this chapter, I first describe the assumptions that characterize our understanding of self-fulfilling prophecy effects in the classroom, explicating the emerging interest in student mediating processes. Next, I review our findings concerned with students' awareness of differential teacher treatment in the classroom and the associated relationships with other student mediating processes, thereby painting a picture of classroom process that grows from student perspectives. Finally, I look at the implications of children's viewpoints for generating alternative models of expectancy influence that impinge on student motivation.

SELF-FULFILLING PROPHECY EFFECTS IN THE CLASSROOM

THE EXISTENCE OF EXPECTANCY EFFECTS

After more than two decades of research following the much-celebrated Rosenthal and Jacobson (1968) study, "Pygmalion in the Classroom," the existence of expectancy effects is well established. As first elaborated by Merton (1948), expectancy effects are described as interpersonal processes whereby a false definition of a situation evokes new behavior, which then makes the original false conception come true. That is, the false belief becomes self-fulfilling.

Although expectancy processes have been studied in a variety of contexts, such as in health and disease, psychological diagnosis, prejudice, and interpersonal interaction (Jones, 1977), the classroom situation has attracted the largest body of research to date. High interest in the effects of self-fulfilling prophecies stems from its capacity partly to explain the consistently low performance of minority students and the widening gap in performance over the course of schooling documented between minority and nonminority students.

Recent meta-analyses and reviews of classroom expectancy research acknowledge consistent support (in both experimental and naturalistic studies) for the proposition that teacher expectations for student performance can function as self-fulfilling prophecies, with effects documented on subsequent student achievement (see reviews by Brophy, 1983; Dusek, 1985; Rosenthal & Joseph, 1983). However, as Brophy (1983) argues, there are differences of opinion among reviewers in their assessment of the magnitude of such expectancy effects and in its generalizability, given the research conducted to date. Correlational studies of naturally occurring expectations in the classroom, while enriching our understanding of the ecology of classroom life, limit our ability to separate student effects from teacher effects on the outcomes of schooling (Mitman & Snow, 1985). Further, there is considerable evidence that while expectancy effects can happen, they do not always happen—there are sizable teacher differences in susceptibility to expectancy effects in the classroom.

MODELS OF EXPECTANCY INFLUENCE

A variety of theoretical assumptions have been proposed to characterize the processes by which expectations (in particular, teacher expectations) can become self-fulfilling. In their earliest model, Brophy and Good (1970, 1974) suggested the following components of a causal process: on the basis of school records and classroom observation, teachers form differential expectations for student behavior and achievement; differential expectations are then expressed in differential treatment toward students; students then respond with behavior that complements and reinforces teacher expectations.

Braun (1973, 1976), hypothesized that in order for students' achievement to be influenced by teacher expectations, students had to first become aware of the expectancy messages contained in differential treatment. Students' interpretation of teachers' expectations would be critical in influencing their self-image and their motivation to learn, which in turn would become reflected in achievement. Braun also speculated about how learner self-image might be an essential factor in determining the potency that teacher expectancy cues might have for different children.

Brophy and Good (1974) characterized this hypothesized route of expectancy influence as an indirect one, in which achievement changes are mediated by student awareness of expectancy cues and changes in student self-image and motivation. They also speculated about a direct course of influence whereby differential treatment, for example, in the form of exposure to material or opportunity to practice such material, would directly impact student achievement gains without necessarily involving children's awareness.

STUDENT MEDIATION: A MISSING LINK

While theoretical developments provided for the role of student mediating processes as critical variables in explaining how differential treatment could result in the enhancement or the deterioration of student academic performance, no empirical evidence about the indirect route of influence was available. The bulk of the research activity was directed toward a documentation of the communication of teacher expectations in differential interaction patterns in the classroom. When student variables were studied at all, attention was largely focused on the endpoint of influence, that is, changes in children's achievement.

This pattern in expectancy research mirrored the long history of educational research in general, where the voices of children were rarely represented. Primary vantage points for study have been the teacher—teacher attributes, attitudes, and behaviors—and teaching materials or the curriculum. When we have looked to the student in the classroom, our focus has been narrowly placed on the end products of educational intervention—that is, on the achievement of students. It is only recently that we have come to appreciate that children are active interpreters of the classroom reality, as of any social reality, and not simply passive recipients of instruction.

This emphasis is not surprising, given the dominance of a behavioral model of explanation. In recent years, the behavioral (or reinforcement-centered) conception of self-fulfilling prophecies has been gradually replaced with a social–cognitive model, which highlights both teachers' and students' perceptions and cognitions about each others' actions (see Brophy, 1983; Cooper, 1979; Cooper & Good, 1983; Darley & Fazio, 1980; Weinstein, 1983, 1985). Such models incorporate student responses as an important interactive factor in the process. As Darley and Fazio (1980) point out, some students may not be socially perceptive at all or if they perceive the teachers' expectations, they may reject it out of hand and disconfirm the expectations with their behavioral response. Such models allow for individual differences in teachers' and students' interpretations or attributions that may affect susceptibility to expectancy effects.

FRAMING AN APPROACH TO THE STUDY OF STUDENT MEDIATION

My early interest in underlying student mediating processes was stimulated by some puzzling findings from a study of expectancy processes and reading group membership in three first-grade classrooms (Weinstein, 1976). In this study, despite a widening in the gap between highs and lows over the course of the year on a variety of outcomes, evidence for differential teacher treatment favoring high reading groups was not found upon examination of dyadic interaction patterns between teacher and students. Instead, low reading groups were favored with more frequent positive and less frequent critical interactions with the teachers.

Yet, qualitative records of teacher statements directed toward the high reading groups revealed ability statements favoring highs. Further, observers pointed out qualitative differences, although not coded, in the kinds of praise given to highs and lows. Which cues were the students reading and how did they interpret the patterns of teacher behavior?—these were the questions in which we became interested. We turned toward the learner: first, as an important source of information about the transmission of expectancy cues in the classroom, and second, as a critical mediator of its potential influence.

There already existed a growing literature concerned with children's perceptions of classroom environments (e.g., Walberg, 1976). Important relationships were found between classroom environmental attributes (as identified by students) and learning outcomes. Children's perceptions of classroom climate became important as a *source of environmental description*. Yet the perceived climate research relied heavily on the classroom mean of students' observations as the index of environment. In contrast, the teacher expectancy problem focused attention on the possibility that there might exist subenvironments for high and low achievers within classrooms and that children may be able to identify these climate differences.

Children's perceptions also proved to be of interest as a critical link in unraveling relationships between teaching interventions and outcomes—that is, as a *mediator* of such relationships. Both Berliner (1976) and Doyle (1977) argued that children's interpretation of teacher behavior or of text material could operate as critical intervening or mediating processes in the causal pathway between educational intervention and educational outcome. As one example of this mediating process, in a study of teacher structuring, soliciting, and reacting behavior, student perceptions of these behaviors were found to be more critical in predicting achievement than the observed teaching behaviors alone (Stayrook, Corno, & Winne, 1978).

This mediating paradigm (in contrast to the environmental descriptor paradigm) suggests the following: First, what students perceive about teaching behavior may not in fact resemble either teacher intent or observed practice; and second, it is the students' perception–cognition that is ultimately the influential element on achievement. Applied to the teacher expectancy problem, this paradigm focuses attention on the student role in actualizing teacher effects on achievement. This paradigm also underscores the importance of the student perspective rather than the observed classroom reality as a focus of study.

There also existed a vigorous literature on developmental social cognition (e.g., Shantz, 1975) which alerted us that knowledge about developmental regularities in the social understanding of children was vitally important for the task of pursuing student mediational processes in expectation effects. Important cognitive changes as children develop may critically alter (1) the social reality children understand at each grade level, (2) the expected congruence between teacher intent and children's understanding, and (3) the kinds of outcomes expected in children's perceptions of self and of others.

These issues framed our beginning attempts to clarify the nature of children's responses that mediate between the communication of teacher expectations in the classroom and the differential achievement outcomes of students.

OUR RESEARCH STUDIES OF
STUDENT MEDIATION

DEVELOPMENT AND PILOT TESTING OF INSTRUMENTS:
THE SUMMER PROGRAM STUDY

Our initial task was to conceptualize and measure the kinds of processes that intervene between differential teacher treatment and other suppressed or enhanced gains in student achievement. The key assumption made was that differential treatment by the teacher *provides cues* to students about expected achievement.

Teacher cues about expected achievement (when perceived as well as understood) were then hypothesized to influence a child's self-view. That is, a child adopts a self-view in accordance with how significant others behave toward him or her. In turn, out of self-image grow self-expectations about the child's own capacity to perform. These self-expectations can come to influence a child's willingness to attend, to respond, or to continue trying—all behaviors that may affect learner outcomes on standardized achievement tests.

Thus, the learner may or may not (based on individual difference hypotheses) *perceive, interpret, internalize* (into self-expectations), and *act on* the information contained in teacher cues about expected achievement. In clarifying the relationship between teacher behavior and student performance, a systematic investigation of *learner perceptions of teacher treatment* was clearly an important place to start. The needed instruments and the designs of the first study and those to follow grew from the following observations.

Influences on the Design

First, while the classroom expectancy literature had tested hypotheses concerning observed (by research observers, not students) differential treatment by the teacher toward high and low achievers as an expression of teacher expectations, *childrens' perceptions of these differential interactions* had not been assessed. In the classroom-climate literature, which has studied children's perceptions of classroom environments, the research has focused on *classroom-averaged* perceptions about the general climate within the classroom, not on the differential experiences of high and low achievers. Because we wished to assess the latter, a new instrument (the Teacher Treatment Inventory) was developed that would incorporate expectancy-related teacher behaviors and *within-class* comparisons.

In developing the Teacher Treatment Inventory, we chose a methodology that *targets* the type of student for whom an environmental description is desired (for example, a hypothetical low achiever) in contrast to the general or self-descriptions of the classroom climate scales. This approach had a number of distinct advantages: (1) We placed the students in the same role as classroom observers—that is, they were required to rate (not count) the interactions the teachers had with different students, *without* making an explicit judgment about differential treatment. (2) In avoiding the direct assessment of differential treatment, we reduced possible bias in that rating—that is, bias that might reflect stereotypes in beliefs or defensiveness and protection of the teacher. (3) We could expand the application of the instrument to the rating of students who differed on a variety of characteristics, such as gender as well as the ability-level distinction studied here, fully replicating the design of classroom observational studies of differential treatment. (4) By specifying a target student for which all students could describe the environmental context, one could look for both agreements and disagreements in perception among different types of children who were doing the rating. General or self-descriptions of classroom climate cannot distinguish between the effects of individual differences on perceptions and the effects of actual environmental differences.

A second design factor suggested by research was that the perspectives of the student and the observer concerning the nature and meaning of classroom events may well differ (Weinstein, 1976). This finding underscored the importance of investigating children's open-ended constructions of the classroom reality as well as children's ratings of researcher-derived categories of differential teacher treatment. Given children's longer and more extended history in the classroom as compared to observers, and given cognitive changes in children's understanding, children may attend to different expectancy cues. Also, it is important to discern the meaning of differential treatment for children. How does differential treatment signal information about ability differences among the students? Thus, we adopted a multimethod approach in our assessments of children's perceptions, and we included a clinical interview as well as an inventory in our studies. A clinical interview was chosen as a vehicle for exploring children's understanding of their relative smartness in the classroom and the ways in which they learn about their relative academic status.

A third feature of our approach grew from the fact that there was little in the classroom expectancy literature about individual differences in the learner that might mediate his/her susceptibility to teacher feedback (except for the Braun, 1976, hypothesis for the importance of learner self-image). Yet research on the perceptual process in general and student perceptions in particular suggested that the perceptions of others appear to be jointly determined both by the perceiver and by the person who is the object of attention. Thus, we were concerned to examine selected groups of elementary-school-aged children, in a varied student population, representing different age groups and a diversity of achievement levels, gender, and ethnic membership. This enabled an exploration of individual and age-related differences in the capacity of children to process social information from classroom interaction and to apply it to themselves in the form of stable self-perceptions, and ultimately an investigation of differential susceptibility to teacher expectancy effects.

Design and Study Sample

Primary goals of the first study were to develop and pilot test two new instruments—the Teacher Treatment Inventory and the Learning about Smartness child interview. Assessments were carried out in a sample of 102 first through sixth graders who were enrolled in summer enrichment classes in math and computer sciences at a university facility. A separate group of 45 first through sixth graders received the structured interview.

We explored whether children perceived (1) differences in the ways in which their teachers worked with high and low achievers in the classrooms and (2) differences in the attributes of high and low achievers. We also explored whether perceptions (3) were shared across students or (4) were moderated by the characteristics of the perceiver. In this study, we varied the grade level, gender, and perceived ability of the student participants. However, we required ratings only of male high and low achievers in order to simplify the design.

Instruments

The Teacher Treatment Inventory. In developing the Teacher Treatment Inventory (Weinstein & Middlestadt, 1979), we turned largely to classroom observation studies of differential teacher treatment to provide us with the teaching behaviors hypothesized to serve as teacher cues about expected performance. Items depicting a wide range of teacher–student interactions were derived from the research literature (1) on the expression of teacher expectations in teaching behaviors, (2) on relationships between teaching behaviors and achievement, and (3) on student perceptions of classroom climate. The pilot interviews with children also provided insights into the kinds of interactions that differentiated the treatment of students in the classroom.

In completing the 60-item inventory, children were given a description of a hypothetical male student who was either a high or a low achiever in the classroom:

> **High achiever form:** John (Anne) is someone who does really well in school. In fact, he (she) always gets the *best* grades in the class. Everyone thinks John (Anne) is very smart.

> **Low achiever form:** John (Anne) is someone who does not do very well in school. In fact, he (she) usually gets the lowest grades in the class. Everyone thinks John (Anne) is not very smart.

After reading the description of the hypothetical student, the children rated each of the 60 items as descriptive (yes/no) of the hypothetical high or low achiever.

Although the children were assessed out of the context of their regular classroom, they were asked to report about the teacher they had at the end of the preceding school year. Assignment of high and low achiever forms of the Teacher Treatment Inventory to the children was counterbalanced by grade and by gender of the responding children.

"Learning about Smartness" Child Interview.   An interview schedule was developed to examine (1) how children understand "smartness" (its causes and perceived stability and the underlying differentiating characteristics of smart and not-so-smart students), (2) how children perceive the consequences of "smartness" (teacher and peer treatment and the meaning of smartness to teachers, peers, and self), and (3) how children come to learn about their own level of smartness in the classroom.

Perception of Differential Treatment toward Male High and Low Achievers

Based on a comparison of treatment perceptions from the two comparable halves of the sample (rating a male high or low achiever), children reported differential treatment across one quarter of the teacher behaviors studied (Weinstein & Middlestadt, 1979). Thus, we had beginning evidence that children saw differences in the ways in which teachers worked with high and low achievers. Teacher interactions with male high achievers, as reported by the children, reflected high expectations, academic demand, and special privileges. Male low achievers were viewed as receiving fewer chances but greater teacher concern and vigilance.

Of interest, in some cases, the perceptions of the target's treatment were shared by all students; in other cases, grade-level differences as well as characteristics of the perceiver colored perceptions. Without controlling for classroom difference effects, it was difficult to interpret these findings, yet they suggest both the congruence of views among children and the possibility of differential perception.

In adjective ratings made of the male high and low achievers, children perceived differences between the highs and lows in both academic qualities and in characteristics that extended into the social realm of popularity and friendship. These perceived differences in qualities of the target students provide evidence that the instructional set for rating teacher treatment is understood by the children. These adjective differences also suggest the children attribute different characteristics to male high and low achievers in the classroom.

The interviews with children illuminated the subtle distinctions that students made between types of teacher behavior—distinctions that rely on nonverbal as well as verbal messages, and distinctions that have not yet made their way into the observational categories used by classroom observers. As one 10-year-old described the types of teacher praise, praise is "a good long compliment, not 'you did good—goodbye,' but a deep down feeling compliment" (Weinstein & Middlestadt, 1979, p. 429). The results with the Teacher Treatment Inventory and the richer understanding gained from the interviews with children encouraged us to begin a more systematic investigation of children's perceptions of differential teacher treatment.

PERCEIVED DIFFERENTIAL TREATMENT IN A CLASSROOM
CONTEXT: NIE STUDENT PERCEPTIONS OF
DIFFERENTIAL TEACHER TREATMENT STUDY

Next Steps

A necessary next step of the work involved a more systematic investigation of children's perceptions of treatment toward the four types of target children within the classroom—that is, including female as well as male high and low achievers, thus replicating the design of classroom observational studies of the communication of expectations in differential treatment. The full representation of the four achiever types would allow for a separation of teacher treatment effects due to the ability of the target student, the gender of the target student, or an interaction of both characteristics.

A second step concerned a more systematic exploration of the effects of learner characteristics on perceptions. Given an interest in the effects of gender and ability differences among raters on perceptions of treatment, it was important to ensure that student raters were equally represented by gender and ability within each of the four rating conditions. Thus, we moved to a selected sampling for the Teacher Treatment Inventory—that is, to use a randomized block design, distributing rating forms to students on the basis of their gender and ability level. In order to study these perceiver differences more carefully, we sampled within one age group of children—older elementary school children from fourth through sixth grades.

Third, the expectancy hypothesis had not been systematically explored across different classroom environments, although such effects had not been found in every classroom. Further, there existed a growing body of research concerned with what students perceive and how they perform in different organizational settings (e.g., competitive versus cooperative classroom structures; Ames, Ames, & Felker, 1977). We hypothesized that the expression and potency of teacher expectancy cues would be lessened in open-plan classrooms as compared to traditional classrooms because of differences in classroom philosophy and process. In open-plan classrooms, teacher dominance over classroom process is reduced and students play larger roles in decision making. Both the nature and context of evaluation are different, with evidence of broader criteria of evaluation, individualized indices of progress, and more private task-completion rates and teacher feedback.

Thus, it was important to examine student perceptions of differential treatment within varying environments and to make assignments of blocks of subjects within classrooms. This would both enable classroom comparisons and control for or equalize the contributions of any classroom differences to the results. This would also allow for any within-class comparisons in the extent of student agreement of perceptions.

Finally, it was critical to begin to examine relationships between awareness of differential teacher treatment and other child variables hypothesized to follow the perceptions of differential treatment—that is, children's interpretations of differential treatment, children's own expectations for performance, and children's academic and social competence.

Study Design and Sample

Thus, the next study was designed to (1) examine perceptions of treatment of both male and female high and low achievers, (2) explore perceptions of teacher treatment within and as a function of classrooms—in particular, within contrasting classrooms of open and traditional structure, (3) systematically explore the influence of student gender and achievement level on perceptions of differential treatment, (4) develop a coding system to explore the clinical interviews about smartness, and (5) relate the extent of children's perceived differential treatment to child outcomes.

In the spring of a school year, the Teacher Treatment Inventory, measures of self-concept, expectations, and sociometic status were administered to 234 fourth, fifth, and sixth graders from 16 classrooms (8 open and 8 traditional in structure, as nominated by principals). In this study, the achievement level comparison of the TTI was assigned to students within classrooms (in counterbalanced fashion), and the gender comparison was assigned across classrooms. Student achievement scores were collected from the prior year and from end-of-the-year records. A subset of these children (133 fourth graders), representing both male and female high and low achievers from each classroom, were further selected for clinical interviews; these interviews were taped, transcribed, and coded with excellent interrater reliability.

Revision and Factor Analysis of the Teacher Treatment Inventory

Revisions of the instrument included reducing the 60-item inventory to 44 clear and differentiating items and substituting a 4-point rating scale for the yes/no judgment. Thus, children were asked to pretend that the target student was a student in their own class and to rate the frequency (on a 4-point scale, indicated by circles of increasing size) with which their own teacher works with John (Anne) in the way described in each item. In all the studies, items were read aloud so that reading level would not affect performance on the inventory.

Four scales were constructed on the basis of findings from a factor analysis of the Teacher Treatment Inventory (Weinstein, Marshall, Brattesani, & Middlestadt, 1982). The first scale, labeled Supportive Help (alpha = .75), describes the variety of ways in which the teacher helps the student and provides support. Scale 2, Negative Feedback and Teacher Direction (alpha = .77), reflects both negative feedback from the teacher and teacher control over the student's activities. Scale 3, Work and Rule Orientation (alpha = .71), describes an emphasis by the teacher on monitoring the student and a focus on learning, getting the work done, and following the rules. Scale 4, High Expectations, Opportunity, and Choice (alpha = .80), reflects trust by the teacher, positive feeling, and feedback, and the provision of opportunities to participate and work in autonomous ways.

Reported Differential Treatment toward High and Low Achievers

The early findings of reported differential teacher treatment were replicated with fourth–sixth graders in the spring of the school year using a revised and factor-analyzed version of the Teacher Treatment Inventory (Weinstein et al., 1982). Here, three of the four Teacher Treatment Inventory scales significantly differentiated the treatment of high and low achievers. Based on a comparison of treatment profiles obtained from comparable subsets of students within each classroom, children reported systematic differences in how the teacher works with high and low achievers in the classroom. Children described low achievers as the recipients of more negative feedback and direction from the teacher and more work- and rule-oriented treatment than high achievers. On the other hand, high achievers were reported to receive higher expectations and more opportunity and choice from the teacher than low achievers.

Differential teacher treatment toward high and low achievers was reported by children regardless of the gender of the target student that children rated. That is, high and low achiever treatment differences were reported for both boys and girls. Further, gender differences in reported treatment on these particular interaction patterns were not large. The salient distinction in treatment that children reported concerned the differential treatment of high and low achievers.

Achievement and Gender Differences in Children's Reports of Differential Treatment

In this more tightly controlled study, where the Teacher Treatment Inventory (TTI) was assigned to students within classrooms in a randomized block fashion, such that equal numbers of male and female high and low achievers within the classroom filled out male and female high and low achiever forms of the TTI, neither high nor low achievers were more sensitive in detecting differential treatment by the teacher toward high and low achieving target student. Further, the gender of the student subject was not related to their perceptions of differential treatment toward high and low achievers (Weinstein et al., 1982).

These findings suggest that children within a classroom, regardless of their gender and their achievement level, share similar perceptions of teacher treatment. That both high and low achievers agree about the extent of differential treatment suggests that a general climate description of a classroom, obtained by averaging the perceptions of all the students about their own experiences, may mask the existence of different climates that coexist for high and low achievers within the same classroom.

Classroom Characteristics and Perceived Differential Treatment

Open–Traditional Structure and Children's Perceptions of Differential Treatment. In this study, we compared children's perceptions of differential treatment in two contrasting types of classroom environments, an open education philosophy (where, on the basis of more individualized instruction, one might expect more equitably distributed positive treatment), as contrasted with a traditional educational approach. In this sample of 16 fourth through sixth-grade classrooms, nominated by administrators as reflective of an open or a traditional philosophy and validated by teacher reports of classroom practices, we failed to find a relationship between classroom type and degree of differential treatment reported by the students (Weinstein et al., 1982).

Classroom Variability in Degree of Differential Treatment Reported by Children. Yet a test of classroom differences in degree of differential treatment reported revealed great variability across classrooms, with students in some classrooms reporting a great deal of differential treatment, and students in other classrooms, very little differential treatment. Of interest, the variability in degree of differential treatment reported was not linked to the average achievement level of the students within the classroom.

Although we could not yet explain this classroom variability in the degree of differential teacher treatment present, this variability was consistent with the findings of the observational literature. This led us in future analyses to distinguish between classrooms, and in this case to do so on the basis of student-perceived criteria. We then constructed a class-level index of the degree of differential treatment perceived by students; using this index to create a median split within each sample of classrooms we studied, we then identified high and low differential treatment classrooms. Given classroom variability in children's reports of the frequency of differential treatment, we wanted to study students' responses to teacher expectancy cues in the context of different classroom environments as well as to identify the correlates in teacher beliefs and teacher practices that were associated with much or little differential treatment as identified by students.

Children's Perception and Understanding of Differential Treatment

Our findings demonstrated that children were aware of differences in the ways that their teacher worked with high and low achievers in the classroom—and in some classrooms these differences were large; in other classrooms, very minimal. In our interviews with a subset of fourth graders, we examined the nature of children's understanding of differential treatment by the teacher and explored the relationship between teacher interaction patterns and children's developing sense of ability in the academic world.

Teacher Practices Provide Clues about Student Ability.   In these interviews, we first asked children to rank their own achievement relative to their classmates and then we asked how they had learned about their own level of smartness in school. Overwhelmingly, children referred to teacher practices (66% of the clues), as the source of information, as compared to self-evaluation, peer, or parental behaviors (Weinstein, 1981). Of interest, feedback practices were the primary teacher cue reported by children in this sample. Over all the teacher cues cited, 79% involved feedback practices, 18% involved instructional practices and 1% involved climate factors such as the quality of teacher–student relationships (2% were noncodable). Marks, checks, display of performance were the most frequent source of feedback cited.

When children were asked to specify what teachers did to alert them to good or poor performance, feedback practices continued to be salient, except that reinforcement behaviors such as praise and criticism were more frequently cited than were marks, and still other instructional practices emerged as important.

Model of Classroom Factors.   We were impressed by the broad range of clues that children reported as informative about their relative smartness and we identified six critical aspects of teachers' strategies that communicated expectations to students (Marshall & Weinstein, 1984; Weinstein, 1986). In addition to feedback practices in the evaluation of performance, children read clues about ability in the differentiation (1) of assignments of tasks to students ("one person will be doing the harder work"), (2) of patterns used to group children for instruction ("I wanted Miss——to put me in a smarter group"), (3) of motivational strategies used for instruction (highs could "read any book they want, lows "can't choose what they read because they need it"), (4) of responsibilities given to learners ("The way you know a person is smart, Miss——always picks them to go different places"), and (5) of quality of teacher–student relationships ("you can really tell just by the way she treats people who are doing well"). (Feedback practices are the sixth aspect of teacher strategies that communicate teacher expectancies.)

Subtle, Complex, Single-Incident Clues. An examination of the interviews also points out the subtle distinctions that children make between types of teacher behavior. Such distinctions give clear information about relative rank in the classroom achievement hierarchy, such as the following example:

> Sometimes she says, "Oh, that's very poor reading" to someone else and she says "pretty good" to me and sometimes . . . I kind of marked myself in the middle on reading because . . . to other people she says "excellent reading." (Weinstein, 1986, p. 243)

Further, not only are children alert to differences in the frequency of teacher behavior patterns toward different children but they also cite single critical incidents that are vividly reported and that convey information about ability, such as the following:

> Well, one person, (X), her pulse is bad, she just jumps up and hollers too much and skips around. She (the teacher) says "Sit down, dumb Dora," my teacher says that and everyone starts laughing. (Weinstein, 1981, p. 11)

Thus, these sometimes subtle, complex, and often infrequent teacher behaviors appear to offer children information about their own ability relative to their classmates.

Children also relate specific teacher behaviors to how they feel about themselves and the effort they are likely to expend. For example, one fourth grader described his feelings as follows:

> She has another funny way of looking at you. Not only that she is not smiling though. She's looking mad, unhappy, disappointed. She gets that look and says "I am very disappointed in you." I hate that feeling. I hate it. I hate when she does

> that. . . . She makes me feel like I've just started school today. It makes me feel like I'm stupid. Just dumb, crazy, stupid, dumb. (Weinstein, 1985, p. 345)

Another fourth grader describes a possible change in attitude:

> Like if the teacher always yells at you whenever you do something wrong—if you don't understand something and she yells at you and says "You should already know"—then you might not do as well. You might say, "Well, I don't like that part."

And another fourth grader mentions a change in effort:

> Between that time I moved up in groups. She (the teacher) says that you could do more better if you try and I think that I just didn't try because other people was just saying—well, you can't do that. So that's one of the reasons why I moved up. I say—well forget them, I'm gonna try at least, and so I did.

Classroom Type and Public Nature of Teacher Behavior Patterns. When fourth-grade children described the kinds of cues they used to learn about their relative smartness in the classroom, children's presence in perceived high or low differential treatment classrooms did not largely affect the kinds of cues they used to learn about smartness and about good and poor performance. However, the extent to which these cues occurred in public varied by type of classroom. For example, 77% of children in perceived high differential treatment classrooms as compared to 57% of children in perceived low differential treatment classrooms reported at least one public teacher communication about poor performance (Weinstein, 1981). As an example, the teacher might "point out the good and bad students" or there might be "a chart that shows how we are doing."

Perceived Differential Treatment and Child Outcomes

Given children's awareness of differential treatment by the teacher toward peers, and given variability by classroom in the reported frequency of such differential treatment, we further explored how reports of differential treatment were related to children's expectations, to their academic achievement, and to their social competence with peers.

Children's Expectations. After controlling for initial student differences in achievement, we compared the degree of association between teacher expectations and student expectations in two types of classrooms that differed in degree of differential treatment reported by the students. Comparisons were made using sets of regression equations calculated separately for students in the eight high- and eight low-differential-treatment classrooms.

Student expectations were more strongly associated with teacher expectations in classrooms where students reported greater differential usage of work and rule orientation and of high expectations, opportunity, and choice, but not of negative feedback and teacher direction (Brattesani, Weinstein, & Marshall, 1984). These findings provide evidence, in this fourth–sixth-grade sample interviewed in the spring of the school year, for greater congruence between children's own expectations and the expectations of teachers in classrooms where children report more ability-related cues from the teacher. This suggests that this information may be utilized by children in forming their own expectations for performance.

Achievement Outcomes.   To what extent does degree of differential treatment present in the classroom moderate the relationship between teacher expectations and year-end achievement among the students. In this NIE student perceptions sample (Brattesani et al., 1984), we repeated the design of analyses that we had conducted for the children's own expectations, and ran separate regression analyses for the eight high and eight low differential treatment classrooms. After controlling for initial achievement differences among the children, teacher expectations predicted more of student year-end achievement in those classrooms which students had identified as high in differential teacher treatment than was predicted in low differential-treatment classrooms. In these high-differential-treatment classrooms, teachers' expectations explained an additional 9% to 18% of the variance in student achievement, whereas in low-differential-treatment classrooms, teachers' expectations explained only an additional 1% to 5% of the achievement variance. These different predictive patterns in high- and low-differential-treatment classrooms as identified by children provide an important source of validation for the children's perceptions and underscore a link between perceptions (awareness) of differential treatment and achievement.

Social Competence Outcomes.   Not only are academic indices affected by teacher expectancy processes, but evidence also exists to suggest that social competence indices are affected as well. Utilizing the fourth-grade NIE student perceptions sample, Botkin and Weinstein (1987) examined children's perceived and actual social competence in the two types of classroom environments. In classrooms where children reported much differential teacher treatment as compared to classrooms with little differential treatment, children's ratings of both their academic and their social competence were more highly correlated with their academic rank in the classroom as measured by teacher expectations.

Further, the salience of differential treatment cues was not only related to perceived competence measures but also to actual friendship choice patterns among the children, clearly an important aspect of being socially competent. Children for whom the teacher held low expectations were more likely to be chosen as work partners on a sociometric measure in low as compared to high-differential-treatment classrooms, whereas no differences existed in the likelihood with which high teacher expectancy children were chosen in the contrasting classroom environments. These differences in nomination however did not hold for play choices. Yet, for both work and play choices, more crossover choices (that is, highs choosing lows and lows choosing highs) occurred in low-differential-treatment classrooms as compared to high-differential-treatment classrooms, suggestive of more social interaction among groups of children differing in academic performance.

Perhaps underlying these differential patterns of friendship choices are attitudes held about the children which are framed by the classroom experience. Our summer program study documented that children perceived the high achiever males (whose treatment they had rated) to be more popular, friendly, competitive, attentive, independent, and successful but not more powerful than the low achiever males (Weinstein & Middlestadt, 1979). The NIE Student Perceptions study interview data revealed that such perceived differences in characteristics between high and low achievers may be in part a reflection of the salience of expectancy cues in the classroom. In low-differential-treatment classes, children saw fewer differences in the task orientation of high and low achievers than they did in high-differential-treatment classrooms (Marshall, Weinstein, Sharp, & Brattesani, 1982).

THE ECOLOGY OF CHILDREN'S ACHIEVEMENT
EXPECTATIONS OVER TIME: DEVELOPMENTAL,
CLASSROOM, AND PARENTAL INFLUENCES IN THE
NIE–NIMH–SPENCER FOUNDATION STUDIES

Further Steps

Following this study of fourth–sixth graders, our next step was to systematically explore age-related differences in children's perceptions and responses to the classroom processes that communicated academic expectations for them. Thus, we utilized a cross-sectional approach, sampling children from classrooms at three grade levels (grades 1, 3, and 5).

Second, we wished to gain a firmer grasp of the ecology in which children's expectations were formed, and we sought a triangulated approach whereby we could learn and interrelate perspectives from the children, the teachers, observers of classroom structure and process, and the parents. Third, we sought to replicate as well as expand upon the measurement of distinct child processes which mediated between differential treatment and achievement outcomes. Fourth, we continued to explore individual differences in children's awareness of and susceptibility to teacher expectancy effects. Finally, we examined these processes at several intervals over the course of the school year so that we could capture change and explore the successive steps through which teacher prophecies for students became self-fulfilling.

Thus, in this study, we were interested in providing a descriptive base of knowledge about how children at different stages of development and at different phases of their elementary-school career perceive and interpret teachers' treatment of male and female students of high and low academic status. Further, our goal was to delineate the relationship between different classroom environments, perceived differential treatment, and student outcomes, as well as to document the specific classroom processes that underlie these relationships. Finally, we hoped to begin the process of integrating parental expectations and actions with teacher expectations and classroom processes in the task of explaining and predicting children's achievement expectations and performance. Knowledge gained from this study would be critical for enlightening our understanding of classroom environments where children can feel competent and achieve.

Design and Samples

The first study (a reliability study) tested 318 children from 26 first, third, and fifth-grade classrooms, again in the spring of the school year, in order to adapt the Teacher Treatment Inventory (TTI) for usage with children as young as first graders and to assess test–retest reliability of the measure.

A second study assessed 579 children, their teachers, and their parents from 30 classrooms, 10 each at the first-, third-, and fifth-grade level during the fall of the school year. Age comparisons in children's reports of differential treatment were specifically explored. In this study, all target comparisons between gender and achievement levels on the TTI were assigned in counterbalanced fashion to children within classrooms. Entering and year-end achievement scores were also available for the children.

A carefully defined subsample of children and their teachers was then followed over time. On the basis of student identification of the extremes of high- and low-differential-treatment classrooms, and representing male and female high and low achievers in each of the selected classrooms, a subset of 144 children and their 12 teachers were chosen for more extensive study (through classroom observation and clinical interviews) and a retesting on all the measures during winter–spring of the school year. This follow-up provided an opportunity to watch the unfolding of self-fulfilling prophecies over the course of a school year and to compare the phenomenon across children of different ages. Analysis of these data still continue; hence, only partial reporting of the results are available here.

Adaptation and Revision of the Teacher Treatment Inventory

A third revision of the TTI was undertaken in order to clarify items and to extend its applicability from upper elementary school age children to children as young as first graders (Weinstein, Marshall, Sharp, & Botkin, 1987). The original 60-item inventory has now been reduced to 30 items, which have been factor analyzed into three internally consistent scales of 10 items each, reflecting *Negative Feedback and Teacher Direction* ("the teacher scolds John/Anne for not trying"; "the teacher chooses the books John/Anne will read in class"), *Work and Rule Orientation* ("the teacher asks other children to help John/Anne"; "the teacher explains the rules to John/Anne"), and *High Expectations, Opportunity, and Choice* ("The teacher trusts John/Anne"; "The teacher asks John/Anne to lead activities").

Stability of Treatment Perceptions.   The reliability study demonstrated that reports of teacher treatment of the targeted students proved stable over a 2-week test–retest period for all the age groups of children studied (Weinstein et al., 1987). Thus, perceptions of the frequency of teacher interaction patterns with different types of students are not spurious reports but reflect somewhat enduring processes in the classroom, available for student interpretation.

Class-Level and Individual-Level Determinants of Differential Treatment.   Within each classroom, the profile for high-rated and low-rated achievers within each gender group were compared, and the resulting difference in the frequency of teacher interactions on each scale reflected children's perceptions of the degree of differential treatment expressed by the teacher. In the previous studies, based on randomized block assignment procedures (by achievement level and gender of the responding student) within each classroom, subsets of comparable students rated the treatment of only one type of targeted student and the profiles obtained from these subsets of students were then compared. In this study, the preceding method was repeated, and, in addition, children rated teacher interactions with both high and low achievers, although at separate times, to yield an individually derived measure of perceived differential treatment.

Self and Brief Versions of the Teacher Treatment Inventory. The format of the TTI has also been adapted to yield a self version—that is, children are asked to describe their teachers' interaction with them. A short version of the TTI has also been developed. This is an 8-item global measure of the degree of differential treatment perceived, based on a selection of the most differentiating items across the three scales, with adequate inter-item consistency.

Age and Classroom Differences in Children's Awareness of Teacher Expectations

This study specifically targeted age comparisons in children's reports of differential teacher treatment, this time examined in the fall of the school year. Again, the results largely replicated earlier findings of reported differential treatment, importantly demonstrating this pattern early in the school year, as compared to our previous studies of children's perceptions of teacher treatment obtained in the spring. No significant age differences between first, third, and fifth graders emerged in reports of differential treatment.

Children as young as first graders reported differences in the teacher treatment of high and low achievers in the classroom—differences that favor high achievers with more positive treatment and differences that appear regardless of the gender of the high or low achiever rated. In children's eyes, low achievers are more likely to have their activities structured by the teacher and to receive help and negative feedback, whereas high achievers are more likely to be trusted, asked to perform, and given freedom of choice (Weinstein et al., 1987).

While age was not a factor with regard to perceptions of differential teacher treatment toward others, age-related differences played a role in children's awareness of how differential treatment applied to themselves. As measured in the fall of the school year, younger children were less accurate than older children in predicting the specific expectations that their teachers held for them. Younger children were also less likely than older children to see their own treatment from the teacher as consistent with their expectancy status in the classroom. Being a member of an identified high-differential-treatment classroom did not accelerate their awareness.

Yet, despite these differences in the accuracy of perceptions, younger children were still likely to report expectations for themselves which were congruent with their teachers' expectations for them in those classrooms that children had identified as reflecting a great deal of differential treatment. Less congruence of teacher–student expectancies was found in low-differential-treatment classrooms (Weinstein et al., 1987). Also, children for whom the teacher held low expectations reported significantly lower expectations themselves than did children for whom the teacher held high expectations, but only in those classrooms where children reported more differential treatment. No significant differences in expectancies were found between high and low teacher expectancy students in classrooms with little reported differential treatment.

Of interest, these classroom differences appeared despite the fact that high- and low-differential-treatment classrooms did not differ at entry in the mean achievement level of their students or in the spread of achievement represented in these classrooms. Further, these patterns held best for first and third graders but not for fifth graders. An examination of the means by grade level in light of an almost significant interaction with grade suggested that by fifth grade, children for whom the teacher held low expectations reported low expectations themselves in both kinds of classrooms. This trend is suggestive of developmental differences that might play a role in differential susceptibility to expectancy processes.

These results underscore critical age or grade differences in children's awareness of and inferred responsiveness to teacher expectations in the classroom, appearing in the fall of the school year. Fifth graders appear to be more sensitive to teacher expectations (or to their academic status), regardless of the salience of differential treatment cues in the classroom. Although younger children demonstrate less awareness, they do identify the presence of differential treatment and for these children, greater perceived differential treatment is associated with greater congruence between children's expectations for themselves and their teachers' expectations for them.

Classroom Correlates of Differential Teacher Treatment

To date in our analyses, we have examined selected aspects of teacher beliefs and teacher practices in contrasting high- and low-differential-teacher-treatment classrooms, as identified by students at three grade levels.

Teacher Expectancy Beliefs.   We have found that teachers' expectations patterns for students vary by classroom (Weinstein, Marshall, Botkin, & Sharp, 1985). In classrooms where, according to student report, teachers greatly differentiated the treatment of high and low achievers, teachers' expectations were more consistent and less changeable from fall to spring as compared to teachers in low-differential-treatment classrooms. Further, in the high- as compared to low-differential-treatment classrooms, despite the lack of classroom differences at entry in the correlation of students' reading and math achievement scores, teachers' expectations for student reading performance more strongly mirrored their expectations for student math performance. This suggests that high differential treatment teachers are more likely to hold a unidimensional concept of ability (Rosenholtz & Simpson, 1984), where smartness in one area suggests smartness in other areas, whereas low-differential-treatment teachers view abilities in reading and math as more distinct.

Teacher Practices.   Our examination of teacher practice differences between the two types of classrooms come from spring observations of classroom structural and interactional patterns in selected first-, third-, and fifth-grade classrooms at the extremes of student-reported (in the fall) high and low differential treatment. Our observation system combined quantitative and qualitative perspectives and attempted to capture the classroom structural and interactional factors that affect children's views of their own ability (Marshall & Weinstein, 1986). Our model of these factors grows from an analysis of the child interview data and pilot classroom observations (Marshall & Weinstein, 1984).

The proposed model is a complex one, in that certain teaching strategies may compensate for or negate the effects of other teaching strategies in influencing children's interpretations and reactions to classroom events. For example, a teacher's expressed attitude about errors as a point of learning can mitigate the negative effects of public errors in a whole-class responding situation.

In conducting an observational study of 12 of the classrooms at the extremes of perceived high and low differential treatment, the intent was not to validate children's perceptions of differential teacher treatment (measured in the inventory at a dyadic and behavioral level). Rather, our goal was to more fully describe the classroom organizational and social processes that are associated with these differences in children's judgments.

The comparisons suggested few quantitatively coded differences between the types of classrooms in the direction of our hypotheses, except at fifth grade, and enormous variability within and between teachers in the use of different teaching strategies (Marshall & Weinstein, 1986). On the other hand, qualitative analyses (for example, of a high- and a low-differential-treatment classroom at fifth grade) suggested far more subtle differences in the ways in which teachers *minimized* or *maximized* the social comparison information available to the students. These differences appeared (1) in the implementation of classroom tasks and accompanying performance opportunities (the holding up of individual answer cards for the teacher's eyes only, in contrast to public responses), (2) in the grouping of students for instruction (the use of heterogeneously grouped families for seating and study periods, in contrast to ability-based seating), (3) in the feedback provided (focus on mistakes as part of the learning process, in contrast to public display of students making errors), (4) in the motivational strategies used (the use of competition between heterogeneous families against the teacher or the prior class record, in contrast to competition between high and low achievers), (5) in the responsibility given to students (in student participation in evaluation, in contrast to teacher control of evaluation), and (6) in the nature of teacher–student relationships (warmth and humor, in contrast to threats and demands). In the low- as compared to high-differential-treatment classroom, more strategies that minimized opportunities for the comparison of student ability levels were documented.

Work in Progress

Analyses of this database are continuing. We are pursuing an examination of the course of expectancy processes over time in child-identified high- and low-differential-treatment classrooms. And we are exploring the role of children's self-concept as a mediator of susceptibility to teacher expectancy effects and examining relationships between individual differences in what children perceive about teacher behavior and their susceptibility to achievement changes. Work is also ongoing concerning the relative contributions of parental and teacher expectations to children's views about themselves.

CONCLUSIONS

Let us look now at these findings as a whole and what they tell us, from the child's point of view, about the unfolding of self-fulfilling prophecies in the classroom. First, these findings suggest that children are observers (and highly sensitive observers at that) of teacher behavior patterns in the classroom. Not only do children monitor their own interactions with the teacher, they also show awareness of how the teacher interacts with other children in the classroom, especially children identified as high and low achievers.

Children report differences in the frequency of teacher interactions with different types of students. High achievers are seen as receiving more opportunities to perform, to be challenged, and to serve as leaders as well as more positive feedback from the teacher. Low achievers are seen as receiving more teacher direction and structure, more help-giving and more frequent negative feedback.

Children also make subtle, qualitative distinctions between types of teacher behavior, and appear influenced by single, critical incidents, which when seen in the context of the particular classroom history, convey meaningful messages to students. Differential treatment cues lie in the tasks children are given, in the experiences that stem from the grouping arrangements used in teaching, in the opportunities to perform and the feedback given for performance, in the strategies used to motivate students, in the responsibilities given students for their own learning, and in the teacher–student relationships that develop. They reflect differences in opportunity, in feedback, and in the climate surrounding learning.

Supportive evidence for children's awareness of differential teacher treatment is also found in a study by Cooper and Good (1983). High teacher-expectancy students, when asked whether these interactions occurred more often, about the same amount, or less often than classmates, reported more frequent favorable interactions than did low teacher-expectancy students. In this study, student estimates of teacher treatment were in the same direction as observational records of the frequency of interactions, although not reaching significance. Mitman and Lash (in press) also report children's perceptions of teacher interactions as both consistent and inconsistent with observer data.

Regardless of whether such perceived differential treatment is consistent with observed patterns of treatment, regardless of whether recurring patterns of differential treatment can be viewed as either appropriate instructional practices (e.g., help-giving) or reactive to large student differences in performance (e.g., the greater use of negative feedback), the continued presence and/or perception of *consistent* differences in treatment patterns is informative about the needs of or expectations for groups of children. One purpose then for children's careful comparative observation and interpretation of teacher interaction patterns lies in the information it yields about one's place in the classroom achievement hierarchy. Thus, children can learn about their relative smartness from the patterns of teacher interaction with peers and with themselves.

Second, consistent with the observational literature (Brophy, 1983), classroom differences emerged in children's reports of the degree of differential teacher treatment. Some, but not all, teachers sharply differentiated the treatment of high and low achievers in their classroom. Such variation in frequency of differential treatment patterns was not found to be linked with teachers expressed philosophy of education, such as open as compared to traditional views of teaching. Yet, despite extremely variability in type of practices within classrooms, evidence for subtle differences in the strategies teachers used emerged between high- and low-differential-treatment classrooms. Teachers in high-differential-treatment classrooms held more stable and global expectations for their students than did teachers in low-differential-treatment classrooms.

Third, children's identification of differential treatment at a classroom level proved to be associated with and predictive of children's academic as well as social competence. That is, children's reports of differential teacher treatment distinguished classrooms where expectancy-consistent processes occurred from classrooms where such processes were not evident. At a classroom level, children's awareness of differential treatment mediated the relationship between teacher expectations and student outcomes.

In classrooms where children reported extensive differential treatment by the teacher toward high and low achievers, the low-teacher-expectancy students, themselves, reported less favorable teacher treatment and lower expectations for their future performance than did high-teacher-expectancy students, and their year-end achievement was more consistent with teacher expectations. These low-teacher-expectancy students also saw themselves as less cognitively as well as less socially competent and were, in fact, less often chosen by peers on sociometric measures, than did high-teacher-expectancy students. In sharp contrast, in classrooms where children reported little or no differential teacher treatment, such differences between the expected high and low performers were not seen. These classroom differences in patterns of children's self-perceptions and performance, which were associated with reports of differential teacher treatment, were evident despite the fact that at the start of the school year, student-identified high and low differential treatment classes did not differ in mean achievement level or in the spread of achievement of its students represented in the classroom.

Thus, in classrooms where achievement cues are more salient to children, differences among students are greater, suggesting that children may utilize the cues available to interpret their own interactions with the teacher and to set their own expectations for future performance. Expectations for success or failure are critical determinants of the degree of effort children expend and ultimately become reflected in performance. Other studies have also documented the powerful mediating effect of classroom context in shaping ability perceptions of students (Mitman & Lash, in press; Rosenholtz & Simpson, 1984). The accentuation of student differences in classrooms with more salient achievement cues extends beyond academic performance to social relationships. Perceived and actual social competence of low performers suffers in classrooms where children report that the teacher differentiates the treatment of high and low achievers.

The important finding here is that these are classroom differences that children identify—that is, children's perceptions mediate children's outcomes, providing support for the increasingly important role of students' thought processes in classroom instruction (Marx, 1983; Weinstein, 1983; Wittrock, 1986). These are also correlational findings and thus we cannot entirely rule out the possibility that student performance differences drive teacher expectations. However, the strength of a teacher effect interpretation lies in the observed relationships between a consensual identification by classes of children about differential treatment and patterns of outcomes among subgroups of children within those classrooms, despite the absence of achievement differences at entry. Also, the consistency of the findings across a wide array of student outcomes is suggestive of a classroom culture that sustains or accentuates student differences.

Finally, there is emerging evidence for both the consistency of teacher expectancies and the individual and developmental differences in children's awareness of and response to teacher expectations in the classroom. This has also been true in recent studies of childrens' perceptions of the ability and the behavior of themselves and their classmates (e.g., Blumenfeld, Pintrich, & Hamilton, 1986; Rohrkemper, 1985; Stipek & Tannatt, 1984). We have strong evidence that a child's achievement level and gender are not related to their perceptions of differential teacher treatment. Thus, for example, both high and low achievers within a classroom have a common understanding of a low achiever's experience. We also have evidence that children as young as first graders do not differ from older elementary school children either in their identification of differential teacher treatment or in the patterns of self-expectations that are associated with the salience of achievement cues. Yet substantial age or grade differences do exist in the extent to which younger children are accurate in predicting their teachers' expectations and in the responsiveness of older children, particularly low-teacher-expectation students, to teacher expectancy cues.

IMPLICATIONS AND FUTURE DIRECTIONS

THEORY

These findings suggest revisions in existing models of the mediation of teacher expectancy effects in the classroom, which have focused largely on the teacher (Brophy, 1983). Our findings point to the central role of **students** in the mediation of such self-fulfilling prophecies: in children's identification of differential teacher treatment and teacher expectations, and in their differential responsiveness to teacher cues, as a function of age or other individual differences. Children's perceptions are an important source of information about classroom expectancy effects.

Children's viewpoints also teach us that the teacher–student dyad is not the only unit of analysis for the transmission of expectancy effects. Instead, teacher treatment of peers is as salient a source of information as teacher treatment of self. A singular focus on the teacher–student dyad does not capture the complexity of how children understand their classroom reality. Thus, the social groupings within and between classrooms become critical arenas for comparative information.

Further, *explanatory models* for the transmission of expectancy cues need to move beyond behavioral theories that place teacher reinforcement behaviors as the critical mechanism underlying student change in achievement toward a cognitive-mediational model of transmission (e.g., Cooper & Good, 1983; Darley & Fazio, 1980; Weinstein, 1985), which takes into account the social–cognitive capacities of children and their awareness and interpretation of different patterns of teacher behaviors and the ensuing implications for their own self-views. Here the incorporation of context is critical—the social, structural, and cultural factors that perpetuate and compound expectation effects and that create norms and a climate whereby achievement differences between students are accentuated. Changes in these explanatory contructs also mean (1) changes in the unit of measurement of expectancy transmission away from behavioral interactions toward more qualitative assessments of structures, norms, and practices that serve to create the culture of the classroom (Marshall & Weinstein, 1986), as well as (2) broadening of the unit of analysis through linkages between teacher expectations for individual students and teacher expectations for intact groups within classes, for intact classes, for tracks, for schools, for school districts, and for nations.

Finally, children's viewpoints underscore the dynamic interrelationships that should be incorporated into our theoretical understanding of expectancy effects in the classroom. As it stands, our current formulations are rather static, with regard to context, time period, and expected outcomes. Insights from children's perspectives suggest that we must distinguish between teachers and classrooms in our search for expectancy effects (teachers vary in their expression of expectations), and we must search for consistencies or inconsistencies across subject matter (expectations may be generalized by both teachers and students). Expectancy processes and children's understanding may well change over the course of a school year, and effects may be compounded and cumulative across school years. Such longitudinal studies will help to separate the relative contribution of student versus teacher effects in the cyclical process of expectancy influence. Thus, we are talking about capturing entire school careers in order to separate developmental change from life experience effects. Only in this way can we come to understand differences in the experiences of low-teacher-expectancy students from fifth grade as compared to from first grade. Our theories must also address the complex interrelationships between the development of academic competence and social–emotional competence. Peer relationships are forged in the context of academic exchanges, and as such, our explorations of the outcomes of teacher expectancy effects must be expanded to include social as well as academic indices.

RESEARCH

That teacher expectation effects exist has been well established. Given existing models of conceptualization and operationalization in current research paradigms, if anything, we may well be underestimating the extent and the impact of such expectancy effects on children.

The next steps in future research require an investigation of the compounded, generalized, and cumulative processes of expectations in schooling—a context-specific and longitudinal study of children's schooling careers where classroom and school effects and academic and social effects can all be integrated. In that context, we must ask what factors lead children to resist teacher expectations; here, parental expectations and age-related changes may prove critical. We must also ask what factors support teachers in their development of more positive classroom environments for all students. In identifying children and teachers at risk for expectancy effects, we must also identify factors that improve resilience. This knowledge will prove critical for developing interventions to prevent the effects of negative self-fulfilling prophecies in the classroom and in schooling. Here, student perceptions of teacher behavior and the instruments developed for our studies can provide important information about classroom life. Student perceptions can be used to identify classroom environments and teachers more prone to teacher expectancy effects and can assess the impact of change.

INTERVENTION

Our findings also underscore the validity of children's viewpoints, in that identification of extreme differential teacher treatment was associated with expectancy-consistent differential outcomes. As researchers, teachers, child clinicians, and parents, we can listen and learn from children's perceptions of their school environment, and we must, at times, advocate for change. Children's perspectives can determine the need for intervention. This means getting a full picture of what school looks and feels like to the individual child—What is the full range of opportunities? Does the teacher see that the child has potential? Does the environment support the building of academic competence and social friendships?—and working toward change. At a classroom level, such information is also useful for teachers and for staff-development efforts.

Few of us, whatever our relationship to elementary school classroom life, may be aware of how actively and how sensitively children monitor teacher behavior and teacher–child interaction patterns for clues about their smartness relative to their peers. A greater understanding about how teaching practices can diminish or enhance children's expectations for mastery in learning might well serve to prevent some of what we come to define as school failure.

ACKNOWLEDGMENTS

This research was supported by grants from the National Institute of Education (NIE-G-79-0078), (NIE-G-80-0071), the National Institude of Mental Health (#R01 MH34379), and the Spencer Foundation. The opinions reflected here do not necessarily reflect the position or policy of these agencies, and no official endorsement should be inferred.

REFERENCES

Ames, C., Ames, R., & Felker, D. (1977). Effects of competitive reward structure and valence of outcome on children's achievement attributions. *Journal of Educational Psychology, 69,* 273–287.

Berliner, D. C. (1976). Impediments to the study of teacher effectiveness. *Journal of Teacher Education, 27,* 5–13.

Blumenfeld, P. C., Pintrich, P. R., & Hamilton, V. L. (1986). Children's concepts of ability, effort, and conduct. *American Educational Research Journal, 23,* 95–104.

Botkin, M. J., & Weinstein, R. S. (1987). *Perceived social competence and friendship choice as a function of differential teacher treatment.* Manuscript in preparation.

Brattesani, K. A., Weinstein, R. S., & Marshall, H. H. (1984). Student perceptions of differential teacher treatment as moderators of teacher expectation effects. *Journal of Educational Psychology, 76,* 236–247.

Braun, C. (1973). Johnny reads the cues: Teacher expectation. *The Reading Teacher, 26,* 704–712.

Braun, C. (1976). Teacher expectation: Socio-psychological dynamics. *Review of Educational Research, 46,* 185–213.

Brophy, J. E. (1983). Research on the self-fulfilling prophecy and teacher expectations. *Journal of Educational Psychology, 75,* 631–661.

Brophy, J. E., & Good, T. L. (1970). Teachers' communication of differential expectations for children's classroom performance: Some behavioral data. *Journal of Educational Psychology, 61,* 365–374.

Brophy, J. E. & Good, T. L. (1974). *Teacher–student relationships.* New York: Holt, Rinehart & Winston.

Cooper, H. M. (1979). Pygmalion grows up: A model for teacher expectation communication and performance influence. *Review of Educational Research, 49,* 389–410.

Cooper, H. M., & Good, T. L. (1983). *Pygmalion grows up: Studies in the expectation communication process.* New York: Longman.

Darley, J. M., & Fazio, R. H. (1980). Expectancy confirmation processes arising in the social interaction sequence. *American Psychologist, 35,* 867–881.

Doyle, W. (1977). Paradigms for research on teacher effectiveness. In L. S. Shulman (Ed.), *Review of research in education* (Vol. 5). Itasca, IL: Peacock.

Dusek, J. B. (Ed.) (1985). *Teacher expectancies.* Hillsdale, NJ: Erlbaum.

Eccles, J., & Wigfield, A. (1985). Teacher expectations and student motivation. In J. B. Dusek (Ed.), *Teacher expectancies* (pp. 185–226). Hillsdale, NJ: Erlbaum.

Jones, R. A. (1977). *Self-fulfilling prophecies.* Hillsdale, NJ: Erlbaum.

Marshall, H. H., & Weinstein, R. S. (1984). Classroom factors affecting students' self-evaluations: An interactional model. *Review of Educational Research, 54,* 301–325.

Marshall, H. H., & Weinstein, R. S. (1986). Classroom context of student-perceived differential teacher treatment. *Journal of Educational Psychology, 78,* 441–453.

Marshall, H. H., Weinstein, R. S., Sharp, L., & Brattesani, K. A. (1982, March). *Students' descriptions of the ecology of the school environment for high and low achievers.* Paper presented at the meeting of the American Educational Research Association, New York.

Marx, R. W. (1983). Student perceptions in classroom. *Educational Psychologist, 18,* 145–164.

Merton, R. K. (1948). The self-fulfilling prophecy. *Antioch Review, 8,* 193–210.

Mitman, A. L., & Lash, A. A. (in press). The consistency of student perceptions of differential academic class standing and class behaviors with other indicators. *Elementary School Journal.*

Mitman, A. L., & Snow, R. E. (1985). Logical and methodological problems in teacher expectancy research. In J. B. Dusek (Ed.), *Teacher expectancies.* Hillsdale, NJ: Erlbaum.

Rohrkemper, M. (1985). Individual differences in students' perceptions of routine classroom events. *Journal of Educational Psychology, 77,* 29–44.

Rosenholtz, S. J., & Simpson, C. (1984). The formation of ability conceptions: Developmental trend or social construction. *Review of Educational Research, 54,* 31–64.

Rosenthal, R., & Jacobson, L. (1968). *Pygmalion in the classroom: Teacher expectations and pupils' intellectual development.* New York: Holt, Rinehart and Winston.

Rosenthal, R., & Joseph, G. (1983). The bases of teacher expectancies: A meta-analysis. *Journal of Educational Psychology, 75,* 327–346.

Shantz, C. U. (1975). The development of social cognition. In E. M. Hetherington (Ed.), *Review of child development research* (Vol. 4). Chicago: University of Chicago Press.

Stayrook, N. G., Corno, L., & Winne, P. H. (1978). Path analyses relating student perceptions of teacher behavior to student achievement. *Journal of Teacher Education, 29,* 51–56.

Stipek, D. J., & Tannatt, L. M. (1984). Children's judgement of their own and their peers' academic competence. *Journal of Educational Psychology, 76,* 75–84.

Walberg, H. L. (1976). The psychology of learning environments. In L. S. Shulman (Ed.), *Review of research in education* (Vol. 4). Itasca, IL: Peacock.

Weinstein, R. S. (1976). Reading group membership in first grade: Teacher behaviors and pupil experience over time. *Journal of Educational Psychology, 68,* 103–116.

Weinstein, R. S. (1981, April). Student perspectives on achievement in varied classroom environments. In P. Blumenfeld (Chair), *Student perspectives and the study of the classroom.* Symposium conducted at the meeting of the American Educational Research Association, Los Angeles.

Weinstein, R. S. (1983). Student perceptions of schooling. *Elementary School Journal, 83,* 287–312.

Weinstein, R. S. (1985). Student mediation of classroom expectancy effects. In J. B. Dusek (Ed.), *Teacher expectancies* (pp. 329–350). Hillsdale, NJ: Erlbaum.

Weinstein, R. S. (1986). The teaching of reading and children's awareness of teacher expectations. In T. E. Raphael (Ed.), *The contexts of school-based literacy.* New York: Random House.

Weinstein, R. S., Marshall, H. H., Botkin, M., & Sharp, L. (1985, April). *The development of student performance expectations.* A paper presented at the American Educational Research Association meetings, Chicago.

Weinstein, R. S., Marshall, H. H., Brattesani, K. A., & Middlestadt, S. E. (1982). Student perceptions of differential teacher treatment in open and traditional classrooms. *Journal of Educational Psychology, 75,* 678–692.

Weinstein, R. S., Marshall, H. H., Sharp, L., & Botkin, M. (1987). Pygmalion and the student: Age and classroom differences in children's awareness of teacher expectations. *Child Development, 58,* 1079–1093.

Weinstein, R. S., & Middlestadt, S. E. (1979). Student perceptions of teacher interactions with male high and low achievers. *Journal of Educational Psychology, 71,* 421–431.

Wittrock, M. C. (1986). Students' thought processes. In M. C. Wittrock (Ed.), *Handbook of research on teaching* (3rd ed.; pp. 297–314). New York: Macmillan.

7

A Cognitive-Processing Analysis of Motivation within Classroom Tasks

Philip H. Winne
Ronald W. Marx

INTRODUCTION

In contemporary research on both teaching and learning from teaching (e.g., Corno & Snow, 1985; Walberg, 1980; Winne, 1985a), the construct of students' motivation plays an important role. Researchers' theoretical interests about motivation parallel teachers' practical concerns. Veenman (1984) reviewed studies that investigated beginning teachers' perceptions of problems they face. He found that teachers ranked problems about motivating students above other obviously important issues such as the effective use of different teaching methods, a knowledge of subject matter, and the effective use of textbooks and curriculum guides.

Research and theory about motivation presented in this and the preceding volumes of this series (Ames & Ames, 1984, 1985) has advanced progressively. Noteworthy in this work is an increasing emphasis on motivation as a phenomenon of thinking beyond one of feeling (Weiner, 1984). In our nonpositivist world, however, there remains yet more to explore and to explain. In particular, several fundamental concerns need further examination: What initiates students' motivational cognitions? How do cognitive activities that concern motivation intermingle with what students know both about themselves and about the knowledge they have and are acquiring about subject matter? What is the experience of motivation while students work on classroom tasks in academic workplaced (Doyle, 1983)?

In this chapter, we attempt to raise a number of questions concerning cognition and motivation and to sketch a framework for seeking answers to them. First, we describe selected aspects of human motivation. This establishes a foundation for considering students' motivation as a subset of this broader topic. Tasks and activity structures are the classroom situations we consider as contexts within which to analyze students' experiences of motivation. Tasks and activity structures are logical models that describe what students are doing in classrooms and the context of their actions. In the chapter's second section, we define and describe tasks and activity structures. Based on these analyses, our final section explores issues about students' motivation per se. Here, we pose questions about motivation in terms of current knowledge about how students perform tasks within activity structures. In partial response to the questions we pose, we also sketch some parts of a framework for future research, attempting to focus on two issues: (1) how motivation "happens," and (2) the role motivation plays in situations where students are expected to learn from instruction.

WHAT ARE THEORIES OF MOTIVATION FOR?

Theory and research about motivation attempt to account for three interrelated aspects of behavior. One aspect concerns which particular behavior a person will perform in a given situation when other potential behaviors could have been performed. For instance, after a teacher has asked a question, why do some students bid to answer the question by raising their hands while others appear to avoid this opportunity as best they can? We take as an axiom that the choice among alternative behaviors is not random. Rather, behavior and the thought that underlies it are purposeful and directed toward goals. Motivational researchers aim to explain how goals are selected and how they influence students' paths toward goals.

A second aspect of behavior targeted in research about motivation is the temperament of the person's behavior. Temperament is a feature of behavior that modulates and colors how the behavior is enacted. Temperamental variables found in previous research include a person's capacity for resisting distraction while enacting the behavior and the "intensity" with which the behavior is enacted. In classroom situations, questions about temperament are common. For instance, why are some students able to ignore the chatter of groupmates whereas some of their peers seem equally as able to disregard the punctuation exercises on the worksheet before them? Why does one student practically "attack" those same exercises, checking and rechecking which rules apply about using apostrophes, while others approach the work with leisure or even indifference?

The third aspect of behavior that has been a focus in motivational research is persistence. Under conditions that allow a person to continue behaving in a particular way, persistence is gauged by the time allocated to or taken up by a particular behavior. In instructional settings, questions about persistence also are typical. Why do some students work tirelessly on dissecting a frog while others' time spent on this activity is minimal?

MOTIVATION IN TEACHING

Two diferent issues about students' selecting, tempering, and persisting at behavior arise in instructional settings. First, teachers are responsible for assuring that students achieve educational objectives. In order to promote, facilitate, or develop students' knowledge and skills in any subject, contemporary research about learning converges on at least one clear prescription: Teachers must arrange for students to engage in cognitive activities in which they manipulate and transform information. Because any form of engagement involves students in selecting, tempering, and persisting at behavior, motivation is a necessary feature of learning in classrooms. According to most theories, motivation influences or determines (1) students' selection of covert and overt means for interacting simultaneously with the subject matter and with the social features of classrooms, (2) temperamental aspects of this interaction, and (3) how long students will interact. In brief, a positive state of motivation is a necessary condition for students to learn from instruction.

The second way in which motivation is important to teaching is that, in addition to being a logically necessary condition for learning by virtue of its definition, motivation is an objective to be achieved. All reasonably exhaustive formulations of educational goals describe educated students as selecting certain behaviors over others (good citizenship, problem-solving approaches to conflict), having particular temperamental characteristics (tolerance, open-mindedness, interest), and persisting to reach personal objectives (self-direction) and sustain societal norms (the right to free speech). In this view, motivation is a product of instruction.

MOTIVATION AND COGNITION

Motivation, then, is both a condition under which instruction can be effective, and it also is a result of effective instruction. These characteristics combine to create two important properties of motivation: it is recursive and simultaneous. By recursive, we mean that motivation depends on and is a function of itself. As a condition for learning from instruction at a particular time, a state of motivation is influenced by prior states of motivation which, in turn, depended on motivation as a condition for behavior that led to reaching those states. By simultaneous, we mean that, at any time that motivation plays a role in behavior, it is both a process and a product, a means and an end. Students' motivation both propels behavior and is a state of being. Theoretically, students update motivational states while simultaneously performing cognitive activities that involve those motivational states.

This feature of motivation, its "recursive simultaneity," is not unique to views of motivation. For instance, models describing how students read for comprehension (e.g., Samuels & Kamil, 1984), work to solve math problems (e.g., Mayer, Larkin, & Kadane, 1984), and reason about information (e.g., Johnson-Laird, 1983) describe cognitive events in much the same ways as we just described motivation. A student can be in a motivated state at the same time that motivation is exercised as a process that transforms behavior. Correspondingly, a student can be in a state of partial comprehension at the same time that further comprehension strategies are being applied to enhance comprehension.

For instance, consider a student who is reading Shakespeare's bawdy dialogue in the opening scene of *Romeo and Juliet*. The language is not contemporary and, without a clear sense of its import, much meaning about the setting of the tragedy is lost. Electing to hypothesize what unfamiliar words mean and then checking those hypotheses by looking at explanatory footnotes at the end of the text is one way to seek understanding. The student might just as well have skipped those words, or substituted best guesses and read on. This student is in a motivated state—she judges herself to be efficacious and perceives that the extra help she seeks in the footnotes is worth the additional effort and is not a sign of stupidity. She is exercising motivational processes as she carries out the cognitive tasks of hypothesizing and monitoring. Correspondingly, she has comprehended enough of the text to frame hypotheses about what new words mean, and she engages a particular cognitive strategy to confirm those hypotheses.

In our view, the overlap of these descriptions about both cognition and motivation is not accidental. Our sense is that cognitive research, which investigates topics such as reading comprehension, problem solving, and reasoning generally, is considered to be more advanced than research on motivation. To the extent that this perception is valid, we believe it is explained by two facts.

First, research about, say, comprehension, problem solving, and reasoning almost always has limited its purview to comprehension, problem solving, and reasoning. Very few studies of these genres complicate methodology and theory with motivational variables (cf. Corno & Snow, 1986). Instead, these genres of research seem to assume that, across individuals and within one individual who is performing several tasks (e.g., several subtraction items on a worksheet), motivation is either a constant or it is a random but uninfluential factor in performance. A students' *capability* to exercise cognition is the focus of these studies rather than the selection, temperament, or persistence of cognition as these three variables are conceptualized in research about motivation. In studies about motivation, students also engage in activities that entail comprehending, problem solving, or reasoning. These activities provide a context for motivational processes to occur and for motivational products to emerge. However, because contemporary theories of motivation posit that students select, temper, or persist at cognitive and behavioral activities partly as a function of their perceived capabilities, motivational research needs to consider cognitive capabilities jointly with motivation. This complicates research about motivation.

Second, more so than motivational researchers, cognitive researchers have paid substantially more attention to what students are doing in the acts of comprehending, problem solving, and reasoning. The state of the art for analyzing tasks that students perform in cognitive research is much more developed and is applied much more regularly than in research on motivation. A major goal of this chapter is to survey means for repairing this imbalance. This will not prove as difficult a job as might be predicted because there is a great deal of common ground between the two areas. In fact, we contend that almost all that is needed is to throw a bit of light on motivational ground using the same lamp as cognitive researchers have used to illuminate what students do cognitively. This lamp—a view of tasks and activity structures—is the tool we use to address the fundamental questions about motivation that we raised earlier.

TASKS AND ACTIVITY STRUCTURES

Since the late 1970s, the concepts of classroom tasks and activity structures have emerged, and have been extended and refined (Berliner, 1983; Doyle, 1983). Both tasks and activity structures are concepts for describing or measuring classroom events. A first order of business is to describe what tasks and activity structures are, and what distinguishes them.

TASKS

Etymological analysis reveals that the word *task* has deep and informative roots. The tap root for the word task reaches into *taxa,* a word of Middle Latin meaning to impose a tax—that is, a payment of money or performance of service for use by a government or for benefit of the public. There also are secondary roots. One of these branches into todays' verb *to apprise,* which is a modification of the past participle of the French verb *apprendre,* meaning to learn. Another root branches into the Latin *reprobare,* today's verb *to reprove,* meaning to address words of disapproval to someone. A third root digs into today's word *to praise.* In turn, *praise* derives jointly from the Latin *pretium* meaning a price; and the Latin *pretiare,* which underlies today's verb *to prize,* to value or esteem highly. If ever there was a word that (1) suggested we address students' motivation and its integration with cognition to support students' learning from teaching, and (2) linked a student with the teacher (*qua* a government or authority) and with classmates (*qua* a public), *task* is it.

Teachers pose tasks for students to perform for at least three different reasons: (1) to collect information about students for instructional decision making, (2) to involve students directly with processing information or practicing skills in order to learn, and (3) to demonstrate knowledge or skill for a group by having one student model it. Tasks also are situations in which students can be reproved or praised by their teacher, their classmates, or themselves. Performing a task has a price that the student must pay. There are two methods of payment: (1) energy expended in performing the task plus (2) forgoing other equally or more valued options. Finally, performing a task may yield something that the student values or esteems highly.

There are many ways to define and model a task. Regardless of the approach one takes, fundamental decisions must be made about two issues. First, where are the boundaries of a task? This issue concerns how a task will be separated from the complex background of the classroom in order to analyze the task. In general, definitional qualities of the boundaries of a particular task must provide rules for differentiating one task from another task and for differentiating tasks from nontasks. Some of the questions that must be answered about the boundaries of a task are (1) When does a particular task start? (2) When does a particular task end? (3) Are there intervals of time during which a student is performing no task?

Second, within the boundaries of a task lies the task's territory, and this territory can be experienced differently depending on one's perception of it. In classroom settings, there are two clearly separable perspectives from which a task can be viewed (Winne, 1985b). One is that of the student performing a task. The second is the perspective of an outsider: either the person who poses the task, such as a textbook author or researcher; or the person who observes a student performing the task, such as a teacher or classmate.

THE COPE MODEL OF TASKS

In earlier work, we have individually (Marx, 1983, 1985; Winne 1985a, 1985b, 1985c) and jointly (Marx, Winne, & Walsh, 1985; Marx & Walsh, 1988) described what tasks are, as have others (cf. Doyle, 1983). This work has led to a model of tasks that can be described in terms of a COPE unit. *COPE* is an acronym representing four facets: conditions, operations, products, and evaluations.

Conditions.   Conditions for a task can be described in terms of three main components, as shown in Table 1. First, a task is about some *content*. From the point of view of cognitive theories about learning from teaching (Winne, 1985a; Winne & Marx, 1987), content can be divided into two separate domains: declarative knowledge and procedural skills (Gagné, 1985).

Declarative knowledge can be further subdivided into three types (Winne, 1985c): (1) primitive structures of meaning called concepts (e.g., a triangle, a friend, pride); (2) propositions in which two concepts are linked by a third, wherein the third concept forms a relationship between the first two (e.g., "good teachers are dedicated workers," "I like science"); and (3) schemata, structured collections of propositions that describe complex, meaningful wholes (e.g., classroom routines such as seatwork and lecture).

TABLE 1

Components of Conditions in the COPE Model of Classroom Tasks

Content	Setting	Presentation
Declarative knowledge	Resources	Medium
Concepts	Social features	Goals
Propositions	Time allocation	Performance cues
Schemata		
Procedural skills		
Pattern recognition		
Action oriented		

Procedural skills have a schematic form: IF a set of conditions is true, THEN an action is performed. Procedures can be subdivided into two types—pattern-recognition procedures and action-oriented procedures—based on what action is required (Gagné, 1985).

Pattern-recognition procedures classify a set of IF-conditions as instances of a concept, proposition, or schema. An example of a procedural skill related to recognizing an instance of a concept is: "IF a mathematics word problem states the rate at which an object is moving and the amount of time that the object is in motion, and IF it requires an answer stating the distance covered, THEN the problem is a rate and distance problem." Pattern-recognition procedures are preliminaries to successful problem solving and, once learned, have been shown to improve performance significantly (Hutchinson, 1986).

Action-oriented procedures invoke operations that transform information or the external environment IF a set of conditions is true. An action-oriented procedure might follow a student's positive identification of a word problem as a rate and distance type. IF the word problem is a rate and distance type, the student could THEN use action-oriented procedures to transform verbal information into an algebraic equation involving d, r, and t; and proceed to solve the equation for the unknown.

These two types of procedures also appear in theories of motivation. For instance, attributions are expressions of declarative knowledge. Techniques for self-regulation (see Corno & Rohrkemper, 1985) embody procedural skills. Whereas differences between declarative knowledge and procedural skills tend to dominate researchers' perspectives, teachers and students typically view content in terms of subject matter topics such as arithmetic, art, or spelling (Doyle, 1986). There is little classroom-based research that has investigated whether declarative knowledge and procedural skills are differentiated by teachers as they teach (Clark & Peterson, 1986) or by students as they grapple with academic tasks (Marx, Winne, & Walsh, 1985; Wittrock, 1986).

The second component of a task's conditions is the *setting* of the task. Setting is an amalgam of environmental variables that surround the task per se. Classroom tasks are embedded within a setting that could be characterized in terms of a potentially huge number of variables, not all of which bear on the task or influence it. Other features of the setting nonetheless may influence how students perceive and perform the task. Examples of setting features can be (1) the resources available while a student works at the task (Doyle, 1983) such as a calculator; (2) social features of interaction between the teacher and student (e.g., Mehan, 1979) and among students in small groups (e.g., Lindow, Wilkinson, & Peterson, 1985); and the time allocated to a task by the teacher or peers. Setting is often assumed to be a constant or near-constant for a given task, although it is likely that features of the setting change during a task (Marx & Walsh, 1988).

The third component of a task's conditions is the *presentation* of the task itself. Three clusters of variables describe presentation: (1) the medium of presentation, (2) the description of a target outcome or goal for the task, and (3) cues embedded in the presentation about how students might or should perform the task. For instance, a task may be presented orally, in which case information about it is transient; or the task may be presented on a worksheet, in which case information about it is relatively permanently and continuously available. The goal of the task may be described clearly and in detail, or it may be withheld, as is common in discovery-oriented tasks. Cues about how to perform tasks (see Winne, 1985b) can be present or absent, and can be of different types (e.g., "Reread . . ." vs. "Mentally rehearse . . .") and more or less directive in terms of what students "should" do (e.g., "Make an outline first . . ." vs. "You might consider the main points before . . .").

Operations.   The *O* in COPE represents operations that are applied when students perform tasks. Operations are cognitive activities that transform information in working memory, along with associated behaviors that manipulate the external environment. We postulate that there are five primitive cognitive operations that process information in the cognitive system: stimulating, monitoring, assembling, rehearsing, and translating (Winne, 1985a, 1985c). These five operations are considered primitive because they cannot be analyzed into more elementary aspects of cognition. By forming an acronym, the five cognitive operations can be referred to as the SMART operations. Each of the SMART cognitive operations can be distinguished from the others by (1) the attributes of information that is input to the operation and (2) the products that each operation produces. Secondarily, each operation can be distinguished by (1) the number of units of information on which it operates, and (2) the control or effort a student must exert to apply the operation.

Stimulating is the operation that transfers information stored in long-term memory to working memory. Information that is presently active in working memory serves as the input to stimulating. The product of stimulating is other information (retrieved from long-term memory) that is made "active" so that it can be operated on. When an item of information is active in working memory, other content in long-term memory that is associated with the item has an increased probability of entering working memory. The principle that accounts for this increase in the probability that information will enter working memory is the principle of *spreading activation* (Anderson, 1983). Spreading activation is like a ripple spreading over a pond. Content closely associated to the information at the center of the ripple is more likely to enter working memory, provided that capacity is not exceeded. Stimulating is a simple operation. It operates on only one item of information at a time, cannot be controlled, and therefore seems effortless.

An example of stimulating is presented by Stein (1986) in her discussion of the acquisition of writing skills. Based on research investigating a wide range of learning and performance situations, from reading and writing to problem representation and solving, Stein argues that students first must form in working memory a context for writing in which focal information is embedded. Only after this context has been formed can the writer proceed to generate written text. Stein illustrates this principle by describing a young girl who, as preparation for a subsequent writing task, was given the prior task of describing her feelings about her aunt's wedding. In order to describe her feelings, the girl first recalled considerably detailed information about events and activities at the wedding. Re-instantiating this detailed information about the events of the wedding, in turn, provided the girl with information she needed in order to stimulate information about her feelings. Once information about feelings was active, the girl could proceed with writing her essay.

Monitoring performs matching or comparison. This operation takes as input features describing two items of information that are active simultaneously in working memory. The features of one item serve as criteria against which features of the second item of information are assessed. Monitoring operations produce a profile of matches and mismatches. These profiles can be coded either as a list of dichotomous hits and misses or along a continuum of similarity. Monitoring is a controlled and effortful operation.

Stein's young writer also provides an example of monitoring operations. As the girl tells her story of events that occurred at the wedding, she also has active in short-term memory information about the task she is to perform, to describe her feelings. As stimulating operations supply information to working memory about what happened at the wedding, each event is compared against her internal propositions about what feelings are in order to determine whether the events contain information about feelings. Matches specify information about her feelings that the girl would write about in her essay.

Assembling takes as input at least two items of information that are active in working memory. Its output is a new relation between two items of information. The output of assembling is often monitored for its fit to another item of information that is active in working memory so that only particular relations are developed—namely, relations that fit criteria for performing the task. Assembling is controllable and effortful.

Returning to the example of Stein's young writer, suppose the girl's teacher had instructed her to use new vocabulary words in the essay about her feelings at the wedding. Suppose further that the teacher had provided a list of feeling words that were not previously in the girl's lexicon. In the presence of task information ("describe your feelings"), these new words are assembled with active information in working memory (the wedding story) to provide new relations. "When my sister walked down the aisle, I was: excited–*thrilled*." "As I saw my sister drive away with Bob, I felt: like I would miss my sister—*regretful*."

It is important for our later arguments to emphasize here that the new relations assembled in working memory, the links between stimulated events about the wedding and new vocabulary words, may or may not be stored in long-term memory. If they were, the girl would then have a new understanding of her feelings at the wedding as well as having a larger lexicon of words to use when asked to describe her feelings in other similar situations.

Rehearsing is the operation that transfers to long-term memory information that is newly placed in working memory or that was created there by other operations. Hence, the product of rehearsal is a change in the network of long-term memory. Rehearsal operates on one item of information at a time. It is highly controllable and effortful. The young writer would be rehearsing if she repeated to herself the newly assembled proposition, "Being excited means the same as being thrilled."

Translating is an operation that recodes one item of information into another code. The output of translating is not new information, but rather a different version of old information. Classic examples of translating involve imagery, although we intend that translating also encompasses alternative encodings of information that do not entail

changes of mode (Bruner, 1966). The young writer would be performing translating operations if she created vivid mental images of what she
looked like when she experienced the different feelings at the wedding,
while the teacher described the meanings of the new feeling words.
Translating is controllable and effortful.

Products.   The SMART operations can be distinguished in part by the
type of products that they yield (see Table 2). For example, the product
of *stimulating* operations is newly active information (transferred from
long-term memory into working memory). The product of *assembling*
operations is a relation between/among items of information that are
active in working memory. *Rehearsal* transfers information from working memory into long-term memory. *Translating* yields information that
has been recoded into a new format. All cognitive operations performed
on content produce such cognitive products. These products are themselves content and, therefore, are either concepts, propositions, or
schemata. In the context of an ongoing task, such as solving a problem in
several steps, it can be useful to conceive of products as updates to
previous content. Over time, as a student works on a task, products
establish successive cycles of newer frameworks for content, that is,
newer conditions.

Also, from the point of view of the classroom teacher, there are
observable products of cognitive operations in the form of student
behavior (e.g., answers to questions, requests for explanations, looks of
puzzlement, and so forth). In our research (Winne & Marx, 1982), we
found that teachers' sense of the word *task* was dominated by these
observable features of students' behavior rather than by conceptualizations of the mental operations that students use to carry out a
classroom task.

Evaluations.   This final attribute of the COPE model for a task reflects
the fact that tasks are occasions for students to approach goals. In order
for the student performing a task to know whether goals have been
reached, the products yielded by operating on the task must be
considered in relation to information that characterizes the goals of the
task. This information, labeled *evaluations* in the COPE model, is
generated when students monitor actual products vis-à-vis criteria that
describe the goals of the task. Thus, evaluations and products are both
information about content, but they are distinguished by one critical
feature: products of a task *are* the goals of the task, or they are
approximations of those goals; evaluations are information *about* those
products vis-à-vis goals. Evaluations can be provided by external sources

TABLE 2

Operations and Products in the COPE Model of Classroom Tasks

Operation	Input	Number of items	Effort	Product
Stimulating	Information in working memory (active information)	1	Effortless	Information in long-term memory is activated, transferring it to working memory
Monitoring	Active information about features; one item serves as a basis for comparison	2	Effortful	Profile of matches and mismatches in working memory
Assembling	Active information	≥2	Effortful	New relation(s) between active items in working memory
Rehearsing	Active information	1	Effortful	Copy and transfer active information into long-term memory
Translating	Active information	1	Effortful	Recoded version of originally active information in working memory

such as a teacher, a classmate, or the answer section of a textbook. Evaluations also are available within the cognitive system as the products of self-directed cognitive operations, the phenomenon commonly labeled *metacognition* (Flavell, 1976).

Two significant characteristics are denoted by the word *evaluation*. First, evaluations can assess products "coldly," in terms that are nonaffective and nonemotional. Second, although it is not necessarily the case, evaluations carry information that can raise a student's values, affects, and emotions to a conscious level. In terms of our earlier analysis of cognition, this is explained by assuming that information in evaluations can stimulate propositions about value, affect, and emotion, thereby making them active in working memory where they are experienced (Zajonc, 1980). In short, an evaluation of a product describes that product in relation to a goal and simultaneously is sufficient to arouse value, affect, and emotion (Buck, 1985; Weiner, 1985).

Recap

In this section, we developed a 4-part typology for describing tasks. We encapsulated this typology in the acronym COPE. The *C* refers to conditions of the environment within which students pursue a task. These conditions were divided into three main sets: (1) *content,* the declarative and procedural knowledge that a student encounters in the external and cognitive environments while performing the task; (2) *setting* factors that may influence how students perceive and perform the task; and (3) the *presentation* of the task as described by its medium, a statement of goals, and cues that can guide students about how the task might be performed.

The *O* in the typology designates cognitive operations that a student uses to perform a task. Five primitive operations, the SMART operations, were described: stimulating, monitoring, assembling, rehearsing, and translating. Each operation was distinguished by the nature of content input to it and output from it.

The *P* of the COPE model reflects products that are the results of operations carried out on content. Products are open to further processing or to storage in long-term memory. New products that are encoded into the network of content in long-term memory constitute the cognitive prerequisites for learning.

Finally, *E* refers to evaluations that update the student about the status of the task vis-à-vis goals. Evaluations can stimulate both neutral information and affect by virtue of the nature of entries in long-term memory.

IMPORTANT FEATURES OF COGNITION INVOLVED IN
PERFORMING TASKS

Research about human cognition in general and about students' cognition in particular has generated rich and extensive findings. We discuss that three features of cognition that influence our analysis of motivation as a phenomenon in students' pursuit of classroom tasks (Calfee, 1981; Winne, 1985b; Wittrock, 1986). These features were identified by applying three criteria: (1) They are highly representative of contemporary theories of cognition, (2) they are firmly supported by empirical research, and (3) they have implications for our later analysis of motivational cognition.

Interactions between Knowledge-Driven and Data-Driven Cognitive Processing

Cognition involved in performing nontrivial tasks is an interaction between top-down or knowledge-driven processing and bottom-up or data-driven processing. *Knowledge-driven processing* means that once a student has characterized a particular task in terms of a known category of tasks, default values are assigned for some features of the task that are not explicitly supplied from the environment. For example, a common task in elementary school classrooms is to learn the spellings and definitions of words in a list. This word-meaning task is highly routinized, and the routine is followed virtually every week of the school year. After the first few weeks of school in the fall, teachers rarely have to specify all of the parameters for this task when it is introduced because students have learned a schema or script (Schank & Abelson, 1977) for it. When they recognize a truncated pattern of features that matches their script for the word-meanings task, they stimulate the script for this task and it supplies default values for parameters that the teacher has not provided.

These defaults have special implications for students' use of schemata in procedural form—that is, in IF–THEN format. In pattern-recognition procedures, knowledge-driven processing provides a mechanism to interpret incomplete or noisy patterns of information obtained from the environment. When information is missing or garbled, pattern recognition procedures assign a default value for such information, based on the student-selected category of tasks in terms of which a particular event is being interpreted. Returning to the word-meanings example, all a student needs to know about the task is that it is "the word meanings for the week." If the list always has 10 words on it and only 9 are written on the chalkboard, the students will invariably ask the teacher what the 10th word is because their pattern of slots for this task specifies that the task involves 10 words. In action-oriented procedures and organized clusters of these procedures that make up what cognitive psychologists label *production systems*, knowledge-driven processing allows chains of action sequences to run off smoothly unless bottom-up pattern recognition contradicts expectations. In the word-meanings example, the students will copy the words into their workbooks and follow the standard script (e.g., copy the definitions of each word from the dictionary and write a sentence using each new word) unless they are unable to complete the task using established production systems (e.g., a student can't find a word in the dictionary and doesn't know its definition).

Knowledge-driven processing has been shown to be influential in a wide range of perceptual and cognitive activities (Neisser, 1976; Wickelgren, 1979). Findings about defaults in action-sequence production systems, for example, are illustrated in research on judging and making inferences (Nisbett & Ross, 1980). Parallel findings about defaults and knowledge-driven processing appear in studies of motivation in the form of findings such as the fundamental attribution error (i.e., the tendency to attribute other's performance to dispositional rather than situational factors; Ross, 1977), people's naive theories of attribution (Weiner, 1985), and students' conventional interpretations of classroom environments (e.g., Rosenholtz & Simpson, 1984).

There are considerable benefits to top-down processing in settings as complex as classrooms. Students' use of defaults allows them to process information quickly and automatically while continuing to stay in contact with developments in the instructional environment. Despite the advantages of knowledge-driven processing, it cannot account for all cognitive activity in instructional situations. Classrooms are fundamentally social arenas (Hamilton, 1983), and such contexts make heavy demands on motivational and social–cognitive processes (Higgins & Bargh, 1987; Pittman & Heller, 1987). When information incoming from complex environments does vary widely from the values assigned as defaults, motivational research reveals that people become more vigilant and begin to process information much more carefully, that is, in a bottom-up mode. For example, when people are deprived of control over their environment, they become much more deliberate processors of incoming data (Pittman & Heller, 1987).

Pittman and Heller suggest that bottom-up processing often may need to supplement top-down social cognition because people rarely maximize opportunities to inform themselves thoroughly about their environment. Rather, it appears people typically sample only enough information to make sense of a situation. As well, teachers purposefully vary tasks so that students encounter novelty, presupposing this to have positive effects such as boosting students' attention and interest. As a consequence of (1) the disposition to sample information incompletely from the environment and (2) teachers' purposeful variations of the instructional environment, students likely must switch dynamically and frequently between top-down and bottom-up processing.

Goal-Directed Nature of Cognitive Tasks

We assume that cognition in such tasks as reasoning deductively, making inferences, solving problems, and creating original products is always goal directed and always involves monitoring progress toward the goal. Without information about an unachieved goal, there is no task. Therefore, cognition used to perform a task is strategic. In making this assertion, we borrow from the widespread theoretical utility and empirical evidence supporting models such as Miller, Galanter, and Pribram's (1960) TOTE unit; Newell and Simon's (1972) means–ends analysis; Chi, Glaser, and Rees's (1982) descriptions of novice and expert problem solving in terms of backward chaining and forward chaining; and Flavell's (1976) concept of metacognition.

In casting students' information processing as goal-directed, it is important to separate claims about students' use of strategies to complete classroom tasks from notions of rationality and effectiveness as assessed by an observer of students' work. A *strategy* is a systematic deployment of resources in an attempt to achieve a goal. One hallmark of a strategy is that different paths toward the goal are followed depending on local conditions that are encountered in the course of performing a task. Students deploying particular strategies are rational in the sense that they reason—that is, can justify—the strategies they adopt and branches in the paths they follow toward the task's goal. Unless they are psychotic, we also must grant that students adopt particular strategies because they believe that particular strategies are effective for achieving the goals that they have understood for the task.

What a student deems strategic may rightly be judged unsystematic or ill informed by a teacher or classmate. For example, when teachers and students share the same understanding about a task, students may use less than adequate strategies because they lack appropriate strategic knowledge (Wong, 1986). However, when a student has misconceptions about a task's content (Anderson, Harding, & DuBay, 1985), or when a student's goal is not the same as the teacher's, even for what appears to be the same task (Winne & Marx, 1982), differences in their views about a correct or optimal strategy for performing the task are explained by the fact that the task the student pursues *is* a different task than the one perceived by the teacher.

If the axiom that students are goal directed in their use of cognitive operations to carry out classroom tasks is tenable, then we can make a strong link between information-processing theories of classroom tasks and motivational theories of those same classroom tasks. As we described in the introduction, one of the three objectives of a theory of motivation is to account for choice. We assumed that choice was directed, not random. This goal also is shared by theories of cognitive processing, which address how goals exert strategic influence over cognitive activities. It follows that theories about information processing and theories about motivation must account for related phenomena—namely, how successive behavior is influenced by prior goals.

This same conclusion was reached by Pittman and Heller (1987) in their review of social motivation and social cognition. Parallel with cognitive psychologists, Pittman and Heller conclude that people behave in a manner that is consistent with their goals, and that they depart from a strategically chosen path only in the face of widely discrepant information. In Pittman and Heller's model, social cognition is characterized in terms of a homeostatic model in which disconfirming information plays a critical role in keeping the motivational and social–cognitive system in balance. Consequently, a negative feedback mechanism is critical in their model of social cognition. Cognitive psychologists' analog to this mechanism is bottom-up, data-driven processing which disconfirms defaults assigned by top-down, knowledge-driven processing and provides information that students use to redirect their path toward a goal.

These alternate motivational and cognitive accounts of goal-directed performance sound very much like what Simon (1969) labels as *satisfi-cing*. Once a person has chosen a goal, then work toward that goal proceeds until overwhelming evidence indicates that alternative actions are required. We find strong parallels between Simon's account of cognition and Weiner's (1984) view of attribution theory in achievement contexts. Motivational cognition should be expected to occur when goals are chosen or when default values are not acceptable and bottom-up processing is required to adjust to the task.

Independence between Cognitive Operations and Information

The SMART cognitive operations are independent of information in the sense that, while they operate on information, they are not items of information per se. Although cognitive operations exist independently of information, they cannot be used or observed until they have information on which to operate.

The label *cognitive processing*, as used in the literature about instruction, usually is *not* meant to be considered independently of information. Tasks that students perform to learn and to participate in classroom events intrinsically involve content. The vast bulk of content in any classroom task has been acquired previously through formal instruction in home and at school, as well as through informal developmental experiences. It is inside tasks, where cognitive operations are entwined with content, that cognitive processing occurs. Consequently, cognitive processing is a joint function of primitive cognitive operations that do the processing (the SMART operations) and the content that is processed.

Similarly, we posit that motivational processing is a joint function of primitive cognitive operations that do the processing (i.e., the SMART operations) and the content that is processed. Because we hypothesize that only one set of primitive cognitive operations is needed to account for both cognitive processing and motivational processing, cognitive and motivational processing are distinguished on the basis of informational content on which the common cognitive operations operate. The content that students process as they carry out acquisition and retrieval tasks in classrooms correspond to topics of curriculum and are usually characterized in terms of disciplines of knowledge such as mathematics or social studies. In contrast, the content cognitively operated on during motivational processing concerns the three main topics upon which motivational theory has focused: choice, temperament, and persistence. Terms for this content appearing in the literature of motivational research include, for example, values, intentions, expectations, and attributions.

Summary about Tasks

Tasks are the events of classroom life that constitute opportunities for students to engage their cognitive and motivational apparatus in the service of achieving personal and educational goals. We have discussed tasks in terms of the COPE model, according to which tasks can be described as consisting of conditions, operations, products, and evaluations. A major focus for this discussion has been on the cognitive elements in the model and the implications of the study of cognition for developing a model of motivation that is grounded in a view of tasks that students carry out in classrooms. The major implication of this argument for the study of motivation is that both cognition and motivation depend on goal-driven processes. If this is tenable, the rich theoretical and empirical literature of cognitive psychology can be brought to bear directly on the study of motivation.

Though classroom tasks constitute the cognitive interface between educational goals and students, classrooms are also social arenas in which tasks are enacted within the context of a socially defined work environment. The elements of this work environment are activity structures, and it is to a discussion of these structures that we now turn.

ACTIVITY STRUCTURES

According to Doyle (1986, p. 398), "the basic unit of classroom organization is the activity." Activities are organized and recurring situations within which teachers and students carry out tasks in classrooms. Activity structures have four defining features (Berliner, 1983; Burnett, 1973; Doyle, 1986): (1) characteristic rhythm or location within school schedule and setting, (2) characteristic educational function that operates across educational tasks, (3) characteristic social roles and normative expectations, and (4) repetitive usage across curricula.

Characteristic Rhythms and Locations. Activity structures have temporal and, generally, physical boundaries. Activity structures usually have typical durations—a 50-minute class, a 5-minute review—often punctuated by structural features of the school day, such as recess, lunchtime, or changes in class periods. Also, in elementary school classrooms, activity structures are usually bounded temporally by clearly specified transition periods. Activity structures may also take place, particularly in elementary schools, in designated areas of classrooms with particular configurations of people and materials.

Characteristic Educational Functions. Participants in activities have at least one, but much more commonly, several interrelated and overlapping tasks to perform in order to fulfill a particular educational function, such as participating in a reading group. Whereas tasks are defined at the level of individual students or of an observer, activity structures are defined jointly by the tasks they comprise *and* the social configurations among teacher and students. Because activity structures include tasks, activity structures inherit all the descriptive features of tasks. Activity structures are differentiated on the basis of functions that they serve in instruction such as re-presenting previously studied information or providing tutorial assistance (cf. Berliner, 1983). Whereas tasks often can be crisply distinguished on the basis of fairly precise features of conditions, operations, products, and evaluations, activity structures are differentiated in terms of functions. For example, two common activity structures are tutoring and seatwork. In both, students usually pursue many of the same tasks. But the functions of tutoring—remediation, motivation, diagnosis—differ from those characteristic of seatwork—enrichment, practice, occupying a group of students productively while orchestrating another activity structure that involves a second group of students.

Characteristic Norms and Social Roles. Activity structures are normative, carrying expectations about how participants may or should perform their individual and interacting tasks. The significance of this feature is that, whereas a task emphasizes cognitive and behavioral action carried out almost entirely by a single student performing the task, activity structures are intrinsically social occasions in which participants have particular roles.

Repeated Cross-Curricular Uses. Activity structures are repeated frequently, sometimes several times within a lesson, but usually at least once per day or several times a week. The import of this feature is that repeated experiences with a given activity structure allow students to develop *scripts* (Schank & Abelson, 1977)—that is, schemata about sequences of events and tasks that compose the activity structure. Scripts, which are top-down, or knowledge-driven structures, have default values for particular elements that appear within them. They also have slots within which information about the current version of the script must be placed in order to instantiate the generic abstract script with its current form in the here and now. For example, by the time they are in middle school, all students in North American classrooms have had literally thousands of interactions in a common activity structure called the *classroom recitation* (Gage & Berliner, 1984). One of the features of the classroom recitation is that teachers call on individual students to answer questions; the rest of the class is expected to participate by listening to the response. The teacher and students are known to develop and follow very systematic methods (turn-taking scripts, Mehan, 1979) in this activity. Violations of this script are rare; when violations appear, they are extremely salient.

Tasks and activity structures create the events in which students engage while doing the work of learning in school. A theoretical account of classroom motivation must address and account for some features of students' performance during these events. In the remainder of this chapter, we sketch some of the properties of such a theory.

MOTIVATION DURING INSTRUCTIONAL SITUATIONS

To this point, we have sketched our view of a cognitive psychology about instruction, and we argued that this view can generalize to encompass some motivation phenomena that characterize students as they perform classroom tasks.

Next, we address two very basic questions: What is motivational processing? What tasks are students motivated about? Our answers are framed in terms of the preceding account of students' performance of tasks within activity structures.

WHAT IS MOTIVATIONAL PROCESSING?

According to our postulate about recursive simultaneity, (1) motivation is a *product* that results from performing instructionally relevant tasks, and, at the same time, (2) it is a *process* that accounts for how students participate in those tasks. As a product, motivational content is stored in students' long-term memory. We hypothesize that (1) motivational content is coded in the same forms as other information—namely, as primitive concepts, propositions, and schemata—and (2) it is operated on by the same primitive cognitive operations as are used to operate on other types of content.

Primitive motivational concepts are emotions or feelings such as happiness, frustration, and sadness (cf. Weiner, 1985). These concepts cannot be analyzed further and account directly for students' affect. As with the word task, the etymology of "emotion" reaches into the Latin *ex* (from) and *movere* (to move), combining in *exmovere* (to move away). Hence, emotions are the source of "motive force." These concepts move students to action, presumably to sustain or diminish the dominance of primitive motivational content in working memory, in students' conscious experience.

Experience (initially) and instruction (later) lead students to assemble primitive motivational concepts with neutral information in working memory about the initial and updated conditions of tasks in which they participate. The products of these operations are propositions that link emotions to information in the propositions that are described in theories of motivation (Winne, 1985c). For instance, one kind of proposition is an *attitude*: "Because I'm usually happy during science period, I guess I like science." A second type of proposition is an *attribution*: "I succeeded in answering that question because I kept at it; I tried hard." A third and fourth type of proposition are *efficacy expectations* and *outcome expectations*. Illustrations are "This task should be easy for me because I've done one just like it before." "If I raise my hand, the teacher will come help me, and that will reduce my frustration."

Schemata, in the form of pattern-recognition procedures and action-oriented procedures, also appear in theories of motivation. These schemata blend motivational content and cognitive operations to produce a parallel to cognitive processing, what we call *motivational processing*. In pattern-recognition procedures, motivational content appears as THEN-components. The attitudinal and attributional propositions just mentioned illustrate this sort of motivational processing. In action-oriented motivational procedures, the motivational content appears in the IF-conditions, which, if matched or satisfied, THEN lead to specific associated actions. Action-oriented motivational procedures are accounts of how emotions, feelings, or more complicated motivational content lead to motivationally guided action. They lie at the core of motivational theories about volition (see Kuhl & Beckmann, 1985), self-regulation (see Corno & Rohrkemper, 1985), and maintenance of self-concept (see Tesser & Campbell, 1985).

Methodology in a study by Schunk and Hanson (1985) reflects how this account of motivational processing functions in self-regulatory or self-maintaining activities. These researchers developed videotapes in which a 10-year-old student modeled positive beliefs about achievement concerning 2-column subtraction tasks that required regrouping: high self-efficacy ("I can do this one"), high ability ("I'm good at these"), low task difficulty ("That looks easy"), and positive attitudes ("I like doing these"). These are motivational propositions: *affect* assembled with *information* about subtraction tasks, which are output by cognitive processing, which in turn recognizes patterns in the information about the task. For instance: IF the problems are subtraction problems that involve regrouping, THEN "I'm good at these" and "I like doing these." Schunk and Hansen also developed videotapes in which the student modeled a progression of coping skills, culminating in self-regulatory expressions such as "I'll have to work hard on this one" and "I need to pay attention to what I'm doing." These illustrate action procedures in which both cognitive and motivational THENs follow upon particular IFs that the student model used to characterize the subtraction tasks.

Our views about motivational content and motivational processing also can characterize several other motivational phenomena. Consider Csikszentmihalyi's (1975) notion of flow states. As people work through a task, updating the task's initial conditions to reflect their current state of work, the products of cognitive operations uncontrollably and effortlessly stimulate content in long-term memory. Some of that content will include motivational content as activation spreads through a network of previously assembled propositions. However, a flow state is one in which the person is so absorbed with the content of the task that motivational content does not intrude into consciousness as the student performs the task. How can this be explained?

At the outset of working on the task, suppose students' pattern recognition procedures stimulate highly positive motivational content such as strong efficacy expectations. In parallel, appropriate subject-matter content about the task also is activated. At this point, the student is both very motivated and cognitively well prepared to initiate work on the task. As involvement with the task progresses smoothly, motivational content that may be stimulated does not differ from that already active. Because (1) updated conditions about the task have not stimulated motivational content that contradicts the initial motivational content, (2) control is sustained, and (3) there is no novel motivational content to attend to, their conscious homeostatic regulation of motivational processing (Pittman & Heller, 1987) remains unnecessary. New motivational content does not take up residence in working memory, and vigilance over motivation is lowered. Consequently, cognitive processing about subject-matter content about the task fully absorbes the limited capacity of working memory. In short, the student experiences a flow state.

Our account of motivational processing also sheds light on how motivational self-regulatory procedures counteract unproductive temperament and persistence (see Corno & Rohrkemper, 1985). Students monitor intermediate products that develop as they proceed through a task. If intermediate products are monitored and characterized as deficient, negative motivational content can be stimulated by spreading activation (see the earlier section on stimulating operations for a discussion of spreading activation). As this new motivational content takes up residence in working memory, it triggers the need for control to return to homeostatis. If the student has available action-oriented procedures that can re-establish control over the task and that progress toward the goal of the task, this will stimulate positive motivational content through spreading activation. Both control and positive feelings about control then re-establish in working memory.

However, what happens if the students lack action-sequence procedures that re-establish satisfactory progress toward the goal of the task? In this case, because THEN-components of action-oriented procedures that achieve progress toward the task's goal are not forthcoming from long-term memory, spreading activation may ripple through long-term memory to stimulate further aversive motivational content. Should this spiral continue uninterrupted, we hypothesize that emotional states such as anxiety or helplessness are established. Learned helplessness, then, is a case where, following repeated experiences of this sort within a particular activity structure, the script for that activity structure reinstates feelings of helplessness as a dominant default for THEN-components of pattern-recognition procedures. Hypothetically, replacing these pattern-recognition procedures with action-oriented procedures lessens helplessness (see Corno, 1986).

Summary. Primitive motivational concepts, the strong feelings that supply force to behavior, are content. When primitive cognitive operations assemble this motivational content with other information about a task, motivational processing occurs. Motivational processing, when examined by using principles that have been developed in research on cognitive processing, can account for several topics in contemporary research about students' motivation, including flow states, self-regulation, and learned helplessness. Phrased simply, motivational processing is neither more nor less than cognitive operations carried out on motivational content. Therefore, principles of cognitive processing account also for motivational processing.

WHICH TASKS MOTIVATE STUDENTS?

There are two answers to this question. The first is trite and circular: Students work on tasks when they expect that evaluations of the task's products are associated with positive motivational concepts. Students avoid tasks when evaluations about the products of the tasks are associated with negative motivational concepts. Because, by the principle of spreading activation, it is plausible that motivational content is stimulated whenever nonmotivational content is active in working memory, then performing every task potentially involves motivation. This line of development expresses a tautology: students approach tasks when they are positively motivated and avoid tasks when they are negatively motivated.

The second answer is more useful, but it is also much more complicated. It begins to address teachers' concerns about situations in which students lack motivation. Such situations involve activity structures within which students (1) do not select instructionally productive tasks to perform, (2) perform those tasks with inappropriate temper, or (3) do not persist at a task long enough to produce an acceptable product. For example, when studying a science chapter at their desks, students may not use a strategy for minotiring comprehension even though that strategy has been mastered.Or, they may behave so that it is clear they do not like having to concentrate—for instance, by stopping frequently to chat with a friend. Alternatively, students may not apply the comprehension-monitoring strategy to every paragraph in the chapter or may not use parts of the strategy despite knowing that using the complete strategy might lead to better understanding and thereby increase the chances of earning a higher mark on a test.

What might account for these kinds of behaviors? We propose two possible paths to account for them. One path introduces a concept that has been addressed in motivational theories, but poorly addressed in research: utility. In following this path, we reconsider the notion about the territory of a task. The second path follows a different line of reasoning based on Winne's (1982) analysis about how students can fail to perform a task.

Utility and "Motivational Reasoning"

Consider the activity structure of a classroom recitation, a particular instance of what Berliner (1983) has labeled *two-way presentation*. In this activity structure, students and the teacher communicate about subject matter with one another as a group. An example would be the teacher and class discussing how changes in the value of the dollar affect the balance of trade and interest rates.

Within this activity structure, the teacher plans to ask several higher-cognitive questions that, theoretically, require students to develop a

product that involves cognitive operations beyond merely directly stimulating information in long-term memory (cf. Winne, 1979, p. 14).
According to rhetoric about higher-cognitive questions, the products
achieved by students who answer them is not merely the acquisition of
new information, but also the development of more advanced methods
of thinking. In our terms, this means that students who answer higher-
cognitive questions also develop new or expanded action-oriented
procedures that can be used in tasks involving near and far transfer (i.e.,
transfer to highly similar or dissimilar contexts, respectively).

When the teacher asks a higher-cognitive question during recitation,
students can answer the question in at least three different ways: (1) A
student could perform the complex cognitive operations as intended by
the teacher to develop an answer to the higher-cognitive question. (2) A
student could apply monitoring operations to search the textbook
seeking a plausible answer. (3) A student could wait until another
student answered it and then rehearse that student's answer. (See Corno
& Mandinach, 1983, for a theoretical model of these forms of cognitive
engagement in classrooms.)

In terms of the COPE model for tasks, these are actually three
different tasks because the configuration of factors in operations,
products, and evaluations differ. These three tasks can be distinguished
not only in terms of what students select to do, but also in terms of
requirements for their persistence. For example, the first task, according
to rhetoric about higher-cognitive questions, requires the most persistence because it entails several cycles in order to work through the task.
A student who consistently performs the third task would likely be seen
by the teacher as unwilling to participate or "low" in motivation.

For teachers (who want all their students to respond as the first
student does because this is believed to have the most educational
benefit) and for motivation theorists (who want to account for students'
selection, temperament, and persistence), the issue of importance is
"Why does a student display one as opposed to another form of task
engagement?" There are four possible answers to this question (Winne,
1982), each with different implications:

1. A student may not engage in the task because the teacher's
question did not register in working memory. This student was not
paying attention—a different task was absorbing cognitive capacity.
That other task may be instructionally relevant (perhaps the student is
taking notes) or it may not be (perhaps the student is daydreaming).

2. A student who attends to the question may perform the wrong task
if the student misperceived the task that the teacher intended by posing

the question. Perhaps the student treated the question as rhetorical rather than one to be answered. In this case, the student's pattern-recognition procedure is flawed either because an IF-component is distorted or because one of the IF-components that was needed in order to produce an accurate classification did not register in working memory.

3. The student who attends to the teacher's question and accurately perceives the task that the question frames may not have the capability to perform that task. This student lacks an adequate action-oriented procedure. The inadequacy may reflect inefficiency (lack of automaticity) if the teacher allows too little time for the student to complete the task, or the inadequacy may stem from missing IFs or THENs in the procedure itself.

4. The student who attends to the question, accurately perceives what the task is, and has the capability to perform it will not necessarily choose to carry out the task of answering the question as the teacher intends. Motivationally, this student may (1) have a clear outcome expectation; (2) view this outcome as having positive value or incentive; (3) have a positive and clear efficacy expectation; and (4) stimulate a supporting attribution; and yet the student still might not perform the task involved in answering the teacher's higher-order question. Why? We propose that, in the student's view, another task can be substituted without importantly diminishing positive motivational content. That substitute task has equal or greater utility for the student.

Utility is gauged in terms of motivational costs and benefits that accrue by performing alternative tasks (Covington & Omelich, 1979). Utility is an output of motivational processing. Specifically, utility results from monitoring motivational content about evaluations that are associated with the products of alternative tasks. The alternative tasks that a student considers are those that are defined as allowable in the script for an activity structure. For example, the conventional script for classroom recitations allows students to engage in either of two tasks: (1) to try answering questions, or (2) to listen to other students' answers. The first task may be affectively risky: IF an answer to the teacher's question (a product of the task) is publicly displayed, THEN evaluations that stimulate positive motivational content are not assured because other students or the teacher may misperceive the information in that answer and wrongly consider it inadequate. The second substitute task has no chance to produce affectively positive evaluations from the teacher or classmates, but it avoids affectively negative evaluations. Its utility may be greater.

A student reasoning this way defines the task differently than the teacher does because the student emphasizes "public display of the product" as part of the task, whereas the teacher minimizes this aspect of the task. The student who elects not to answer the question based on the relative motivational utility of this action as compared to answering the teacher's question in public substitutes a different task for the teacher's—one that is allowable within the script for this activity structure.

Suppose the rhetoric is correct in saying that students' answering higher-cognitive questions helps students to develop transferable action-oriented procedures (see Winne, 1979). The student who elects not to answer the teacher's questions suffers important losses in the long term because this student chooses not to engage in the more instructionally appropriate cognitive processing. Repeated over thousands of lessons, this engagement within the activity structure of recitations may develop a pattern-motivated behavior and level of procedural knowledge in which students learn how to perform substitute tasks that get them through an activity structure; tasks that "satisfice" (Simon, 1981), but that ultimately retard or prevent their achievement of important educational objectives. Here are the makings of a downward spiral of motivation and learning.

In summary, one answer to the question about which tasks students are motivated to perform is that students perform the task with the most immediately perceptible utility. Outcome (**O**) and efficacy (**E**) expectations, attributions (**A**), and incentives (**I**) feed into the IFs of a motivationally targeted pattern-recognition procedure. Output from this procedure is a THEN proposition that describes the relative utility (**U**) of alternative tasks. This kind of "motivational reasoning" involving a constellation of AEIOUs characterizes classroom activity structures whenever an activity structure allows students to participate by performing substitute tasks. Territoriality thus becomes an important issue to consider. While the teacher may intend students to perform a particular task, activity structures in classrooms often permit students to substitute different tasks and yet still appear to the teacher to participate in instruction as the teacher intends. Some types of substitutions may have detrimental effects on both motivation and competence.

Effects of Features of Task Presentation on Failure

It sometimes appears to teachers or researchers that students are not motivated to perform a task. As just developed, one explanation for this observation is grounded in the notion that, when activity structures permit latitude in the tasks that students can perform, students engage in "motivational reasoning" to select the task with the greatest utility. A second explanation also can be posed—one that has fundamentally nothing to do with motivational reasons as these are applied by the teacher or researcher. This explanation merits consideration simply because, when either teachers or researchers attribute students' failure to perform a task to motivational cause, they may be mistaken.

Previously, we outlined three prerequisite conditions that must be met in order for a student to perform a particular task as posed by the teacher (Winne, 1982). These were that the student: (1) attend to information about the task so that it is registered in working memory, (2) accurately classify what the task is—that is, perceive it in the same way as the teacher, and (3) have the capability to carry out the task. When any one of these three prerequisites is not satisfied, the student cannot perform the task that the teacher poses. Instead, the student will perform another task, one for which motivational reasoning can be wholly different from what the teacher or researcher assumes.

Research has shown that these three prerequisites are influenced by factors within the conditions facet of a task (Brown, Bransford, Ferrara, & Campione, 1983; Jenkins, 1979). The main types of factors that we identified are the medium of presentation, the goal(s) set for the task, and cues about how to perform the task provided to the student by the teacher or another source. For instance, when the teacher speaks rather than writes the directions for writing an essay, the medium of presentation limits whether students can refer back to those directions.

A fundamental question that needs to be raised in addressing students' motivation about tasks is whether they are approaching the same task as the teacher intends or the researcher supposes. If students do not register information pertinent to what the task is, misperceive the goal, or lack the capability to perform part or all of a task, the student approaches a different task. Consequently, the constellation of efficacy and outcome expectations, attributions, incentives, and utilities that the student stimulates may differ substantially from what the teacher or researcher supposes. When such category errors are not detected, the student may be judged by the teacher or researcher to lack motivation or to engage in insufficient motivational processing. In fact, the student may have been motivated about a task that he or she understood to be the task posed, but that task may not have been the task the teacher or researcher intended to request.

Thus, a second answer to the question about which tasks students are motivated to perform is that they perform the task they have understood, based on the information they have. Conditions of the presentation of a task—the medium, the description of goals, and delivery of cues—can lead students to perform tasks that differ from tasks posed by a teacher or researcher. If this difference is not recognized by the teacher or researcher, and because motivation exists in relation to a particular task, a category error may be made in describing the student's motivation.

CONCLUSIONS

A complete theory of motivation in the context of instruction is traditionally viewed as having to account for why students behave in classrooms as they do. This explanation of student behavior has three facets: (1) what students elect to do, (2) the temperament with which they act, and (3) their persistence in the presence of obstacles or alternatives. We postulate that these behavioral manifestations are reflections of underlying mental events. This led us to probe into what those mental activities might be and how they might function.

We hypothesize that mental representations for information do not differ fundamentally across topics. Instead, basic research from both cognitive and motivational fields leads us to propose that all information, regardless of whether it is about a subject matter or an affect, is represented in memory as concepts, propositions, and schemata. We hypothesize further that the mental operations that work with information—the SMART cognitive operations—do not vary as a function of the informational content on which those operations work. Consequently, the fundamental difference between what we labeled *motivational processing* as opposed to *cognitive processing* is the information that students think about, not how they think about it.

Because the forms for mentally representing information as well as the means for mentally operating on information appear highly similar regardless of whether we are considering motivation or cognition, we propose that there is little difference between these two mental phenomena. Adopting this perspective, we were able to account for several motivational phenomena by straightforwardly drawing on accounts provided by cognitive psychological models. These included accounts that addressed fundamental issues such as when students become motivated, how motivation guides task performance, and how students select to perform one task instead of others.

When addressing the classroom events that create opportunities for students to think and feel, we analyze them in terms of tasks that are embedded within activity structures. Tasks can be analyzed in terms four facets: conditions, operations, products, and evaluations. Students work at tasks by applying both top-down and bottom-up processing, both of which are governed by a goal that the student perceives about the task. When the scripts that students have learned for activity structures allow them to substitute tasks for one another, they select a task to pursue based on utilities that "satisfice." The tasks that students do perform also determine what information they acquire about subject-matter topics (such as signed numbers) and about motivational topics (such as attributions). Also, the tasks that students actually perform lead them to develop the patterns for processing subject-matter content in situations such as classroom recitations and for processing motivational content such as principles of self-regulation.

In short, we propose that previous integrations of models about cognition and models about motivation overlap even more than has been thought heretofore. By capitalizing on the strengths of each area, we expect that a truly productive blend will emerge.

ACKNOWLEDGMENTS

Portions of this chapter were written while the first author held a research professorship at Simon Fraser University, British Columbia, Canada and was a Distinguished Visiting Professor at the Max Planck Institute for Psychological Research, Münich, F.R.G. Support from both organizations is gratefully acknowledged.

REFERENCES

Ames, R., & Ames, C. (Eds.) (1984). *Research on motivation in education: Vol. 1. Student motivation.* Orlando, FL: Academic Press.

Ames, C., & Ames, R. (Eds.) (1985). *Research on motivation in education: Vol. 2. The classroom milieu.* Orlando, FL: Academic Press.

Anderson, C. W., Harding, T., & DuBay, J. (1985, April). *Effects of instruction on student conceptions of respiration and photosynthesis.* Paper presented at the meeting of the American Educational Research Association, Chicago, IL.

Anderson, J. R. (1983). *The architecture of cognition.* Cambridge, MA: Harvard University Press.

Berliner, D. C. (1983). Developing conceptions of classroom environments: Some light on the T in classroom studies of ATI. *Educational Psychologist, 18,* 1–13.

Brown, A. L., Bransford, J. D., Ferrara, R., & Campione, J. (1983). Learning, understanding and remembering. In J. H. Flavell & E. Markman (Eds.), *Mussen handbook of child psychology: Vol. 3. Cognitive development* (4th ed., pp. 77–166). New York: Wiley.

Bruner, J. S. (1966). *Toward a theory of instruction*. Cambridge, MA: Harvard University Press.

Buck, R. (1985). Prime theory: An integrated view of motivation and emotion. *Psychological Review, 92,* 389–413.

Burnett, J. H. (1973). Event description and analysis in the microethnography of urban classrooms. In F. A. J. Ianni & E. Storey (Eds.), *Cultural relevance and educational issues: Readings in anthropology and education* (pp. 287–303). Boston: Little-Brown.

Calfee, R. C. (1981). Cognitive psychology and educational practice. In D. C. Berliner (Ed.), *Review of research in education* (Vol. 9, p. 3–73). Washington, DC: American Educational Research Association.

Chi, T. H., Glaser, R., & Rees, E. (1982). Expertise in problem solving. In R. J. Sternberg (Ed.), *Advances in the psychology of human intelligence* (Vol. 1, pp. 7–75). Hillsdale, NJ: Erlbaum.

Clark, C. M., & Peterson, P. L. (1986). Teachers' thought processes. In M. C. Wittrock (Ed.), *Handbook of research on teaching* (3rd ed., pp. 255–296). New York: Macmillan.

Corno, L. (1986). The megacognitive control components of self-regulated learning. *Contemporary Educational Psychology, 11,* 333–346.

Corno, L., & Mandinach, E. B. (1983). The role of cognitive engagement in classroom learning and motivation. *Educational Psychologist, 18,* 88–108.

Corno, L., & Rohrkemper, M. (1985). The intrinsic motivation to learn in classrooms. In C. Ames & R. Ames (Eds.), *Research on motivation in education: Vol. 2. The classroom milieu* (pp. 53–90). Orlando, FL: Academic Press.

Corno, L., & Snow, R. E. (1986). Adapting teaching to individual differences among learners. In M. C. Wittrock (Ed.), *Handbook of research on teaching* (3rd ed., pp. 605–629). New York: Macmillan.

Covington, M., & Omelich, C. (1979). Effort: The double-edged sword in school achievement. *Journal of Educational Psychology, 71,* 169–182.

Csikszentsmihalyi, M. (1975). *Beyond boredom and anxiety*. San Francisco: Jossey-Bass.

Doyle, W. (1983). Academic work. *Review of Educational Research, 53,* 159–199.

Doyle, W. (1986). Classroom organization and management. In M. C. Wittrock (Ed.), *Handbook of research on teaching* (3rd ed., pp. 392–431). New York: Macmillan.

Flavell, J. H. (1976). Metacognitive aspects of problem solving. In L. B. Resnick (Ed.), *The nature of intelligence* (pp. 231–235). Hillsdale, NJ: Erlbaum.

Gage, N. L., & Berliner, D. C. (1984). *Educational psychology* (3rd ed.). New York: Houghton-Mifflin.

Gagné, E. D. (1985). *The cognitive psychology of school subjects*. Boston: Little-Brown.

Hamilton, S. F. (1983). The social side of schooling: Ecological studies of classrooms and schools. *Elementary School Journal, 83,* 313–334.

Higgins, E. T., & Bargh, J. A. (1987). Social cognition and social perception. In M. R. Rosenzweig & L. W. Porter (Eds.), *Annual review of psychology* (Vol. 38, pp. 369–425). Palo Alto, CA: Annual Reviews.

Hutchinson, N. L. (1986). *Instruction of representation and solution in algebraic problem solving with learning disabled adolescents*. Unpublished doctoral dissertation, Simon Fraser University, Burnaby, British Columbia.

Jenkins, J. J. (1979). Four points to remember: A tetrahedral model of memory experiments. In L. S. Cermak & F. I. M. Craik (Eds.), *Levels of processing in human memory*. Hillsdale, NJ: Erlbaum.

Johnson-Laird, P. N. (1983). *Mental models*. Cambridge, MA: Harvard University Press.

Kuhl, J., & Beckman, J. (eds.) (1985). *Action control: From cognition to behavior*. New York: Springer-Verlag.

Lindow, J. A., Wilkinson, L. C., & Peterson, P. L. (1985). Antecedents and consequences of verbal disagreements during small-group learning. *Journal of Educational Psychology, 77*, 658–667.

Marx, R. W. (1983). Student perception in classrooms. *Educational Psychologist, 18*, 145–164.

Marx, R. W. (1985). Classroom organization and perceptions of student academic and social status. In I. E. Housego & P. P. Grimmett (Eds.), *Teaching and teacher education: Generating and utilizing valid knowledge for professional socialization* (pp. 75–100). Vancouver, British Columbia: Western Education Development Group.

Marx, R. W., & Walsh, J. (1988). Classroom tasks and academic learning. *Elementary School Journal, 88*, 207–219.

Marx, R. W., Winne, P. H., & Walsh, J. (1985). Studying student cognition during classroom learning. In M. Pressley & C. J. Brainerd (Eds.), *Cognitive learning and memory in children: Progress in cognitive development research* (pp. 181–203). New York: Springer-Verlag.

Mayer, R. E., Larkin, J. H., & Kadane, J. (1984). A cognitive analysis of mathematical problem solving ability. In R. J. Sternberg (Ed.), *Advances in the psychology of human intelligence* (Vol. 2, pp. 231–273). Hillsdale, NJ: Erlbaum.

Mehan, H. (1979). *Learning lessons: Social organization in the classroom.* Cambridge, MA: Harvard University Press.

Miller, G. A., Galanter, E. H., & Pribam, K. H. (1960). *Plans, goals, and the structure of behavior.* New York: Holt.

Neisser, U. (1976). *Cognition and reality: Principles and implications of cognitive psychology.* San Francisco: W. H. Freeman.

Newell, A., & Simon, H. A. (1972). *Human problem solving.* Englewood Cliffs, NJ: Prentice-Hall.

Nisbett, R., & Ross, L. (1980). *Human inference: Strategies and shortcomings of social judgment.* Englewood Cliffs, NJ: Prentice-Hall.

Pittman, T. S., & Heller, J. F. (1987). Social motivation. In M. R. Rosenzweig & L. W. Porter (Eds.), *Annual review of psychology* (Vol. 38, pp. 461–489). Palo Alto, CA: Annual Reviews.

Rosenholtz, S., & Simpson, C. (1984). The formation of ability conceptions: Developmental trend or social construction? *Review of Educational Research, 54*, 31–63.

Ross, L. (1977). The intuitive psychologist and his shortcomings. In L. Berkowitz (Ed.), *Advances in experimental social psychology* (Vol. 10, pp. 173–220). New York: Academic Press.

Samuels, S. J., & Kamil, M. L. (1984). Models of the reading process. In P. D. Pearson (Ed.), *Handbook of reading research* (pp. 185–224). New York: Longman.

Schank, R. C., & Abelson, R. P. (1977). *Scripts, plans, goals, and understanding.* Hillsdale, NJ: Erlbaum.

Schunk, D. H., & Hanson, A. R. (1985). Peer models: Influence on childrens' self-efficacy and achievement. *Journal of Educational Psychology, 77*, 313–322.

Simon, H. A. (1981). *The sciences of the artificial* (2nd ed.) Cambridge, MA: MIT Press.

Stein, N. L. (1986). Knowledge and process in the acquisition of writing skills. In E. Z. Rothkopf (Ed.), *Review of research in education, 13*, 225–258. Washington, DC: American Educational Research Association.

Tesser, A., & Campbell, J. (1985). A self-evaluation maintenance model of student motivation. In C. Ames & R. Ames (Eds.), *Research on motivation in education: Vol. 2. The classroom milieu* (pp. 217–247). Orlando, FL: Academic Press.

Veenman, S. (1984). Perceived problems of beginning teachers. *Review of Educational Research, 54,* 143–178.

Walberg, II. J. (1980). A psychological theory of educational productivity. In F. H. Farley & N. Gordon (Eds.), *Psychology and education* (pp. 81–108). Berkeley, CA: McCutchan.

Weiner, B. (1984). Principles for a theory of student motivation and their application within an attributional framework. In R. Ames & C. Ames (Eds.), *Research on motivation in education: Vol. 1. Student motivation* (pp. 15–38). Orlando, FL: Academic Press.

Weiner, B. (1985). An attributional theory of achievement and emotion. *Psychological Review, 92,* 548–573.

Wickelgren, W. A. (1979). *Cognitive psychology.* Englewood Cliffs, NJ: Prentice-Hall.

Winne, P. H. (1979). Experiments relating teachers' use of higher cognitive questions to students' achievement. *Review of Educational Research, 49,* 13–49.

Winne, P. H. (1982). Minimizing the black box problem to enhance the validity of theories about instructional effects. *Instructional Science, 11,* 13–28.

Winne, P. H. (1985a). Steps toward promoting cognitive achievements. *Elementary School Journal, 85,* 673–693.

Winne, P. H. (1985b). Cognitive processing in the classroom. In T. Husen & T. N. Postlethwaite (Eds.), *International encyclopedia of education* (pp. 795–808). Oxford: Pergamon.

Winne, P. H. (1985c). *Retrieval tasks in instruction.* (Social Sciences and Humanities Research Council of Canada Final Report, No. 410-84-0398). Burnaby, British Columbia: Instructional Psychology Research Group, Simon Fraser University.

Winne, P. H., & Marx, R. W. (1982). Students' and teachers' views of thinking processes for classroom learning. *Elementary School Journal, 82,* 493–518.

Winne, P. H., & Marx, R. W. (1987). The best tool teachers have—their students' thinking. In D. C. Berliner & B. Rosenshine (Eds.), *Talks to teachers; A festschrift for N. L. Gage* (pp. 267–304). New York: Random House.

Wittrock, M. C. (1986). Students' thought processes. In M. C. Wittrock (Ed.), *Handbook of research on teaching* (3rd ed., pp. 297–314). New York: Macmillan.

Wong, B. Y. L. (1986). Self-questioning in instructional research. *Review of Educational Research, 55,* 227–268.

Zajonc, R. (1980). Feeling and thinking: Preferences need no inferences. *American Psychologist, 35,* 151 175.

8

Family Structures and Student Motivation: A Developmental Perspective

Joyce L. Epstein

INTRODUCTION

Across the school years, families and schools simultaneously influence student motivation to learn. The concurrent influences on children by families and schools may be similar or different, positive or negative, and more or less effective—but the influence is inescapably synchronous from preschool through high school. Earlier volumes in this series on motivation in education focused on individual behavior and on characteristics of classrooms (Ames & Ames, 1984b, 1985). This chapter initiates a discussion of the family's role in motivating children to learn.

We define motivation to learn, much as Brophy (1986) does, as the students' desire or willingness to engage and persist in academic activities in school. Motivation to take the role of student is different from motivation as an appetite for knowledge or as a competitive force to surpass others. Students fall along a continuum of purposeful learning, just as they do along a line of yearning for learning, ranging from weak to strong motivation to do assigned schoolwork. This type of motivation may be less dependent on ability or achievement than other types (cf. Weiner, 1979, 1984). Motivation to take the role of student, to learn, complete assignments, earn credentials, and move on to the next

259

phase of education or work, applies to all children—not to just a few with unusual traits, skills, or goals.

We extend the boundaries of influential settings to include the home as one of the major settings where this type of motivation is developed, supported, and demonstrated. Motivation to learn at home is evident in children's commitment to study, their completion of homework, their discussion of school experience with the family, their work at school that draws on activities at home, and their persistence in school to graduation. For over 20 years, research has shown that students benefit from family conditions and practices that emphasize and encourage schooling (Coleman, Campbell, Hobson, McPartland, Mood, Weinfeld, & York, 1966; Epstein & McPartland, 1979; Leichter, 1974; Marjoribanks, 1979, 1980; McDill & Rigsby, 1973).

Despite clear and consistent reports on the importance of family environments for student success, there have been few efforts to identify the specific, alterable structures of home environments that create conditions that support children's learning and development. There has been even less attention to the mechanisms by which family organization and practices motivate children to develop behaviors and attitudes that characterize successful students.

We have argued that the degree of overlap in family and school environments helps to explain patterns of student motivation, learning, and development. (Epstein, 1987c). We suggest that "school-like" families accumulate knowledge and practices that demonstrate to their children direct connections with school organizations and curricula. In this chapter, we detail what we mean by family–school overlap by identifying key structures in families that are parallel to structures in schools and that affect interpersonal interactions, motivation, and student outcomes.

There are theoretical and practical benefits from characterizing schools and families in parallel terms to study environmental effects and person–environment interactions (Holland, 1973; Stern, 1970). Using structurally consistent concepts and measures, Epstein and McPartland (1979) examined the effects on students of family and school authority structures. Epstein (1983a) extended this approach with consistent measures in a three-way, longitudinal, person–environment– environment model to account for the simultaneous influence of child, family, and school characteristics on student development.

Using this interactive model, we examined how students changed when they experienced similar or different patterns of decision making at home or at school. We found that students who were developmentally ready for decision making gained more in independence over 1 year if their families and schools offered many opportunities for decision making. There also were some compensatory patterns of socialization. For example, students who were ready for the challenge gained more in independence if their schools offered opportunities for decision making, even if their families did not.

In reviewing our and others' studies, Hess and Holloway (1984) suggested that the fit between home and school deserves more detailed analysis. In this chapter, we introduce six major structures at home that affect children's motivation to learn. These are directly analogous to structures at school that organize classroom instruction and management. We discuss the developmental nature of these structures, as well as their influence on motivation and on academic and nonacademic outcomes.

FAMILY STRUCTURES AND STUDENT MOTIVATION: TARGET STRUCTURES IN FAMILIES

Which family variables influence motivation and commitment in school? We could discuss warmth, affection, or encouragement—the affective qualities of family interactions. But these terms are too general to help us understand how particular, manipulable aspects of home life affect student motivation to learn. Six variables that help teachers organize classroom instruction (Epstein, 1988) have important analogs in the family: the **T**ask, **A**uthority, **R**eward, **G**rouping, **E**valuation, and **T**ime (TARGET) structures. The structures have been ordered heuristically in an acronym to suggest aspects of family organization that should be the target of attention to improve family influence on children's motivation to learn.

TASK STRUCTURE

The *task structure* (**T**) at home concerns the range of children's activities, including household chores delegated by parents; learning opportunities designed by parents; homework assigned by teachers; and play and hobby activities selected by children. It includes all activities directly or indirectly related to school learning that are conducted at home by children alone, with parents, siblings, or others.

From family to family, children's tasks vary in type, number, and frequency. Some children do many household chores every day and few school assignments. Others do many school tasks and few chores. Tasks vary in the degree of independence or the amount of contact and cooperation with siblings, parents, or friends permitted or required for completion. Variations in sequence, scope, variety, and interdependence are manipulable and measurable qualities of the task structure at home that affect whether children are challenged and motivated to think, act, and learn.

Family attention to learning starts in infancy when parents teach their toddlers to walk and talk—basic motor and cognitive skills. Family tasks concerning learning continue in the child-rearing activities that prepare the child for entry to school and for interactions with teachers, children, and others outside the home. These may include self-care, (buttoning clothing), self-monitoring (telling time), academic skills (listening to stories), reading readiness (identifying shapes, telling address), or reading skills (writing names or letters). Research suggests that learning opportunities provided by parents are important for building conversational skills (Snow, 1977), other reading and linguistic skills (Hess, Holloway, Dickson, & Price, 1984; Marjoribanks, 1979; Tizard, Schofield, & Hewison, 1982), and abilities to solve problems and anticipate the future (Sigel, 1981).

There is wide variation among families in the types and sequences of school-like activities conducted with infants, toddlers, and young children prior to their formal entry to school. But research consistently shows that preschool preparation by families contributes to children's readiness for "real" school, initial positive attitudes toward school, fewer grade retentions, and continued advantages for achievement in school (Andrews & associates, 1982; Gordon & Breivogel, 1976; Lazar & Darlington, 1982; Leichter, 1974; Rubin, Olmsted, Szegda, Wetherby, & Williams, 1983; Schaefer, Hunter, & Watkins, 1986; Sigel & McGill-icuddy-DeLisi, 1984; Weikart, Epstein, Schweinhart, & Bond, 1978; Zigler & Valentine, 1979).

Activities at home are likely to be more diverse in their origin and design than activities at school. Tasks for children may be originated by parents, teachers, children, siblings, other relatives, friends of the child or family, contacts in the community, religious groups, or technology (e.g., television, radio, computers, video recorders). Unlike many classroom tasks, activities at home are usually more active than passive. Schools have been criticized for encouraging teachers to lecture while students sit and listen (Goodlad, 1983; Sizer, 1984). But most tasks at home involve physical movement, exchange of ideas, help if needed, and flexible time for completion—characteristics that encourage children's learning.

Families also arrange activities that are not available at the school (e.g. sports, music, drama, volunteer work, foreign language). Although a few children show early talent or unusual interest in particular subjects (Bloom, 1982), most children build a repertoire of talents and interests over the school years. The task structures at home and at school largely determine the range of options from which children select their special interests.

Although some families continue to plan and conduct school-like tasks with their children through the high school grades, (Baker & Stevenson, 1986; Clark, 1983; Epstein, 1983a; McDill & Rigsby, 1973), most families need help from the school to understand how to structure tasks at home that are challenging and appropriate for their older children (Epstein, 1986a; Rich, 1985). The school can and should provide useful information to parents on the school curricula, specific objectives for learning, course requirements and options, and other information. Regardless of parents' education, family activities and discussions about school and other topics contribute to the growth of children's cognitive skills, positive attitudes about schoolwork, and improved daily work in school. When home activities concerning school or learning are based on useful information from the school, the task structure at home overlaps the task structure at school and may strongly and positively influence student motivation and school success.

AUTHORITY STRUCTURE

The *authority structure* (**A**) at home concerns the types and frequency of children's responsibilities, self-directed activities, and participation in family decisions. Patterns of children's participation in decision making vary from family to family. In some cases, parents make all or most decisions and exercise near-total control over children's behavior at home. In other settings, children have real and frequent input both to decisions about their own activities and to many family decisions. Some parents fear that sharing authority with youngsters will reduce their ability to control their own children. Other parents extend too much authority too soon to their children, leading to inappropriate activities, poor decision-making skills, poor parent–child relations, and weak motivation for school learning.

The authority relations within a family affect parent–child relations and influence children's motivation in school. If children and parents have a history of sharing decisions and discussing ideas together, children may be more likely to discuss issues and topics raised at school, describe problems, and seek help from parents. In contrast, if children and parents share few decisions, children may be less likely to talk about school problems or ask for help on schoolwork, thereby maintaining some personal control over that aspect of their own lives. Children who are included in important decisions at home may be at an advantage at school if their interactions with family members prepare them to interact successfully with their teachers and participate in discussions and projects with other students. These skills increase students' positive attitudes toward school and improve the quality of their experiences in school (Epstein, 1981).

There is a convincing literature, starting with Lewin, Lippitt, and White (1939), that suggests that authoritative (not authoritarian) relations lead to more self-reliant, explorative behavior in young children (Baumrind, 1971) and in older students (Elder, 1971; Epstein & McPartland, 1979). By including children in the family decision-making process, parents help children learn that their decisions lead to their own successes and failures. This feature of family life is not restricted to families with highly educated parents or to students with advanced abilities. Low- and high-achievers become increasingly self-reliant through opportunities for decision making at school (Wang & Weisstein, 1980), and through opportunities for self-direction at home (Epstein, 1983a).

REWARD STRUCTURE

The *reward structure* (**R**) at home concerns the procedures and practices that recognize children's efforts and accomplishments. Parents decide by their practices to pay attention to few or many types of behaviors, achievements, or talents of their children. They may acknowledge small or great gains in skills, and they may emphasize effort or ability in learning. The reward structure includes the overt and subtle practices that demonstrate parents' warmth, affection, and appreciation of their children.

Parents' praises, prizes, and punishments differ by type and frequency, but a key factor for children's motivation to learn is whether parents place more or less value on school-related skills and improvements. Thus, parents who reward sports, mechanical, music, or reading skills will differently influence their children's beliefs about the importance of these skills. When families emphasize, minimize, or ignore the importance of school activities, they show the depth of the connections between their home and the school and influence whether and how children are motivated to invest their time in schoolwork.

Many parents recognize and reward the major cognitive and motor accomplishments of infants and toddlers with intangible rewards—hugs, excitement, encouragement—or tangible rewards—candy, toys, and so on. The child's first steps, first words, new songs, crayon scribbles, and other new skills are given recognition. During the preschool years, parents assist and reward children for writing their names, learning the alphabet, for painting a picture. Early rewards help establish these behaviors in the child's evolving internal motivational system. Young children consider walking, singing, saying the alphabet, bike-riding, and painting as skills that are enjoyable and rewarding for their own sake. They work to master these skills and to continue learning.

Once children are in school, however, many parents lack information about how to monitor and reward children for increments in their school learning. Although most parents say they value education, few systematically and knowledgeably reward their children for the actual progress they make in schoolwork. Schools need to help parents understand, monitor, and reward students' attitudes and achievements. With each new grade level, parents need more assistance from teachers, administrators, guidance personnel, and others to understand where their children are starting from, what they are working toward, and how to recognize and reward progress in order to maintain or boost children's motivation to learn.

GROUPING STRUCTURE

The *grouping structure* (**G**) at home is the analog of one at school that determines whether, how, and why students who are similar or different on particular characteristics (e.g., gender, race, SES, ability, goals, or interests) are brought together or kept apart for instruction, play, or other activities. Families, like schools, guide their children's contacts and interactions in peer and friendship groups (Epstein, 1983c, 1986a). In so doing, they directly and indirectly influence motivation to learn.

Patterns of interaction within the family influence children's personalities and interpersonal skills outside the family. "Warm" children may make friends easily, whereas "aloof" children may not (Maas, 1968). Families provide opportunities that encourage nurturing behavior such as child care responsibilities (Whiting, 1986), or care of elderly family members. Family training in prosocial behaviors such as comforting, sharing, defending, helping, and cooperating (Sigel, Dreyer, & McGill-icuddy-Delisi, 1984) influence children's social relations with their peers and their success on learning tasks that require cooperation with others.

Patterns of interaction arranged by the family shape the grouping structure at home. Parents bring toddlers and preschoolers together in formal or informal play groups at home or in the neighborhood. Families may select day care, nursery, kindergarten and other schools to provide or prevent their children's interaction with other groups of children. At one extreme, some parents "home-teach" their children in order to *prevent* children from attending the same school with "less desireable" peers (Williams, Arnoldsen, & Reynolds, 1984). At the other extreme, parents send their children to boarding school to *assure* their membership and total immersion in a group of peers. Private or public schools may be selected so that children interact with or avoid particular groups. Family choice of schools and other influences over peers and friends affect children's motivation to learn because the peer group is a powerful social context with expectations for the attitudes and behavior of group members.

Families influence their school-aged children's selection of friends by their attitudes and discussions about children in the neighborhood, and their attitudes toward cross-sex, cross-race, and other friendships. Parents' attitudes and their own behaviors toward children and adults of different races, ethnic groups, family backgrounds, physical features, and disabilities encourage or discourage their children's contacts and friendships. For example, parents' racial attitudes influence the chil-drens' racial attitudes and their cross-race choices of friends (McPart-land, 1969; Patchen, 1982).

Family practices influence how children balance their loyalties to parents and to peers. Open communications at home increase the likelihood that children will approach parents as well as their peers for advice and information (Isherwood & Hammah, 1981; Youniss & Smollar, 1985).

Parents help create a grouping structure at home by their invitations to children and by their interactions with the parents of other children. In some families, children's activities with friends are based on sports; in others, on trips to the library, museum, children's theater, and other school-enriching places and events. Peer-group activities at home that support school-like activities influence children's motivation to learn and demonstrate family and school connections.

Most families lack information to understand and to influence peer and friendship groups across the school years in ways that boost motivation and learning. Schools need to help families understand the importance of the peer group, their children's social skills, the organization of groups in school, and how to support their children's peer relations. Schools can help establish a strong contextual effect among families for supporting students' schoolwork (e.g., by guiding attitudes and behaviors about homework, providing family phone directories or the names of family–school liaisons to encourage communication among parents about school-related activities). Parents can encourage their children and their friends to give high priority to schoolwork and homework by establishing family rules about completing homework before doing other activities. If homework habits are coordinated across families in neighborhoods, the peer group at home will be more likely to support learning at school. Families also demonstrate their support of school programs by attending assemblies, team sports, demonstrations, award ceremonies, performances, or other activities in which their children and their friends and classmates participate.

EVALUATION STRUCTURE

The *evaluation structure* (**E**) at home concerns (1) the standards that are set by parents and children for learning and behavior, (2) the procedures for monitoring and judging the attainment of those standards, and (3) the methods for providing information about performance or needed improvements. Because these judgments may lead to rewards or punishments, the evaluation structure is closely linked to the reward structure.

Evaluations of children at home about academic, social, or other matters may be public, private, or personal; comparative or individual; and frequent or infrequent. Public evaluation is open for others to hear. At home, evaluation of one child may take place in front of siblings, other relatives, or friends. Private evaluation is between the child and one other—a parent, sibling, friend, or another relative—but always without any other audience. Personal evaluation is conducted by the child alone, in accordance with his/her own goals. Personal or intrinsic evaluations rely on the values and standards adopted from the family, but the messages, ratings, and course of action for improvement are self-initiated and self-directed. Each type of evaluation may prompt different motives in children about learning and school activities, with positive public, individual, or personal and intrinsic evaluations more productive than negative public or comparative ones.

Comparative evaluations require each child to be judged according to a fixed standard or in relation to what others do (e.g., compared to a top scholar, a sibling, a friend, a parent at the age of the child). Individual evaluations are based on the child's history and patterns of improvement. Depending on other factors, frequent evaluations may reflect either responsive monitoring or overcontrol by parents; infrequent evaluations may reflect either parental neglect or faith in the children's abilities to proceed independently.

Parents readily evaluate their children's behavior at home, but they are often at a loss about the procedures and criteria to use to evaluate progress and effort that concerns school work. Schools should assist parents by providing information on learning objectives, testing and grading policies, programs for remedial and enrichment activities, and other factors that involve the school's evaluation of students. Parents also serve as their children's advocates by monitoring the school processes to assure fairness in the evaluation practices, testing procedures, and children's placements.

Families can balance or minimize the negative impact of some school evaluations that reduce student motivation and interest in school, such as those that are solely based on comparisons of one child against another. Or, families can support the positive influence of school evaluations that recognize children's efforts and progress. Either approach requires that families have useful information both about the school goals and programs and about their children's progress. The success of the family's evaluation structure for influencing motivation to learn depends, also, on the parents' demands on themselves for high-quality work, and the public ways they analyze their own efforts.

The evaluation structure at home offers or limits access to rewards from the family. If the parents' standards are too high, or if the evaluation procedures are not clear, family practices will lead to failure, disappointment, or alienation for many children. Under these conditions, children will not measure up to the parents' expectations, and will not qualify for rewards and support. An ineffective evaluation structure reduces motivation by withholding information needed to improve performance. By contrast, an effective evaluation structure at home leads children to a higher level of understanding about their own effort, abilities, and improvement.

If the parents and children set clear, sequential, and attainable standards, the evaluation structure at home will challenge and support the success and satisfaction of most children and will encourage their continued motivation to learn. If the messages are immediate, corrective, constructive, and offered with affection (as opposed to delayed, uninformative, destructive, and uncaring), children's efforts are more likely to be directed toward learning and improvement. Parents' frequent, informative, and individual evaluations that focus on the child's improvements are important supplements to schools' heavily summative evaluations.

TIME STRUCTURE

The *time structure* (**T**) at home concerns the schedules families set for children's activities and assignments. Families do not usually set rigid 50-minute periods for work or play, as most schools do. But too much flexibility or unplanned time may result in a lack of dedication to schoolwork at home. In some families a laissez-faire attitude about time management may be translated into school lateness, absence, incomplete or forgotten work, or poorly executed homework. In other families, so many activities are planned that a fixed-time schedule is needed to fit in music lessons, sports, homework, and other requirements. This, too, may diminish the family's emphasis on schoolwork, reduce the time the children spend on homework and reduce the quality of the work completed. Other qualities also come into play. Families are rarely silent, but the level of noise influences whether time for schoolwork at home is used effectively (Levine, 1983, 1984).

A 1984 study of adolescents shows that, on average, 41% of adolescents' waking hours are spent at home compared to 32% in school and 27% in other settings (Csikszentmihalyi & Larson, 1984). Home time is divided into leisure, eating, personal care, chores, and academic activities. Time spent at home can be structured to help a child carry out the role of student (Asp & Levine, 1985).

Students' assignments and personal rates for learning determine the time needed to complete homework or other tasks. For example, at the elementary school level, *slower* students spend *more time* on homework than brighter students (Epstein, 1985; Levine, 1984). Elementary school teachers tend to assign all students in a class about the same amount of homework, so slower learners take longer to complete the work. At the high school level, we find the more expected pattern—*brighter* students spend *more time* on homework (Keith, Reimers, Fehrmann, Pottebaum, & Augey, 1986; Pennsylvania State Department of Education, 1984). These students are in more demanding courses where teachers assign more homework, and they have developed more intrinsic motivation to learn and initiate more work on their own.

Schools need to inform parents each year about the amount of time students need at home to complete homework assignments on most school nights and weekends. Then, family schedules and activities can be arranged to support students' school responsibilities. Informed communications by families with their children's schools can assure that slower learners in middle, junior high, and high schools are not "written off" or short-changed in their courses and assignments just because they take more time to learn. Parents, teachers, and children need to understand how time for learning at home can accommodate students' needs and boost motivation for learning.

The promising fact is that there is almost immediate payoff to students in better schoolwork and report-card grades that result from family schedules and support for homework. At the elementary and high school levels, parents' involvement (i.e., time spent) assisting or monitoring homework has positive effects on students' attitudes and achievements, net of ability and family background (Epstein, 1982, 1985, in press; Keith et al., 1986). Epstein (1986a) shows tht the teachers' practices make the difference for whether parents are involved at home on learning activities that assist their children in school. Thus, teachers play a critical role in providing information to parents how to use their time productively at home in ways that directly assist their children as students.

LINKS AMONG TARGET STRUCTURES

The TARGET structures at home are linked to each other and to the parallel structures at the school. For example, homework is a *task* designed and assigned at school, but completed and discussed at home. Completing homework requires an appropriate *time* structure at school and at home. At school, the teacher must be sure that enough instructional time was allocated to teach the skills needed for the homework activity, and that the assignment was designed to be completed in a reasonable time period for students of all abilities. At home, the family schedule must provide time for homework among other chores. Doing homework happily at home requires that the children participate in *decisions* about how, when, and with whom to do the work. Continuing to do homework every night year after year, requires *peer group* norms that place high priority on homework. Students also need to know that parents and teachers recognize and reward their efforts. At school, teachers must use clear, fair, and encouraging *evaluation* procedures that tell students how to improve their work and that inform parents how to help their children on needed skills. Thus, it is clear that changing one structure (e.g., designing more appropriate homework tasks) requires changing other TARGET structures if the change is to succeed in family and school environments.

There are many potentially important links between and among the TARGET structures at home and between home and school. We do not yet know which connections are especially important for children's motivation to learn, but we offer some ideas and hypotheses about a few of them.

The *task, authority,* and *reward* structures are importantly linked, for example, when children are permitted to choose tasks or choose among tasks for their own reasons (e.g., to suit their personal feelings of competence and interests). Good and Tom (1985) report that when students are permitted to choose tasks they consider challenging, they are more motivated to work, even for fewer rewards. There are many opportunities at home to permit children to choose among equally important tasks to help them build skills in decision making and self-confidence.

The *task* and *reward* structures at home are linked in several ways. For example, if parents reward performance and ability instead of effort and improvement, many children will avoid challenging tasks (Dweck, 1984). Rewards define children's successes and lead to their preferences for particular tasks or subjects. Extrinsic rewards tend to focus students' attention on the results of tasks rather than on the learning that takes place.

The *task* and *grouping* structures at home combine to determine whether and which children work together on assignments. Doing schoolwork with siblings or friends at home may increase mastery of a skill and promote social support for learning.

There are connections, too, between the *reward* and *grouping* structures. Rewards based on comparisons with others, instead of measures of personal improvement, tend to focus children's attention on their often fixed, relative positions in a group, rather than on their own increasing abilities. There should be different results in students' attitudes and behaviors if reward structures emphasize personal improvement instead of competition between individual children and their friends or peers.

The *task* and *time* structures at home are closely linked. If the tasks are inappropriate, or if the time to do them is inadequate, children will not be motivated to do the tasks. When the links between task and time structures are productive, students will increase their accumulated knowledge. For example, educationally oriented homes are organized so that children spend more time reading than doing household chores (Asp & Levine, 1985). And, the organization of time at home for learning extends beyond the school year. Heyns (1978) suggests that time at home during the summer months on school-related tasks affects how well students succeed in school the following fall.

Effective connections among the *task, authority,* and *time* structures at home may assist student motivation and learning at home. Scott-Jones (1980) distinguishes between two types of learning activities of first-grade students that she observed in the homes of black, low-income families. Among brighter students, *the children* initiated learning activities as part of their play, and were assisted by a parent as needed. Among slower students, *the parents* initiated learning activities in ways unrelated to the child's play. Child-initiated activities may be inherently more interesting. Parent-initiated activities that are neither integrated with play, designed or guided by teachers, not coordinated with school expectations and requirements, may be uninteresting and disruptive to learning. Schools can guide parents of children with learning problems to understand how to help their children at home on specific "family-friendly" tasks that boost student motivation to learn as they provide practice on needed skills.

If children lack motivation to learn, parents need to examine the TARGET structures at home, singly and in combination, to see if the organization of family practices is working against children's commitment to schoolwork. In the next section, we discuss how these structures and their related practices must change as children change in order to continue to influence motivation to learn.

TARGET STRUCTURES AT HOME AND STUDENT DEVELOPMENT

The TARGET structures at home must be responsive to the changing abilities, needs, and accumulated skills of children and parents. Lipsitz (1984) suggests that schools promote student motivation when they are designed to meet the developmental demands created by changes in children's biological, cognitive, personal, and social growth. Stipek (1984) summarizes important developmental issues in achievement motivation. Epstein (1988) discusses how teachers design TARGET structures in classrooms to respond to student development and diversity. Similarly, the TARGET structures at home need to respond appropriately to changes in child development.

From childhood to adolescence, youngsters increase in independence, responsibility, understanding abstractions, understanding themselves and others, resolving conflicts, memory skills, and other academic and social skills (Ruble, 1980; Simmons, Blyth, Van Cleave, & Bush, 1979; Stipek, 1984). Parents' skills, knowledge, and parent–child relations also change (Maccoby, 1984; Sigel et al., 1984). Although many parents *gain confidence* about interacting with their children, many others *lose confidence* in their ability to help their older children (Epstein, 1986b). Parents need to understand how family organizations must change as children mature in order to provide support and challenges at home for continued learning and development.

TASK STRUCTURE

The task structure at home meets developmental demands by including increasingly challenging activities for older children (Ruble, 1980; Veroff, 1969). Research suggests that older students prefer challenging tasks. And, regardless of age, the more able a student feels, the more likely he or she is to seek challenging tasks to test knowledge and extend accomplishments (Kukla, 1978). Thus, children who have mastered a skill will be motivated by more challenging tasks, and older children who have experienced repeated failure will be especially likely to avoid certain tasks.

Many families understand that tasks for infants, toddlers, and preschool children must be appropriate, challenging, enjoyable, and based on the youngster's prior levels of ability and changing interests. Parents buy toys and games that are recommended for certain ages to motivate play and learning. Or parents teach toddlers or preschoolers new words and skills based on what the child already knows. Relatively easy and familiar tasks lead to mastery, feelings of success, and readiness for new levels of difficulty. Families enjoy preschoolers' repetitions of familiar tasks as children build efficient and proficient learning behaviors. Most families are not well-informed, however, about age-appropriate tasks or useful repetitions for school-aged children that will motivate learning and school success. Schools play important roles in helping families design and revise the task structure at home to provide students' with opportunities to practice, increase efficiency, and master needed skills, by providing information, examples, and specific activities for home learning (Becker & Epstein, 1982; Epstein, 1986a, 1987a; Rich, 1985).

AUTHORITY STRUCTURE

The authority structure at home responds to student development by providing older children with increased opportunities for independence, responsibility, self-direction, and participation in family decisions. The transfer of power from parent to child occurs more slowly than had been supposed (Maccoby, 1984). A period of cooperative coregulation, shared decision making, parental supervision, and children's self-direction occurs in middle childhood, as children move slowly toward independence. Youniss and Smollar (1985) note that there is greater parent control and child consensus up to about age 10, and an increase in parent–child negotiation, compromise, and revisions of requests in later years. In our studies, we found that the number of family rules and regulations *decrease* and opportunities for student participation in family decisions *increase* from ages 10 to 18 years (grades 5–12).

There are some contradictory patterns that occur in schools. For example, school programs become more participatory and permit more decision making from grades 5 to 12 (Epstein, 1984a). Students make more choices of courses and activities, and some teachers offer less direct and less constant supervision. At the same time, some classes for older students may become more formal and stylistic, with more lecturing by teachers and less active learning by students. Thus, contrary to expectations for developmental increases in opportunities for autonomy, some middle, junior high, and high school classes become *more* restrictive, *less* challenging, and permit *less* independence than classes in earlier grades (Brophy & Evertson, 1978; Eccles, Midgley, & Adler, 1984).

Similarly, there are wide variations among families in the number of rules, types of participation, and rates of change in these family practices. In some families, the opportunities for decision making and independent action increase as the children mature, whereas in other homes, the types and levels of participation remain the same, despite changes in children's abilities. Contradictory practices occur at home if parents expect older students to be more responsible, but, at the same time, they set overly restrictive rules or engage in less communication with their older children. The rates of change in family rules and decision making have independent effects on student attitudes and behaviors. Families that withhold or prevent increased participation in decision making may seriously limit student motivation and learning (Epstein, 1983a, 1984a).

A responsive, changing authority structure at home may actually *increase* parental authority and prolong parental influence. Older children may be more willing to seek advice from parents when they have continuing evidence that their own ideas are taken seriously. Parents who are aware of the need for changing authority structures are more likely to monitor the practices at home and school to assure that their children are offered increasing opportunities for independence and self-direction. This may be especially important for slow learners who often need remedial academic instruction, but who, like all children, need opportunities for independence and self-direction to match their social skills and to maintain their motivation to learn.

REWARD STRUCTURE

The reward structure at home meets developmental demands created as children gain in self-confidence and as they revalue different kinds of rewards and recognitions (Maccoby, 1984; Ruble, 1980). Young students or students starting to learn a particular subject or skill may need more frequent rewards, recognition, and encouragement, whereas older students or those with clear strengths in a subject may need less frequent recognition to maintain their motivation to learn new skills. Young children may respond to small, frequent, demonstrative recognitions and social reinforcements (hugs, praise, candy, ribbons, stars) while older children may be bolstered by less frequent but more dramatic awards (e.g., money, a trip to a ball game or movie, trophies, small gifts related to an accomplishment) or by more subtle recognition (e.g., privately offered praise and encouragement). The rewards older children value are different and more varied than those of younger children. But, whether frequent or intermittent, attention and recognition from the family continues to be important for children at all grade levels. The goal is to create conditions at home so that, over time, children feel intrinsically rewarded by learning.

There are some intriguing contradictory patterns of results in research on children's understanding and use of the concepts of effort and ability, how "success" is measured, and how rewards are distributed. Some researchers report that young children place high value on effort, whereas older children place greater value on ability (Kun, 1977). Young children believe that if they try hard, they are successful, regardless of their results. Older children believe that if they get high grades they are successful regardless of their effort. These beliefs and definitions may reflect parents' and teachers' increasing attention and rewards for high marks and little attention to effort.

Other researchers suggest that older children (ages 10–12) begin to recognize the importance of *effort* in judging whether they and others deserve rewards for completed tasks (Weiner & Peter, 1973). The discrepancies in whether older children recognize effort or ability or equate effort with success may have to do with whether the child is focusing on rewards for him/herself or for others, or whether the environment distributes many or few rewards of different value. Older children are more sensitive to the social justice in giving *some* recognition for effort, but giving *more* recognition for success and ability. These patterns are not fixed. The reward structures at home and at school may be designed in ways that encourage older children to continue to value effort and improvement.

The conflicting ideas about the effects of age on children's beliefs and attitudes toward effort and ability are complicated by the fact that as students enter middle school or junior high, their report card grades tend to go down, even as their overall competencies go up (Peterson, 1986). Middle and junior high schools are larger than elementary schools, and students are compared with new groups of students. With more demanding tasks and more competitive rewards in the middle grades, many students who had received top grades receive just average grades. Or, those who had been average elementary students are rated below average in the middle grades. The same redistribution of report card grades occurs at entry to high school, when new tasks and greater competition in larger schools again revise the schools' evaluation and reward structures. For many students, report card grades in middle school and high school decrease even as their knowledge and competencies increase.

These changing patterns of rewards in schools have important implications for family reward structures. Most families lack information about older students' achievements and progress in school at the very time the children would benefit from knowledgeable guidance and discussions at home. If such information were provided to parents by schools, more families would be able to help children understand and deal with the discrepancies between lower report card grades in school and greater personal abilities outside of school. Older students benefit from family support to maintain a sense of self-esteem, maintain their motivation both to learn and to complete high school, and gain intrinsic rewards from learning.

GROUPING STRUCTURE

The grouping structure at home needs to change as students expand their social circles. Family control over peers and friends changes over the years from infancy to adolescence. Early childhood contacts with peers are controlled largely by the family. Later, contacts with peers are controlled more by the school than the home. Older students interact with peers and select their friends from wider boundaries and more settings than younger students.

There is a delicate, changing balance between peer pressure and family expectations as children mature. Youniss and Smollar (1985) note that parents continue to guide adolescent children at the same time relations among peers and friends are becoming more complex and intense. Epstein (1983b) shows that there are simultaneous patterns of influence of parents and friends (and schools) on students from grades 6 through 12. Awareness of the developmental patterns in children's social groups, peer pressures, and dating patterns may help families maintain a healthy balance between family and peer influence. If children think their families are not interested in their friends, they may overemphasize the importance of conformity to peer standards and values, and repudiate family and personal values including the importance of learning at school.

EVALUATION STRUCTURE

The evaluation structure at home should be developmentally responsive to students' increasing abilities to understand the causal connections between plans, actions, and results in learning. Young children do not usually pay attention to the causes of their performance, nor do they analyze how to improve their work (Harter, 1978; also see Stipek, 1984). An effective evaluation structure at home focuses children's attention on their own work and efforts. Older children benefit from family evaluations that provide detailed reasons for the judgments about their schoolwork, attitudes, and behavior, and useful suggestions and plans for improvement. Families need to increase the extent to which older children are involved in setting standards for and judging progress on their own schoolwork and learning. Over the years, there should be a decrease (but not disappearance) in the frequency of parents' evaluations as children increase their abilities to evaluate themselves.

TIME STRUCTURE

The time structure at home needs to change as students increase their ability to work intensively. School activities, hobbies, talents, leisure activities, and part-time work become more complex and time-consuming. Over time, family practices must support the deeper and more sustained investments of time that children require to master school subjects. When time structures at home do not make these adjustments, children will lack the mastery of skills that provide older students with self-confidence as learners.

There are important connections between time in school and at home. As the number of structured, achievement-related activities in school increase, students receive more homework from several teachers and need more time for work and study at home. Many parents do not know how to continue to monitor and guide older children's time at home while they also try to promote independence and self-direction. Families need information from the schools each year through high school to make needed changes in increasingly complex time structures for school work at home, and to guide their children's decisions about time use.

LINKS AMONG DEVELOPMENTAL CHANGES IN TARGET STRUCTURES

Earlier, we discussed a few of many connections among the TARGET structures. There also are connections among the developmental changes in these structures. For example, a family may change the level of challenge in the *tasks* assigned to older children at home, but this will be more successful if concurrent changes are made in the *authority* structure to give children increasing control over their own activities. And, the *task* and *reward* structures need to change together so that as tasks become more challenging, appropriate rewards are offered as incentives for effort and as official recognition of valued work.

The *authority* and *evaluation* structures also need to change in concert. Along with increased opportunities for decision making, families must permit children to bear the consequences of their decisions and help them evaluate their choices and the results. If parents and children set goals and standards together, the children will better understand the evaluations they receive, feel pride at meeting standards, and raise their own expectations for their performance.

Changes in the *task, authority,* and *time* structures are linked as families help children accept increasing responsibility for planning their time for weeknight and weekend homework and study, as well as their time for household chores, hobbies, time with friends, and later, part-time work.

The TARGET structures combine to influence motivation in the broadest sense. For example, intrinsic motivation to learn—to get pleasure from a task itself and to feel rewarded by new knowledge— shows a curvilinear pattern in development. For most children, there seems to be less intrinsic motivation about learning school tasks during the school years (Maehr, 1984). This may be due, in part, to (1) inappropriate designs or inadequate change in tasks, rewards, patterns of participation, and (2) other organizational weaknesses in the TARGET structures in school and at home. On average, intrinsic motivation to learn increases again in late adolescence and adulthood, as interests crystallize and as youngsters gain greater personal control over their time and their activities.

Families assist their children in many ways across the school years. Children must adjust to *expected changes* in schools, such as promotion to new grade levels or transitions to elementary, middle, or junior high school, and *unexpected changes* such as transfers to new schools because of family moves or school closings or redistricting. Family discussions, shared planning, monitoring problems, and other preparations help children meet changes that are part of the natural order of school life. Family TARGET structures can assist children to make smooth transitions to new school grades, instructional groups, or demands in school and to maintain positive motivation for learning at difficult times across the school years.

Family practices deeply influence children's values, goals, and school-related behaviors and achievements. In the next section, we examine how family TARGET structures affect motivation to learn and influence particular student outcomes that are important for school success.

TARGET STRUCTURES AT HOME, MOTIVATION, AND OUTCOMES

TASK STRUCTURE

We suggest that the TARGET structures at home relate to *different* motivational forces and student outcomes, as shown in Table 1. The top section of the table, for example, suggests that the *task structure* at home is linked especially to the student's level of *curiosity* and *anxiety* about learning (see Column 2). Well-designed tasks increase curiosity and challenge students to think and work without creating undue anxiety about learning. This will occur when tasks are appropriate for the

TABLE 1

Family TARGET Structures, Student Motivation, and Outcomes

TARGET structures at home[a]	Influence on motivating forces[b]	Influence on student outcomes[c]
Tasks (T) at appropriate levels of difficulty Balance in the number of kinds of household chores, school assignments, and leisure projects Family discussions of school activities and assignments Parent–child interaction about schoolwork Novelty and variety in tasks Change in tasks for new levels of ability	Curiosity Interest Low anxiety about school Task involvement Challenge Need achievement/ achievement striving	Attitudes toward homework and schoolwork Performance of role as son/daughter, student and individual Interest in school skills Learning/knowledge/ achievement Understanding concepts of ability and effort Understanding options for special interests, advanced skills, talents, occupations Other competence/ incompetence outcomes
Authority (A) based on shared decision making by parent and child Emphasis on children as active participants Opportunities for choice and autonomy Change in rate and type of participation according to age, grade, and new abilities	Internal locus of control Personal responsibility Low fear of authority Efficacy Approach success and avoid failure	Ability to solve problems, choose appropriate actions Attitude toward authority Knowledgeable use of authority resources and structures Independent, wise use of counsel to learn self-directed behavior Initiative, leadership, exploration Flexibility of behavior Other independence/ dependence outcomes (e.g., education and career plans)
Rewards (R) based on parent recognition of improvement as well as excellence	Self-esteem/self-concept of ability Affection/attachment/low guilt	Feelings of self-worth Awareness of behaviors and attitudes valued by others

TABLE 1 (*Continued*)

TARGET structures at home[a]	Influence on motivating forces[b]	Influence on student outcomes[c]
Recognition of many different skills and talents, including school-related activities Rewards for both cooperative and competitive behavior Responsive incentives Appropriate balance of tangible and intangible rewards Extrinsic rewards and development of intrinsic rewards Change in rewards to meet new needs and abilities	Expectations for success/failure Intrinsic motivation (to please self)/extrinsic motivation (to please others)	Cooperative/competitive behavior with parents, siblings, relatives, friends, classmates Improvement and performance goals and goal attainment Attitudes about learning Attention to finished products Other confidence/doubt outcomes
Grouping (*G*) that encourages interactions with other children with similar/different abilities, talents, and backgrounds Family discussions of friendship, social behavior Opportunities for social contact at home with siblings, friends, other relations that involve school-related activities Grouping patterns and family emphases that change as peer group relations are revised	Social status Influence Security Social motives, goals Empathy	Attitudes toward peers Tolerance, acceptance, appreciation of group and individual differences Popularity/acceptance from others Negotiation, compromise, sharing, cooperation, and other interpersonal skills Social responsibility Family identity Other conformity/ individuality outcomes, and other prosocial behaviors

(*continued*)

TABLE 1 (*Continued*)

TARGET structures at home[a]	Influence on motivating forces[b]	Influence on student outcomes[c]
Evaluations (*E*) that establish family standards and clear expectations for school skills Informative messages from parents for improvement of school skills Monitoring and information systems that change with children's age and abilities	Certainty/uncertainty Information value Prediction of success Prediction of required effort	Awareness of improvement–progress Internalized standards Ability to compare self and others Fairness in judgments Plan for improvement Setting future goals Reasoning Other outcomes of understanding/ misunderstanding personal goals and skills
Time (*T*) that respects diversity in children's rates of learning Opportunities for intensive study on subjects of interest Balance in household chores, school assignments, hobbies with high priority on school-related tasks Change in timing to match the level of task difficulty and children's ability	Sense of purpose Commitment Persistence	Completion of homework Knowledge of personal pace for work and learning Accumulated knowledge Improved skills in management and organization—e.g., planning, scheduling, completing tasks Development of expertise in one or more subjects Continued interest in learning Other completion/ quitting outcomes

[a] The TARGET structures are described in terms of positive qualities. It should be understood that each component of each structure listed here or discussed in the text represents a continuum (e.g., more or less appropriate level of task difficulty, more or less shared authority).

[b] The motivating forces are discussed in these and related terms in numerous chapters in Ames and Ames, 1984b, 1985; Ball, 1982; Fyans, 1980; Weiner, 1979, 1984. The simple terms in this column stand for complex concepts, and each represents a continuum (e.g., more or less curiosity, more or less anxiety).

[c] Each outcome is a variable that ranges along a continuum (e.g., children may be more or less positive in their attitudes, have low or high achievement, more or less independence). Although the table is set in three columns, the entries represent a continuing loop of 2-way and 3-way influences. Structures and their component practices, motivational forces, and interim outcomes change and affect each other over time, and they need to be researched in nonrecursive models.

students' abilities and prior knowledge, and when they include a degree of novelty and excitement to minimize boredom and maximize interest. Poorly designed tasks that are too easy for students will minimize curiosity and those that are too hard will maximize anxiety. Either inappropriate level of difficulty will create negative motivations that increase student withdrawal or alienation from school or home tasks.

If curiosity is energized and anxiety is controlled, positive outcomes should result, such as those described in Column 3. Interesting, challenging tasks that awaken curiosity produce positive attitudes about schoolwork and homework. And, if there is a good mix of school, household, and leisure tasks at home, the child develops a balanced set of interests and goals, which should lead to more successful performance of the roles of student, son/daughter, and unique individual. Thus, appropriately challenging tasks conducted by children at home increase curiosity and involvement and lead to increased knowledge, mastery of skills, achievement, and other competencies. If the task structure is too predictable or rigid, children will not be engaged intellectually and will not proceed with maximum learning.

The entries in the rest of the table show connections between the authority, reward, grouping, evaluation, and time structures with particular motivating forces and different student outcomes. Here, we discuss a few examples shown in the table.

AUTHORITY STRUCTURE

We link the *authority structure* at home with the development of students' *locus of control* (see Column 2 in the section on authority structure). For example, high participation in decision making at home increases both children's feelings of internal control of their environment and their attributions of success to personal actions. These motivating forces promote such outcomes as positive attitudes toward authority, more successful independent judgments, and better use of the school organization (see column 3). Students who assume greater responsibility for their own work have less reason to blame their parents or teachers for their failures and more reason to feel pride in personal successes. Greater self-direction means that students are making demands on themselves, and this may make them less antagonistic and more positive toward other authority figures, such as their teachers at school (Epstein, 1981) or parents at home.

In an earlier study, we found that family authority practices that sequentially increase children's decision-making opportunities tend to increase feelings of internal locus of control and promote growth in independence (Epstein, 1983a). Greater internal control may also boost youngsters' abilities to state their own interests, make education and job plans, and improve other independent behaviors.

Others, too, suggest that parent authority based on reasoning and shared power leads to more internal attributions and, potentially, to more positive attitudes toward school and learning. By contrast, parental force and coercion are likely to promote external attributions in children (Dix & Grusec, 1983). Restrictive, authoritarian family practices and practices that are not developmentally appropriate put the child in the role of the "pawn," described by deCharms (1976, 1980), instead of being the "origin" of behavior. Instead, children see that others are, in fact, in control of their successes or failures. Thus, if the authority structure is too hierarchical or restrictive, children will not experience the high internal locus of control or sense of purpose needed for effective school learning and behavior. Dependent, externally controlled children are not likely to initiate ideas or actions or lead others nor will they seek ways to make the school organization work for them.

REWARD STRUCTURE

Positive *reward structures* at home increase children's *self-confidence,* reduce *guilt about success,* and increase motivation to *continue learning.* These qualities result in greater effort and commitment to schoolwork. Some families reward children only for high test scores or letter grades (such as A's on report cards). These grades are not attainable by all students, even with great motivation and effort. A family reward structure based on top scores or comparisons with other siblings or other students may increase children's motivation to avoid failure rather than to improve skills. By contrast, some families monitor and reward improvement—or "personal bests"—criteria that can be met by all students with motivation and effort. This reward structure focuses on changes in the accomplishments of individuals and may encourage purposeful work (Ames & Archer, 1987; Nicholls, 1984; Stipek, 1984). High self-esteem is likely to be produced, maintained, and increased for more children if the reward structure at home emphasizes improvement rather than top grades. The positive sense of self is a motivating force that helps children develop positive attitudes toward learning, attention to improvement, pride in completed projects, and other outcomes that, in turn, confirm and strengthen self-confidence.

GROUPING STRUCTURE

Positive *grouping structures* at home help children improve their *social status, social motives,* and *feelings of security.* Students who have a sense of social support are able to concentrate on their academic assignments. Other students may spend time and energy thinking about their status in their family or peer group instead of thinking about their schoolwork (Marjoribanks, 1979). Children's self-concepts are influenced, in part, by others' reactions to their ideas and behaviors (Minuchin, 1977). Learning problems may develop if children lack the social skills that help them work together and make friends in school with other students. Families build children's social skills through their practices that relate to the peer group at home. Strong social skills should promote students' appreciation of and cooperation with others in school or home activities.

EVALUATION STRUCTURE

The *evaluation structure* at home provides information to children about their efforts and attainments. This information promotes children's *sense of certainty* about sequences of actions for learning and their ability to predict the *level of effort* needed to reach standards that they and their parents set. This, then, results in more (1) successful strategies for improvement, (2) willingness and ability to obtain help when it is needed, and (3) intrinsic and honest understanding of personal goals and skills.

Unfair or unclear evaluations at home may create critical gaps in children's ability to execute school assignments successfully, even if the children were initially motivated to learn. Uncertainty creates barriers to action—reducing children's willingness to invest effort in learning. Most families have high expectations, but many children do not reach the family's goals. The effectiveness of the evaluation structure at home may largely determine whether parents and childrens' high hopes become actual attainments.

TIME STRUCTURE

Time structures at home that reflect the time needed for learning increase children's *sense of purpose, persistence,* and *performance* on assigned tasks (Maehr, 1984). These motivating forces lead to better homework completion, greater accumulated knowledge, and improved time management. These skills may contribute to the development and maintenance of children's abilities to plan, control, and complete their work, and they help students see how school and learning are important investments in their lives.

IMPLICATIONS FOR RESEARCH

Table 1 is far more complex than it looks at first glance. Although each TARGET structure is linked in the table to particular motivational forces and specific outcomes, the "true" influence process is overlapping and multidirectional. For example, each of the TARGET structures may contribute in different ways to self-confidence about learning, and many of the motivational forces may work together to boost academic achievement. Research supports some of the specific influence patterns suggested in Table 1 such as authority structure ⟶ internal locus of control ⟶ positive attitudes toward teachers (Epstein, 1981, 1983a), or time structure ⟶ commitment ⟶ completion of homework and accumulated knowledge (Levine, 1983, 1984). But most of the connections and the directions of influence still require painstaking research.

Table 1 must not be read as a causal model. It is not suggested that family structure ⟶ (leads to) motivation ⟶ (leads to) outcomes in a one-way, fixed process. For example, children's motivations and actions (such as high anxiety or low self-esteem) in response to family task structures may cause the family to revise practices. This would reverse the influence arrows to suggest family structure ⟵ motivation, or more likely, dual influences: family structure ⟷ motivation. Outcomes such as improved skills or failure, in turn, influence motivation. Thus, we suggest that children's motivations about learning affect the design of the TARGET structures at home, as much as the other way around. And outcomes of learning and development, such as those shown in Column 3 of the table, influence student motivation and prompt revisions in family TARGET structures. Indeed, our discussion of developmental changes requires that new outcomes direct new structures and motivations. Thus, the table represents the components that require testing in recursive and nonrecursive models, as well as in longitudinal and cross-sectional studies, to improve an understanding of the complex and continuous connections between family organization and student practices, motivations, and outcomes.

The table should not be interpreted to mean that the connections are solely the responsibility of the family. The family's successful organization of the TARGET structures concerning their children's motivation to learn in school depends heavily on the quality and quantity of information from the schools about children's programs and progress. Research clearly shows that families want assistance from the schools to understand how to help their children at home, and that if such assistance is provided, families are more responsive and productive partners in their children's education (Epstein, 1986b, 1987a). Schools have an important responsibility (based on their understanding of children at specific stages of development and the skills required for success at each grade level) to help families increase the degree of family–school overlap in ways that promote more effective students (1987b, 1988).

"Academic press" at home is a familiar concept that has been variously represented by the number of books in the family, parents' education, school supplies at home, or other measures of family characteristics, routines, and schedules that may impact student achievement (Asp & Levine, 1985; Brookover, Beady, Flood, Schweitzer, & Wisenbacker, 1979; McDill & Rigsby, 1973). The theory of family–school overlap and the TARGET structures provide substance and actual practices to the useful but often ill-defined concept of "academic press." Research is accumulating that indicates that the alterable *practices* of families—such as those that result from the design and execution of the TARGET structures at home—affect motivation and success in school as much as or more than the fixed family structures or static measures of family resources such as family income, parents' education, family size, and parents' marital status (Clark, 1983; Epstein, 1984b; Heatherington, Camera, & Featherman, 1981; Laosa, 1982; Scott-Jones, 1984).

Table 1 is a starting place. We need to understand motivation both as an important outcome (e.g., What factors promote curiosity, high self-confidence, and the desire to learn?) and as an influence on other school-related outcomes (e.g., How does curiosity affect the amount and kinds of learning students obtain? How does self-esteem lead to tolerance of others?). We suggest that the TARGET structures at home are important determinants of motivational forces that promote academic and nonacademic outcomes that have implications for success in school. And motivational forces and outcomes help to determine the design, revision, and rates of change in family structures.

DISCUSSION

Parents do not usually discuss family practices using terms like "the task structure" or "the authority structure." But, parents do talk about their children's activities (Tasks), increasing independence (Authority), the parents' reactions to their children's good and bad behavior (Rewards), their children's friends, acquaintances, classmates, clubs, and cliques (Grouping), how parents judge their children's progress and needed improvements (Evaluation), and how the children and parents spend time (Time). The TARGET structures, then, are part of everyday life, although families differ widely in the extent to which they purposely organize and revise the practices that operationalize these structures. Positive family environments support and challenge children to learn. Negative environments distract childrens' attention from school, set up emotional or cognitive barriers to success, or misinform students in ways that reduce motivation about school activities. Our discussion leads to the following conclusions:

1. Family warmth, understanding, and belief in the importance of education are necessary but not sufficient qualities for building and maintaining children's motivation to learn. These affective dimensions must be linked to specific practices that organize family life and that demonstrate the importance of education.
2. Motivation has been variously characterized by curiosity, high internal locus of control, attribution of success and failure, high interest in achievement, sense of purpose, expectations for success, affection and attachment, low anxiety, high self-esteem, self-confidence, and other energies that can be applied to learning. These qualities are influenced by different treatments, opportunities, interactions, and experiences that occur under different family and school TARGET structures.

   Motivation to learn is at once an external and internal process (Ames & Ames, 1984a; Ball, 1982). Students are motivated to learn by external conditions at school and at home that promote interpersonal interactions with significant others—mainly teachers, parents, and peers. And students are motivated to learn by internal forces—individual ability, the desire for information, knowledge, or success, or the desire to please others or fulfill their own or others' expectations. External conditions at home include the TARGET structures—tasks offered or assigned, decision making opportunities and experiences, rewards and recognitions, peer and friendship relations, fair judgments and advice for improvement, and the time allocated for various activities.

3. Family environments have the power to increase or decrease student motivation and maximize learning and development. The TARGET structures at home are manipulable variables that help parents create positive conditions and correct negative ones. Low motivation to learn and poor achievement or inadequate social skills may not be due to low ability or low effort in an individual, but rather to the poor design of the TARGET practices at home or at school. Inappropriate tasks, uninformed instruction, inadequate opportunities for involvement, narrow or exclusionary rewards or recognitions, fixed or unfair competition with others, inappropriate or unfair evaluations, or inadequate time for learning may produce low motivation and unsatisfactory learning in otherwise capable children.

4. The TARGET structures must change as children change. Families need to be aware of child and adolescent development and organizational management in order to effectively design and revise family practices to meet their childrens' needs and capabilities. If these structures do not change as the children change, youngsters may be at a real disadvantage in their school achievement and attitudes.

5. There are potentially important connections among the TARGET structures, particular motivational forces, and student outcomes. These connections suggest that families can purposely design new practices to promote more positive motivations and more productive attitudes and behaviors in their children. And families can take cues from their children's skills and behaviors to revise practices in order to promote increasingly advances skills and experiences.

6. The TARGET structures at home do not operate separately. The more coherent the connections among the TARGET structures at home concerning schoolwork, the more powerful the influence of the family on student motivation, learning, and other important outcomes.

7. The TARGET structures at home and at school simultaneously influence student motivation across the years that students are in school. It is not the family's responsibility alone to improve student motivation and success in school. Nor can families be expected to know automatically how the TARGET structures at home can be designed and revised to support positive conditions for learning. It is, in large part, the school's responsibility to communicate with the

family every year about the specific objectives and opportunities for learning, and about how the family can support the efforts of the school to maintain or increase their children's motivation. Parents with a deep understanding of their own children need to assist teachers by providing information about a child's talents or special needs. The two-way communication between parents and teachers bolsters motivation if it results in positive attention to student progress.

Parents need to be aware of the importance of influencing their children's motivation as well as outcomes. It is as important for schools to help parents know how to increase their children's curiosity or boost self-esteem as it is to help parents focus on achievement skills or completed homework. The TARGET structures and their links to motivation and outcomes provide useful terms for discussing family practices and interactions.

We have selected an analytic scheme that defines family organization in the same terms that we use to describe effective classrooms (Epstein, 1988). We call attention to the changes needed in these structures at home and at school to meet new levels of children's academic skills and social development. Families motivate children to learn by giving them a chance to think, to participate at home, to make choices among activities, to feel challenged in family discussions, to feel successful, to interact with others to test ideas and goals, and to take control of the way they plan and spend time. The discussion shows the diversity and depth in child-rearing practices and in children's actions and reactions to those practices that occur across the school grades. It is imperative to study the family along with the school to understand contextual effects on student motivation and learning. Family structures and resulting practices have serious consequences for school behaviors that characterize successful students.

REFERENCES

Ames, C., & Ames, R. (1984a). Systems of students and teacher motivation: Toward a qualitative definition. *Journal of Educational Psychology, 76,* 535–556.

Ames, C., & Ames, R. (Eds.) (1985). *Research on motivation in education: Volume 2. The classroom milieu.* Orlando: Academic Press.

Ames, R., & Ames, C. (Eds.) (1984b). *Research on motivation in education: Volume 1. Student motivation.* Orlando: Academic Press.

Ames, C., & Archer, J. (1987). Mothers' beliefs about the role of ability and effort in school learning. *Journal of Educational Psychology.*

Andrews, S. R., Blumenthal, J. B., Johnson, D. L., Kahn, A. J., Ferguson, C. J., Lasater, T. M., Malone, P. E., & Wallace, D. B. (1982). The skills of mother: A study of parent–child development centers. *Monographs of the Society for Research in Child Development* (6, Serial No. 198), 47.

Asp, E., & Levine, V. (1985, April). *The social context of home environment and achievement at school.* Paper presented at the annual meeting of the American Educational Research Association, Chicago.

Baker, D., & Stevenson, D. C. (1986). Maternal strategies for school achievement: Managing the transition to high school. *Sociology of Education, 59,* 156–166.

Ball, S. (1982). Motivation. In H. Mitzel (Ed.), *Encyclopedia of education* (5th ed.). New York: Free Press.

Baumrind, D. (1971). Current patterns of parental authority. *Developmental Psychology Monographs, 4* (1, part 2).

Becker, H. J., & Epstein, J. L. (1982). Parent involvement: A study of teacher practices. *Elementary School Journal, 83,* 85–102.

Bloom, B. S. (1982). The role of gifts and markers in the development of talent. *Exceptional Children, 48,* 510–522.

Brookover, W. B., Beady, C. H., Flood, P. K., Schweitzer, J. H., & Wisenbacker, J. M. (1979). *School social systems and student achievement: Schools can make a difference.* New York: Praeger.

Brophy, J. (1986). *Socializing students' motivation to learn.* East Lansing, MI: Michigan State University. (Mimeo).

Brophy, J., & Everston, C. (1978). Context variables in teaching. *Educational Psychologist, 12,* 310–316.

Clark, R. (1983). *Family life and school achievement: Why poor black children succeed and fail.* Chicago: University of Chicago Press.

Coleman, J. S., Campbell, E. Q., Hobson, C. J., McPartland, J. M., Mood, A. M., Weinfeld, F. D., & York, R. L. (1966). *Equal educational opportunity.* Washington, DC: Office of Education, Department of Health, Education and Welfare.

Csikszentmihalyi, M., & Larson, R. (1984). *Being adolescent.* New York: Basic Books.

DeCharms, R. (1976). *Enhancing motivation: Change in the classroom.* New York: Livingston.

DeCharms, R. (1980). Competence and achievement motivation in personal causation. In L. J. Fyans, Jr. (Ed.), *Achievement motivation: Recent trends in theory and research.* New York: Plenum.

Dix, T., & Grusec, J. E. (1983). Parent socialization techniques: An attributional analysis. *Child Development, 54,* 645–652.

Dweck, C. S. (1984). Motivation. In R. Glazer & A. Lesgold (Eds.), *The handbook of psychology and education.* Hillsdale, NJ: Erlbaum.

Eccles, J., Midgley, C., & Adler, T. F. (1984). Grade-related changes in the school environment: Effects on student motivation. In M. L. Maehr (Ed.), *Advances in motivation and achievement* (Vol. 3, pp. 283–331). Greenwich, CT: JAI Press.

Edler, G. H., Jr. (1971). Parental power legitimation and its effect on the adolescent. In J. P. Hill & J. Shelton (Eds.), *Readings in adolescent development and behavior* (pp. 179–190). Englewood Cliffs: Prentice-Hall.

Epstein, J. L. (1981). Patterns of classroom participation, student attitudes, and achievements. In J. Epstein (Ed.), *The quality of school life.* Lexington, MA: Lexington Books.

Epstein, J. L. (1982, April). *Student reactions to teachers' practices of parent involvement.* Paper presented at the annual meeting of the American Educational Research Association, New York City.

Epstein, J. L. (1983a). Longitudinal effects of person–family–school interactions on student outcomes. In A. Kerckhoff (Ed.), *Research in sociology of education and socialization* (Vol. 4), Greenwich, CT: JAI Press.

Epstein, J. L. (1983b). The influence of friends on achievement and affective outcomes. In J. Epstein & N. Karweit (Eds.) *Friends in school: Patterns of selection and influence in secondary schools.* New York: Academic Press.

Epstein, J. L. (1983c). Selection of friends in differently organized schools and classrooms. In J. Epstein & N. Karweit (Eds.) *Friends in school: Patterns of selection and influence in secondary schools.* New York: Academic Press.

Epstein, J. L. (1984a). A longitudinal study of school and family effects on student development. In S. A. Mednick & M. Harway (Eds.) *Handbook of longitudinal research.* New York: Praeger.

Epstein, J. L. (1984b). Single parents and the schools: The effects of marital status on parent and teacher evaluations (Report 353). Baltimore: The Johns Hopkins University Center for Social Organization of Schools.

Epstein, J. L. (1985). Homework practices, achievements, and behaviors of elementary school students. In *ERS information folio: Homework (1987).* Arlington VA: Educational Research Service.

Epstein, J. L. (1986a). Friendship selection: Developmental and environmental influences. In E. Mueller & C. Cooper (Eds.), *Process and outcomes in peer relations.* New York: Academic Press.

Epstein, J. L. (1986b). Parents' reactions to teacher practices of parent involvement. *The Elementary School Journal, 86,* 277–294.

Epstein, J. L. (1987a). Teacher practices of parent involvement: What research says to teachers and administrators. *Education in Urban Society, 19,* 119–136.

Epstein, J. L. (1987b). Toward a theory of family–school connections: Teacher practices and parent involvement across the school years. In K. Hurrelmann, F. Kaufmann, & F. Losel (Eds.), *Social intervention: Potential and constraints.* New York: de Gruyter.

Epstein, J. L. (1988). Effective schools or effective students: Dealing with diversity. In Ron Haskins & Duncan MacRae (Eds.), *Policies for America's public schools: Teachers, equity, indicators.* Norwood, NJ: Ablex.

Epstein, J. L. (in press). Effects of teacher practices of parent involvement on student achievement in reading and math. In S. Silvern (Ed.), *Literacy through family, community, and school interaction.* Greenwich, CT: JAI Press.

Epstein, J. L., & McPartland, J. M. (1979). Authority structures. In H. Walberg (Ed.), *Educational environments and effects.* Berkeley: McCutchan.

Good, T. L., & Tom, D. V. H. (1985). Self regulation, efficacy, expectations, and social orientations: Teacher and classroom perspectives. In C. Ames & R. Ames (Eds.), *Research on motivation in education: Vol. 2. The classroom milieu.* Orlando: Academic Press.

Goodlad, J. I. (1983). *A place called school.* New York: McGraw-Hill.

Fyans, L. J., Jr. (1980). *Achievement motivation: Recent trends in theory and research.* New York: Plenum.

Gordon, I., & Breivogel, W. F. (1976). *Building effective home–school relationships.* Boston: Allyn and Bacon.

Harter, S. (1978). Effectance motivation reconsidered: Toward a developmental model. *Human Development, 21:* 34–64.

Heatherington, E. M., Camera, K. A., & Featherman, D. L. (1981). *Cognitive performance, school behavior, and achievement of children from one parent homes.* Washington, DC: National Institute of Education.

Hess, R. D., & Holloway, S. D. (1984). Family and school as educational institutions. In R. D. Park (Ed.), *Review of child development research* (Vol. 7). Chicago: University of Chicago Press.

Hess, R. D., Holloway, S. D., Dickson, W. P., & Price, G. G. (1984). Maternal variables as predictors of children's school readiness and later achievement in vocabulary and mathematics in the sixth grade. *Child Development, 55,* 1902–1913.

Heyns, B. (1978). *Summer learning and the effects of schooling.* New York: Academic Press.

Holland, J. L. (1973). *Vocational choices: A theory of careers.* Englewood Cliffs, NJ: Prentice-Hall.

Isherwood, G. B., & Hammah, C. K. (1981). Home and school factors and the quality of school life in Canadian high schools. In J. Epstein (Ed.), *The quality of school life.* Lexington, MA: Lexington Books.

Keith, T. Z., Reimers, T. M., Fehrmann, P. G., Pottebaum, S. M., & Aubey, L. W. (1986, April). *Direct and indirect effects of parent involvement, TV time, and homework on academic achievement.* Paper presented at the annual meeting of the American Educational Research Association, San Francisco.

Kukla, A. (1978). An attributional theory of choice. In L. Berkowitz (Ed.), *Advances in experimental social psychology* (Vol. 1). New York: Academic Press.

Kun, A. (1977). Development of the magnitude-covariation and compensation schemata on ability and effort attribution of performance. *Child Development, 48,* 863–873.

Laosa, L. M. (1982). School, occupation, culture, and family. *Journal of Educational Psychology, 74,* 791–827.

Lazar, I., & Darlington, R. (1982). Lasting effects of early education: A report for the Consortium for Longitudinal Studies. *Monographs for Research in Child Development, 47* .(2–3, Serial No. 195).

Leichter, H. (Ed.) (1974). *The family as educator.* New York: Teachers' College Press.

Levine, V. (1983, April). *Time allocaiton at home and achievement at school.* Paper presented at the annual meeting of the American Educational Research Association, Montreal.

Levine, V. (1984, April). *Time allocation at home and at school, and school achievement.* Paper presented at the annual meeting of the American Educational Research Association, New Orleans.

Lewin, K., Lippitt, R., & White, R. (1939). Patterns of aggressive behavior in experimentally created social climates. *Journal of Social Psychology, 10,* 271–299.

Lipsitz, J. (1984). *Successful schools for young adolescents.* New Brunswick, NJ: Transaction Books.

Maas, H. S. (1968). Preadolescent peer relations and adult intimacy. *Psychiatry, 31,* 161–172.

Maccoby, E. E. (1984). Middle childhood in the context of the family. In W. A. Collins (Ed.), *Development during middle childhood: The years from 6–12.* Washington, DC: National Academy Press.

Maehr, M. L. (1984). In R. Ames & C. Ames (Eds.), *Research on motivation in education. Vol. 1. Student motivation.* Orlando: Academic Press.

Marjoribanks, K. (1979). *Families and their learning environments: An empirical analysis.* London: Routledge & Kegan Paul.

Marjoribanks, K. (1980). *Ethnic families and children's achievement.* London: George Allen & Unwin.

McDill, E. L., & Rigsby, L. (1973). *Structure and process in secondary schools: The academic impact of educational climate.* Baltimore: The Johns Hopkins University Press.

McPartland, J. M. (1969). The relative influence of school and classroom desegregation on the academic achievement of ninth grade students. *Journal of Social Issues, 25,* 93–102.

Minuchin, P. P. (1977). *The middle years of childhood.* Monterey: Brooks/Cole.

Nicholls, J. G. (1984). Conceptions of ability and achievement motivation. In R. Ames & C. Ames (Eds.), *Research on motivation in education: Vol. 1. Student motivation.* Orlando: Academic Press.

Patchen, M. (1982). *Black–white contact in schools: Its social and academic effects.* West Lafayette, IN: Purdue University Press.

Pennsylvania State Department of Education. (1984). *Manuals for interpreting elementary, intermediate, and high school reports.* Harrisburg: Educational Quality Assessment Program.

Peterson, A. C. (1986, April). *Early adolescence: A critical developmental transition?* Invited presentation (Division E) at the annual meeting of the American Educational Research Association, San Francisco.

Rich, D. (1985). *The forgotten factor in school success: The family.* Washington, DC: Home and School Institute.

Rubin, R. I., Olmsted, P. P., Szegda, M. J., Wetherby, M. J., & Williams, D. S. (1983, April). *Long-term effects of parent education on follow-through program participation.* Paper presented at the annual meeting of the American Education Research Association, Montreal.

Ruble, D. N. (1980). A developmental perspective on theories of motivation. In L. J. Fyons, Jr. (Ed.), *Achievement motivation.* New York: Plenum.

Schaefer, E. S., Hunter, W. M., & Watkins, D. B. (1986). *Parenting and child behavior predictors of retention in grades K, 1, 2.* Paper presented at the annual meeting of the American Education Research Association, San Francisco.

Scott-Jones, D. (1980, April). *Relationships between family variables and school achievement in low-income black first graders.* Paper presented at the annual meeting of the American Educational Research Association, Boston.

Scott-Jones, D. (1984). Family influences on cognitive development and school achievement. In E. Gordon (Ed.), *Review of research in education* (Vol. 11). Washington, DC: American Educational Research Association.

Sigel, I. E. (1981). Social experience in the development of representational thought: Distancing theory. In I. E. Sigel, D. Brodzinsky, & R. Gulinkoff (Eds.), *New directions in Piagetian theory and practice.* Hillsdale, NJ: Erlbaum.

Sigel, I. E., Dreyer, A. S., & McGillicuddy-Delisi, A. V. (1984). Psychological perspectives of the family. In R. D. Parke (Ed.), *Review of child development research: Vol. 7. The family* (pp. 42–79). Chicago: University of Chicago Press.

Sigel, I. E., & McGillicuddy-DeLisi, A. V. (1984). Parents as teachers of their children: A distancing behavior model. In A. D. Pelligrew & T. D. Yawker (Eds.), *The development of oral and written language in social contexts* (pp. 71–92). Norward, NJ: Ablex.

Simmons, R. G., Blyth, D. A., Van Cleave, E., & Bush, D. (1979). Entry into early adolescence. *American Sociological Review, 44:* 948–967.

Sizer, T. (1984). *Horace's compromise.* Boston: Houghton Mifflin.

Snow, C. E. (1977). The development of conversation between mothers and babies. *Journal of Child Language, 4,* 1–22.

Stern, G. G. (1970). *People in context: Measuring person–environment congruence in business and industry.* New York: Wiley.

Stipek, D. J. (1984). The development of achievement motivation. In R. Ames & C. Ames (Eds.), *Research on motivation in education: Vol. 1. Student motivation.* Orlando: Academic Press.

Tizard, J., Schofield, W. N., & Hewison, J. (1982). Collaboration between teachers and parents in assisting children's reading. *British Journal of Educational Psychology, 52,* 1–15.

Veroff, J. (1969). Social comparison and the developmental of achievement motivation. In C. P. Smith (Ed.) *Achievement related motives in children.* New York: Sage.

Wang, M. C., & Weisstein, W. J. (1980). Teacher expectations and student learning. In L. J. Fyans, Jr. (Ed.), *Achievement motivation: Recent trends in theory and research.* New York: Plenum.

Weikart, D. P., Epstein, A. S., Schweinhart, L., & Bond, J. T. (1978). *The Ypsilanti preschool curriculum demonstration project: Preschool years and longitudinal results.* Ypsilanti, MI: High School Educational Research Foundation.

Weiner, B. (1979). A theory of motivation for some classroom experiences. *Journal of Educational Psychology, 71,* 3–25.

Weiner, B. (1984). Principles for a theory of student motivation and their application within an attributional framework. In R. Ames & C. Ames (Eds.), *Research on motivation in education: Vol. 1. Student motivation.* Orlando, FL: Academic Press.

Weiner, B., & Peter, N. (1973). A cognitive developmental analysis of achievement and moral judgments. *Developmental Psychology, 9,* 290–309.

Whiting, B. B. (1986). The effect of experience in peer relationships. In E. Mueller & C. Cooper (Eds.), *Process and outcomes in peer relations.* New York: Academic Press.

Williams, D. D., Arnoldsen, L. M., & Reynolds, P. (1984, April). *Understanding home education: Case studies of home schools.* Paper presented at the annual meetings of the American Educational Research Association, New Orleans.

Youniss, J., & Smollar, J. (1985). *Adolescent relations with mothers, fathers, and friends.* Chicago: University of Chicago Press.

Zigler, E., & Valentine, J. (Eds.) (1979). *Project Head Start: A legacy of the War on Poverty.* New York: Free Press.

PART III

Discussants

9

Thoughts about Motivation

Martin L. Maehr

INTRODUCTION

The four chapters that are the subject of this review reflect four important programs of research that have had and that are likely to continue to have an important influence on motivation theory and research. It would be surprising, and in my view unfortunate, if they do not also increasingly influence educational practice. To the reader's delight, the research they report is characterized by a variety in the problems addressed. There is also in evidence a rich variety of methods employed. Yet, a careful reading will also reveal complementary and convergent lines of thought, a similarity in themes that is characteristic of the literature generally. Both the nature of the perspectives shared as well as the points of divergence deserve comment.

SIMILAR THEMES

THOUGHTS, PERCEPTIONS, AND MOTIVATION

Even a quick reading of these chapters suggests the existence of a theme that plays throughout the review of different programs of research: the importance of thoughts and perceptions in guiding and directing behavior. Cognitive theory, of course, has not only been a force in psychology generally but has, in particular, increasingly dominated the study of human motivation. While this observation is hardly novel, the onset of this trend, how these chapters reflect it, and the implications for pursuing a cognitive approach in the study of motivation do deserve comment.

In their brief historical introduction, Csikszentmihalyi and Nakamura suggest that the resurgence of cognitive theory gave the study of motivation a new life. If it did not make the study of motivation possible, it gave considerable encouragement to such study so that the now very lively interest in this area is at least partially attributable to the cognitive revolution. Some historians thinking back on Freud, Hull, and perhaps also McClelland and Atkinson may raise their eyebrows at such a suggestion, but there is an important point or two to be made in this regard. Whether a cognitive perspective has in fact saved the study of motivation or increased interest in it is hard to say. It certainly can be argued that the focus on intrinsic versus extrinsic rewards reflected in these chapters, as well as in the literature generally, have been given new and special life through the rebirth of cognitive theory. But beyond that, it seems fair to argue that the cognitive perspective has drastically revised what the study of motivation is all about.

When David McClelland (see for example, McClelland, 1951, 1961; McClelland, Atkinson, Clark, & Lowell, 1953) initiated his ground-breaking program of motivational research, the focus was on individual differences in motivation: how these might be acquired through early socialization experiences and the degree to which these would be evident in a variety of contexts and under varying conditions. It was assumed that motivation was essentially an unconscious emotive–dynamic process that could only be assessed indirectly through fantasy measures.

When Bernard Weiner (see for example, Weiner, 1972; Weiner, Frieze, Kukla, Reed, Rest, & Rosenbaum, 1971) argued that those high or low in need for achievement were likely to think differently about success and failure, it signaled the beginning of a different era in the study of motivation. If thoughts, or attributions in particular, were to be the critical variables, there was precedent aplenty for moving from the study of individual personality orientations to the role of context as this may affect thoughts. After all, the study of attributions (see for example, Heider, 1958; Jones, Kanose, Kelley, Nisbett, Valins, & Weiner, 1971) was especially concerned with such thoughts about situations and how meanings change as contexts change. In short, Weiner's modest attempt to insert attributions into the achievement motivation equation in fact transformed the focus of motivation research. The situation and its meaning became the focus. Individual differences and personality waned in importance.

In any case, a cognitive perspective on motivational questions prevails. The effects of social context (e.g., Ames, 1987), task design, and structure (e.g., Hackman & Oldham, 1980) on motivation are now understood in terms of mediating cognitions: not only cognitions of control and competence but also perceptions of purpose and meaning (cf. Maehr, 1984; Maehr & Archer, 1987). This cognitive emphasis has, of course, affected how we study motivation and how we can enhance it. In an earlier era, the study of human motivation was almost tantamount to the study of personality. That is hardly the situation today.

In the first instance, the four chapters that are the subject of this discussion all reflect this trend. In fact, they really serve significantly to identify the issues, the problems, and the possibilities of this current perspective on defining and understanding human motivation. They also reflect considerable variety in the problems addressed and even greater diversity in the methods employed for addressing them. But a careful reading will reveal complementary and convergent lines of thought that may be seen as making contributions to a shared understanding of human motivation—a shared understanding that could prove to be a working basis for integrating the diverse and varied research into a unified framework for guiding both research and practice.

The commonality in perspective, of course, is generally evident in the fact that thoughts, broadly construed, are assumed to be the major antecedents of the direction, intensity, and duration of behavior. But at a more spefic level, there is also an emerging common interest around two kinds of thoughts. Though this interest is evident in various degrees and is more or less explicitly stated by the authors, one senses (1) the obvious importance of thoughts about self and (2) the emerging importance of purposes and goals.

THOUGHTS AND PERCEPTIONS OF SELF

Through earlier periods of emphasis on external reinforcers, unconscious mechanisms, or physiologically based needs and drives, there were always a few who continued to remind us of an enduring role of concepts of self in organizing and directing behavior. The writings of Allport (1955) and Rogers (1951, 1961) repeatedly held the banner of selfhood high among the multiplicity of motivational variables evoked in discussion of behavior—even in a period when some did not "need the motivation hypothesis" or considered motivation to be an esoteric area of study at best. The use of self constructs in the 1950s and 1960s was, to say the very least, diffuse. When self-perceptions or concepts were viewed as a determinant of behavior, the hypotheses were often vague and uncertain. Thus, Rogers and his colleagues went little further than to suggest or assert that individuals behaved so as to maintain and enhance their perceived self. Moreover, what little research was conducted in this period was not characterized by rigor in design or measurement—or relationship to well-articulated theory.

Incidentally, it is probably fair to say that it was especially difficult to get a handle on studying how individuals might behave so as to *enhance* their concept of self. Attitude theory (e.g., Festinger, 1957) provided some basis for understanding how one behaved so as to retain a particular view of self—one acted in a way that was congruent with one's view and selected experiences that were likely to confirm that view. But how one might effectively and systematically study self-enhancement or self-actualization was problematic.

Certainly, one important impediment to progress in the understanding of the motivational role of self-concepts was definitional. In particular, the global way in which selfhood was initially defined doubtless did not facilitate its use in motivation research. With the increased interest in cognitive interpretations of achievement motivation in particular, concepts of self have been specified in such a way that they now can and do play a major role in various approaches to understanding motivation (see e.g., Covington, 1984; Deci & Ryan, 1958).

Interestingly enough, it appears that the current interest is now more in how individuals behave so as to enhance their view of self than in the matter of self-maintenance. That is, the focus is not limited to how individuals behave so as to protect and retain a certain picture of themselves. Rather, with the rediscovery of self within the context of achievement research, the focus increasingly is on how individual's behave so as to enhance that view of self. It is the aspiration to increase one's sense of competence, for example, that is at the heart of current achievement motivation reasearch and theory (cf. Harter & Connell, 1983; Maehr & Nicholls, 1980).

To some degree, all of the chapters reflect this state of affairs, but the Schunk chapter focuses most directly and extensively on the role of such cognitions in affecting behavior. In the first instance, Schunk's chapter calls attention to the wide range of research that has been conducted on what might be termed *perceived competence*. Indeed, he presents a nicely organized and representative summary of this research. Arguably, judgments of competence are among the most commonly employed variables in motivational research, especially research on motivation and achievement. His presentation is framed in terms of *self-efficacy theory* (Bandura, 1982). In addition to organizing and interpreting a wide range of research in terms of that formulation, he also describes his own interesting program of research. The amount of research by Schunk and others concerned with self-efficacy is prodigious. It also has come to have major implications for educational practice. Indeed, one of the major contributions of Schunk's chapter is that he not only shows the importance of the concept of self-efficacy in understanding human motivation but also, more generally, illustrates how one can put motivation theory to work in classroom settings.

To return to the central point, reading of these chapters emphasizes what is evident in the literature more generally. Among the thoughts that are influential in the motivational process, there are none more important than thoughts about self. The shared perspective that is apparent in motivation theory today is one that gives special weight to the role of selfhood—even though the nature of that selfhood may be variously defined.

THOUGHTS AND PERCEPTIONS OF PURPOSES AND GOALS

In addition to selfhood, these chapters prompt consideration of at least one other critical feature of a cognitive analysis of motivation: intentionality. Purposes and goals, if not consistently and similarly referred to in these chapters, nevertheless emerge as factors to be considered in the data reported. At the very least, these chapters prompt a consideration of an issue that is becoming increasingly important in current motivational theory and research.

Recent analyses of motivation, especially achievement motivation, have exhibited a special interest in the role of purposes, intentions, and goals (cf. for example, Dweck, 1985). Of course, goals have been a part of the motivational language for some time. To the general reader, it might seem strange that it could be otherwise. After all, what is motivation about anyway? However, as in the case of the use of self-concept variables, the definition and use of *goals* and other purpose-suggesting constructs has been given renewed and enriched life with cognitive theory. Further, the emergence of goals in discussions of motivation has stimulated new lines of inquiry and prompted reformulation of the questions asked and the answers given. Thus, the explicit as well as the implicit use of the concept of goal in these chapters deserves some comment.

The concept of *goal* is characteristically used in one of two ways in current motivation research. In the first place, it is used to refer to a performance standard to be reached. This performance standard may be viewed as a level of aspiration held by the performer(s) or it may be viewed as a level set, at least initially, by someone other than the performer. In either case, the focus is a specified level of performance, and one might label this a "quantitative" use of the term. A second use of the term might be described as "qualitative" in nature. Thus, the term *goal* may be used to refer to qualitatively different purposes or intentions in pursuing a task. The concept is employed in both ways in these four chapters.

Considering the so-called quantitative use of the term, one should call special attention to recent and extensive research on motivation in work organizations that has focused on goal-setting. Briefly, this research has indicated that the establishment of performance goals for a work group enhances productivity (Locke & Latham, 1984; Locke, Shaw, Saari, & Latham, 1981). There remains some question of how participation in the setting of goals and/or the degree to which the worker's acceptance of the goals may modify the relationship (Erez, Earley, & Hulin, 1985; Erez & Kanfer, 1983). Yet, there is considerable evidence that setting a goal for a work group is a direct and effective method of enhancing work motivation.

Precisely *why* such performance goals should have direct effects on worker motivation is an interesting—but still not fully answered—question. Locke and his colleagues have been more concerned with the empirical findings and their applicability than they have been with some of these theoretical issues. Moreover, while it would seem that these findings are ripe for an analysis from a cognitive perspective, surprisingly little attention has, in fact, been given to perceptions of performance goals. How does the method of establishing goals affect perceptions? How do such perceptions in turn modify performance?

This questioning of the functions of the role of performance goals demands an updated cognitive analysis. While such an analysis is not attempted in any of these chapters, at least one of the chapters takes this issue seriously and examines some of the issues carefully. Schunk calls attention to the importance of goal-setting generally. Further, he initiates an exploration of why performance goals might influence motivation in important ways. His explanation relates to the effects of attaining goals on self-efficacy. I cannot as yet be persuaded that self-efficacy or a sense of competence or perhaps any sense-of-self variable can fully explain the effectiveness of goal-setting in the world of work, but Schunk has made a good case for the interpretive role of self-efficacy in understanding the function of goals in learning and achievement settings. His analysis reminds one of earlier work on level of aspiration that should perhaps be reconsidered in this connection. However, the thrust of Schunk's chapter, as that of Locke's, is on the pragmatic function of goal-setting in intervening to enhance motivation. That is an important focus. But also needed is a theoretical analysis that fully incorporates the full range of research on goal-setting. At least, we could hope for an interpretation which would bring Locke et al's results into the mainstream of cognitive theory.

The second use of *goal* is broadly evident in the achievement theory literature and has been featured in earlier volumes in this series (see for example, Ames, 1984; Maehr, 1984; Nicholls, 1984). In their different ways, these researchers have each stressed how the intention, the goals, and the purpose in performing a task affects the nature of that performance. Thus, Ames (see for example, Ames & Archer, 1987, in press) has followed a pattern similar to that prsued by Dweck (1985) and specified two important achievement goals present to varying degrees in classroom settings and in the interaction between parent and child.

One of the two goals is referred to as a *mastery goal*. Under this goal, behavior is oriented toward self-improvement, irrespective of the performance of others. The second goal is referred to as a *performance goal* and the focus is on social comparison and competition. The reigning intention of a performance goal is to demonstrate that one can exceed the performance of others, that one is better than others at a particular task. Current research has explored the role of goal orientations in a wide range of contexts and settings, including especially the classroom (see for example, Ames & Archer, 1987, in press; Ames, Maehr, & Archer, 1987).

Results to date indicate support for several different assertions. First, it appears that environments that stress performance goals are especially debilitating for individuals who are lacking in confidence or in perceived ability or skill. However, environments that stress mastery tend to reduce such debilitating effects. Second, environments that lay differential stress on mastery and performance goals are likely to eventuate in different learning strategies. In brief, students are more likely to seek out challenges and be open to novel experiences when mastery goals are stressed. Performance goals seem to induce a conservative approach to learning: Students do not wish to risk failure. Third, there is reason to believe that students will not only feel more positively disposed toward learning tasks under mastery (compared to performance) goal conditions, but may also be more likely to exhibit continuing interests in the task area. Finally, there is some reason to believe that creativity is more likely to be fostered by mastery rather than performance goal conditions. Given these major assertions, it may seem as if mastery goal orientations are overwhelmingly "good," and performance goal conditions overwhelmingly "bad." That may be too simplistic, because it is possible that for certain situations and for certain learning outcomes a performance orientation may not only be desirable but necessary.

In any event, it can be readily seen that this use of the concept of goals focuses on qualitative motivational changes that occur as the perceived purpose and goal orientation of the activity varies. Moreover, it stresses the fact that judgments about *self* are likely to have different effects, depending on perceptions of the perceived purpose of the activity.

Such a concern with intentionality and goal functions is sometimes explicit, but perhaps more often only implicit in the chapters reviewed here. Only Dodge, Asher, and Parkhurst talk explicitly and at length about goal orientations as modifiers of motivation. It is not difficult, however, to read a goal orientation into the other chapters or to interpret the research reported there in terms of goals. While the other chapters do not use the same type of goal-oriented language, the focus and concerns reflected therein are compatible with goal analyses of motivation. Thus, the way Csikszentmihalyi and Nakamura and Lepper and Hodell discuss extrinsic and intrinsic reward conditions is certainly related to the use of the concept of mastery and performance goals. Indeed, it might be suggested that these results on extrinsic and intrinsic rewards could readily and conveniently be incorporated into the motivational goal paradigms suggested by Ames (1987), Dweck (1985), Nicholls (1984), and others. To some considerable degree, of course, they already have been. Goal theorizing has made ample and explicit use of extrinsic/intrinsic reward research. At the very least, it may be argued that a goal theory framework is at least one viable framework for interpreting the fascinating research reported by Csikszentmihalyi and Nakamura and Lepper and Hodell. It is a framework that can prove, and indeed already has proven, most fruitful.

TOWARD A COGNITIVE THEORY OF MOTIVATION

Whether or not I have stretched a point or two in trying to see convergence around two major cognitive constructs, it seems evident that all of these chapters play off a common theme: the importance of thoughts and perceptions in guiding behavior. Therewith, the research conducted within these separate programs is, to a considerable degree, complementary. There is, accordingly, some reason to suggest that these chapters and the broader literature they reflect will all eventually add up to a more complete theory of motivation. If such convergence does eventuate, we will indeed be able to speak of a prevailing *cognitive* theory of motivation.

VARIATIONS ON SIMILAR THEMES

COMMENTS ON VARIATION IN FOCUS, APPROACH, AND CONTRIBUTION

But aside from such convergence of interest and perspective and the use of similar constructs, there is considerable variation in method and focus among the chapters. In general, the special kinds of contributions of each of the chapters deserves to be highlighted.

Csikszentmihalyi and Nakamura

Through an innovative time-sampling methodology Csikszentmihalyi and his colleagues have mapped out the ebb and flow of conscious experiences of individuals as they go about the business of living. They have gathered data from a wide variety of groups—in different settings and in different cultures. This variation and diversity of persons and groups studied is truly impressive: chess masters, rock climbers, basketball players, music composers, surgeons, high school students, teenage members of Japanese motorcycle gangs, long-distance sailors.

In this chapter, however, the authors choose to focus especially on adolescents in their several school and out-of-school worlds. Such a focus on adolescence, although appearing here primarily for illustrative purposes, is nevertheless notable. Adolescence is virtually a wasteland so far as psychological research is concerned. Yet, it is during this period that motivational problems seem to loom largest—if one talks to teachers, parents, and others who feel they have a responsibility to motivate them.

Csikszentmihalyi and Nakamura's use of cross-cultural comparisons is also worthy of some comment, even though it is admittedly not the most important feature of their chapter or their program of research generally. Beyond the not-unimportant value it has within the context of the present chapter, the use of cross-cultural evidence prompts a more general commentary. For the most part, cross-cultural research on motivation is notable for its absence. Since the appearance of *The Achieving Society* (McClelland, 1961), there have been all too few examples of cross-cultural research on motivation. This situation has prevailed in spite of the fact that most researchers are Americans who live and work in an increasingly pluralistic and culturally diverse society, a society where motivational "problems" are often associated with cultural background.

Moreover, the cross-cultural results Csikszentmihalyi and Nakamura choose to report in this case are provocative. Thus, the comparisons of Italian and U.S. adolescents are well worth pondering. While the general pattern of experience is seemingly comparable for "bright normal" adolescents in the two cultures, there is a reason to believe that school is less likely to be seen as a positive experience for U.S. adolescents, especially those who are talented. This is disturbing but accords well with Nicholls, Patashnick, and Nolen's (1985) work, which prompts one to believe that U.S. schools have often served to make learning seem like "work." That is, they have defined the educational experience as an instrument to other ends and therewith reduced its intrinsic interest for many students. That this apparently happens in a special way with talented youth is disturbing—but probably inescapably—true.

In any event, Csikszentmihalyi and Nakamura report that the learning environment of the talented youth whom they studied were rarely in the "flow state," and spent a large part of their time bored. Even more serious, perhaps, is the fact that a considerable portion of their boredom was experienced in academic settings. While the talented youth in their study were apparently ready to enjoy high challenges, they rarely found such challenges in their daily lives and especially not in the school settings where they could capitalize on their talents in a productive way. Even though this aspect is not really the major point of this chapter, it is certainly a point worth mentioning in a book purporting to deal with motivation in education.

Lepper and Hodell

While Lepper and Hodell share Csikszentmihalyi and Nakamura's interest in intrinsic motivation, their approach is manifestedly different. Their results, however, are no less fascinating. Following more conventional paradigms of experimental social psychology, they have proceeded to systematically study the negative effects of extrinsic rewards.

Beginning with a now-classic study (Lepper, Greene & Nisbett, 1973), Lepper and his colleagues have conducted a series of studies directed, first of all, to identifying the key variables in reducing intrinsic motivation. Starting with the rather straightforward finding that children who receive extrinsic rewards for intrinsically interesting tasks exhibit a loss of motivation, Lepper and his colleagues have proceeded to examine variation in both the independent and dependent variables. More specifically, on the independent variable side, they have moved from an initial concern with rewards or incentives to consideration of the role of evaluation and performance feedback, social control, task design, and structure. On the dependent variable side, Lepper and his colleagues have moved beyond the initial focus on continuing motivation to an exploration of effects on problem solving and creativity. Parallel to this work, of course, a number of other researchers (e.g., Deci, 1975, 1980; Deci & Ryan, 1985) have pursued similar programs of research. The result is that today there is available a large body of research on what might be generally termed intrinsic motivation, but most especially on the negative effects of extrinsic rewards on continuing task interest.

In many respects, this chapter is most useful as it makes a strong case for the negative role of extrinsic rewards in educational practice. In spite of repeated arguments to the contrary, extrinsic rewards, constraints, and external control are a pervasive part of educational practice. The authors sketch out some useful suggestions for classroom practice and, above all, raise some interesting questions for future educational research. They summarize in a convenient way the advice that has eventuated from research in this area regarding what should *not* be done in order to maintain the "natural" intrinsic interest of children in learning. They also venture an initial idea or two regarding how one might deal with the problem of creating intrinsic interest—or any interest at all—where there apparently is none. In this regard, I was especially intrigued with the discussion of possible use of fantasy in stimulating interest. Anyone who has observed "good" teachers at work is cognizant of the effectiveness of asking students to "imagine," to play "as if" games, etc. This suggestion—only minimally covered in this chapter—is one that deserves further amplification and exploration if motivation theory is to contribute significantly to pedagogical theory.

It might be noted in closing off comments specific to the Lepper and Hodell chapter that it serves as an important complement to the chapter authored by Csikszentmihalyi and Nakamura. Collectively, the two chapters reinforce the view that a major burden of motivation research in the area of education must be the development of understanding of intrinsic interest—why it is there, when it is there, how one maintains it, and how one gets it when it has been lost. As cannot be said too often, the interest that may be commanded in the classroom is not the only interest that counts. Optimum educational development must involve a continuing interest that reaches beyond the learning setting, that invades all of life, that is self-maintaining.

While complementing Csikszentmihalyi and Nakamura in several significant ways, Lepper and Hodell expand the range of discussion on intrinsic motivation considerably. First, their method as well as the variables they have considered have led and should continue to lead to a more detailed understanding of the critical variables affecting intrinsic motivation. Their work has focused attention on the quality of teaching–learning environments that may be important in this regard. Thus, the Lepper and Hodell chapter not only yields a basic framework for understanding intrinsic motivation in educational settings but also suggests specific ways in which it might be fostered.

Schunk

While most of the chapters concentrate primarily on what might be termed the purpose factor, Schunk focuses on concepts of *self*, especially on the individual's perceived ability to perform the task effectively. That certainly is a distinguishing feature of Schunk's chapter. There is yet another. He seems to be especially concerned with the question, "So what?" And in this regard, he has directed his research in a special way toward developing intervention strategies. Of course, given his theoretical bent, these are strategies that stress changing motivational patterns through changing *self-efficacy*. But the strategies Schunk reviews have revelance beyond the confines of self-efficacy theory. They are strategies to be considered by anyone interested in effecting motivational change. As such, his survey of self-efficacy change strategies is a useful component of this chapter, particularly to those who teach or to those who teach teachers. One cannot comment on all of the strategies, of course. And referring to any of them while ignoring others may be hazardous. However, there is one strategy that especially intrigues me, partly I suppose because it had not previously figured significantly in my thinking: the suggestion that modeling can serve as a strategy for enhancing self-efficacy.

Taking the Lepper and Hodell and the Schunk chapters together, one has a sound basis for beginning to develop intervention strategies and programs. The two chapters are complementary in this respect, as they focus differentially on the two facets that I have suggested are key to a cognitive perspective on motivation: goal orientations and self-concepts. But as stressed earlier and at some length in this chapter, it is not just the utility of Schunk's work that is important. By systematically exploring self-efficacy, he has most certainly helped to establish concepts both of self in general and of self-efficacy in particular as important variables to be considered in constructing a general theory of motivation.

Dodge, Asher, and Parkhurst

In several ways, the Dodge et al. chapter is the one that is most manifestly different from the other chapters—and not just because it deals with social skills and interpersonal relationships rather than achievement—although that difference is interesting and worthy of note.

As already indicated, Dodge et al. are the only authors who explicitly, and at some considerable length, concentrate on goal orientations as modifiers of motivation. As such, they make a special contribution to how one might emply goal constructs in motivation research and theory. For example, they reinforce a notion not always emphasized in those motivational approaches that take goals seriously—namely that individuals typically hold or must deal with a number of different goals in any performance situation. Therewith, they point out that behavior is significantly not only a function of trying to handle a variety of goals but also a function of trying to resolve conflicts between competing goals. That particular idea deserves broader consideration among those who choose to consider the motives that guide, direct, and "energize" achievement patterns.

Complementary to this, Dodge et al. also call attention to the necessity to begin viewing goals—their development, their nature, and their function—as a complex cognitive scheme. Moreover, while a number of the authors seem to be viewing motivation as, in part, a function of information processing, none of the authors attempt to spell this out to the same degree as Dodge et al. Further, as one views motivation as part of a complex cognitive scheme, one is prompted to raise questions about developmental changes in motivation patterns. Certainly, one cannot expect the 2-year-old to exhibit the same cognitive scheme as the 16-year-old—and how does this affect the understanding of motivation in the two cases? While Dodge et al. do not attempt to provide definitive answers here, they do broach this issue and place it squarely on the agenda for future motivational research.

Finally, as Dodge et al. do concentrate especially on social interaction and not on achievement per se, they make a special contribution to this collection. First, they make an interesting point about goals—one that would not as readily flow from a concern with achievement per se. In the realm of interpersonal relationships, one cannot only concentrate on the type of goals that the individual might be considering or following; one has also to consider the individual's perceptions regarding the goals that other persons hold. We conform our behavior significantly to our perceptions of the goals that others hold in their relationship with us. I suspect that this type of perception also occurs in the realm of achievement and in fashioning achievement goals, but it is certainly not as well researched or understood in that domain—if indeed it is even recognized as a relevant component.

A second contribution to be mentioned in closing is more general. At the very least, the Dodge et al. chapter may serve to call attention to the possibility of developing a more comprehensive theory of motivation—one that not only embraces achievement but also human behavior more generally. Certainly, a complete theory of motivation in educational settings must somehow incorporate the concerns that drive the work of Dodge and his colleagues.

CONCLUSION

In this review, I have searched hard—perhaps too hard—for similar themes and perspectives that might suggest a step along the way toward a new integration of what we know about human motivation. I think I have found some convergence here and there and a degree of complementarity that suggests the eventual emergence of a general—and widely accepted—scheme for understanding motivational processes. Admittedly, these chapters concentrate, for the most part, on reporting results of self-evidently important programs of research.

Yet the results are interesting. They are important—not only for solving practical problems but also for the more extensive theory building for which I hold out hope. Indeed, they seem to reflect a transition stage in which some of the positions (social learning, attribution, etc.) have ceased to have independent importance and where we are groping for one or two new conceptions to put forth that may guide the next stage of research on human motivation. In any case, the work contained in these chapters will certainly serve as building blocks for any new perspectives or next stages that might evolve in the search to understand human motivation.

Aside from the interest in theory building, there is a justified concern with the practical implications of the work reviewed in these chapters. So what can one learn about what to do to improve teaching and learning? These chapters are especially rich in this regard. Not that they presume to spell out lists of "how-to-do-its." While specific suggestions are indeed made here and there, the contributions of these chapters lies mainly in that they suggest a perspective on education, on pedagogy theory, perhaps ultimately on educational philosophy.

These chapters direct themselves heavily toward undergirding arguments for the importance of fostering intrinsic motivation. They present arguments for emphasizing choice and freedom in learning. There is considerable grist for the humanist mill in what is said here. And, it can hardly escape the reader that much of what is said might have been better received in an earlier period, when "open education" was in vogue, than it will be presently. The current stress on effectiveness, productivity, and on "the basics"—while it need not take this form—has tended to emphasize testing, external control, and extrinsic rewards. There is much that is said in these chapters to suggest that the stress on such externalized control of the learning process may not be facilitative of motivation. But regardless of the receptivity of the message on the part of educational policy makers, it is now more than ever that the educational establishment needs to hear what is said in these chapters.

REFERENCES

Allport, G. W. (1955). *Becoming: Basic considerations for a psychology of personality.* New Haven: Yale University Press.

Ames, C. (1984). Competitive, cooperative, and individualistic goal structures: A cognitive-motivational analysis. In R. Ames & C. Ames (Eds.), *Research on motivation in education: Vol. 1 Student motivation* (pp. 177–207). New York: Academic Press.

Ames, C. (1987). The enhancement of student motivation. In M. Maehr & D. Kleiber (Eds.), *Advances in motivation and achievement: Vol. 5. Enhancing student motivation.* (pp. 123–148). Greenwich, CT: JAI Press.

Ames, C., & Archer, J. (1987). Mothers' beliefs about the role of ability and effort in school learning. *Journal of Educational Psycology. 79*, 409–414.

Ames, C., & Archer, J. (in press). Achievement goals in the classroom: Student learning strategies and motivation processes. *Journal of Educational Psychology.*

Ames, C., Maehr, M. L., & Archer, J. (1987). *The motivational environment of the classroom and student motivation.* Work in progress.

Bandura, A. (1982). Self-efficacy mechanism in human agency. *American Psychologist, 37,* 122–147.

Covington, M. (1984). The motive for self-worth. In R. Ames & C. Ames (Eds.), *Research on motivation in education: Vol. 1. Student motivation* (pp. 77–112). New York: Academic Press.

Deci. E. L. (1975). *Intrinsic motivation.* New York: Plenum.

Deci, E. L. (1980). *The psychology of self-determination.* Lexington, MA: D. C. Heath.

Deci, E. L., & Ryan, R. M. (1985). *Intrinsic motivation and self-determination.* New York: Plenum.

Dweck, C. S. (1985). Intrinsic motivation, perceived control, and self-evaluation maintenance: An achievement goal analysis. In C. Ames & R. Ames (Eds.), *Research on motivation in education: Vol. 2. The Classroom Milieu* (pp. 289–305). New York: Academic Press.

Erez, M., Earley, P. C., & Hulin, C. L. (1985). The impact of participation on goal acceptance and performance. *Academy of Management Journal, 28*(1), 50–66.

Erez, M. & Kanfer, F. H. (1983). The role of goal acceptance in goal setting and task performance. *Academy of Management Review, 8,* 454–463.

Festinger, L. (1957). *A theory of cognitive dissonance.* New York: Harper.

Hackman, J. R., & Oldham, G. R. (1980). *Work redesign.* Reading, MA: Addison-Wesley.

Harter, S., & Connell, J. P. (1983). A structural model of the relationships among children's academic achievement and their self-perceptions of competence, control, and motivational orientation in the cognitive domain. In J. Nicholls (Ed.) *Advances in motivation and achievement: Vol. 3. The development of achievement motivation* (pp. 219–250). Greenwich, CT: JAI Press.

Heider, F. (1958). *The psychology of interpersonal relations.* New York: Wiley.

Jones, E. E., Kanose, D. E., Kelley, H. H., Nisbett, R. E., Valins, S., & Weiner, B. (Eds.) (1971). *Attribution: Perceiving the causes of behavior.* Morristown, NJ: General Learning Press.

Lepper, M., Greene, D., & Nisbett, R. (1973). Undermining children's intrinsic interest with extrinsic rewards. *Journal of Personality and Social Psychology. 28,* 129–137.

Locke, E. A., & Latham, G. P. (1984). *Goal setting: A motivational technique that works.* Englewood Cliffs, NJ: Prentice-Hall.

Locke, E. A., Shaw, K. N., Saari, L. M., & Latham, G. P. (1981). Goal setting and task performance: 1969–1980. *Psychological Bulletin, 90,* 125–152.

Maehr, M. L. (1984). Meaning and motivation. In R. Ames & C. Ames (Eds.), *Research on motivation in education: Vol. 1. Student motivation* (pp. 115–144). New York: Academic Press.

Maehr, M. L. & Archer, J. (1987). Motivational factors in school achievement. In L. Katz (Ed.), *Current topics in early childhood education* (pp. 85–107). Norwood, NJ: Ablex.

Maehr, M. L., & Nicholls, J. (1980). Culture and achievement motivation: A second look. In N. Warren (Ed.), *Studies in cross-cultural psychology* (Vol. 2) (pp. 221–267). New York: Academic Press.

McClelland, D. C. (1951). *Personality.* New York: Sloane.

McClelland, D. C (1961). *The achieving society.* New York: Free Press.

McClelland, D. C., Atkinson, J. W., Clark, R. A., & Lowell, E. L. (1953). *The achievement motive.* New York: Appleton-Century-Crofts.

Nicholls, J. G. (1984). Conceptions of ability and achievement motivation. In R. Ames & C. Ames (Eds.), *Research on motivation in education: Vol. 1. Student motivation* (pp. 39–73). New York: Academic Press.

Nicholls, J. G., Patashnick, M. E., & Nolen, S. B. (1985). Adolescents' theories of education. *Journal of Educational Psychology, 77,* 683–692.

Rogers, C. R. (1951). *Client-centered therapy.* Boston: Houghton-Mifflin.

Rogers, C. R. (1961). *On becoming a person.* Boston: Houghton-Mifflin.

Weiner, B. (1972). *Theories of motivation: From mechanism to cognition.* Chicago: Markham.
Weiner, B., Frieze, I., Kukla, A., Reed, L., Rest, S., & Rosenbaum, R. M. (1971). Perceiving the causes of success and failure. In E. E. Jones, D. E. Kanose, H. H. Kelley, R. E. Nisbett, S. Valins, & B. Weiner (Eds.)., *Attribution: Perceiving the causes of behavior* (pp. 95–120). Morristown, NJ: General Learning Press.

10

Furthering Our Understanding of
Motivation and Environments

David C. Berliner

INTRODUCTION

These comments are about classroom processes (Weinstein), classroom tasks (Winne & Marx), the appropriateness of particular kinds of
environments for particular kinds of students (Eccles & Midgley), and
the ways that activities in the homes of students match or fail to match
the activities that occur in schools (Epstein). They are a wide ranging set
of annotations, criticisms, elaborations and the like, around the loosely
unifying theme of these chapters: how environments and motivation
for school are related. Each chapter is discussed in the order just noted,
then some common themes are extracted from these different views of
motivation and issues of schooling.

PERCEPTION AND MOTIVATION

Weinstein provides us with an example of that rare and wonderful
quality in science—seen too infrequently—an ongoing research program. A simple but profound truth that emerges from this cumulativ
set of studies is that environments do not influence motivation in a

direct fashion, rather, it is the perception of those environments that influences motivation. In line with the renaissance of cognitive concerns in psychology, we have increasingly come to view ourselves as something other than mere responding systems. We see ourselves now as thought-ful moderators of the stimuli we encounter, thinking before acting when we choose to. And that is a key phrase and an element missing in the description of the work given us by Weinstein—thinking before acting when we choose to.

CONATION

In the descriptions of the studies by Weinstein and her colleagues, the issues surrounding volition are nowhere to be found. These studies do reveal to us a thinking (or at least perceiving) child who reacts to nuance in interpersonal relationships, and, with each passing year increasingly recognizes these sometimes subtle characteristics of the environment. Yet we develop no picture of an active cognizer from the descriptions of the students in these research studies. As well as their social sensitivity to significant others, the one characteristic that marks youngsters in the grades that Weinstein and her collaborators studied is willful or voli-tional behavior. Perhaps we should talk here of cognitive styles, of personality variables, or—more broadly—of conation. Conation is not often discussed these days, but the privilege of being a discussant allows one to raise the odd idea for examination. Conation deals with the intrinsic unrest of the organism. It is the tendency to act, rather than the tendency to be passive. It is the opposite of homeostasis. *Conation* refers to volition—the purposive act (English & English, 1958).

Through misinterpretation, the students in Weinstein's studies may be thought of as overly passive cognizers or simple seekers of homeostasis in interpersonal relations when, in fact, there may be great individual differences in how they process and interpret the information they receive from teachers about their own behavior in the classroom. While a teacher in a high-differential-treatment classroom may be recognized by virtually all the students in a like manner, confirming the reliability and the validity of the measurement system, the reaction to the teacher's behavior may be quite different across different students. For students, *as a group,* the perception of the teacher's behavior is probably the initiator of a set of complex cognitive responses that ultimately leads to some congruence between what the students do and what the teachers communicate that they are expected to do. Thus, in accordance with this kind of passive model of students, the communication of expectations should result in lower or higher self-concept and/or lower and higher academic performance. But for *individual* students in that classroom, the teachers' behavior may be unrelated to any new actions on their part. They are resistant, impervious, autonomous, or some such word that captures the conative, volitional, purposive aspects of their behavior. These students appear to be more inner directed, more under self-control, more autonomous, and therefore more resistant to environmental influences than is the behavior of others.

The anecdotal evidence for thinking that these students exist in some numbers is frequently found in biography. As some minorities, or women, or children of poverty distinguish themselves in some way, these students often write about their personal drive to overcome impediments to their success. These impediments are often very much like those described in classroom research—low expectations for performance by significant others. Additional evidence that large numbers of individual students resist conforming to the teachers communication of expectations can also be found in the frequency of use of the term "overachiever," which, in my opinion, is one of the least useful terms in all of pedagogy. To *overachieve* means to outperform expectations, as if the expectations were real and performance were not. So when educators and parents talk of overachievers they are talking of children who do not succumb to the low expectations that are held for them. Similarly, "underachievers" are resisting communications that they can perform much better than they do.

Still more evidence for the importance of the conative elements in behavior come out of new conceptions of childhood that emphasize the adaptability, resiliency, and malleability of children after trauma, rather than the permanence of the effects of the trauma on the child's life. From what we ordinarily think of as intolerable and destructive environments, where child abuse, alcoholism, sexual trauma, and violence are everyday events, come some well-functioning human beings. Scars may be evident, but permanent damage to the child does not always occur. Apparently there exists in some children the ability to discount, to ignore, to overcome environmental conditions that are crippling to other children. And this aspect of personality is not given prominence in the Weinstein chapter, which describes, instead, the main effects of such conditions—not the kinds of interactions that might be found on further delving into the data. That is not a fault of the investigators—rather, it is a comment on what research is also needed to round out these studies and to understand how affective, cognitive, and conative abilities interact. Weinstein clearly notes this, as well, in her section on needed research.

There are few doubts that person–environment interactions generate compensatory, conciliatory, and and inhibitory processes that significantly affect the cognitive processing of information (Snow, 1980). Weinstein and her colleagues describes for us the inhibitory qualities associated with cognitive activity that are by-products of the interactions in classrooms staffed with high-differential-treatment teachers. And these researchers inform us, as well, about the conciliatory qualities that exist in the classrooms of the low-differential-treatment teachers. But a full psychological account of the individual differences among children in these classrooms also calls for the opposite. That is, what is called for are studies of children who are successful academic achievers and who hold positive attitudes while in the classrooms of the teachers showing high differential treatment and studies of the children who do not fare well in the classrooms of teachers who show low differential treatment. Thus, we might call for conative-treatment interaction studies. Conative processes are aptitudes; thus these studies would be a subset of studies that follow the approaches more generally called research on aptitude–treatment interactions (e.g., Snow & Farr, 1987).

NORMAL BEHAVIOR

Missing from this review of research is much discussion of the normal, anticipated, or ordinary nature of the actions of teachers who demonstrate high differential treatment. I do not mean to condone such behavior by labeling it normal. Such behavior cannot be condoned on moral grounds, any more than can cheating behavior, which also is ordinary and normal behavior in some school and classroom environments. Moreover, such behavior should not be condoned when it is clearly possible to find teachers who are capable of running classrooms in such a way that lower levels of differential treatment of students are noted, where more morally acceptable behavior is demonstrated, and where more desirable outcomes for students occur. By Weinstein's demonstration that such teachers exist, any arguments that the behaviors that we value are like pie-in-the-sky—unachievable by ordinary teachers in ordinary circumstances—are dropped from consideration right from the start.

We must keep in mind, however, that the low-differential-treatment classrooms discussed and valued in these studies are those that were merely lower than some others in perceived differential treatment. The sample of teachers studied were those who were in the upper and lower half of the distribution of perceived differential treatment. It is quite likely that in *all* classes the amount and explicitness of the achievement cues from teachers through which students determine their ability was too high. If we believe that social comparisons, public evaluations of performance, and blatant disparagement ("Come on dumb Dora!") are simply improper behaviors for teachers to use, than we should be greatly troubled by these data. Yet it appears to be normal, typical, ordinary, and apparently in daily use in America's classes, whether we approve of it or not.

The behaviors of families and teachers always exist in a cultural matrix. After all, families and schools are supposed to socialize students to the society in which they live. In contemporary America, from a cultural perspective, the behaviors of the teachers that Weinstein and her colleagues describe for us are neither improper nor immoral. It is sad but true, I believe, that many people would argue that one of the legitimate functions of schools is to sort and classify in order for the "best" students to be identified—a kind of social Darwinism at work. Not everyone can achieve well, the argument goes, so the sooner students learn that, the sooner that they will have realistic expectations for themselves. It is a disservice, the argument continues, to keep students from the truth about their ability. Public evaluations, competitive achievement situations, and the like, make that information available to students in unequivocal ways. Many parents often unknowingly commuicate their approval of this position when they say to a teacher "I'm glad you think she's doing fine, but what I want to know is how she's doing in comparison to other kids in this class?" Most of Weinstein's teachers, then, were acting in congruence with some mainstream American positions and thus should not be thought of as evil or bad or uncaring people. They are merely individuals representing their own culture, and, as we all know, one's own culture is likely to be hardest to discern. Perhaps when we think about these studies we need to recognize that "cultural deviants" may well be an appropriate label to describe the teachers who showed *lower* rates of differential treatment of their students!

LEARNING NEW TEACHING BEHAVIORS

Let us grant, then, that most of the teachers that Weinstein studied are behaving in ways that are quite compatible with the cultural mainstream. But as educators and advocates for children, we may not want our schools to be quite that representative of our culture. If that is the case, we then must ask what can be done during the education of these teachers such that they learn to discern the unhappy consequences of perfect cultural reproduction? We could start by ensuring that teachers learn about multiple abilities and try to break the strong norm in our culture that favors a single-ability conception of intelligence. But getting teachers and school administrators to accept the work of Gardner (1983) and others—that intelligence comes in many forms—is much like teaching Newton's laws in physics. Despite being able to pass advanced courses in physics, sometimes with a grade of "A," students maintain their naive beliefs about physics. Despite education, they continue to hold completely false beliefs about the nature of a situation, such as identifying the forces at work on an object when you throw it into the air. Naive scientific beliefs, like deeply embedded cultural beliefs about the nature of intelligence or the appropriateness of competition, are hard to change. Nevertheless, we are slowly learning that naive scientific beliefs can be changed by certain kinds of educational confrontations with evidence (Anderson & Smith, 1987). Where in teacher education, we should inquire, are the experiences that might change the deeply held beliefs of teachers from unidimensional and global conceptions of ability, as Weinstein describes them, to multidimensional and contextualized conceptualizations of ability, as we might desire them? I do not think that any systematic attempts to do this currently exist in programs of teacher education.

If one wanted to confront deeply held beliefs with evidence that might induce change, it would not be hard to do. A longitudinal study of childrens' personal achievement motive, completed in Europe, should be enough to convince even the most rabid upholders of the benefits of competition that it can have unexpected large negative effects for the majority of students (Trudewind & Kohne, 1982, cited in Hechhausen, Schmalt, & Schneider, 1985). In that study, the achievement motivation of 311 students in 26 classes was assessed over 4 years, from first to fourth grade. In the classrooms where students competed against performance standards that they created, measures of achievement motivation went up dramatically. On the other hand, initial levels of achievement motivation went down rapidly in those classes where social comparisons were the primary source of evaluative information. Thus, we find evidence that in classrooms with competitive, norm-referenced, public evaluations, we can expect to see decreases—not increases—in achievement motivation as time in school goes by.

The ends that many members of society want (young people that are motivated go-getters, achieving entrepreneurs, strivers after excellence, etc.) are actually achieved in larger numbers by different means than they might ordinarily guess. The evidence from many sources (e.g.

Ames & Ames, 1984; Covington, 1984) rather consistently goes counter to the position some might hold about the ways needed to develop highly motivated individuals for contemporary society in a capitalistic country. But we have no research programs studying interventions in teacher education to learn how to change these deep, wrong, and unconsciously held beliefs about the "proper" ways to run classrooms. As noted here previously, we are not dealing with teachers who are evil or uncaring individuals; we are dealing with mainstream representatives of our culture who are not trained in the manner I believe they should be trained. Weinstein and others have data that suggest we need to do more to create classrooms where teachers' achievement cues are less salient, where differential treatment of students is minimized. Even if real differences in student performance are driving teacher behavior, as Weinstein recognizes is possible, the moral obligation for educators to provide environments for children to take pride in personal accomplishment is not diminished. But, the evidence suggests that this is not the case. Rather, relative accomplishment is what is valued and relative standing in the smartness hierarchy is communicated clearly to children. Where in the educational program of teachers will these notions be addressed in enough depth that a change in attitudes might be likely?

Other implications for policy and practice in teacher education may be derived from these studies. For congruence with a multiple-abilities conception of intelligence, we should require that teachers receive some of their training in multidimensional classrooms, rather than unidimensional classrooms, during the time they are learning to teach. In multidimensional classrooms, where many tasks are occuring simultaneously, students have different and multiple ways to achieve status. In classroom environments where different tasks occur simultaneously, there is evidence that more different kinds of ability are recognized by teachers and therefore, more students in that classroom feel competent. We might want, as well, to see novice teachers proficient in running cooperative learning programs. This too could reduce the competitiveness of the typical classroom. Currently, prospective teachers usually read about such technology and its beneficial effects, but they see it in use infrequently and almost never have any chance to practice running a cooperative learning group. We might also try in our teacher education programs to design some courses following a mastery orientation, and vow never to use norm-referenced tests ourselves. In this way, we might model ways to use criterion-referenced tests so that students in teacher education programs have some experience with classes that do not rely on socially referenced evaluation. Unfortunately, we may expect teacher educators and teacher education to change slowly. And for some time to come, the placement of student teachers is more likely to be based on convenience than it is on the pedagogical considerations of the kind suggested by these interpretations of Weinstein's data. Thus, some of the teacher behavior that we dislike we must also recognize as normal, ordinary, typical teacher that is likely to continue as a dominant form of instruction for many years to come.

MOTIVE INTERACTIONS

The negative effects of certain teacher behavior, as seen through the eyes of students, permeates this set of studies. But not featured in any prominent way is the construct of anxiety. And it may be necessary to complicate the interpretations of these studies by throwing in that construct and, I fear, other constructs as well. Motivation is a field vexed by more than difinitional problems. There is the clear realization that behavior is never adequately explained by attributing the causation of behavior to a single motive pattern. No matter how we design our research, we always know it will be an oversimplification of a world in which many different motives are in dynamic interaction. It is the patterning and salience of these various forces at a particular moment in time that affects the probability to act in certain ways. One of these many motivational variables—anxiety—is more likely to be present in one kind of classroom studied by Weinstein than it is in the other.

In the classrooms characterized as high in differential treatment, students show more consistency in their matching of the teacher's expectations, and less positive feelings about their social competence. We should also expect less overall achievement in these classes. Recent work by Helmke (1988) looked at elementary classes that showed the achievement-impairing effects of anxiety. These were classrooms where the correlation of test anxiety with performance was high and negative—as high as $-.81$. The characteristics that stood out when the classrooms showing large achievement-impairing effects were compared to those where the correlation between test anxiety and achievement was much less (though still negative) were quite similar to those classrooms characterized by Weinstein as high in differential treatment of students.

If we can generalize, it is likely that in the classes that had high differential treatment of students, we will also see the maximum amounts of test anxiety. And then the questions arise: How are these various motivating factors combined? In what ways will the distribution of achievement be different in classes where anxiety is high, and does that affect the interpretations about the ways that teacher expectation influences student perception and achievement? Is the variance in student achievement that is accounted for by teacher expectancy working in a direct manner, or is it moderated by the anxiety–achievement relationship? We might hold very different interpretations of the data and design very different interventions for classrooms if the path through which teacher expectancy affected student achievement was through test anxiety rather than in any direct path. Interactions, moderating variables, indirect paths among classroom variables that have motivating properties all complicate the issues about how motives in classrooms operate. Those who would pursue this line of research need to explore these complications if they would attempt to design environments in which children experience failure less frequently then they do now. A worthy goal, I believe, and deserving of much more research support than is now given to the study of school motivation.

MOTIVATION THEORY
AND EDUCATIONAL TASKS

Winne and Marx provide us with something as rare as Weinstein's systematic and cumulative research on teacher's prophecies and students perceptions and behavior. They offer us theory. A good deal of research in psychology and education is only tied loosely to theory, so it is worth praising those who dare to posit grand ideas. Reading and rereading Winne and Marx, as I searched for ideas that are worth a reviewer's comments. increased my admiration for their ability to categorize (COPE, SMART, the four factors that do this, the two ways to answer that, etc.). I also came to admire their audacity and the heuristic value of what they have written. As might be expected, however, I inevitably searched also for problems in their presentation. To test their ideas against my own experience is, of course, a reasonable test of theory concerned about that very fundamental human process—motivation.

MEDIATION BY STUDENTS

As with Weinstein, and as a result of the cognitive concerns of contemporary researchers, we again find a general truth about student mediation to be an important concern in this explication of ideas about motivational processes. That is, it is the tasks that students perceive that determines what they will do. It is not the tasks that a teacher or researcher sets that is nearly as important. Teachers and researchers must keep in mind that the most important version of reality is not the task we think we set for students (nor, as in Weinstein's work, is it the communication we think we direct to students), rather, the important version of reality is the student's perception of the task (or of the communication). That is, the students version of reality should be the one that counts the most for those who study the effects of teachers, classrooms and schools on students. This is made explicit in this chapter, and that is worth noting.

RECURSIVITY AND SIMULTANEITY

It is also worth noting that Winne and Marx call attention to the recursive and simultaneous characteristics of motivation. The emphasis by school people, focused as one might expect on daily life in classrooms and schools, almost always leads to an emphasis on the process of motivation and not on motivation as a product. The daily ebb and flow of motivation, while of crucial significance to the classroom teacher, charged as they are with the need to maintain a heterogeneous group's interest in learning, is of only mild interest to the parents, school researcher, and society at large. Teachers and school administrators focus on motivation as process, because they have to; the rest of us more often focus on motivation as product. Readers of Weinstein's studies are moved by the data and interpretation because she gives us insight into how school failure can be turned into something that is trait-like or enduring, not state-like and ephemeral. The import of her research findings on our thinking about motivation in the classroom is that they are concerned about motivation as a product of life in classrooms. Almost all agree that the end products of schooling have to be more than high or low levels of raw learning. They must include dispositions to act in valued ways—that is, the outcomes of school learning must include motivational characteristics.

Winne and Marx, while clearly noting the differences between the process and the product aspects of motivation, focus on the tasks in which students engage. This is a form of microanalysis of motives and does not illuminate the equally important (perhaps the more important?) issue of motivation at a macrolevel, such as the enduring nature of motives as suggested by Weinstein. Although intimately related, the analysis of motivational processes in instructional tasks may not give us the insights we need to understand motivation in the form of a school product—the enduring motive patterns that characterize one's likelihood to achieve in academic ways, to continue in high school until the end, to obey school rules, to act responsibly in social relationships.

Somehow, we will need to think about these broader products of schooling, and that is not easily handled in this chapter, which deals with more molecular issues. Here we see primarily a focus on the processes that occur when students engage in the tasks that make up the educational activities. These activities, as a body, then constitute the means of instruction for delivery of the curriculum that a community wants taught. This becomes the experience we call "schooling in classrooms." The tasks are nested in other complex events and motivational webs, and we need to be reminded that the processes that describe instructional tasks may not be the same ones that are useful to describe activities at other levels of analysis.

ACTIVITIES AND TASKS

As Winne and Marx sharply distinguish between activity structures (lecturing, recitation, seatwork and so forth) and the tasks that must be accomplished by students within those activity structures, they also reveal to us that the choice of a teaching method is probably much less important than we first might have thought. The cognitive tasks engaged in by students in one instructional form (e.g., lecturing) can resemble the cognitive tasks engaged in by students instructed by some other means (e.g., self-study). Or the cognitive tasks of two students, both in a recitation activity, may be vastly different. Each of the different means of instruction has characteristics associated with it that circumscribe what students are likely to do and not do—the prescriptions and proscriptions that are recognizable parts of any teaching pattern, activity structure, or teaching method. But learning and motivation are much more likely to be affected by the tasks students work at within those instructional means than they are by the means itself. The description of activity structures has much to recommend it, since we in education often have finely grained measures of cognitive outcomes and only the coarsest measures of instructional treatments (Berliner, 1983). Thus, activity structures are useful descriptions of educational environments. They can help us to provide ways to characterize treatments. But in this chapter we see how they too can be overly coarse descriptions of treatments or environments. The cognitive task, therefore, is likely to be a better unit for analysis of what is salient for learning and motivation. The COPE unit for task description, with its SMART operations is worthy of serious consideration as a descriptive system or a heuristic for examining cognitive tasks. But whether it can really be useful for understanding the ways in which motivation works is less clear to me, perhaps because I do not find that the analysis of cognitive tasks has obvious usefulness for the analysis of motivation.

COGNITIVE AND MOTIVATIONAL PROCESSES

The hypothesis that there is sufficient identity in cognitive and motivational processes to use the former in understanding the latter is at the heart of this analysis by Winne and Marx. They see only that the information processed is different while claiming that neither the representations nor the operations used for processing information would be different. But this needs to be questioned, despite their sensible arguments.

I find it hard to associate affective responses with many kinds of cognitive processes, and I find it easy to associate affective responses to many kinds of motivational processes. When I am doing statistical analysis I am aware of few affective responses. When I succeed at doing a complex statistical task, and I attribute it to my ability, I feel pride, my self-esteem rises, my pleasure is overwhelming. But when I fail to solve a statistical problem, and I attribute that to my lack of ability, I feel shame, incompetence, depression. My expectation of future success and failure and my willingness to engage in future statistical tasks is information about motivational processes and may be subject to analysis like all other cognitive information. That is why Winne and Marx can find overlap between the study of cognition and the study of motivation. But their formulation does not help me when it comes to the affective responses that I might generate while doing statistical tasks—emotions like shame, pride, anger, indifference, or guilt. These internal responses have powerful motivational properties. Moreover, there is reason to believe that affect (and therefore the kinds of motivational characteristics that are associated with particular kinds of attributions) is completely independent of cognition (e.g., Zajonc, 1980, 1984). In fact, Izard (1984) and Zajonc would argue that affect often occurs without cognition, has primacy over cognition, and may be controlled by different anatomical structures. So my personal feelings that cognitive processes may often be "cool" (likely to be affect free) while cognition that deals with motivational processes may often be "hot" (loaded with affect), is not without scientific backing.

My problem is that concerns about affect are not evident in the explication of Winne and Marx, and this leaves me wanting a more encompassing theory. People murder for love, for hate, out of jealousy and greed. Emotions such as these—the passions—are acceptable as causal explanations for behavior by the general public, demonstrating how important they are to our thinking about motivation. But in the theory of Winne and Marx, affect is not prominently featured, and thus we seem to be missing an entire class of variables that could help us in understanding the causes of behavior. Classrooms, as important social settings for young people, do elicit powerful affective responses, and these will organize and regulate cognition for the students. Weinstein's chapter is an example of this truth. These affective responses may not be elicited during a good deal of cognitive information processing, but they are elicited much more often when motivational information is being processed. Therefore, the equating of cognitive with motivational processing (while one is usually "cool," and the other usually "hot") is not to be accepted without questioning this premise. Though the theorizing of Winne and Marx has heuristic value, it is lacking for me because it is too cool, too rational. And that raises another important issue about their thinking, to which I now turn.

RATIONALITY AND MOTIVATIONAL THEORY

Winne and Marx insist that people act in a manner that is consistent with their goals, that both cognition and motivation depend on goal-driven processes, that students, unless psychotic, are goal directed. This purposive and volitional behavior, the conative aspects of action, are as conspicuous here by their presence as they were conspicuous by their absence in the studies by Weinstein and her colleagues. Moreover, for Winne and Marx, without goals, there can be no tasks, and thus any discussion of motivation and classroom tasks would have limitations.

I have a personal problem that now must be confessed publicly. I do not always act rationally. I am not always goal directed. Tasks are often undertaken in order for me to find goals, rather than the other way around. I first thought that this revelation may be too self-deprecating but then found, instead, that I may be in good company. March and Olsen (1976) and Snow (1980) discuss a common situation for organizations and individuals to find themselves in—one where goals are not easily discernible, are hazy, changing, ambiguous. On many school days, seatwork in classrooms may have those qualities. The information-processing psychologists (and Winne and Marx follow their mode of thinking) assume that goals are given or discernible.

But that simply is not always the case. "Interesting people and interesting organizations," say March and Olsen, "may as frequently engage in action to find goals, as they justify actions in terms of goals." People often need ways of doing things for which they can provide no good reason. They often need to act before they think. They supplement their rationality with foolishness. They need opportunities to be playful. Through play, we get a chance to act "irrationally," "unintelligently," "foolishly," and thereby find goals we might never discover if we had acted purposively and rationally.

Thus, tasks may not just be misperceived or undertaken to achieve different goals than those of the teacher or the researcher, as Winne and Marx posit, tasks may be engaged in for no really good reason at all! They may simply be intrinsically interesting, as when a child stops reading her history textbook to spend 20 minutes playing with a ladybug, or fails to continue in the computer drill-and-practice program when she finds that she can make the computer draw fractals. Playful tasks and goal-searching tasks (engaged in to find goals) are as much a part of school life as are tasks that are rational and goal directed. A theory of tasks and human motivation will need to find an explicit place for issues like these. In summary of the last two issues, then, I find us with a heuristic set of ideas about cognition, motivation, and classroom tasks, but I also believe that these ideas may suffer from a paucity of emotionality and a surfeit of rationality.

SCHOOL ENVIRONMENTS AND MOTIVATION

The lack of attention to affective concerns in the chapter by Winne and Marx is now in even sharper focus as we look at Eccles and Midgley. They, like Weinstein, are concerned not just with cognitive issues, but also with the role that is played by perceptions, attitudes, opinions, and beliefs, along with their inevitable affective tones, in the development of youngsters. The case is convincingly argued by Eccles and Midgley that there is a developmental mismatch, with unfortunate consequences, between young adolescents and the school environments they experience. I would argue, however, that they may be simply too restrictive in their conclusion that young adolescents, in particular, have suffered in the school learning environment. Schools are not now, and only rarely ever were, designed to accommodate children's needs or to optimally promote learning. Perhaps the Pestalozzian school or the kindergarten of Froebel once did what Eccles and Midgley would like to see happen again—the design of a developmentally appropriate curriculum and school. But in recent years in our country, we have seen academic tasks being pushed down into kindergarten, tests for entrance and exit from kindergarten, behavioral designs for raising "super-kids," and so forth. Over time, the kindergarten, like junior high and middle school, seems to have evolved (or devolved?), and in doing so may have lost many of its most humane qualities. This chapter forces us to think about the loss of purpose of the junior high. And, when the authors of this chapter ask if the assumptions upon which junior high are based are reasonable, I cringe and ask myself what happened, and what we can do about it. One thing we certainly should do is lobby for more research on these issues. And some proposals come immediately to mind.

CULTURE, SOCIAL CLASS, AND SCHOOL CHANGE

In presenting their review Eccles and Midgley inadvertently, I'm sure, portray students as some kind of homogeneous group. They are not. Ethnic, racial, and social class differences abound, and these differences influence what we can learn from our research. Would the transition to a particular junior high school environment be the same for the child of recent oriental immigrants, with upward mobility a driving force, as it is for the third generation Hispanic in a mining town of the southwest? Do suburban, college-bound children have the same kinds of attitudinal and emotional shifts when they enter junior or senior high school as do poor inner-city black children? Searching for person–environment matches, a laudatory but difficult task under any conditions, is only made more difficult by ignoring heterogeneity among the persons. Pooling information, rather than disaggregating it, will hide more than it will reveal about the interactions between persons and environments. Perhaps some of the inconsistency in the data reported in this review is due to such aggregations of dissimilar data.

The cultural issue was also neither commented on by Weinstein nor addressed by Winne and Marx. Yet we might hypothesize that students' perceptions are likely to differ as a function of their culture, ethnic, and social-class backgrounds, thus moderating some of the effects of teachers' prophecies on student behavior. And the issue of what is "hot" cognition and what is "cold" will also be affected by these characteristics of students. With great heterogeneity in the makeup of the North American school population, it is more than just good science to look for interactions between student characteristics and treatments. It is also necessary for developing school policy.

While Eccles and Midgley forcefully suggest that we are not doing right by most children because we fail to design environments that match their needs, they do not raise the issue that the environments for different types of children may also need to be different. I would argue that a plan for a humane transition to junior high in the Hispanic barrios of the southwest would take on a different character than one dealing with the transitions of rural Anglo children in Indiana. These are, of course, important research questions if our goal is to help all of our youngsters to achieve as much as they can in as pleasant an environment as we can provide. But a continuing problem for all who think about ways to improve education, and a particularly frustrating problem for those interested in person–environment interactions, is that we have a scarcity of genuine differences in environments. There is a scarcity of diverse means of instruction. While we have thousands of ways to characterize persons, we have a deeply rooted feeling that the school environments we see simply do not show much variation and we have few ways to characterize environments.

CHARACTERIZING ENVIRONMENTS

Winne and Marx used activity structures and tasks to try to cope with the problem of describing the events that impinge on students in classrooms. Some kind of taxonomy of environments, which is not now available, is what they need to understand the issues that they want to study. In the Eccles and Midgley chapter, too, we see the need for more and better ways to discuss educational environments. Eccles and Midgley fully recognize that "middle school" or "junior high school" do not in any way communicate precise information about the salient aspects of these environments. Surely their line of research and other studies of schooling would improve if taxonomic work on the nature of classroom tasks and activities were undertaken with some vigor. Alas, a government that values both guns and butter cannot spare much for basic research in education. And that raises a point about the kinds of research that can be done in this area, given such constraints.

BASIC RESEARCH AND ACTION RESEARCH

The facts that (1) basic research on important issues has not yet been done, and (2) it will take years to sort out some of the existing conflicting findings in this field do not mean that other forms of research cannot proceed. In fact, we have sufficient evidence now that young adolescents may often behave in ways we do not value but that appear to be a direct function of our school programs, school designs, teachers' attitudes, and so forth. Action research, or the creation of demonstration sites with strong evaluation programs, can certainty be undertaken to find solutions to these problems even before all the basic information we need is collected. The evidence presented us by Eccles and Midgley is sufficient to launch experimental programs to remove the harshest characteristics of the transition from one level of schooling to another. They inform us that some adolescents do not show the expected negative effects and that there seems to be some relationship between certain kinds of school organization and the magnitude of these effects. From that information can come school designs worth careful study. And as more is learned about the developmentally appropriate classrooms for young adolescents, we might learn something about the more general case of how change of schools can be made less stressful for our young people.

CHANGE OF SCHOOL AS A BROADER TOPIC

Developmental psychologists and like-minded people have focused on the age–stage–environment issues and have convincingly argued that a problem exists at the junior high school level. The issues of discontinuity as one makes a transition between, say, elementary school and junior high school, however, are a subset of a larger problem for youngsters in our society; discontinuity when moving from school to school. We live in a society where many school administrators think of themselves as stable in population turnover if they have only 20% of their students turnover during the year. It is not unusual at all to have 50% turnover among students in many schools—an educational problem that has not been adequately recognized by designers of school programs or those who criticize the schools.

Because large numbers of families move each year, we can almost always find many 6th graders who have been in 4 or 8 or more different schools. As these children have moved from environment to environment, they have experienced (1) both structured and unstructured classrooms and schools, (2) both distant and caring teachers, (3) both evaluation systems that are public and those that are private, (4) both comparison to others and evaluation in terms of personal growth, and (5) both harsh and lenient grading. These children should also be of great concern to society.

Whenever someone generates a list of the top 10 stressors in adult life we see noted "transitions to new jobs," "making new friends," "moving to a new locale" and so forth. It seems odd, therefore, not to have recognized the possibility of such events being even more stressful for young people as they take on their new job—their work as a student at a new school. It is likely that *all* school changes for youngsters have a greater probability of leading to temporary negative rather than positive effects on motivation to learn, self-concept, and academic and social development. The long-term effects of such moves probably depend on the ways new children are received at their new school. Research and practice that was guided by humane concerns about our young people should have led us to an understanding of how to make transitions from school to school easier for the many students that now experience the negative effects of relocation. District and school programs should have been developed to soften the negative consequences of this common occurrence in contempory American life. Apparently few such programs exist. Usually, each teacher is independently responsible for figuring out what to do. An effort at developing more systematic programs to help youngsters as they move from school to school would have to address the broad issues of transition first, I think, and the specific issues of developmentally appropriate transitions—schools that fit student needs—second. The transition to junior high for young adolescents is a particular case of the more general one—the need to design school programs that are caring about children whenever they must move from one environment to another.

FAMILY ENVIRONMENTS AND MOTIVATION

In Epstein's work, we see again an example of cumulative studies, as in the work of Weinstein, and that of Eccles and Midgley. Her analysis and description of the TARGET structures in families, and their relationship to TARGET structures in school is an important one for three reasons: (1) The formulation deals with descriptions of environments, (2) it is possible to test the relationship, and (3) most important of all, it gives the school a bigger role to play in the development of students.

DESCRIPTIONS OF ENVIRONMENTS

To help make sense out of the complex activities that characterize classrooms, Epstein and her colleagues invented the TARGET structures. These descriptions of classroom environments seem to apply equally well to the study of a student's life at home. This is a good sign. As noted before, it is terribly important to have adequate descriptions, category systems, or taxonomies of environments. This one does appear to be a fruitful one to use—albeit one with a decided sociological bent. Note how this level of analysis would be too molar for Winne and Marx, who must posit, instead, a much more molecular vision of tasks, one that focuses on internal cognitive processes.

TESTABILITY

In Table 1 of Epstein's chapter we have the beginnings of a theory about the causal connections among TARGET structures, motivational variables, and student outcomes of various types. This logical analysis, however, is not likely to receive a great deal of support once empirical testing is begun. I predict this because of the primitive nature of our measurement system for looking at environments (e.g., tasks or activities), for measuring motivational variables (e.g., personal responsibility), and for measuring any student outcomes besides achievement (e.g., tolerance of group differences). Nevertheless, in principle, the linkages described are all testable and can provide researchers with a blueprint for conducting empirical studies for the next several years.

THE ROLE OF THE SCHOOL

However much help Epstein's analysis may prove to be for scientists, it is of little practical use unless school personnel redefine themselves and shed the isolation they have nurtured within their communities. A home–school linkage, with improved student learning and social behavior as its goal, is possible only if school personnel find ways to reach out and communicate to the adults in the student's homes. School people need to discuss with the adults at home, in a professional manner, what might be done to make home and school life more compatible. There is some reason to be hopeful that a program of outreach from schools to parents can be helpful, particularly for minority students in low-income families. Work by Clark (1983) and Goldenberg (1984) suggest that the compliance rates for school messages sent home to parents will be about the same across social classes. That is, the parents of low-income black or Hispanic children seem to comply as well to school requests for some action to be taken as do the parents of white middle-class children. A lack of financial resources and/or limited English proficiency were not factors. Thus, we learn from this work that when parents are given professional advice about what they might do to help their children, they took it. Possessing this useful bit of knowledge, however, suggests problems for our society. Teachers are already busy people. Adding the responsibility for parental involvement as a job requirement of teachers who already lead busy lives is not possible. Thus, we are left wondering who from the school will take on the role of communicating with the parents?

If schools are not proactive in these matters, only the parents who know how to deal with schools will seek ways to help their children. These will be people who were successful school attenders, generally middle-class parents. The teenage mother, herself a child and probably a school failure, is not likely to show up and ask middle-class teachers for advice about what she can do in her home to foster her child's achievement. These parents are no less concerned about their children than other parents in our society, but they are less skilled at getting information from middle-class institutions, and they probably have less freedom when it comes to organizing home environments to promote school achievement.

What is so intriguing about Epstein's formulation, even before all the data we might want is in, is that it calls for action, like the studies of Weinstein and those of Eccles and Midgley. The TARGET classroom structures are a way to analyze life in homes and may be used to suggest sensible ways that the home life of students can be made more helpful in promoting school achievement. What is needed are some persons who, for a few years, will take on this new role for schools, and other personnel who will do formative evaluations of such programs. When school dropout rates for certain ethnic groups exceed 70%, as is true of Puerto Ricans in New York City, and we also know that Puerto Rican family life is strong and parental values are compatible with those of other members of society, then it is long past the time for schools to become proactive. While funding for persons who could take on this new role for schools will be difficult to find, it is important to remember that even small changes in dropout rates would have large fiscal payoffs for society. Savings in welfare costs, juvenile delinquency, medical benefits, as well as increased revenues from taxes by wage earners could more than pay for such a program in the long run. It is odd that nobody is starting to enlarge the role of the school in this way, to see if it might help those students most in need.

Although well thought out, the descriptions of the TARGET structures are not without problems. A few of these are pointed out herein.

TASK STRUCTURES AND CULTURAL DIFFERENCES

Only in rare instances do Epstein's descriptions of TARGET structures explicitly deal with the notion of cultural difference. An easily recognized truth, for example, is that we might find different task and authority structures to be in use in different cultures. Less evident is that there could be dramatic discontinuities between the task structures in use in school and those found in the homes of some culturally different children. The *magnitude* of these differences may not be as obvious as is the fact that differences will occur across cultures. For example, Yaqui Indian children in Tucson and Phoenix take on great reponsibility during the 40 or so days of their Easter celebration. Their festival melds a pagan pre-Colombian religion with a 16th-century Catholic service to form a special New Year's rite that blends into the Catholic Easter celebration. Children start at a very young age to have important roles to play in the celebration, including public performances of religious obligation, often throughout the night. For days on end, the children maintain mature interactions with the adults of the tribe. But at the same time that they are taking up these complex and important sacred duties in their tribe, they find themselves in school environments that are vastly beneath them in complexity and the level of responsibility that is required of them. Being treated in school as a child sometimes belittles them, and the simple tasks they are asked to perform may bore them. The activity structures they have engaged in at home are not just different, as we might expect them to be across cultures, they also show very little continuity with the children's school experiences.

The caretaking and cooking behavior that some children engage in for their families may be classified in the same way, as would a child's participation in a family business. These home task structures provide experiences that are far more complex and call for far more responsibility, at a much younger age, than anything being provided by school. This produces a problem to which Epstein only partly attends—namely, that school can be deadly dull compared to the lives some children lead outside of school. She recognizes that home may provide more interactive or more diverse activities. But I believe that it goes farther than that: In different cultures, the activities in which children engage at home may not have any analog at all to the activities in which they engage at school. To make the home task structures more compatible with the school structures might call for a "dumbing" down or a decomplexifying of the home structures.

Perhaps, if school personnel did reach out to the families of the children they serve, as in the Yaqui example, teachers would learn about these home activities and design school programs for these students that capitalize on their maturity. Too often, we think of children who occasionally are up with adults all night, or who care for their siblings, or who work in their parents' store in the evening, as deprived. It might be just as easy to consider them advantaged, because the activity structures they engage in help them develop responsibility and maturity beyond that of many of their age-mates. The instruction we design for them should be different, as they are different.

AUTHORITY STRUCTURES AND SCHOOL NORMS

I do not believe that Epstein's views of home and school authority structures are completely thought out. She believes that children who are fortunate enough to be included in decision making at home have an advantage at school. I could argue the opposite point. When the home authority structures allow for genuine decision making, the student is likely to experience more discontinuity than if the home authority structures were more authoritarian or fostered more dependency in the child. Schools simply do not reward independent learners, independent thinkers, independent decision makers. As a rule, students are allowed to ask few questions in their classrooms. Those questions that they do ask are generally at a low level of complexity, dealing with procedural matters. They rarely initiate conversations; rather, they are the recipients of low-level inquiries by their teachers. They are constrained in their choice of activity. In virtually every way, their behavior is constrained. Compliance to rules is rewarded; challenges to those rules are discouraged and punished. In this way, most schools have more in common with prisons and hospitals than they do with families. When we think of many behaviors (e.g., toilet behavior, posture when sitting, choice of reading material) we find that even authoritarian family structures rarely regulate student behavior as completely as do schools. Thus, Epstein's assumption that parents who develop their children's decision-making capabilities are helping their children succeed in school is not, in my view, accurate. Furthermore, many parents are against their children learning these kinds of skills. The recent flight from public schools to private fundamentalist schools by parents who are against their children learning such horrendous things as "critical thinking skills," "values clarification," and "higher-order questioning" (all noted by a conservative columnist as programs that should be boycotted in the schools) attests to the fact that parents are not always desirous of children who can think for themselves. Tragically, such contemporary trends have affected the school curriculum, such that genuine decision-making opportunities for students in schools may now be in shorter supply then they ever were, lest some of the community's parents be alienated.

My analysis leads me to believe that a parent who raises a child to be a mature decision maker and expects that child to demonstrate those capabilities in schools is likely to be raising a child who will be in trouble throughout their school careers. This is not incompatible with Epstein's findings that when family authority practices sequentially increase children's decision-making opportunities, the children gain in feelings of internal locus of control and in feelings of independence. My point is that institutional norms are incompatible with this form of child-rearing, however desirable Epstein or I may find it.

SOME SUMMARY COMMENTS AND DIRECTIONS FOR RESEARCH

The two chapters tied closely to data (Eccles & Midgley; Weinstein) and the two chapters that offer us ways to conceptualize motivational issues (Epstein; Winne & Marx) are all very different yet focus on some common problems. For example, they all deal with the problem of how to conceptualize environments. Those who wish to build on Weinstein at the classroom level or Eccles and Midgley at the school level need to look for more precise ways to talk about how environments affect children. A start at that is seen in the work of Winne and Marx and Epstein, along with that of Berliner (1983), Doyle (1983), and others who try to take the ecological psychologist's perspective. The entire body of work in this tradition needs to be brought together to provide a guide for researchers interested in teaching and classrooms. Until we have adequate ways to characterize environments, we will always have some difficulty in conducting and reporting our research. This deficiency in scientific understanding leads to inadequate measures of treatments and hampers us, as well, in evaluating the fidelity of treatment when replicating or installing instructional programs. Thus, we see revealed in these chapters an important problem and a direction for future work.

Future work must also examine the influence of cultural differences and the impact these could have on the issues that each of the writers tried to address. Culture (and we include here gender, ethnic, and social class differences, as well) affects motivational theories in subtle ways. Unless a researcher is especially sensitive to such issues, effects may be hidden from view. One example will suffice. What does it mean to be an educated person? Because motivational theories concerned with educational phenomena must at some time address this issue, it would be a problem if this question meant slightly different things for different kinds of people. I think that is the case. There is the possibility that in one cultural group, among the answers you would receive to this question is "polite, well-mannered." In this case, the child's deportment is as important as is her or his achievement. In another culture, answers to that question may include "having a college degree." In this case, schoolwork is instrumental and has no value besides the certificate that it brings. In still another culture, the answers might include "being a good conversationalist" or "knowing the facts that are in the books." The former leads a group of students to display school motives that have decided social ends; the latter view leads to school motives that are easily directed toward mastery of mathematics and science, rather than the humanities.

A similar perspective comes from Entwistle's (1981) research on cognitive styles and motivational processes. In that work, three learning styles of students were described: One in which students sought understanding, the *meaning* oriented style; a second where students sought to memorize, a *reproduction* oriented style; and a third in which students sought high grades, an *achievement* oriented style. Culture, as I have described it here, acts like the learning styles described by Entwistle. Perhaps learning style is the psychological variable through which culture exerts its influence. Culture and learning styles both may be characterized as ordering and regulating perception. Therefore, their influence must be understood if motivational theories and research are to be useful in a heterogeneous society like ours.

Individual perceptions of activity structures and other environmental characteristics are likely to come to the foreground in the near future. Thus, we are likely to see renewed attempts for incorporating individual differences (and therefore, research on aptitude–treatment interaction) into our theories about environments and motivation. One potentially fruitful way to start thinking of ways to include measures of individual differences into these research studies is to start thinking about cognitive styles (Messick, 1987). Cognitive styles influence the organization of cognitive structures, regulating many aspects of cognition including encoding, storage, retrieval, strategy selection, and decision making. Cognitive styles moderate affect and perception. Because of these factors, these stable individual differences in functioning may provide us a way to examine individual differences in response to different kinds of teacher expectations, or in response to activity structures and school organizations. Thus all these authors, when writing about individual differences, as they someday must, are likely to find the cognitive style literature a useful one.

A final word about research and practice is required. Critics of educational research abound, including highly placed government officials who claim that few research studies ever lead to any useful action (Finn, 1988). But from these chapters, I have noted that sensible actions may be derived with regard to teacher preparation and school organization and management. These research programs, though underfunded and as yet incomplete, are already able to guide school persons who would like some data to help them improve whatever parts of the school system for which they have responsibility. Contrary to some critics' views, I think we see in these chapters evidence of a rather productive research community. The chapters provide us not only with guides for the improvement of research and ideas about how we might be able to improve practice, but also with concepts to better understand educational phenomena. In the long run, that may be the biggest benefit of all.

ACKNOWLEDGMENTS

I thank the Spencer Foundation and the Center for Advanced Study in the Behavioral Sciences for their support while this chapter was written.

REFERENCES

Ames, C., & Ames, R. (1984). Goal structures and motivation. *The Elementary School Journal, 85*, 39–52.

Anderson, C. W. & Smith, E. L. (1987). Teaching science. In V. Richardson-Koehler (Ed.), *Educators' handbook.* White Plains, NY: Longman.

Berliner, D. C. (1983). Developing conceptions of classroom environments: Some light on the T in classroom studies of ATI. *Educational Psychologist, 18*, 1–13.

Clark, R. (1983). *Family life and school achievement: Why poor black children succeed or fail.* Chicago, IL: University of Chicago Press.

Covington, M. V. (1984). The self-worth theory of achievement motivation: Findings and implications. *The Elementary School Journal, 18*, 39–61.

Doyle, W. (1983). Academic work. *Review of Educational Research, 53*, 159–199.

English, H. B., & English, A. C. (1958). *A comprehensive dictionary of psychological and psychoanalytic terms.* NY: Longmans, Green.

Entwistle, N. (1981). *Styles of learning and teaching.* NY: Wiley.

Finn, C. E. (1988). What ails education research. *Educational Researcher, 17*, 5–8.

Gardner, H. (1983). *Frames of mind.* NY: Basic Books.

Goldenberg, C. N. (1984). *Roads to reading: Studies of Hispanic first graders at-risk for reading failure.* Unpublished doctoral dissertation, School of Education, University of California at Los Angeles.

Helmke, A. (1988). The role of classroom context factors for the achievement-impairing effect of test anxiety. *Anxiety Research, 1,* 1–15.

Izard, C. E. (1984). The primacy of emotion in emotion-cognition relationships and human development. In C. E. Izard, J. Kagan, & R. Zajonc (Eds.), *Emotions, cognitions, and behavior.* NY: Cambridge University Press.

March, J. G. & Olsen, J. P. (1976). *Ambiguity and choice in organizations.* Bergan, Norway: Universitetsforlaget.

Messick, S. (1987). Structural relationships across cognition, personality, and style. In R. E. Snow & M. J. Farr (Eds.), *Aptitude, learning, and instruction: Volume 3. Conative and affective process analyses* (pp. 35–75). Hillsdale, NJ: Erlbaum.

Snow, R. E. (1980). Intelligence for the year 2001. *Intelligence, 4,* 185–199.

Snow, R. E., & Farr, M. J. (Eds.), (1987). *Aptitude, learning, and instruction: Volume 3. Conative and affective process analyses.* Hillsdale, NJ: Erlbaum.

Trudewind, C., & Kohne, W. (1982). Bezugsnorm-Orientierung der Lehrer und Motiventwicklung: Zusammenhänge mit Schulleistung, Intelligenz und Merkmalen der hauslichen Umwelt in der Grundschulzeit. [Orientation of teachers and the development of motivation: Relationships to school achievement, intelligence, and the environment of the primary school classroom]. In F. Reinberg (Ed.), *Bezugsnormen zur Schulleistrungsbewertung: Analyse and Invervoution.* Dusseldorf, Germany: Schwann. (Cited in Hechhausen, H., Schmalt, H-D., & Schneider, K. (1985). *Achievement motivation in perspective.* Orlando, FL: Academic Press.)

Zajonc, R. B. (1980). Feeling and thinking: Preferences need no inferences. *American Psychologist, 35,* 151–175.

Zajonc, R. B. (1984). On the primacy of affect. *American Psychologist, 39,* 117–123.

Index